MORE PRAISE FOR *DYNAMIC HEDGING*

"A truly unique work . . . enjoyable, practical, and, for risk managers, essential reading."

> —*A. Kreysar*
> Head Foreign Currency Options Trader
> SBC Warburg, a division of Swiss Bank Corp.

"A fascinating and impacting book, it entirely changed my course on hedging."

> —*Nicole El Karoui*
> Professor of Probability Theory and Mathematical Finance
> École Polytechnique and Universite Paris 6

"Truly oriented to the reader . . . Does not get bogged down in the mathematical formulas. *Dynamic Hedging* has enlightened me on the hidden risks of exotic options."

> —*Robert K. Friedberg*
> Chief Currency Options Trader
> Credit Lyonnais

"*Dynamic Hedging* is the only book that teaches risk management in a true world environment, not in an unrealistic academic framework. It is mandatory reading for risk managers and consultants."

> —*J. P. Frignet*
> Chairman
> KPMG-Strategic Risk Management

"I laughed, I cried, I hedged Dgamma Dvol."

> —*David DeRosa*
> Quadrangle Investments, LLC

"A rare combination of trading experience and intellectual insight."

> —*James R. Piper, Jr.*
> Partner
> O'Connell & Piper Associates

"A must study for both option traders and more importantly for risk managers. There are a number of major institutions in dire need of this work."

> —*Brian P. Monieson*
> Chairman
> GNP Commodities
> and Past Chairman, Chicago Mercantile Exchange

"This is absolutely the best book that has been written on trading and hedging derivatives. This is the essential missing link for students of finance, who wish to enter the 'real world.'"

—S. Rao
Meridian Derivatives Consultants Inc.

"*Dynamic Hedging* deals with issues in risk management and valuation from an intuitive perspective that only a pioneering practitioner and researcher like Taleb can provide. Taleb has done a masterful job of addressing the fundamental risk management dilemma of reconciling differences in the real-world price behavior with that expected by theoretical modeling. He combines anecdote with rational, brilliant insight to present a powerful treatise on derivatives risk."

—Nicolas Hatzopoulos
President
Derivatech Consulting Inc.

Dynamic Hedging

Wiley Series in Financial Engineering

Series Editor: Jack Marshall
Managing Director of the International Association of Financial Engineers

Structured Financial Products
John C. Braddock

Derivatives for Decision Makers: Strategic Management Issues
George Crawford and Bidyut Sen

Interest-Rate Option Models
Riccardo Rebonato

Derivatives Handbook: Risk Management and Control
Robert J. Schwartz and Clifford Smith, Jr.

Dynamic Hedging: Managing Vanilla and Exotic Options
Nassim Taleb

Dynamic Hedging

MANAGING VANILLA AND EXOTIC OPTIONS

Nassim Taleb

JOHN WILEY & SONS, INC.

New York • Chichester • Brisbane • Toronto • Singapore • Weinheim

To

Cindy, Sarah, and Alexander.

To the memory of my cousins
N. J. Nasr (1970–1996) and B. Y. Kozami (1950–1995).

This text is printed on acid-free paper.

Excel is a registered trademark of the Microsoft Corporation.

Mathematica is a registered trademark of Wolfram Research.

Copyright © 1997 by Nassim Taleb.
Published by John Wiley & Sons, Inc.

Library of Congress Cataloging-in-Publication Data:

Taleb, Nassim.
    Dynamic hedging : managing vanilla and exotic options / Nassim Taleb.
      p.   cm. — (Wiley series in financial engineering)
    Includes bibliographical references and index.
    ISBN 0-471-15280-3 (cloth : alk. paper)
    1. Options (Finance) 2. Hedging (Finance) 3. Derivative
securities. I. Title. II. Series.
HG6024.A3T35 1996
332.64'5—dc20   96-34283

Printed in the United States of America

10 9 8 7 6

Preface

After closing about 200,000 option transactions[1] (that is separate option tickets) over 12 years and studying about 70,000 risk management reports, I felt that I needed to sit down and reflect on the thousands of mishedges I had committed.

I clambered up to my attic where, during 6 entire months, I spent 14 hours a day, 7 days a week, immersed in probability theory, numerical analysis, and mathematical statistics (at a Ph.D. level). Then I began to write this book.

Like George Soros[2], I believed in a **greater uncertainty principle** (more acute than Heisenberg's) that largely invalidates social science theories based on physics-like methodology and weakens the notion of modeling outside of the natural sciences. *It ain't physics,* I kept warning my trainees throughout my career.

My other argument against being scientific was that, even if it were a "science," option theory (while perhaps on the right track) would be too young to be reliable. I then needed to warn the public (and the regulators) against taking an unseasoned and new field and applying some of its still misspecified models to reality. Many of the market risks that have been well known to traders since imperial Rome (like squeezes and the snowballing liquidity holes) have not yet been rediscovered by the scientific risk managers. I am convinced that the financial system is largely threatened by the proliferation of risk management advisory services run by former scientists who bullied their way into financial markets. My intention was to downgrade hedging and risk management from the status of science to that of a craft, until further notice.

This book is about **hedging** the risks of standard and exotic options, as part of the larger framework of risk management. No road map was available since little has been written on this subject (in contrast to the extensive literature for valuation).

Dynamic hedging is more like medicine than biology. It is learned by gaining practical experience as well as by studying published research. The wrinkles of the marketplace often dominate other complex issues, which can lead option theoreticians onto a wrong path. Traders' lore can only be transmitted through practice. This book will meld matters of practical (not necessarily anecdotal) importance with fundamental theory.

The major theme is to present traders and risk managers with the tools to navigate around the difficult notion of manufacturing financial products through book-running. This book will introduce the arcane world of dynamic monitoring of risks. The core of dynamic hedging includes:

- The need for a methodology for the implementation of the Black-Scholes-Merton[3] replicating process for options or any other nonlinear security under the **constraints** imposed by the marketplace.
- The need to generalize the Black-Scholes-Merton framework to cover other parameters than the underlying security in the replicating process (like volatility or interest rates).
- The awareness that transaction costs and frequency can cause a departure from the canons of continuous time finance.
- The awareness that distributions are unstable and hard to model.

Much of the common option literature has been concerned with details of the pricing of instruments (some of which remain untractable).[4] These works often provide insignificant answers to insignificant problems, such as the search for precision in the pricing of American options with constant volatility or interest rates (penny wisdom and dollar insensitivity). In addition, the nontheoretical option literature, departing from the Black-Scholes-Merton framework, has been ensconced in static risk measurement. Most documents introducing traders to conventional risks show only the static, not the dynamic, risks. A derivatives position that is dynamically hedged will be subjected to an entirely different risk profile and, given the limitations of such hedging, will therefore be subjected to **path dependence** (a key word for an option manufacturer).

Readers will not find a magazine-type proliferation of traded exotic structures that delineate infinite variations and combinations; instead, the analysis is limited to the nondecomposable structures (the SDF, **smallest decomposable fragment**). A structure that is the addition of two products will be therefore excluded (except in few cases of *nonadditivity*, where the combination has some merit for the dynamic hedger). The objective of this book is to provide the traders and risk managers with the **tools,** not the ramifications.

Readers should use this book like a roadmap, searching out topics that interest them and moving freely from topic to topic. The formal definitions serve as anchors between categories.

More advanced mathematical topics are relegated to the modules at the back of the book. An attempt has been made to avoid mathematical language and to explain issues in plain English. Formulas do not appear until Chapter 22. In addition, in the presentation of mathematical elements, the book avoids the measure-theoretic framework (required for most proofs in probability theory) and follows an intuitive path. Most mathematical concepts surrounding the topic can be explained with an intuitive verbal description accompanied by graphical hints.

Option Wizards provide a lighter note for many serious topics. Since these sections are designed to be read independently, readers can flip between them at their discretion.

Finally, throughout this book, the pronoun *he* is used as a stylistic convention for ease of reading. This use should always be construed as gender neutral.

- **Part I** (Chapters 1–6) defines **market microstructure and products.** The markets are viewed from the vantage point of broker speaker boxes and market pits, but also are defined in the formal setting of market microstructure theory.

- **Part II** (Chapters 7–16) defines the **basics of vanilla option risk** and presents **measurement** tools.

- **Part III** (Chapters 17–23) describes the **risks of exotic options**.

- **Part IV** (Modules A to G) presents more quantitative tools of analysis and bridges a practitioner's world with **option theory.** These modules, however, should not be construed as appendixes: Most of their content belong to the core of the text.

NOTES ON THE TEXT

Given that I did not initially learn about options in the literature but directly from the market (through observation and experimentation), most of my reasoning remains highly intuitive. I apologize to people with more scholastic tastes who may not be used to such a presentation. Most examples in this book are presented as generic situations. The volatility will be defined as 15.7% (to make one standard deviation equal to 1% daily move). The markets will be scaled to trade at 100.[5] For the purposes of pure option situations, the forward is equal to spot, and the financial carry is insignificant (except in the rare difficult cases where it matters). All options will be European style except for the exotic options where a term structure may be introduced if it becomes relevant for the exercise.

Showing the profile of a butterfly, for example, will involve using 98/100/102 generic calls and studying a calendar spread looking at the three-month 100 against the 6-month 100 calls, and so on.

The creation of generic examples will standardize all cases and help in equating situations throughout the book. When dealing with a purely conceptual option problem, it is necessary to strip out the underlying particularities. *Optionality* transcends the details in most cases. Where these particularities are essential, we will revert to a singular example taken from a specific market.

Notations

P/L	Profit and loss on a position
V or F	Reserved for the value of a generic derivative security
K	Strike price
S_0 or U_0	Underlying asset at time 0
H	Outstrike (barrier strike)
H_H and H_L	High and low outstrikes for a double barrier
r	Interest rate for the numeraire (also r_d)
r_f or d	Rates for the counter-currency or the dividend payout for a stock
y_t	Zero-coupon yield period t
t	Time between present until expiration (except in cases where t_0 is the present, where it becomes $t - t_0$)
σ_i	Standard deviation of the natural log of the prices of the asset i
$\rho_{i,j}$	Correlation of the natural log of the prices between assets i and j
$E_0(S_t)$	Conditional expectation at times 0 of the price of the asset at times t

Jargon

Many terms may be linguistically ambiguous for people from outside the industry. Even option books written for practitioners do not seem to pick up our vernacular.

The same designation delta is used for both the rate and the total equivalent exposure (rate times face value). The same for gamma, vega, theta, and other Greeks.

By "volatility" is always meant implied volatility, not historical. By "15 volatility" read 15% implied volatility for the instrument in annualized terms.

By "underlying" is meant underlying asset, which is also called spot, cash price (as opposed to forward or future).

By "50 cents price" for an option is always meant .5% of face value. By "1 dollar" is meant 1%. By "tick" or "pip" is meant .01% of face value.

By "long the 100" read long the 100 strike.

By "shorter" and "longer" option read "option with shorter time to expiration."

By "leg" is meant one side of a trade in a strategy.

By "Black-Scholes-Merton" is meant the Black-Scholes-Merton option valuation model, as well as its extensions to more complex securities.

By "stopping time" or "first exit" read expected stopping time or expected first exit time.

By "high correlation matrix" read a correlation matrix with most parameters close to 1.

By "integral" is often meant stochastic integral. By "sensitivity to a parameter" is meant comparative static sensitivity to a parameter change. By "the delta vanishes asymptotically" is meant that the delta vanishes asymptotically to the asset price.

By $x/2\ y$ is meant $(x/2)\ y$ and $a + b/2$ means $a + (b/2)$.

Finally, the term *derivative*, can mean either a derivative security or the mathematical rate of change. When possible, the text will specify if it is a mathematical derivative; otherwise it should be construed as being a security.

Nassim Taleb

Larchmont, New York
November 1996

Acknowledgments

This work reflects the help and knowledge of many. First, I want to thank two people who participated in every phase of the manuscript's development: Raphael Douady, a mathematician and Howard Savery, an exotic options trader. Both have extremely intuitive and fast minds. They asked me to adopt a language that would be neutral enough for both to understand. Many of the ideas of the book were discussed and belabored to the point of my being incapable of distinguishing between my original ideas and the ones that they suggested to me. Raphael, in addition, composed an academic paper on *stopping time* (in French no less) to help with some of the pricing tools for the book.

The pedagogical method of defining the issue and explaining it intuitively prior to expanding any point was inspired by the coaching of Marty O'Connell and Jim Piper with whom I, along with Richard Laden, gave a series of seminars on simple methods for hedging complicated options.

The following people either generously reviewed sections of the manuscript and offered comments or discussed some of the topics with me. Nicole El Karoui, David DeRosa, Marco Avellaneda, Dean Weaver (who detected the highest number of undetectable typos), Peter Tselepis, Jamil Baz, Stan Jonas, Yuri Gonorovsky, Bob Freedberg, Steven Monieson, Doug Monieson, Brian Monieson, Scott Kerbel, Antonio Paras, Bob Whittacre, Didier Javice, Richard Laden, Dan Mantini (who detected the first misplaced decimal), Shivagi Rao, Richard Kates, Jimmy Powers, Nick Hatzopoulos, Jean-Philippe Frignet, Rick Welsh, Leon Rosen, Shaiy Pilpel, Tony Glickman, Andrei Pokrovski, Julian Harding, Philibert Kongtcheu, Maroun Edde, Bruno Dupire, David Donora, Hélyette Geman, Bill Margrabe, Henry Zhu, Ram Venkatraman, Nakle Zeidan, Marc Weissman, Thomas Artarit, and Michel Jean-Baptiste.

All mistakes that have been overlooked are mine. I would also like to thank Pamela van Giessen, my editor at Wiley, as well as Mary Daniello, the book's production manager at Wiley, and Nancy Marcus Land, at Publications Development Company.

For any inadvertent omissions that emanate from my absentmindedness, I apologize. Please accept my unspoken thanks.

Data were provided by Banque Indosuez, Steve Monieson, Tradition Financial Services, and Pierre Wolf.

N. T.

Contents

Part II

Measuring Option Risks

PART III

TRADING AND HEDGING EXOTIC OPTIONS

PART IV

MODULES

Dynamic Hedging

As these events are beyond our understanding let us fake being their instigator.

Jean Cocteau

PRINCIPLES OF REAL WORLD DYNAMIC HEDGING

■ **Rebalancing the gamma** corresponds to buying and selling the underlying security in order to replicate the payoff of the option.

Even if traders knew the exact future volatility but hedged themselves (rebalanced the gamma) at discretely spaced increments, they would still have difficulty predicting the final P/L. Option pricing eliminated, by necessity, the transaction costs. If however, they traded every millionth of a second at the screen mid-market they would get a P/L with certainty.

Increasing the frequency of adjustments would compress the results as shown in the following chart:

Mathematically, the shape of the distribution is simply determined by $\sigma/\sqrt{n}$ (functional central limit theorem). An intuitive explanation is that an average will tend to the mean at a speed of $1/\sqrt{\text{number of draws}}$. In this case, the mean is the Black-Scholes-Merton value of the security. In Chapter 16, a case study shows the magnitude of the adjustment luck in the tracking of the P/L.

The increase in transaction frequency would have the effect of increasing the dynamic hedging costs (owing to transaction costs) by moving the center of the distribution to the left,[1] as seen in the following chart:

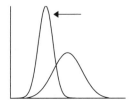

Market makers hence face the continuous dilemma between:

- Variance of returns on one hand. (Option replication is not a risk-free proposition.)
- Transaction costs on the other.

When an option trader sells a structure that is worth 5.00 on his theoretical value sheets, he can expect, baring transaction costs, to manufacture it for somewhere between 4.00 and 6.00. However, the more parameters he needs to be protected against, the higher the management costs.

> ***Risk Management Rule:*** The more volatile parameters the option trader needs to be protected against, the more allowance is necessary against both the volatility of the parameters and the expected transaction costs.

The thesis of this book is that the more parameters fly around (interest rates, volatility term structures, etc), the more arduous the dynamic hedging. Unlike the Black-Scholes-Merton world our trading environment requires us to hedge more than the gamma. Every possible second derivative will be costly. We must hedge the vega convexity, the exposures to the rates and so on as they are not stable. Chapter 15 shows the effect of stochastic volatility and provides the intuition for the vega convexity. Chapter 10 includes a description of convexity broadly defined.

As Black-Scholes-Merton includes the cost of gamma in computing the time value of the option, so will we need to add the convexity of all non linear parameters to it (an Ito term, see Module G). A position that is short gamma on interest rates in addition to the Black-Scholes-Merton gamma needs to be priced accordingly, with the proper markup (or down). The Option Wizard, *The Contamination (or Convexity) Principle*, provides an intuitive explanation of the issue. Problems will occur where the moves in the parameters might be correlated.

Positions that require vega neutrality in a concave vega (short volatility of volatility) will then be inferior in value to others that do not require such dynamic hedge owing to linear vega and so on.

The need to understand the replicating process more thoroughly with exotic options reflects their greater hedging costs.

GENERAL RISK MANAGEMENT

In the immature modern financial jargon, *risk management* is usually interpreted as either coping with the financial risks inherent to an otherwise nonfinancial businesses or the market risks incurred by providers of financial instruments (such as trading firms, exchange traders, banks, and other dealers). The latter will be the concern of this book. Books on risk management abound by people who try to explain sophisticated financial tools to treasurers of corporations or pension funds managers. Because providers face daily risks in the manufacturing of the financial products and instruments, this book focuses on the risk transfer between a static product (corporate risk) and a dynamic one (the market maker's), the delta-neutral operator in Black-Scholes-Merton's world.

There are two levels of risk management: micromanagement and macromanagement.

> **Micromanagement** occurs at the level of one product line or one coherent book run by a unit (e.g., exchange local or "upstairs" trading desk). This encompasses the intimate knowledge of the behavior of every derivative product with respect to time and market movement and the thorough thinking in multiple dimensions required by the derivatives trader's function (the fruit of lengthy apprenticeship).
>
> **Macromanagement** takes place at the level of a general firm. This is a generally more quantitative, more theoretical function perfected by a general watchdog. Somehow by magic, the sum of the risks does not add up to the total risks. Some books match one another, while the risks of others become additive. However, the measurement tools, like diversification and correlation, so celebrated in modern finance appear to be still imprecise and of weak predictive powers. Their use can dangerously lull the risk managers into a false sense of statistical security.

The macromanager's function is to allocate risk (defined as total possible variance) across products and units to maximize the utilization of a trading firm's most valuable resource: *risk*. Figure I.1 illustrates the relationship of dynamic hedging to risk management.

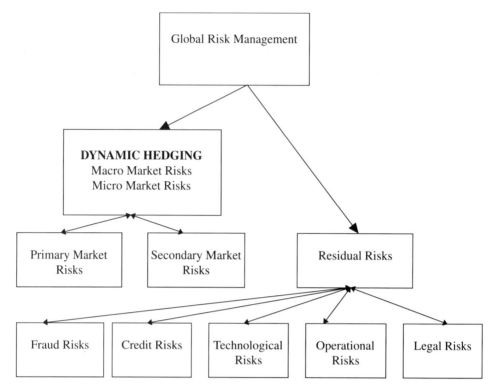

Figure I.1   The larger risk management framework.

There has been a growth in the number of "risk management advisors," an industry sometimes populated by people with an amateurish knowledge of risk. Using some form of shallow technical skills, these advisors emit pronouncements on such matters as "risk management" without a true understanding of the distribution. Such inexperience and weakness become most apparent with the value-at-risk fad or the outpouring of books on risk management by authors who never traded a contract.

There is no shortcut method of risk management. Every person who needs to be acquainted with the activity should work hard at trying to make sense of the dynamic interaction of portfolio components relative to time and combinations of market movements. Every derivative user or trader needs to be able to account for the effect of either the passage of time or the movement of the underlying assets on the portfolio. Issues of pricing are therefore overstated: Most money is made or lost because of market movement, not because of mispricing. Often the cause is mishedging. Most commonly, losses result from a poor understanding of liquidity and the shape of the statistical distribution.

Option Wizard: Culture Shocks

There are spectacular communication problems between traders and *quants* (research assistants) owing to many factors:

- People who have completed a Ph.D. program develop a tendency to be thorough.
- Traders, by contrast, are impatient and need brief simplistic descriptions, something someone who spent most of his adult life solving complex problems is often unable to provide. Traders tend to see matters in "flashes," a type of nonlinear epistemology. Such desire for the highest level of possible abstraction is sometimes mistaken for "short attention span."

This leads to Brecht-like amusing exercises in *incommunicability* between traders and their quants. One trader (himself a former quant) built the following strategy in dealing with the research department people. When communicating with him, they were advised to do the following:

1. In a single sentence, explain the conclusion, before discussing the subject matter.
2. In a single sentence, explain the subject matter.
3. If unable to perform 1 or 2, then abandon the entire project.

This method helps the quant understand the major difference between the less challenging matters of the real world and the thrills of science. In addition, it provides him with a way to learn to focus like a businessperson.

Richard Feynman,* one of the greatest minds of our times, was comfortable enough with his subject matter to write an intuitive book on quantum physics without a single formula.

---

*Richard Feynman, QED (1985) Princeton: Princeton University Press.

PART I

MARKETS, INSTRUMENTS, PEOPLE

Chapter 1

Introduction to the Instruments

Understanding a theory means (. . .) understanding it as an attempt to solve a certain problem.

Sir Karl Popper

In this chapter, we will rapidly but formally define the instruments and present their major characteristics. It is recommended that all readers, even those knowledgeable in this area, study the following definitions, as they will provide the framework of analysis used in the book.

DERIVATIVES

■ A **derivative** is a security whose price ultimately depends on that of another asset (called underlying). There are different categories of derivatives, ranging from something as simple as a future to something as complex as an exotic option, with all the shades in between.

The best way to look at derivatives is to separate them into two broad categories: **linear** and **nonlinear** derivatives. A linear derivative is easy to hedge and lock in completely, whereas a nonlinear one will present serious instability and require dynamic hedging.

■ A **nonlinear derivative** with respect to a parameter is one that presents a second derivative (or partial derivative with respect to that parameter) different from 0.

The option wizard presents a graphic linear or nonlinear derivative view of the concept of nonlinearity.

> ***Risk Management Rule:*** All nonlinear derivatives are time-dependent in their price.

This rule is explored in the contamination principle and will be discussed throughout this book. For now, it is enough to state that nonlinearity

Option Wizard: The Greeks

The "Greeks," as option traders call them, denote the sensitivity of the option price with respect to several parameters. The following are basic definitions for use in Part I. These terms will be explored in greater detail later in this book.

Delta Sensitivity of the option price to the change in the underlying asset price.

Gamma Sensitivity of the option delta to the change in the underlying asset price.

Vega Sensitivity of the option price to the change in implied volatility.

Theta Expected change in the option price with the passage of time assuming risk-neutral growth in the asset.

Rho Sensitivity of the option price to interest rates or dividend payout.

"Long gamma or vega" means a positive sensitivity to the Greek (a higher P/L at a higher parameter).

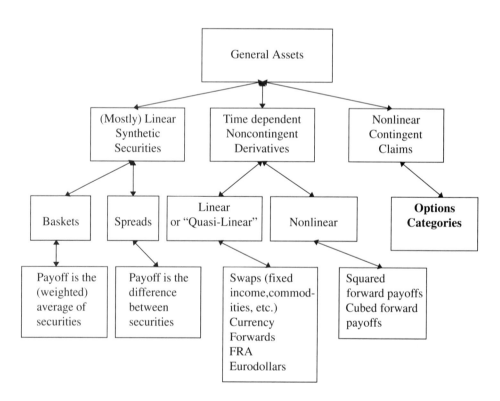

Figure 1.1 Classification of derivatives.

Option Wizard: The Hedger's Viewpoint

Throughout this book, think of a derivative in terms of its replication costs. For this purpose, the world is divided into two categories: the user and the manufacturer. Their utility function and even results will be entirely different. The user is involved in terminal value (usually), while the manufacturer engages in dynamic hedging (when he is doing his job right), which markedly alters the product.

A dynamic hedger will not be interested in whether he owns a put or a call (first-order hedges will make them identical). What matters is the strike and the expiration.

is gamma (or more generally called convexity) and that gamma needs to be accompanied by time decay (the "rent").

Derivatives are not always linear, convex, or concave across all moves (see Figures 1.2A–D). A test of local linearity of a derivative security (that is a function of the underlying asset) between asset prices S_1 and S_2, with $0 < \lambda < 1$, will satisfy the following equality :

$$V(\lambda S_1 + (1 - \lambda)S_2) = \lambda\, V(S_1) + (1 - \lambda)V(S_2)$$

It will be convex between S_1 and S_2 if:

$$V(\lambda S_1 + (1 - \lambda)S_2) \leq \lambda\, V(S_1) + (1 - \lambda)V(S_2)$$

It will be concave if:

$$V(\lambda S_1 + (1 - \lambda)S_2) \geq \lambda\, V(S_1) + (1 - \lambda)V(S_2)$$

Option Wizard: Linear and Nonlinear Securities

Although we are initially considering linearity with respect to the underlying asset, this notion will be later extended to other parameters such as interest rates and volatility.

As the graphical representation at the top of page 12 shows, a linear security constantly behaves like a line. In option parlance, it will have a delta but no other Greeks,* and certainly no curvature. Linear securities require little or no dynamic hedging.

---

* The Greeks initially represented the various derivatives of the Black-Scholes-Merton formula. By extension, it became any sensitivity of a derivative security with respect to a particular market parameter.

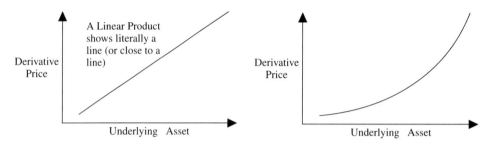

Figure 1.2A Linearity.

Figure 1.2B A nonlinear derivative: Convex security.

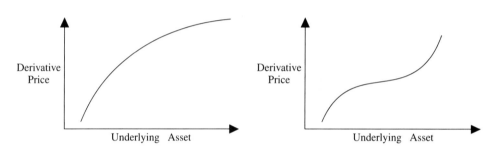

Figure 1.2C A nonlinear derivative: Concave security.

Figure 1.2D A mixed nonlinear derivative.

Many securities exhibit some linearity until the test of fire. These instruments are called "quasi-linear" securities. Convexity affects many financial instruments, even those least suspected.

The contamination principle, we will see, dictates that every nonlinear security commands time value, positive if the security is convex and negative if it is concave.

Synthetic Securities

■ A **synthetic security** is a linear combination of two or more primary instruments in the markets.

A basket's price is derived from a weighted combination of existing primary instruments. For example, Standard & Poor's 500 (SP500) contract is a weighted average of the components. It can therefore be exactly replicated with a mixture of the components (for those who have the time and patience to leg the 500 stocks). A European currency unit (ECU) is another example

Option Wizard: The First Derivative Trade

The earliest option trade on record in Western literature was a bet on future crop by Thales of Miletus, which Aristotle recounted with great pride in his *Politics.** To benefit from a better than expected olive crop, Thales put a deposit on every olive press in the vicinity of Miletus. As demand for these grew, he sublet the facilities for profit, mostly to make the point that philosophers who so desire can achieve material success. The dichotomy between the "MIT-smart" and the "Brooklyn-smart," today prevalent on Wall Street, was already apparent in fifth-century Asia Minor. Thales used the first **derivative** instrument, actually an option on a future, a second-order derivative at that! He did not trade olives, which he would have had to sell short, but chose to buy the equivalent of a call on the olive presses, for fall delivery, with the knowledge that all he could lose was his deposit.

---

* See Russell (1945).

---

of an arithmetic average. A basket composed of 20% stock A and 80% V stock B can easily be replicated with the purchase of every component.

Synthetic securities are not always linear, but exceptions are rare enough for us not to bother with them. For example, when the average of the instruments is not arithmetic, some oddities can result. The U.S. dollar index, traded on FINEX will present some convexity owing to the geometric nature of the averaging and will therefore trade at a premium to the underlying securities for that reason. The nonlinearity that results from the convexity can cause a neutral person to benefit from a market move either way, which can make one side of the arbitrage more desirable. Convexity, which will be defined later on, usually commands a price since Wall Street rarely grants free lunches.

> *Example:* The Elevator Bank issues its own "mother of all baskets" and emits some notes, the payoff of which is indexed off the basket. The official reason is that the basket effectively tracks inflation or some other indicator. The true reason is that the basket will have a lower volatility than the sum of the instruments and is believed to be easy to hedge.

TIME-DEPENDENT LINEAR DERIVATIVES

■ **Time-dependent linear derivatives** are instruments separated from the original asset through time.

Option Wizard: The Contamination (or Convexity) Principle

The most important notion in option hedging and trading is the contamination principle: It is the fundamental principle of dynamic hedging. It means roughly that if there is a possible spot in time and space capable of bringing a profit, then the areas surrounding it need to account for that effect.

The contamination principle is similar to the notion of heat transfer.* If a spot is located near a source of heat, then its temperature will rise accordingly. If the asset price nears a level that would bring a sizable profit to the portfolio then the area surrounding it should cause a modicum of profit as well.

In the following chart, a derivative will pay $1 million should some event take place in the market. Starting at a given point, the security pays on the node to the right. It would then be unreasonable to think that such a security would be worth nothing at Point So. One standard deviation move should result in a payoff of $1,000,000 (or part of that sum).

The Contamination Principle

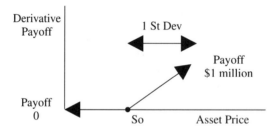

Every experienced trader, seeing the payoff and the probability attached to it, would buy the derivative security. The derivative would then be worth more than 0, and it is easy to see time value taking shape in the following chart:

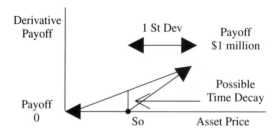

However, time value means time decay. As shown in the following chart, with everything remaining the same, the option would decrease in time value at the standard deviations as the payoff becomes less likely:

(Continued)

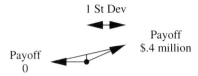

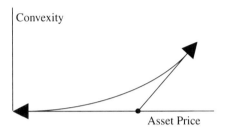

The final chart shows that when the points are far from each other (as in option prices), a convex line forms.

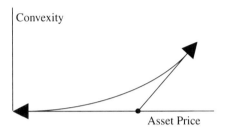

This example suggests why an option has "convexity."

---

* The origin of the designation *contamination* resides in the price of an option "contaminating" those around it. When an option becomes expensive, those around it need to follow. Likewise, one can see that if an Arrow-Debreu price rises those around it need to increase as well. They are then said to contaminate each other.

A swap is a linear (or quasi-linear) derivative, as the second-order derivative with respect to the asset price is equal (or close to) zero. In trader's parlance, its hedge ratio is not supposed to change relative to movements in the underlying asset, although it can be argued that there is no such thing as a purely linear derivative.

Time-dependent linear derivatives include:

- *Forwards.* They are agreements to swap some proceeds in the future.
- *Floating Rate Agreements (FRAs), Eurodollars.* They will, for the purpose of this book, be forward-forwards that can be broken down into strips of products that start period t and end period $t + 1$.
- *Swaps.* Whatever their end use (this is not of any concern here), they can be composed into a combination of Eurodollars or FRAs. Most of their complexity comes from being detail-heavy, but they otherwise exhibit well-behaved features.[1]

Aside from the correlation between a future price and its financing, most of the difficulties of these assets lie in the problem of interpolation between two points. The way time treats them is not always easy to ascertain. A lesser, but no small, difficulty resides in the multiplication of minute details such as the conventions on the delivery or the 360/365-day basis and other rules that no trader was ever known to memorize.

Noncontingent Time-Dependent Nonlinear Derivatives

■ **Noncontingent time-dependent nonlinear derivatives** represent instruments that are convex, concave, or mixed (with respect to the underlying asset) but that are not options (i.e., noncontingent).

The infamous LIBOR-square (London Interbank Offer Rate) for example, provides a lurid example of such convexity. The LIBOR cube will have a third derivative (a convexity of the curvature) but the product does not appear very likely to sell heavily. Despite their payoffs, however, these instruments do not constitute an option since both parties are obligated to swap the proceeds. The strangeness of their payoff is that they are generally convex above a point and concave below, or vice versa. The acceleration of the positive payoffs on one side is balanced by the acceleration of the negative payoffs on the other.

> *Example:*   The Elevator Bank sells to its customers in the area surrounding Cincinnati, Ohio, a note paying to its holder the square of the interest rate move (between inception and some predetermined time in the future). The customer, stressed out by low interest rates, would thus be compensated in an accelerated way against further rate drops. The note looks like an option, and being (on the surface) arduous to hedge, it will sell for higher than "fair" value.

Options and Other Contingent Claims

The price of options depends on contingent events. They represent the bulk of this study. They are the culprit, the topic of this book. A swap is a linear derivative while a path-dependent swap will present uncertain payoffs. In the past, operators defined these instruments as tools with "optionality," where one party had a right to choose and the other one was under an obligation.

We will study options at two levels. Level 1 is a conventional presentation of the product, as if the exotic option markets did not exist. Level 2 will go into a more generalized presentation of the option markets that would encompass both vanilla and exotics (Chapter 2).

Option Wizard: The Contamination Principle and LIBOR Square

LIBOR square is a contract with a mixed payoff: convex in one zone and concave in another. At the origin (where the contract is set), it is neither. According to the contamination principle, the contract needs to be higher than its value on the line in areas where it is long gamma and lower in areas where it is short.*

The contract pays:

$$q(x - x_0)^2 \text{ if } x > x_0$$
$$-q(x - x_0)^2 \text{ if } x < x_0$$

with q the quantity, x_0 the origin, x the present LIBOR price.

Therefore, its delta is

$$2q(x - x_0) \text{ if } x > x_0$$
$$-2q(x - x_0) \text{ if } x < x_0$$

And the gamma is

$$2q \text{ if } x > x_0$$
$$-2q \text{ if } x < x_0$$

The following chart illustrates the valuation process:

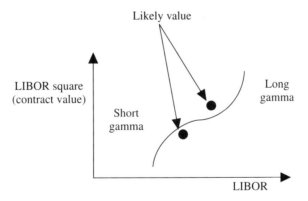

The discussion of option trading will clarify the concept of cells contamination: The arbitrage derived value of any security will depend on its delta-neutral replication.

---

* LIBOR square is a contract that pays to one party the square of the difference between the origin and a higher price and obligates it to pay the square of the difference between the lower price and the origin.

Simple Options

Options are contingent claims, and thus distinguish themselves from other products in being a potential asset for one party and a potential liability for another. This contingency in their value subjects them to probability theory. All option pricing consists therefore in dealing with probability.

- A **put** is the right to sell an instrument at a certain price (the **strike price**) within some time frame. A **call** is the right to buy the instrument.

  With the opening of many new instruments, puts or calls can be confused. They depend on the numeraire. For a currency pair, a put on Mark/Dollar (the right to sell Marks and buy dollars) is a call on Dollar/Mark. Similarly, a put on yields is a call on bonds, a matter of some confusing importance since one illustrious exchange defined a contract on yield (thus inventing an asset), while most cash instruments are traded according to their price.

  An interesting extension is that a call on the SP500 is a put on cash for someone whose P/L is computed in SP500 units (the case of indexed fund managers). More on that later.

- A **European option** can only be exercised on the last day. An **American option** can be exercised any time between its inception and the end date. A hybrid, the **Bermudan option** can be exercised on a set number of days between inception and expiration.

- **Intrinsic value,** for a call, or the in-the-money part of an option is the difference between the asset value and the strike price if that difference is positive. It is zero if the difference is negative. For a put, it is the reverse. For a European option (an option that is only exercisable on one date), the intrinsic value is typically expressed by traders (by convention) as the difference between the strike and the corresponding forward. Since the option is not exercised before expiration, the only price that matters is the term market price of the asset (for delivery on the expiration of the option).

The best way intuitively to test whether any particular instrument is an option is to see if the payoff is asymmetric and if there is a strike price (Figure 1.3). A call option is priced at expiration as the

$$\text{Max } (S - K, 0)$$

with S the asset price at expiration and K the strike price. It is read as the *greater of the difference between the asset price at expiration and the strike or zero.*

This simple formula means in English that the owner collects some amount (intrinsic) or nothing, whichever is greatest. $S - K$ is the difference between spot and strike. When it is negative, the operator would prefer to receive nothing.

A put option will be expressed as

$$Max\ (K - S, 0)$$

■ **Forwards and futures** are contracts to unconditionally exchange an asset at a predetermined date for an agreed-on price.

They are straight claims, with assets and liabilities on both sides of the fence (as opposed to options where one party has an asset and the other a liability). They also distinguish themselves from options because the payoff does not give any party the element of choice. As will be explained later, some minor technicalities in the definition of the futures contracts (truly, very minor) such as the bond futures[2] spawned an entire cottage industry of arbitrageurs, analysts, and the like.

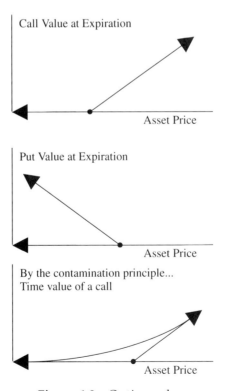

Figure 1.3   Option value.

Another intuitive way to understand an option is to think of it as half the forward or future: The long partakes of the upside (above a certain point, called the strike price) and the short partakes of the downside, for a fee. It is no wonder that being long a put and short a call replicates entirely the future (of course, there are questions of early exercise that we will ignore initially).

Options proliferate in daily life, some of which people are long (they own the choice) for some of which people are short. A chief executive officer owns, by virtue of his position, an option. The manager can partake of the upside of the company and get a bonus when the performance is acceptable. Should the industry experience a downturn and the company go bankrupt, the CEO's sole risk would be his job or some unpleasant but otherwise financially harmless castigation. He will not be asked to appear before the board with his checkbook in hand. It is easy to see that the strike price for the bonus is the required performance and that the shareholders sold (or, rather, gave) that option to the manager.[3]

Forwards, options, and futures represent the bulk of derivatives instruments. A later section in this chapter will present a more advanced version of options.

Hard and Soft Optionality

■ **Optionality** is a broad term used by traders to describe a nonlinearity in the payoff of an instrument. It is often applied to convex instruments or to situations like a "stop loss" or a known order in the market.

As an extension of *the contamination principle,* every item with optionality needs to trade at a premium and the shrinkage of premium with the passage of time (owing to the narrowing of the probability measure of events) will mean necessarily that every item with optionality will have time decay.

It is convenient to call hard optionality the situation where a contract has a strike price and soft optionality the situation where the contract has a built-in convexity but no real strike price. Soft optionality presents generally milder gamma and other Greeks but will present more stable features across time.

Basic Rules of Options Equivalence

Below are the basic rules of what traders call "option algebra."

- Put-call parity for a European option: Long call/short put = Long forward, provided they are all of the same strike.

Warning Expiration: "Pin Risks" (described in Chapter 13) cause put-call parity not to hold for listed options.

Replacing a long with a "+" sign and the short with a " − " sign allows for the following simple arithmetic:
Position equivalence:

$+C - P = F$. A long forward is equal to a long call/short put of the same strike.

Hence:

$+C = P + F$. Long a call is equivalent to long a put/long a future.

And

$+P = C - F$. Long a put is equivalent to long a call/short a future.

- For a "soft" American option (see definition later in this chapter), the put-call parity rules hold but with a weaker equivalence.
- For "hard" American options, the rule becomes more slippery. More complex rules are described in Chapter 15. It is recommended for the nonspecialist to completely ignore put-call parity.

Example: Assume that the 3-month 102 Put trades for $1.975, that the 3-month 102 Call trades for $2.9625, and that the forward for the exact delivery date for both trades for 101.00.
   At expiration, assuming financing at 5%, the call will cost $1.975 × .05 × (90/360) = .025 and the put will cost .0375. We will then have the P/L shown in Table 1.1.

Table 1.1   Static Put/Call Parity

Asset Price	102 Call P/L	Forward Contract P/L	102 Put P/L	Total Forward P/L + 102 Put P/L
106	2	5	−3	2
105	1	4	−3	1
104	0	3	−3	0
103	−1	2	−3	−1
102	−2	1	−3	−2
101	−2	0	−2	−2
100	−2	−1	−1	−2
99	−2	−2	0	−2
98	−2	−3	1	−2
97	−2	−4	2	−2

Table 1.1 shows the profile at expiration. If two trades are identical at expiration *everywhere* on the map of possible prices, and if they expire on the same day, then the trades will have the same risk and profit/loss profile during their life.

The following rule applies to all markets, properly rescaled, provided they are European and present liquid forwards. To make that rule acceptable for the future, proper allowance needs to be made for the "tailing" (see Chapter 7).

Mirror Image Rule

1 unit of a put + x% of the unit in forward = 1 unit of a call + $(100 - x)$% of the unit in forward, all of the same strike and expiration.

This rule is obvious: A put delta neutral at 30% is equal to $P + .3F = (C - F) + .3F = C - .7F$. If a 103 put has a forward delta of 30% the 103 call will have a forward delta of 70%. This formula uses forward delta, not cash deltas that need to be adjusted for. Most risk management systems disclose the cash, not the forward delta, as does the canonical Black-Scholes-Merton formula.

Warning: European options need to be hedged with the forward,[4] not cash. However, most commercial pricing systems tend to disclose the spot hedge instead, which often can be misleading. Traders often have recourse to cash for short-term hedges owing to the lack of liquidity in the forwards. This habit generally leads them to forget the exact conditions for adequate put/call parity.

■ A **forward delta** for a European option is the equivalent cash position with the same delivery date as the underlying asset.

For an American option, a forward delta is typically of uncertain duration. Such a duration, however, is generally calculated and called the "omega" (discussed later in this chapter), but will be too unstable for us to use for adequate equivalence.

Consequently, a straddle will be equal to two calls delta neutral or two puts delta neutral (of the same strike). Assume that the forward delta of a put is 30%:

Straddle = $2P + .6F = 2 (C - F) + .6F = 2C - 2F + .6F = 2C - 1.4F$

Consequently, a call calendar spread will have the same profile as a put calendar spread (assuming interest rates constant).

A put butterfly will have the same price as a call butterfly. Examine the 98/100/102 butterfly (buy one 98 call, sell two 100 call, buy one 102 call):

$$
\begin{aligned}
1\ 98C - 2\ 100C + 1\ 102C &= 1\ (98P + F) - 2\ (100P + F) + 1\ (102P + F) \\
&= 1\ 98P - 2\ 100P + 1\ 102P + 1\ F - 2\ F + 1\ F \\
&= \text{Put Butterfly.}
\end{aligned}
$$

A call butterfly 98-100-102, a put butterfly 98-100-102, and a condor 98-100-102 will have the same exposure.

A 98-100-102 condor is defined as long a 98 put, long a 102 call, and short the 100 straddle:

$$
\begin{aligned}
&= 98P - 100P - 100C + 102C \\
&= 98P - 100P - (100P + F) + (102P + F) \\
&= 98P - 100P - 100P + 102P - F + F \\
&= 98P - 2\ 100P + 102P \text{ a put butterfly, which we established is} \\
&\qquad\qquad\qquad\qquad \text{equivalent to the call butterfly.}
\end{aligned}
$$

To gain an intuitive feel the reader can verify that Figure 1.4 shows the same P/L profile for the following:

Long 98, long 102, short twice the 100, all calls or all puts.
Long 98 puts, long 102 calls, short the 100 straddle.
Long the 98 calls, long the 102 puts, short the 100 straddle.

A result of these rules is that the volatility of an out-of-the-money put should be exactly equal to that of a corresponding in-the-money call of the same strike.

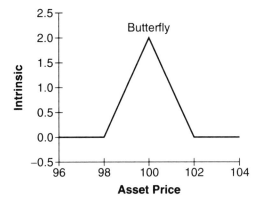

Figure 1.4 Butterfly profile.

Risk Management Rules:

Traders should never carry put-call parity rules outside of a strike.

Some of the preceding rules can be used with soft American options, except when the delta of the option becomes too high.

AMERICAN OPTIONS, EARLY EXERCISE, AND OTHER HEADACHES (ADVANCED TOPIC)

An American option poses more problems than European options because the path followed by the underlying asset can lead to possible early exercise. With a European option, pricing is a simple matter: One can just discount the final payoffs on expiration day.

Without getting immersed in the pricing complications of American options, it is safe to say that the complexity arises because uncertainty about the date of occurrence of the early exercise makes it difficult to model.[5] The rules depend on time and the amount of intrinsic value, which makes the early exercise rules too uncertain.

Such early exercise is generally determined two ways: the soft (or easy) rule and the hard rule.

Soft American Options

■ A **soft American option** (also called a pseudo-European option) is only subjected to early exercise from the standpoint of the financing of the intrinsic value.

An **extension** of this definition is that only one interest rate, that affecting the financing of the premium for the operator, impacts the decision to early exercise.

For risk management and trading purposes, soft American options will be largely similar to the European options, except when interest rates become very high relative to volatility. The reason they are often called pseudo-European options is that they behave in general like European options, except when very deep in the money. The test of early exercise is whether the total option value is less than the time value of the money between the time of consideration and expiration.

Example: Assume that an asset trades at $100, with interest rates at 6% (annualized) and volatility at 15.7%. Assume also that the 3-month 80 call is worth $20, at least if it is American. Forgoing early exercise would create an opportunity cost of $20 \times 90/360 \times .06 = .30$ cents, the financing of the $20 premium for 3 months. The time value of the equivalent put is close to zero (by put-call parity), so the intelligent operator can swap the call into the underlying asset and buy the put to replicate the same initial structure at a better cost. He would end up long the put and long the underlying asset.

Hard American Options

■ A **hard American option** is an option subjected to early exercise tests from the standpoint of both the financing of the intrinsic value and the carry costs of the underlying asset until the nominal expiration.

By extension, two rates, that of the premium for the operator, and that of the carry of the underlying asset impact the decision to early exercise.

An early exercise can thus be attributed, in addition to the soft American rule, to the yield benefits of an early position in the asset. The following filter needs to be taken into account at all times during the life of the option: Would the operator do better if he owned an interest-bearing asset than if he owned the equivalent position through the options?

Example: The operator owns the same call as earlier, but the underlying asset is a currency that pays 20% interest while domestic rates are 6%. The option trader has the additional benefit of exercising the call because, on top of the financing, he can own the currency that pays the high interest rates against his home currency, which costs him only 6% to short, therefore earning approximately 14% annualized on the same value. The benefits of early exercise from the asset ownership are much higher than in the previous case: $.14 \times 100$ (face value) $\times 90/360 = \$3.5$. In addition to that, the trader has the value of getting the cash much earlier, which was computed in the previous case at $.30. The operator should perhaps have exercised the option much earlier to benefit from this extra kicker.

Likewise the put on the high-yielding currency will not be subjected to early exercise. Take the following rule: A market trades at 100. The 120 put with $20 of intrinsic value will be better held till expiration since the operator would have to pay $3.50 to hold the equivalent short position in financing differential. True, the 30 cents of financing the premium would be deducted from that value in the cost-benefits analysis. So the put would not be early exercised by an optimal operator. It will trade and will be considered for all intents and purposes as a European instrument.[6]

These rules of hard early exercise extend to the following instruments:

- *Bonds with a Positive Carry.* American calls are early exercisable when the bond is financed more cheaply than its yield. American puts will therefore be similar to (but not quite the same as) European puts.

- *Bonds with a Negative Carry.* The reverse is true.

- *Equities.* When the equities are negative carry (and the dividend payout is known), the calls resemble European ones and vice versa.

Never trust the price for an American option[7] on a cash instrument. There may be changes in the parameters throughout the life of the instrument (nondividend paying stocks starting to pay, changes in interest rates, reversal of the interest rate differential) that can affect its future value. Parameters, unfortunately, are not frozen.

Options on futures, therefore, will be considered subject to the soft exercise rules. We will generally fold them within the category of European instruments for the purpose of our analysis. At all times, the test will be that of the financing of the premium; differences only become pertinent between European and American options for deep in-the-money instruments.

European instruments tend to prevail where there are differences in the pricing mechanism. The market generally seems to go to the most liquid instrument, and operators—by shying away from complicated options—make them less attractive to trade. European options dominate with the currencies, and represent close to 99% of the volume of those with a high differential.

Option Wizard: The Simplicity Rule

A major rule should be taken into account: **The market always tends to flow to simplicity.** Complexity is generally costlier to both monitor and produce, and somehow in the long run, demand moves away from the complex in favor of the simple. New, elaborate contracts certainly attract people, but typically the novelty wanes. Operators will then try to satisfy their needs for protection by seeking the cheapest possible way.

Complex products cost more to replicate. An optimal operator becomes cost conscious and avoids enriching the financial institutions when he can satisfy his interests more economically. This becomes noticeable with the life or death of listed financial instruments. It is the recipe for the survival of exchange contracts. That rule will be discussed in the study of exotic options.

A Brief Warning about Early Exercise Tests

Most operators have their risk management system flag an early exercise and routinely terminate the option. This is often less than optimal (and downright dangerous) for the following reasons:

- One should refine the test by using a proper volatility for the corresponding out-of-the-money option of the same strike. Most risk management systems do not apply the proper volatility smiles correctly. For example, if the option early exercise test is done at a volatility of 16% and the strike price concerned trades at 20%, the early exercise flagged by the system would be erroneous.

- An additional refinement should be the use of a volatility term structure by retesting with a longer or shorter duration, inputting the highest possible volatility between time zero and the expiration of the option.

- When dealing with a large-size position, dealers, upon exercise, synthetically become short an out-of-the-money option. It is recommended to test for the liquidity of such strike in the market and compute the replacement costs.

- A war story: The day before the stock market crash (of 1987) X, a market maker in the Eurodollar options, found a deep-in-the-money "reversal" in his books (*a reversal means that the trader is long a put, short a call, short the future*). According to his risk management system, the put was early exercisable. He exercised the put staying naked the calls. The following day, the market experienced a 10 standard deviation rally on the open, putting him out of business and, worse, causing his story to become a legend. Ironically, X belonged to the category of "wings" buyers (people who always own out-of-the-money options). He never shorted "wing" options and ended up hurt by a synthetic (and entirely accidental) short.

Consequence: Smile-Calendars (Advanced Topic). The volatility of options of the same strike needs to be equal to allow for put-call parity equivalence. While this rule applies unconditionally for European options, many operators mistakenly apply it to the American variety. In some cases, the rules can be applied, and in other cases they need to be lifted.

When a strong skew is impacting the market, the put-call parity can be weakened considerably by the following:

- A rising volatility curve could separate the put and calls from each other because the nonexercisable leg would follow the nominal maturity, whereas the exercisable one would have a considerably shorter expected life.

Example: Assume that 3-month options trade at 15.7% volatility but that the 1-day options traded at 13%. An exercisable 80 call would be priced at 13%, whereas the nonexercisable leg (the 80 put) would trade at 20%.

- A strong smile (defined as an implied volatility that is a function of the strike price and time to maturity) can present worse results.

Example: As shown in Figure 1.5, assume that the 80 strike for the 3-month option trades at 20% volatility (point A), while the at-the-money trades at 15.7 for 3-month (point B) and 13% for 1-day options (point C). The 3-month 80 call will trade at 13% volatility (point C), while the 80 put would trade at 20%.

> *Risk Management Rule:*   Hard American options are more valuable than European options of the same expiration, because they harbor a compound option on interest rates or volatility. The difference between them increases with either the *volatility of volatility* or the level and volatility of interest (or carry) rates.

The rule is easy to explain to traders who had to live in highly unstable interest rates or fluctuating implied volatility (vvol). The American option gives the owner the right to pay the carry to "extend" the option one additional day and therefore make a bet that the option may no longer be

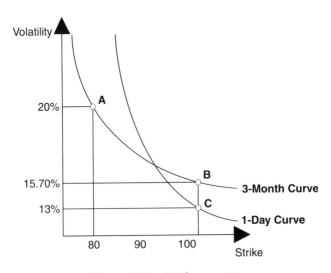

Figure 1.5   Smile curves.

exercisable. As such it becomes an extendible option (for a discussion of compound options see Chapter 21).

American Options Nobody Ever Exercises. Some contracts for American options do not present any early exercise value. They are the options on futures where there is a marks-to-market daily. For example: London Interbank Financial Future Exchange (LIFFE) option products are margined as a future. The profits can be taken out daily and can thus earn interest. Buying a deep-in-the-money option requires a much smaller outlay of cash than other markets.

FORWARDS, FUTURES, AND FORWARD-FORWARDS (ADVANCED TOPIC)

■ A **forward contract** between two parties obligates both of them to buy and sell a given asset on a specified date, or to exchange payments according to a formula.

■ A **future** is a standardized forward contract listed on an exchange with set maturities where the exchange clearing house is the counterparty. Trades take place in an open outcry system and the liquidity is improved by the standardization and the interchangeability between contracts.

There is a difference in hedge ratios between the forward and the future. In the forward, the exchange of payments takes place at a terminal date, while with the future there is a variation margin system of pay-as-you-go. The parties need to exchange payments that correspond to their daily profit or loss. A winner can thus earn interest on the profits. Such difference can be substantial for long-dated instruments.

To hedge a forward with a future, the trader needs to "tail,"[8] to adjust for the difference between a present value claim and a cash one. The hedge (number of units of futures for one unit of forward) is:

$$h = e^{-rt}$$

where t is the number of years and r is the zero-rate until the forward delivery.[9]

Example: A 3-month listed future on the Chicago Merchantile Exchange (CME) in the Deutsche Mark (DEM) against the U.S. Dollar (USD) trades at .70 cents per dollar (one whose expiration happens to fall exactly 90 days from today). The 90-day forward, by arbitrage, also trades at .70 (expressed in spot at 1.4286).

What is the equivalent Deutsche mark (DEM) amount to 100 futures (a future on CME represents 125,000 DEM)? Assume 90-day interest rates are 6%.

Total face value is DEM 12,500,000. The hedge ratio h is Exp $[-.06 \times .25] = .985$, number of futures for one forward. The hedge in the forward is therefore: $12,500,000/.985 = 1,269,000$.

If the DEM future immediately moves to .71 the profit on the future leg will be $125,000 deliverable immediately. The profits in the forward will be $126,900 but will be only a mark-to-market realizable in 90 days.

Credit

Credit is another difference between futures and the forwards. Generic swaps, caps, and floors (with futures equivalent dates) are easy to hedge with strips and Euro options. Going to the over-the-counter market would create a mismatch that consumes two-way credit facilities. If Credit Syldavia engages in a swap with Banca Nazionale del Lavoro, both parties will reduce their credit lines to each other and swell their contingent balance sheets. Should both unwind their side of the trade at different times with different counterparties who in turn trade with each other, the numbers would multiply: Each of the four parties would reduce the size of its books and have its lines to the rest of the world reduced as well. Had all the trades taken place on a standardized exchange, everyone would be flat.

Typically, the way market makers operate is to use the exchange when initiating a trade (when they act as a customer) and to trade a forward when they are acting as a market maker, with other parties calling them and dealing on their prices.

Marks-to-Market Differences

The marks-to-market rules create non-trivial differences between the forwards (and similar instruments) and the futures (see Table 1.2). Forwards are self-marked by operators according to some convention. A few points are updated by the trader and the back office and all the intermediate points on the curve are computed by whatever algorithm is used by the system.

The future, on the other hand, is marked by the exchange through some well-defined rules. The Eurodollar curve, about 40 contracts, is not generated through computer algorithms but with the last trade or bid/offer in mind, even if the resulting curve becomes jagged. An operator who marks the same curve with fewer points will generally have a smoother result.

Another issue lies in the timing. It is called the *nonsynchronous* marked-to-market problem. Many operators carry positions on one exchange offset against positions on another. Exchanges do not have the same settlement time. A future marks-to-market would not accurately portray the resulting P/L.

Table 1.2   Differences between Forward and Futures

	Forward	Future
Marks to Market	Institutional, self-created	Official settlement
Variation Margins	None	Daily
Credit Risks	Depends on the institution	Almost nonexistent:* systemic rather than limited to one institution
Instrument Hedge	Delta is present valued (see Greeks)	Delta is "raw," not present valued
Trading Risks	Higher exposure to illiquidity as the contracts rapidly move away from the liquid maturities	Higher liquidity but fewer "pillars" of trading
Trading costs	Direct costs are generally low Indirect costs are higher, as the bid/offer spread generally larger	Direct costs are high: commission, clearing charges, exchange fees Indirect costs are lower: "spread" is tighter
Sensitivity to Financing	Nonsensitive to the correlation with the financing rate	Sensitive to the correlation between price and the financing rate

*Except, of course, in "emerging" markets.

Example: An arbitrageur plays the forwards in USD-JPY (Japanese yen) by trading forwards in the over-the-counter market against EuroYen futures in Singapore and the Eurodollars in the United States. The bank marks the positions at 4:30 P.M. New York time, while the Singapore futures are marked before he starts his day in New York and the Eurodollar at 3:00 P.M. New York time. His resultant P/L will never reflect the accurate liquidating value of his position.

The Correlation between the Future and the Financing (Advanced Issue)

In the preceding situations, there is independence between the financing rate of the P/L stemming from the future and the expected moves in the future. A correlation between the financing and the future will translate into a convexity or concavity of the future compared with the forward.

Risk Management Rule: When there is a positive correlation between the financing rate r and a future contract F^{10} (on any possible underlying asset) subjected to marks-to-market rules, the future will be convex and will trade above the forward of the same delivery.

Converse: Whenever there is a negative correlation between the financing rate r and a future contract F, the future will be concave and will then need to trade at a lower rate than a corresponding forward.

An illustration of the rule in provided in Chapter 10.

Forward-Forward

■   A **forward-forward** is a contract to exchange an asset at one period against the reverse trade at a later period.

For quasi-linear derivatives, such as fixed-income instruments, it is the price ratio between two forwards.

$$FF(t1, t2) = F(t2)/F(t1)$$

The forward-forward rate is determined by the existing rates in the market interpolated to solve for the break-even rate for the period between $t1$ and $t2$.

The Eurodollar futures are forward-forward deposits, and ironically, the forward-forward often sets the spot (the tail wagging the dog, as often repeated in future circles).

For options, the forward-forward is computed with the nonlinearity of time in mind. This will be dealt with in Chapter 9.

CORE RISK MANAGEMENT: DISTINCTION BETWEEN PRIMARY AND SECONDARY RISKS

Market risks can be primary or secondary, but sometimes the distinction can be counterintuitive; some instruments and markets present more danger in the fringe risks than in their primary exposures.

A primary risk is one that constitutes the bulk of the variance of profits and losses (the P/L), and is where most hedging efforts should be concentrated. Since markets move rapidly, it is easy to see the primary risks as those a trader would cover first, and the residual risks are those that can usually wait until the end of the trading session.

The following classification of risks excludes the party-spoiling correlation-based products (like options of one of two instruments and other goodies).

- **For an equity derivatives portfolio,** market risks are almost entirely directional, with all the possible permutations concerning the derivatives of the effect of the underlying equities. Matters pertaining to interest rates are deemed secondary, as the thrust of the positioning is not at the level of these parameters. Someone can be hurt from the indirect effects of an interest rate change on a long dated stock position (through the effect on the pricing of the forwards), but such variance would be insignificant compared with that caused by the price action and the changes in volatility. Such analysis does not reflect the possible effect of the interest rates move on the equity markets, just their effect on the time structure or equity prices. The health risks of passive smoking are not seriously significant to a man already diagnosed with cancer.

- **For a fixed income derivatives book,** however, both the underlying asset (that is the cash flow schedules as discounted by the interest rates) and the general structure of the interest rate curve need to be taken into account as primary risks. This is mostly attributable to the consideration that fixed-income positions react to a schedule of prices spread over time, not just to one price like an equity or a currency. Every coupon paying fixed income security is a simple sum of smaller zero-coupon securities with different expirations. A 10-year swap's price will principally be affected by the 10-year rates. It will also be affected by the 4-year rates, everything else being equal, because of the effect on the reinvestment over the period. A term structure becomes an integral part of the risks and rewards of every instrument and should therefore be considered a primary risk.

- **For a currency book,** the exchange rate of the currency pair and the volatility are the primary risks. But both the interest rate differentials and the term structures of interest rates are preeminent; they become part of the primary risks with some categories of developing markets that experience a high interest rate volatility.

Such classifications need to adapt to most possible instruments: Those who have tried to come up with a generalized theory of risk management have so far failed in their laborious attempts. No two instruments will be equal. Traders, therefore, must search initially for common points between instruments.

Tables 1.3 and 1.4 will apply to the SDF (smallest decomposable fragment).

Liquidity is preeminent as a risk (the *invisible risk* as traders concede). It will be examined in this book at all levels without fitting it in any category. Liquidity is the source and the cause of everything in trading and it should remain in the back of every risk manager's mind.

Since all options are basically alike this text adheres, whenever possible, to a standardized example. Most examples in the book depict option risks for a generic asset with a flat forward. This approach simplifies the effect of the projection into the future and isolates the pure option risks of the instruments.

In other words we rescale everything to a numeraire. Hence the forward will trade at 100% of cash regardless of the expiration. Such simplification allows a focus on the option risks, without invalidating the real issues. Where the simplification leads to inaccuracies, a tradable instrument will be used taking into account its particularities. The drift and the notion of Girsanov change of probability will be introduced in cases where it affects the hedging technique.

Initially, readers will measure the risks of the derivatives, with simple cases where a "pure" portfolio is created. The basic "Greeks" (vega, gamma,

Table 1.3   Primary and Secondary Risks by Market

Market	Primary Market Risks	Secondary Market Risks
Equities	The underlying equity Volatility	The domestic interest rate Dividend payout Volatility term structure
Fixed Income	Rates Term structure of rates Volatility	Higher order derivatives Risks of pricing formula Volatility term structure* Stability of the covariances between maturities
Currencies	Price Volatility	Rates in each currency Volatility term structure
Commodities	Price Volatility Term structure of prices	The domestic interest rate Storage costs Volatility term structure

* It is assumed that a cap or a floor are decomposed into caplets and floorlets.

Table 1.4   Primary and Secondary Risks by Instrument

Instrument	Additional Primary Market Risks	Additional Secondary Market Risks
Barrier Options	Term structure of rates	Skew
	Term structure of volatility	Volatility of volatility
	Liquidity at the barrier	
Asian Options	Term structure of rates	Model Risk
	Term structure of volatility	Skew
	Variance ratio	
Lookback Options	Mean reversion	Volatility of volatility
		Arcsine law
		"Driftwood" effect
Compound Options	Volatility of volatility	Mean reversion
Multidimensional Options	Correlation measure	
	Volatility of volatility (hence correlations)	

time decay) will be examined before readers modify their measures as practitioners do routinely, whether they are conscious of these transformations or not. This will be followed by a thorough presentation of the modified delta, the modified vega, the modified theta, and the modified gamma. This blanket method should be possible to apply to all instruments.

The generating blocks of some exotic options—bets, barriers, and correlation—will be the final objects of study. Readers will be shown a road map for extending these principles to other, complex instruments. To apply these techniques to a book of specific instruments, it is important to learn to decompose the option risk from the residual risks proper to the instrument. This is best done through the decomposition of the instrument into liquid traded segments (see Figure 1.7).

APPLYING THE FRAMEWORK TO SPECIFIC INSTRUMENTS

A swap is simply a multiasset instrument composed of correlated segments often entirely decomposable into very liquid Eurodollar strips. The framework on multiasset options and the techniques of stacking with correlation matrices should be sufficient for the trader to adapt the principles of dynamic hedging to swaps. As for index-amortizing swaps, the use of

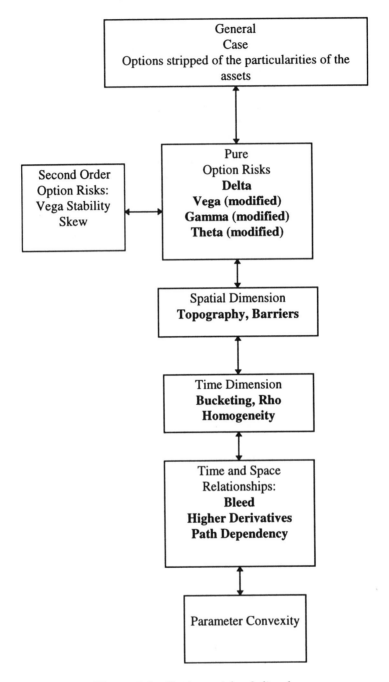

Figure 1.6 Options risks defined.

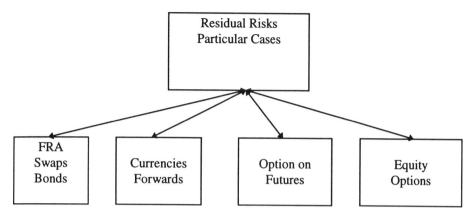

Figure 1.7   An analysis of residual risk by groups of instruments.

American digital options should perform the task, mixed with some knowledge of compound options where applicable. The problem with most fixed-income traders is that they tend to limit their knowledge to the intricacies of the instrument rather than focus on the generating blocks. This method is considerably easier than the holistic Heath-Jarrow-Morton approach.

Chapter **2**

The Generalized Option

A drunk man will find his way home. A drunk bird may get lost forever.
Kakutani[1]

Most traders distinguish between vanilla and exotic options. The vanilla option and vanilla forward are easily priced in the market and benefit from liquid markets. A nonconventional structure would then be called exotic. On the Chicago Board Options Exchange (CBOE), where puts were introduced in 1978, Jim Piper[2] recounts that puts were then exotic and calls vanilla.

There is no true functional difference between the products, except that pricing exotic options often seems to be more complicated. For risk management purposes, six dimensions of analysis are crucial for understanding and pricing options (see Figure 2.1).

STEP 1. THE HOMOGENEITY OF THE STRUCTURE

■ A **time-homogeneous structure** refers to a payoff structure that does not contractually change through time. The contract is said to be uniform with respect to time, between inception and expiration.

Some structures have restrictions on them as the payoff depends on whether some event took place before or after a specified date. So the first question to ask is whether the structure has any time-changing characteristics.

Example: The characteristics of a deferred strike option will depend heavily on whether an event takes place before the day when the strike is set or after. More practically, the option will appear to have no delta and no gamma,[3] but will have some vega between inception and the strike setting time. After the strike setting, generally the settled spot price on a given date, it becomes a normal vanilla (boring) option. The contract for such an option defines two periods—Period 1 when the option will be (on paper) gamma-less and so on, and Period 2 when the option will present vanilla features.

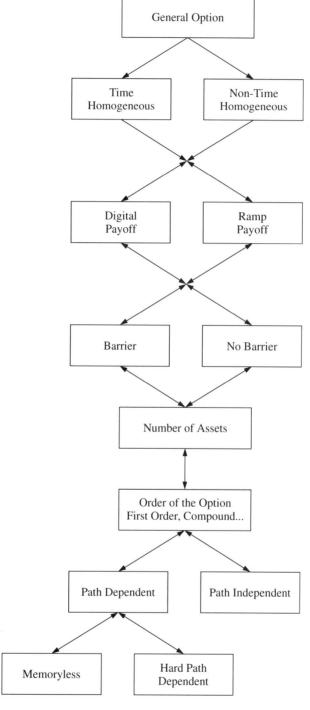

Figure 2.1 The general option.

Option Wizard: The Smallest Decomposable Fragment of a Structure

Every structure for risk management purpose needs to be decomposed into smaller units until it is no longer deemed decomposable.

The term *decomposable* means "composed of structures added together."

- A *double barrier option* is not the addition of two barrier options.
- A *strangle,* however, is the addition of a put and a call.
- A *European double bet* is decomposable into two European single bets. An *American double bet* ("either or") is not decomposable.
- An *option on a basket* is not decomposable into smaller options on the components. Likewise an *option on a spread* is not decomposable into two options on the components.
- *Cap* or *floor options* are decomposable into "caplets" or "floorlets." An option on a swap, called *swaption* by some, is not decomposable (it is akin to an option on a basket).
- A *European barrier option* will not be covered in this book as it is a simple addition of a digital and a call spread.
- Some options are *limit decomposable:* They can be broken down into smaller options but in either infinite amounts or in strike pairs that are infinitely narrow. A lookback option is decomposable into an infinite series of knock-in and knock-out with strike prices infinitely close together. A binary call is limit decomposable into an infinite amount of infinitely narrow call spreads, and that knowledge is useful in trading and pricing although nobody ever tried to perform the replication.

A reminder: For a risk-conscious dynamic hedger (and subjected to transaction costs), the returns of a sum of SDF in a portfolio will be markedly different from the sum of the returns of independently managed SDF.

All options intrinsically change over time. The question here is whether the contract is written in such a way as to alter the payoff after certain dates. Figure 2.2 shows the time to expiration "sliced" in periods. Each period will have its own associated payoff. For example, a window option is a barrier option where the barriers are lifted after a certain period. With a flexible barrier option, the barriers can widen by a percentage point every month. First month: The barrier is at 109 (with, as usual, the spot at 100); second month, the barrier is at 110; third month, at 111; and so on.

Nontime-homogeneous structures can be quite difficult to manage. Later chapters will describe their risks and how to handle Greeks that can accommodate the changes over time.

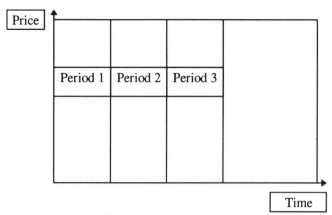

Figure 2.2 Slicing time.

They also can be the most difficult to price, though not always. The model needs to take into account that the payoff changes according to the period. Quants often have difficulties with options that are very easy to hedge (like American options) and find it often trivial to deal with options that are arduous to trade (like bets and binary options).

STEP 2. THE TYPE OF PAYOFF: CONTINUOUS AND DISCONTINUOUS

■ **Digital (discontinuous) and ramp (continuous) payoffs** are the two kinds of payoffs (Figures 2.3 and 2.4). Ramp payoffs are continuous between points, and digital payoffs pay "all or nothing," with no shade in between. They are akin to bets between two people on the outcome of an event.

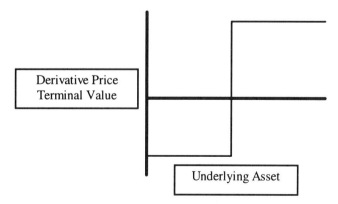

Figure 2.3 Digital payoff.

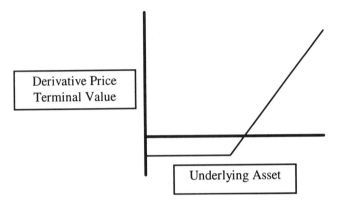

Figure 2.4   Ramp payoff.

Example: Assume that a person bets on the outcome of a well-publicized murder trial, as traders often do, in the amount of $1,000. There will be no intermediate payoff between the loss of $1,000 and the gain of $1,000. The payoff is then said to be discontinuous.

There are two (good news/bad news) points to consider when dealing with the discontinuous payoff options.

1. The bad news is that almost all available hedges in the market are continuous payoff products, therefore creating imperfect or unstable hedges. There may be constructions that provide an accurate hedge (such as vertical spreads), but these constructions are too costly to execute and generally are unavailable.

2. The good news is that the bet option has a small bite. It is a relatively harmless product for those who trade it as it should be traded—as a bet. Dynamic hedging is to be avoided with these situations.

This distinction between payoff types is ever present in structures. There are bet options that are American and pay "if touched" and bet options that pay if some condition is met on expiration. They also provide us with good grounds for the transition to barriers.

Example—European: A three-year dollar denominated note pays 7% every coupon date when dollar-yen is above 100 and 4% otherwise. This note could be constructed with a regular note of the same maturity and a strip of digital call options struck at 100 expiring on the coupon dates.

Example—American: The same note as before except that it pays 8% unless the yen trades at 110 at some point during its three-year life.

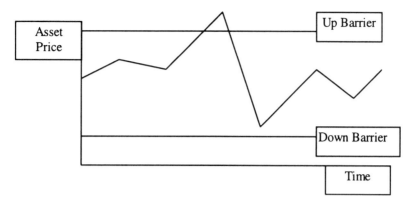

Figure 2.5 Crossing a barrier.

STEP 3. BARRIERS

■ A **barrier** is a price level in the market (called a trigger) that, when reached, markedly alters the payoff of the structure.

Perhaps the most entertaining aspect of option trading is the barrier. Many traders have witnessed "trigger" prices being crossed with heavy heartbeat. They are also interesting for the researcher because they call on a colorful branch of mathematics (probability theory).

The trader must ask whether the structure has a barrier terminating it (knock-out) or initiating it. Figure 2.5 shows an asset price crossing the up barrier.

■ A **high barrier** (or up barrier) is a barrier located above the present spot. A **low barrier** (or down barrier) is a barrier located below the spot.

STEP 4. DIMENSION OF THE STRUCTURE AND THE NUMBER OF ASSETS

■ The **dimension** of the structure is 1 + the number of variables affecting its value (one is for time).

As shown in the tutorial introduction to the random walk in Module A, the conventional "vanilla" option has two dimensions: the asset and time. With two pieces of information: the asset price (y axis) and the time (x axis), the information can be represented in a two-dimensional graph. The market could be illustrated by the classical random walk of a drunk man down Madison avenue.

When more than one variable is involved in the structure, traders need to deal with the notions of correlation and independence.

There are many types of higher dimensional structures: In the "hard" 3D structure, there is more than one strike price; in a "soft" 3D structure (e.g., a convertible), the level of interest rates matters in the construction itself.

An American currency option is particularly sensitive to interest rates and the curve. It is therefore considered a structure of higher dimension.

The custom of derivatives traders to hedge themselves in liquid instruments causes all the instruments to become multiasset (higher dimension by construction).

■ A **multiasset structure by construction** is one that results from the hedge of an illiquid structure with liquid options. When an option in an illiquid market is hedged with a "similar" option in a liquid one, the "similarity" becomes a risk.

This increase in the dimension of the structure is generally necessary with strange instruments.

Example—Multiasset 3D by Construction: A trader at a bank sold to a customer (oh no!) a DEM-AUD (Deutsche mark-Australian dollar) cross option. The option is clearly hedgeable with the underlying asset (the DEM-AUD spot and forward markets). However, the spot market in that country is not very liquid. So the trader breaks up the structure into two units: USD-DEM and AUD-USD. He will hedge his spot and forward exposure there, thus getting into some first order (delta) neutrality. The reader will find in Module C, the meaning of the orderings between two currencies or between a currency and the numeraire "base currency."

The trader, being wise, requires further hedging to reduce the volatility risks of the book. He therefore buys some of the volatility in USD-DEM and some in AUD-USD, as these are liquid in the market. (The proportion will be analyzed later.) He will now have a multiasset portfolio, with the following prices: USD-DEM and AUD-USD, whereas previously he only had one of them to consider. The concept is hard to understand but the two different assets will yield three different volatilities (one for each resulting pair) linked together by two correlations.

Example—Multiasset 4D by Design: The trader in the earlier example received a phone call with bad news and, as a result, had to trade a Greek Drachma-Australian dollar large option position (symbol GDR-AUD). He broke up the volatility risk into liquid subcomponents: GDR-DEM, USD-DEM, AUD-USD and traded each one of those against it (3 assets + time = 4 dimensions).

Option Wizard: How to Get in Trouble Hedging

Financial markets history is littered with stories of traders who bought an instrument and tried to reduce the risks by selling a "highly correlated" one against it, only to discover that they doubled their risks. The trader after seeing on the screen the price of one of the two instruments go down (the one he is long, of course) and the other go up (the one he is short) will blame markets for not being well behaved.

A deeper analysis would show that, typically, some of the instruments that are easy to buy against easy-to-sell "correlated siblings" are invitations for trouble. They act as a trap that will attract many hedgers and arbitrage traders then force them into noisy liquidations. This effect can lead to disastrous results on gullible managers using such apparatus as the "value at risk."

Example—Swaps and Bonds: Swaps would be easy instruments to trade, except that the exact maturity and coupon are never as liquid as operators wish. These swaps will need to be matched, alternatively, with other swaps that, with a different coupon, will trade on their own. When hedged with strip (Eurodollar futures added up in a weighted manner), swaps will become sensitive to the correlation between the components .

STEP 5. ORDER OF THE OPTIONS

- **Higher order options** refer to contingent options. An option on another option is a second-order option. An option on a second order option is a third-order option, and so on.

Higher order options are becoming more and more common with financial products. Many options, called extendible, have built into them a renewal of the contract at a certain price. They can be extended, say five times, for a predetermined $1 each. However, should the option not be renewed at any extension period, the entire structure expires worthless or the underlying asset is delivered at the strike price like a regular delivery.

As the trader goes into higher and higher orders, he becomes confronted with the contingency of a contingency. Positions will move further out-of-the-money, and the risks will become less and less linear. The compounding of a probability with a second-order option reduces the certainty of the payoff and will therefore require less hedge than a regular option. The delta will be lower but very unstable, to the point of carrying little risk disclosure. Delta and fist-order Greeks will be less meaningful and their instability will require the risk manager to have recourse to higher order derivatives, such as the third and fourth *moment,* to assess the portfolio risks.

> *Example:* A common use of compound options is with warrant issues. The price of the warrant is set at some point, say at $2, but the investor has a few hours or days to make up his mind as to whether he wants to buy into it or not. The option dealer is thus short an option on the warrant.

Step 6. Path Dependence

■ **Path-independent options** are options whose payoff depends exclusively on the events upon expiration, regardless of the route taken. A **path-dependent option** depends, in addition to the final price, on at least one price in the path taken to get there.

A European option's price for the buyer depends exclusively on the final price. If someone buys the 104 calls, he stands to benefit if the security gets above 104 upon expiration; otherwise, he would lose his premium. How the spot gets to that point is theoretically irrelevant. The option is therefore said to be path-independent. As will be shown, such path independence is a myth. Every security is path-dependent for a person, including an end user, who has a marked-to-market and the power of a decision throughout its life.

Figure 2.6 shows two paths leading to the same terminal value.

There are two types of path dependent categories: the soft and the hard path dependent options.

■ The **soft-path-dependent option** (also called "memoryless path dependent) depends on one piece of information. The **hard-path-dependent option** (also called "path-dependent with strong memory") will present

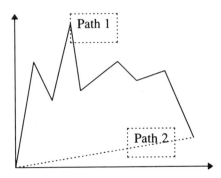

Figure 2.6 Two paths leading to the same terminal value.

a payoff that is entirely dependent on the path taken during some interval. It is therefore truly path-dependent because all the roads do not lead to Rome in the same fashion.

A barrier option is a soft-path-dependent option because at any time it depends on whether the asset traded at or through the barrier or not.

A lookback option is another soft-path-dependent option because it depends on one piece of information from the path: the extremum. What succession of events lead there is not relevant (the lookback options are somewhat related to the barriers in the sense that they can be decomposed into series of knock-in and knock-out options).

Options on averages are hard-path-dependent. Every observation will count and the value will depend on every step taken by the security. Density, however, affects how strong the memory is, and what constitutes a path dependence. A dense path-dependent option cares about every piece of information, whereas a lighter one cares about infrequent ones.

Example: An Asian option will present dense path-dependent features if it is based on hourly prices and light features if the sampling is monthly or quarterly. The effect this has on the final hedging will be discussed later in the book.

Chapter *3*

Market Making and Market Using

Anybody can buy and sell.
James C. Powers

The goal for this chapter is to describe the modus operandi of the various participants in the market (see Figure 3.1).

Pit traders' jargon identifies a three-tier classification of the market participants: the *local*, the *paper*, and the *arb*.

- The **local** is a floor market maker. A pure price-sensitive lot, locals are entirely liquidity driven in their trades. They are the party benefiting from the time and space advantage.

- **Paper** means end customers. Their name is a reminder that in the past a runner would carry their order (literally running) through the floor of the exchange written on a piece of distinctive paper. Locals are always eager to trade with paper because they feel that they have the edge. A local who wants to trade with other locals generally needs to disguise his order to make it look like paper.

- **Arbs** are arbitrageurs or a mixture between market makers and end users. They are the ones carrying the infamous program trading in the SP500 (a cash-future arbitrage) and transfer liquidity from one market to another (for a small fee, of course).

BOOK RUNNERS VERSUS PRICE TAKERS

Book runners, also called market makers, perform this task with a product against an inventory, generally called a "book." Book runners generally post some price at which they are willing to buy (their bid) and some price at which they would be consenting sellers (the offer). They consider that they can benefit from positive expected returns, the fair odds, because they hope to earn a large part of the difference between the middle of the market and the bid or offer, thus achieving transaction positivity (while most other

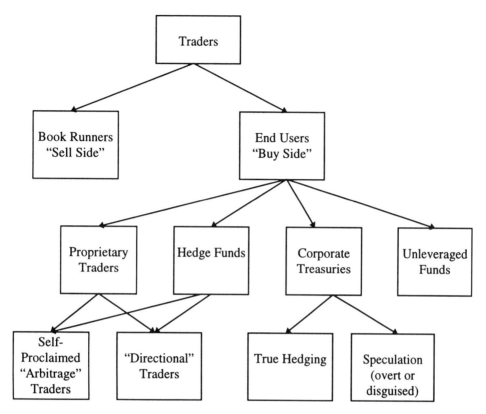

Figure 3.1   Classification of market participants.

participants in the market incur transaction costs in proportion to the liquidity of the instruments involved).

Price takers are market users, a function diametrically opposed to that of the book runner. A market maker acts as a liquidity conduit, standing between end users, for a compensation. The principal difference in attitude between a book runner and an investor lies in their relative price sensitivity. A market maker's willingness to take on a position will increase as the price becomes more attractive; not so for the market user (except in the event of liquidity holes). A market maker reflecting a strong view in all of his trades would ultimately bankrupt his firm as the volume of his transactions would then become one-sided and cause an extravagant accumulation of positions.

Most of the academic literature distinguishes between "upstairs" and floor traders. "Upstairs" traders refers to price takers. Nowadays market makers in complex products are located "upstairs."

No operator is entirely a market maker (that is always devoid of opinion) and no investor is entirely price insensitive. Most investors try to minimize transaction costs, sometimes even earn the spread by working limit orders. Effective market makers "lean" on a position, that is try to keep a core long or short position and skew their prices. Typically their bias is defensive. In a trending bull market, book runners intuitively fear their getting short from the overabundance of buy orders and reflect the preference for a long position by shading their bids and offers upward (and conversely in a bear market). Similarly price takers might delay entering a trade as the price becomes less attractive although occasionally they take an opposite position than intended as a sole result of a price adjustment. Sometimes price sensitivity may be negative: An operator with a belief in trends might be enticed to buy when prices get higher or sell when prices drop.

Finally the difference between a market maker and a market user lies in that the former needs to be defensive whereas the latter has the freedom to be aggressive.

COMMODITIZED AND NONSTANDARDIZED PRODUCTS

There are two types of markets: "commoditized" products that have entered their liquid phase and "nonstandardized" ones where the instruments are still immature and new (see Figure 3.2). Commoditized products exhibit a high volume and high degree of liquidity but relatively small edge, a narrow bid-to-offer spread, and a general overcrowding of talent. Their advantage principally is that the market makers can make up for the narrow spread with the high volume—"a fast nickel is better than a slow dollar," as the adage goes. They are so competitive that they require a certain sophistication in addition to *market sense,* a notion that most traders use and understand but that nobody has been able to define accurately.

Commoditized products have standard agreements in place, eliminate most surprises, and typically trade between dealers where constant matching of risks takes place. The existence of an interbank market is the test of standardization. They rank from the very simple cash products to some lower forms of exotic options (e.g., single barrier knock-outs). Commoditized products are price sensitive, but the volume is high and traders can fine-tune their portfolios in a way to capture their edge.

Nonstandardized products, like structures, have payoffs that are peculiar to the instrument itself and require special pricing capabilities, such as an on-staff mathematician. In contrast, the commoditized products can be priced and managed with the aid of commercially available software products (generally faulty). It can become necessary to design programs for every trade, with a higher incidence of pricing "bugs." An option with a payoff attached to several assets, with a barrier that is reset six times and an uncertain expiration date (it can be extended) will not be easily *booked* in a commercial risk management system. It will require a special computer subroutine to track its "Greeks."

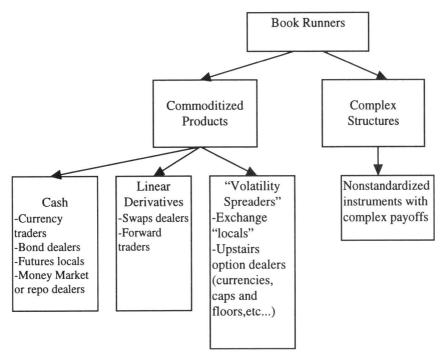

Figure 3.2   Different categories of derivatives book running: Commoditized and nonstandard products.

The real difference between commoditized and nonstandard products is that one type is tailor-made, with a high price tag attached to it and smaller traffic, while the other has the features of a discount store with standard sizes and prices, but a higher volume. Table 3.1 lists these and other major differences. All successful nonstandard products become commoditized. When many of us started trading options, these were mostly nonstandard but the markets moved rapidly from one category to the other. Swaps structures that were difficult to price only five years ago are now given to junior traders.

Trading Risks in Commoditized Products

Cash Products.   Thanks to the competition, these products represent less rewards as they are usually more liquid and require no sophisticated risk management tools. However, they allow the traders to completely offset the risk of their trades and avoid the necessity of warehousing contracts for any length of time. A cash trader will hold a position over his horizon by choice only.

Table 3.1 Commoditized and Nonstandard Products

Commoditized Products	Nonstandard Products
Price sensitive	Product designation sensitive
Supermarket-like products	Tailor-made products
Narrow bid/offer spread	Wide spread, even absence of two-way markets
Trade interbank, often through a broker	Only trade between a financial institution and an end user
Standard pricing formulas	Unseasoned pricing
Trading talent and experience required	Pricing ability required, mathematical sophistication
High volume	Low volume
Standard risk management systems	Tailor-made systems, needs on-staff programmers

Option Wizard: Trader Decay

As products increase in sophistication, traders become rapidly obsolete. This is becoming significant in most markets.

Unlike practitioners of most professions, traders are not given time (or do not give themselves enough time) to adapt to the new products or learn new techniques. Traders are constantly under profitability pressures that force them to focus on "producing" lest they join the ranks of laid-off Wall Streeters. The trader finds himself a niche and milks it until its (and his) termination.

In addition, holding a trading position requires such an intellectual commitment that the trader may feel consumed to the point that other functions of the mind slow down. One comparison is the RAM of a personal computer that is heavily burdened by a program running in the background.

Firms on Wall Street that in the past invested in employee development have been squeezed into "cleanups." A trader is generally "as good as his last trade."

This explains partly the segregation between commoditized products and complex derivatives in most firms. Newcomers present inexpensive sophistication but no trading experience. They, in turn will rapidly decay and will be replaced by the new PhD crop.

S, a thoughtful trader with some intellectual curiosity, once told the author about his dilemma: taking a learning sabbatical and giving up his present job with the possibility of not being able to return, or remaining on the job and becoming richer but obsolete.

Linear (or quasi-linear) Derivatives. Traders hedging a forward or a swap become subjected to maturity mismatches. Their hedge ratios, however, do not change with time and pricing levels. They rarely incur transformation in hedging parameters (assuming no meaningful convexity differences) except for some extrinsic ones (e.g., correlation coefficients). A swap trader on a deserted island can always summarize his position (but not his P/L), whereas an option trader needs to check volatility, spot, interest rates, and so on to know his.

The sensitivity of these portfolios remains constant across time or variation in the market prices. The fact that the hedges might not work in consequence to yield curve shifts or other phenomena does not necessarily make these derivatives nonlinear. The trading complexities reside in the difficulties in gauging the hedge ratios and the relative volatilities and covariances of the different maturities. In addition, swaps are an area where the accuracy of the pricing and interpolation are evident.

Nonlinear Derivatives. These are options-related instruments and fixed income securities with high convexity that change in sensitivity with the passage of time or with market levels (see Chapter 11 for a discussion).

Book running in these derivatives is less accommodating than that in cash or linear products: The trader is ready to warehouse a trade for a given amount of time, generally until expiration, against a fee. Because the hedge ratios and the particularities of the instruments change according to time or market movement, the book runner needs to engage in dynamic management of the position. Novice option traders are taught that there is only one way to hedge the sale of an option: by buying back the same one. The inherent instability of derivative positions and their dependence on time and market levels makes it clearly impossible to define oneself as completely "flat," except when the book is empty of trades, a rare occurrence.

Profitability

Derivatives market making in both standard and nonstandard products is an attractive occupation because although every option is relatively illiquid, the market as a whole for the Greeks is very liquid. Unlike a market maker in an illiquid commodity that is uncorrelated to a more liquid one, the option market maker can easily find cheap alternative hedges.

The compensation for traders comes from offsetting the Greek risks (delta, vega, gamma) more rapidly than predicted. That privilege arises because market makers have decided to run a book and incur the costs associated with the book management. The barriers to entry become their running the book as an ongoing business. Option locals who warehouse strike risks can easily find ways to reduce the variance of the portfolio with combinations of available options.

Proprietary Departments

The distinction between market makers and customers exists within most trading firms and banks. The firms usually benefit from the "franchises" or "customer flows," two buzzwords connected with the book-running function that represent its original mission of trying to service the customer for a fee (except that here the service becomes the risk and the fee becomes the bid/ask spread). Banks saw the success of their hedge fund customers in the early 1990s and tried to replicate their customers' successes by creating internal hedge funds. Many failed and had to liquidate rather rapidly, moving their orientation back toward their conventional way of plying the book-running trade.

The reasons to start a proprietary function were obvious. They had an overspill of back-office capability, which made the marginal cost of manufacturing trading profits very low. They were privy to very fresh information on order flows into the market whether or not it turned out to be relevant in trading. They also had, like everybody, excessive capital freed up from conventional uses such as lending against the receivables of iron nails manufacturing companies.

Their performance, however, did not match expectations for the following reasons: They had a different utility curve than the funds, their executives and managers were operating under a different utility function than the fund managers; and they had different expected returns (the funds were riskier traders). The funds managers had a collection of funds that each presented the features of an option. Bank managers had one option on a collection of generally uncorrelated assets. According to the *Basket Rule* (to be discussed later in this book), the expected returns from such a basket would be considerably lower. In addition, banks sought "diversification," something that seemed to be a good fashionable idea, but that lowered the price of the manager's option.

In a totally random but "fair" return (the expected profits are zero, a martingale, or "fair dice"), one option on a volatile instrument is more valuable or, at worst, equal to a portfolio of options. Such a rule would apply even if the returns were not a martingale, to a point. It resembles the pricing of an option that is more sensitive to the volatility than the expected drift (Figure 3.3).

A trader with a "synthetic capital" of $10 million (i.e., the virtual capital allocated to him by the bank) has often more earning power than a manager with a higher amount of capital under him, because the manager will have to face the "diversification"—the offsetting returns from traders.

Example: A trader has $10 million "synthetic capital." His yearly "swing" is 25%: He will either make $2.5 million or lose $2.5 million. His draw, in addition to his salary will contractually specify 20%. The trader cannot be thrown out before the termination of the contract.[1]

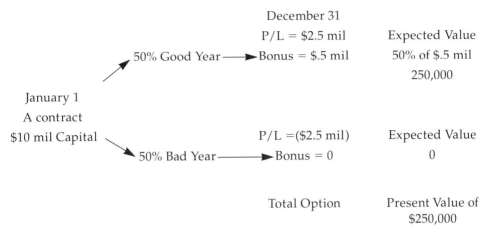

Figure 3.3 Expected returns from a proprietary position: A mediocre trader.

The expected returns for the trader will increase with volatility.

In comparing the good trader to the bad trader, what determines the price of the option is the volatility, not the expected returns from the position. Of course, the example is simplistic: Bad traders do not have easy access to capital; one needs (sometimes, but not always) something that remotely resembles a track record (Figure 3.4).

The manager in a financial institution, in contrast, runs a large group of traders. He is paid 10% of a much larger pie: he will hence have the illusion of partaking of a larger upside. Wrong. The net sum of traders, particularly if they are not proficient, will be worth less than the P/L of one person. What is the solution? Avoid diversification at all costs. Hire one volatile trader, bad or good (the distinction is of small

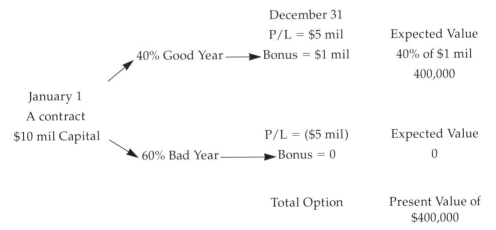

Figure 3.4 Expected returns from a proprietary position: A bad trader.

relevance). If needs be, make sure all the traders carry the same position, without anyone offsetting the other. It is quite dispiriting for a manager to see traders carry positions on opposite sides of the market: While one of them will be profitable and would buy a new car, the net will lock in a loss because of hedging costs. A firm cannot ask its traders to pay for their losses unless they are losing back some of their profits. A deep-in-the-money option resembles a future: A trader with profits loses the optionality since his compensation would decrease with losses.

Compare that with a fund manager who has three *independent* funds. He can draw 20% of each fund, regardless of the outcome of the others. Unlike the manager of a trading desk, he benefits from the sum of the three options. He can enhance his returns by being diversified across separate funds, perhaps even negatively correlated between each one of them. The only way a bank trading manager could achieve an equivalent position would be to maintain three jobs simultaneously at three different banks with a percentage payout in each.

This example shows why proprietary trading departments ended up closing down while fund managers thrived.

TACIT RULES IN MARKET MAKING

Market making in derivatives is subjected to a host of unwritten rules that vary according to the market for each instrument. These rules evolve continuously as the market reaches a semblance of maturity. They are necessary for dealers to coexist and correspond to the needs of an ambiguous relationship between them: Dealers are at once accomplices and competitors; they need each other as trading counterparties but compete for customer business. Generally, if a trade is too large for a dealer, proper risk management forces the dealer to split it with the rest of the market, for a fee. The need to ensure liquidity and the adequate spread of information for one another (without weakening any of the parties) leads to well-defined rules of behavior.

A market maker in a cash product, for example, by asking another one for a price, is giving up information about his position against the consummation of a trade that would reduce that position. The trade-off will be further enforced because he will now have an accomplice.

Example: A large corporation buys 500 million British pounds from Witibank. The Witibank traders, unwilling to hold such a large position, "call out" for prices, contacting other dealers for £20 million each. Dealers need to produce the price without knowing beforehand whether

Witibank is a buyer or a seller. They would realize that Witi has a relatively large amount to execute and know that by getting £20 million they would be handicapped as the market might be flooded by the trade for a certain period. However, they cannot escape their obligation to quote Witibank as they would require the same favor should they be on the other side quoting large amounts to their own customers. By trading, they will also gather a valuable piece of information, the suspicion of a large order weighed against the possibility of a bluff. By trading with Witibank they will then become partners in a secret.

Very liquid products have thus highly developed rules, down to how long a person can wait before the quote becomes invalidated. Also, it is not acceptable to come back to the same dealer after "passing" (avoiding the trade) on a market, to quote too much without trading, or to pass on a "choice" market; that is, when the counterpart shows the same price as a bid and as an offer.

On the floor of the exchanges regulated by the Commodity Futures Trading Commission, market making for futures and options is usually subjected to the open outcry rules. The trader needs to continuously refresh his bid or offer and specify a quantity for which his market is valid; otherwise, he could be asked to honor his price for larger amounts than his capital would allow. Traders have no obligation to respond to the brokers nor to other traders: They hawk their wares to generate business and create advertising for themselves.

In the "upstairs" markets, there are subdivisions that depend on the level of liquidity of the product. The more established and liquid ones, such as short-term currency options, trade like cash, with mature rules and tacit obligations between dealers; whereas structured notes are not an interbank market and have no clear rules. A trader has neither the obligation—nor the need—to quote them to another dealer.

MARKET MAKING AND THE PRICE FOR IMMEDIACY

A theory by Sanford Grossman and Merton Miller[2] states that the market maker function is to provide the price for immediacy. The price taker pays the market maker in order not to have to wait and incur the risks that rise with the square root of time. The price for immediacy is then reached as an equilibrium between buyers and suppliers of immediacy.

Started by Garman in 1976, *Market Microstructure* is still a young branch of financial theory. Most of its motivations are grounded on the awareness that prices do not reach equilibrium immediately in a big Walrassian auction meeting. Customers need market makers to fill gaps arising from imperfect synchronization between buyers and sellers. Bid/offer spreads will then depend on competition between market makers.[3] Some of the theories developed will be explored later in the book.

MARKET MAKING AND
AUTOCORRELATION OF PRICE CHANGES

Briefly, a positive autocorrelation of a price change means that an up-move is more likely than not to be followed by an up-move and a down-move by a down-move. A negative autocorrelation means the opposite: The following move is more likely to be of the opposite sign than the previous one.

The horizon of such effect also needs to be defined. A first-order autocorrelation means that the effect is immediately a function of the move that just happened. In simple terms, a higher order one means that there might be a lag before such an effect is felt.

Many studies report the existence a first-order negative autocorrelation of price changes. Such autocorrelation of prices reflects the "positive edge" of market makers.[4] Most studies report an autocorrelation for price changes when the observations are very frequent, as well as the vanishing of the correlation when observations are separated by more than a few minutes. The most recent, Guillaume et al. (1995) reports a correlation between prices in the dollar/DM currency pair extremely significant up to four minutes for data observed between 1987 and 1993. Figure 3.5 shows the correlation of the changes (the logs of the difference) and the rapidity with which such autocorrelation washes out. Because the 4-minute price volatility is lower than the bid/offer spread, it becomes conceivable that only a market maker can capture such advantage. An average dollar/DM trader will execute a trade every 18 seconds[5] during liquid times, which falls within the zone of high negative autocorrelation.

This first-order autocorrelation of prices (i.e., a short-term memory for events preceding it) does not force us to depart from the notion of a "fair dice," or martingale, once we translate the difference into some positive transaction costs for a market maker. Only a market maker can benefit from a submartingale (that is a favorable dice) and in a limited way at that.

The issue of autocorrelation of returns will be further discussed in the context of the variance ratios in Chapter 6.

MARKET MAKING AND THE ILLUSION OF PROFITABILITY

Market making in complex products can show immediate rewards and future thorns. Mostly profits are shown after the trade because the mark-to-model process generally implemented derives security prices off a mid-market.

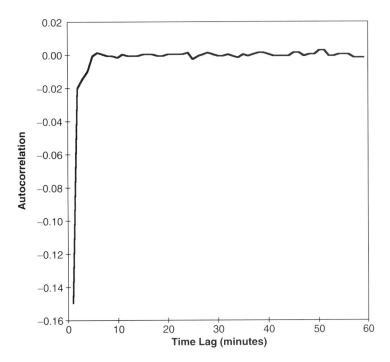

Figure 3.5   Olsen & Associates autocorrelogram of changes, 1987–1993.

Traders usually find a fair value and mark the derivative up, then recognize most or all of the difference between the fair value and the selling price as a profit. This method does not allow for the future costs incurred in the management of an option book. The more complex the security, the more subsequent dynamic hedging will be required, and that in more than one market (a cross-currency structured note needs to be readjusted in the Euro-Strips of both currencies and in options on the cross currency, options need to be rolled as they come close to expiration, etc.). Heavy *slippage* will be incurred when the position attains some large size. All this would eat up the initial profit, but would often be concealed from the trader who receives a steady flow of such profit-booking trades. It would be difficult for the trader to espouse a more aggressive stance and reduce transaction costs by observing the different behavior of the multifaceted subcomponents: Market makers are crippled by the size of their positions in relation to their appetite for risk.

Complex derivatives usually come in batches causing either the initial firm or the competitors to sell more of a successful product. Ideas that sell are rapidly imitated, and customers buy them with the comfort that others are doing the same. That bandwagon makes all the incremental hedges of the product more costly because their liquidity dries up. A costly example is the Mexican peso range notes that make the issuing bank short out-of-the-money puts on the currency. Their demand was widespread before

Option Wizard: Market Making and the Burnout of Traders

Option book runners constantly want to retire into proprietary trading departments. The strains of a position can be unrelenting, particularly when the traders become driven by their books; they then manage positions so defensively as to pay the price of liquidity for each trade. Typically, market makers are given structures by their salesforce and asked to manage the risk and protect the "profits." In distinguishing between primary and secondary trades (the first being a trade that corresponds to the initiation of a position, the second a defensive, dynamic hedge), accelerating the number of trades of the second kind generally causes both fatigue and an erosion of profits. The unpredictability of the results, added to the rarity of a vacation (usually heavy in long-distance calls) causes the eventual combat fatigue.

While a hedge fund manager can exit all his positions with one phone call, the option book runner can only put Novocain™ on the wound; uprooting the problem is impossible. Personal stress usually results from the trader's inability to set his pace: the difference between the hunter and the prey. Most traders are hunter types, possessing an aggressive streak that is hardly compatible with the behavior of a prey.

Exchange traders usually do not suffer the same fate because they have a better control over their inventory and the small number of expirations in their books. It is not uncommon to see exchange traders completely liquidating their book before a telephone-free trekking trip to Nepal.

Another advantage to exchange traders is their freedom to make markets (some exchanges, however, force them into a token obligation). They can rapidly identify a regime shift and widen markets, something a trader at an institution cannot afford to do lest the customers call the boss. Typically, they can refrain from showing one side of the market when markets heat up (as they did during the stock market crashes of 1987 and 1989).

---

the 1995 devaluation and dealers found it difficult, even before the scare, to repurchase the puts or hedge in the synthetic forward without heavy costs.

Adverse Selection, Signaling, and the Risk Management of Market Makers

Adverse selection is a condition well known by insurance companies. They have a tendency to get the less desirable policies since a dying person is more likely to buy insurance than a healthy one. It is also difficult to distinguish between customers since a sick man can withhold information about his health. Likewise, traders have a tendency of moaning that they tend to acquire the garbage from the market *(bad distribution).*

Traders experience another type of problem: a counterparty who buys from them may have information they do not have. We will examine, later in the chapter, the effects such information can have on fair-value pre-trade and fair-value post-trade. Such **signaling** has been investigated extensively in microeconomics and financial theory (see O'Hara, 1995, for a survey). But unlike an insurance company, a trader might find the signal valuable. A trader who traded with a central bank will certainly lose on that particular trade. He will, however, end up winning if he uses the information to "piggy back" the central bank.

Many traders compare market making to being short an option. Typically, leaving the price "out" guarantees the trader a trade if his bid becomes highest or his offer lowest owing to market moves. Even though the market maker's price is valid for only a few seconds, market makers can thus be exposed to being "picked off" when information comes out during that time and the market maker cannot officially change his quotes.

It is well known that market makers lose money chronically when markets experience shocks but produce profits in normal conditions when they can earn the spread without much risk. In that respect, market makers appear to be short volatility.

Option Wizard: Comparative Lifestyles of Traders

X traded options "upstairs" for 10 years, mostly as a book runner or arbitrageur, and for a few years on the floors of the Chicago Mercantile Exchange in currencies, SP500, and minor soft commodity contracts. Both positions had their advantages. As an upstairs trader, he kept his mind occupied and was able to watch a variety of markets, but he had no flexibility and, owing to the size of his positions, was saddled with difficult (but profitable) positions all the time, which prevented him from taking real vacations. Every day for him was like maneuvering a large aircraft carrier, but his job was intellectually rewarding.

As a local, he felt the exhilaration of freedom but was physically limited with markets and instruments. It felt like a blue-collar job but with a higher payout. In addition, he no longer got the respect large traders usually command: Brokers who in the past had toadied up to him now hardly gave him the time of day—not a great loss as he had matured by then.

The best lifestyle X ever experienced was that of a carefree wind-surfing and bicycling fanatic who "scalped" options in the pit only on days when the wind was unaccommodating. X closed his positions in the winter and drove from Chicago to California. What was surprising was that the sports bum was, besides, an excellent pit trader.

What considerably mitigates the risks of a market maker is the management of the liquidity of the market available to book runners. They typically have enough outlays to offset the risks so that being stuck with a position for a long duration becomes exceptional.

VALUE TRADING VERSUS THE GREATER FOOL THEORY

There is a running dichotomy among option traders whether it is preferable to warehouse a trade because of its intrinsic attractiveness or to trade according to other people's desires. Here are the two parties:

1.   The school of value trading favors only accumulating positions that, warehoused until expiration, represent a positive expected return. The traders should be capable of sustaining a lack of trading for an extensive period. As these value trades generally go against the market, the trader needs to have a certain measure of indifference to marks-to-market losses (e.g., buying a "cheap" calendar spread where the back month is heavily discounted owing to structural supply; buying out-of-the-money calls in equity markets owing to the strong discount brought about by the oversupply of covered-writes).

2.   The school of the greater fool theory suggests a trading attitude more accommodative to the marketplace. It reflects the belief that traders are conduits. Value resides as much in the discounting of the final payoff (a net payoff of the trade minus the cost of hedging a book) as in the possibility that someone may "pay up" for the option. A trader would not mind holding an expensive option provided that a greater fool could come to relieve him from it. Playing greater fool is often indispensable with market makers of liquid products owing to their large volume and frequency of trades. Because market makers hardly ever carry trades for a significant period, they find it interesting to value options in terms of their extrinsic rather than their intrinsic value.

This theory is best described in Schwager's *New Market Wizards* (1992), where Jeff Yass, an outstanding market maker, describes his approach to option trading in terms of conditional probability. Somehow "value" is conditional on the most recent information rather than the overall picture. If a market operator is *given* a position by someone else, he receives more than a position: He gets information, and that information would necessarily eradicate the edge. So there are two values: (a) value that was there before the trade (*prior* value) and (b) value that is conditional on the trade, which will be necessarily higher (if the operator is short) or lower (if the operator is long) than the original one (*post* value).

Table 3.2   Value Trading versus Greater Fool Methods

Value Trading	Greater Fool Trading
Only inventory net option positions that harbor a positive expected return.	Only buy the options that might turn out to be in great demand. Only sell the options that someone else might want to get rid of.
Focuses on intrinsic value.	Focuses on extrinsic value, the signal from the market.
Fund manager's approach: slow volume, small turnover.	Market maker's approach: high volume and turnover.
A market maker with new products or a fund manager with liquid products.	A market maker with liquid products.
Time is expected to work in favor of the position, as the value is amortized as expiration nears.	Time works against the position. Sometimes the trader is long expensive options or short cheap options and the gamma differential could be heavy (see topic).
The positions do not "mark" well, that is typically the initial mark-to-market works against the trader.	Positions mark generally well.

Table 3.2 lists the attributes of the two methods.

Example: Two option traders would eventually make money on two diametrically opposite trades, provided they remained consistent with their trading styles. The first one, a value trader, would go against the skew in biased assets markets by buying calls and selling puts for a volatility differential that is not justified by the real skew of the distribution. However, he needs to hedge his deltas as if he were going to stick to his trade until expiration, without changes in the process that would make him sell futures in dips as if volatility were higher.

The second one would buy puts and sell calls, knowing that the difference is not warranted by the distribution. He is aware, however, that someone along the way is very likely to panic at the first dip and buy the expensive puts from him at a higher price. He also can often detect a massive anxiety in the market once it starts to feel heavy. His danger, however, is that warehousing such a trade until expiration would cause him to lose money.

"An expensive option does not come alone," the saying goes. When an option trader sells an option in the market, he would tend to find that the series would become more expensive, owing to the structure of imbalances. The best way for greater fool traders to exit is for them to see the series of options start softening up.

Monkeys on a Typewriter

The Statistical Value of Track Records

There is an application of a mathematical lemma called the Borel-Cantelli Lemma[6]: If one puts an infinite number of monkeys in front of (strongly built) typewriters and lets them clap away (without destroying the machinery), there is a certainty that one of them will come out with an exact version of the *Iliad*. Once that hero among monkeys is found, would any reader invest his life's savings on a bet that the monkey would write the *Odyssey* next?

The same applies to traders. There is tendency on the part of people with a small knowledge of probability laws to select proprietary traders and fund managers based on the following principle: It is very unlikely for a trader to be up money in a consistent fashion without his doing something right. Track records, therefore, become preeminent. So they call on the rule of the likelihood of such a successful run and tell themselves that if someone performed better than the rest in the past then he has a great chance of performing better than the crowd in future days. I have never seen anyone count the monkeys. Nobody counts the traders in the market to calculate—instead of the probability of success—the conditional probability of successful runs given the number of traders in operation over a *finite* market history.

One of the key properties of probability laws is that they are counterintuitive. People look at a casino seeing how a small "edge" translates into virtually certain profits and infer that the same rules apply to a man rolling the dice. The sums of random walks (net profits from the sum of roulette tables) act differently from the final sum of a random walk (a gambler's net results at the end of one session on one roulette table). A modest advantage on a sum of random walks translates into certain profits. The same advantage of one roulette table is generally drowned by the volatility of the random walk itself. The reader could test the difference by generating series of tosses on a spreadsheet using a random number generator and looking at the discrepancies in the results. Even with a small advantage, a counterintuitively high number of negative runs would mar the party. The only way to reduce the frequency of negative runs would be to increase the number of trades and make the bets smaller.

One could think of a roulette table and view the edge of a trader who has negative odds with a system that gives him a 45% chance of winning. What is the probability of the person betting $1 being in the black after 30 throws? Using the cumulative binomial distribution, he has at least a 35% chance of ending up profitable. If the gambler sliced the bet into pieces of $0.10 and compensated with 10 times more bets, the final number of positive results would be 4.6%. This provides a vivid illustration of the reasons to use caution when considering the notions of "edge" and "skilled traders." In a long Wall Street career, I have often heard the adage: "You are as good as your last trade." Often the behavior of the managers of traders is dictated by their latest run. Investors somehow are not as easily fooled.[7]

More Modern Methods of Monitoring Traders

After the ravages of February 1994, people wised up to statistics and started examining new methods to distinguish the truly skilled trader from the lucky monkey on a typewriter. Bill Fung,[8] a consultant to hedge funds, introduced a nonparametric method of assessing the relative performance of a trader to the market. It takes into account that some markets trend and (remember 1993) that some traders were simply lucky to be long those securities that happened to trend. In addition, he monitors the transaction frequency to ascertain the fit between the trader's intention and the actual events in the market: The higher the frequency of trades, the higher the statistical significance of the trader's performance. This method is grounded on the same awareness of the fit of the distribution as the one described in the dependence of a dynamic hedger on the transaction frequency. An option trader who frequently rebalances his book would capture the true distribution with more certainty (for the better or the worse) than his colleagues who hedges himself only occasionally.

Where the fund manager "sits" on a long or short position, therefore depending entirely on the underlying market, the investor can save himself considerable fees, a cut in the expected return, and some headaches, by buying a liquid future on the commodity itself and completely bypassing the fund manager.

The Fair Dice and the Dubins-Savage Optimal Strategy

How aggressive a trader needs to be depends highly on his edge, or expected return from the game:[9]

- When the edge is positive,[10] (the trader has a positive expected return from the game, as is the case with most market makers), it is always best to take the minimum amount of risk and let central limit slowly push the position into profitability. That is the recommended method for market makers to progressively increase the stakes, in proportion to the accumulated profits. In probability terms, it is better to minimize the volatility to cash-in on the drift.

- When the edge is negative,[11] it is best to be exposed as little as possible to the negative drift. The operator should optimize by taking as much risk as possible. Betting small would ensure a slow and certain death by letting central limit catch up on him.

- At any rate, when the trader owns an option on his profits (i.e., gets a cut of the upside without having to share into the downside), as is the case with traders using other people's money, it is always optimal to take as much risk as possible. An option is worth the most when the volatility is highest.

The ArcSine Law of the P/L

Another counterintuitive phenomenon affecting traders concerns the distribution of their P/L. One would think that in a fair game (a totally random P/L), the most likely time spent in the "black" or in the "red" would hover around 6-month per annum. In reality, the probability of spending 1 month or 11 months in either is markedly higher. As a matter of fact, the probability of spending 6 months in the black or in the red is the lowest of all!

That striking law is called the ArcSine law for a random walk[12] and affects us in more than one instance. It also applies to the distribution of the maximum and the minimum and will be covered in Chapter 23.

Figure 3.6 shows the expected amount of time a "fair" trader is expected to spend in the black (or the red). Notice that the drift does not alter the distribution until it becomes very strong. The arcsine law makes commonly used methods of comparing the cumulative performance of traders erroneous. It shows how unjustified most of the conventional measurements can be.

Risk Management Rules

- When judging a nonmarket-making trader, remember that a large share of his profitability is attributable to luck.

- The ratio of luck to skills decreases with the transaction frequency. For a proprietary trader, it is very high, for a market maker it will be very low.

- In general, traders become extremely arrogant and difficult to manage when they are very profitable. A trading manager must be able to face wrongly profitable traders without being influenced by their P/L.

- Do not use Sharpe ratios with nonlinear products, particularly options, or with linear products traded in a nonlinear manner (such as a stop loss).[13]

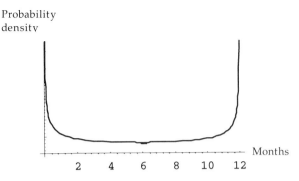

Figure 3.6   Arcsine law for the P/L.

We end on this final problem: A trader is given a stop-loss of $100,000 in any given month (i.e., he would have to close the books and go home until the end of the month). Another trader is allowed $200,000. Assuming that both traded the same size in one uniformly volatile market (constant volatility) and that their profits and losses were (as with most traders) random, which one has a higher expected return?

Answer: They have the same expected profitability. They share the same expected returns but the trader with the smaller stop loss will incur more frequent losses. His P/L will have a strong, positive, "skew": frequent small losses and infrequent large gains.

Chapter 4

Liquidity and Liquidity Holes

The market is a large movie theater with a small door.
An options veteran

This chapter should be read prior to studying barrier options.

LIQUIDITY

Liquidity[1] in a market is defined by the ease with which an operator can enter and exit it for a given block of securities.

If one were to summarize what trading (as opposed to investing) is about, the best answer would be adequate management (and understanding) of liquidity. Liquidity is the source of everything related to markets.

■ **Slippage** is a practitioner's measurement for liquidity. It is computed (for a given quantity to execute) by taking the variation between the average execution price and the initial middle point of the bid and the offer. Slippage is not always a precise measure of liquidity for a particular commodity, but it provides a reliable comparative measurement of liquidity between markets.

Academics offer a number of measurements for liquidity, mostly using the numbers of transactions or the bid/offer spread.

Example. Slippage: A fund manager needs to go long the JPY currency against the dollar. The 115 calls on the Chicago Mercantile Exchange are quoted 88/92 which means that the middle market in theory is at 90. He would then assume that for buying 4,000 contracts, he would have to pay 92 for the first 1,000, 93 for the next 1,000, and up to 98 for the balance of 2,000 as he would drive the currency itself higher thanks to option traders hedging their deltas. His weighted average will then be 95.25 and he will count an overall slippage of 5.25 ticks for his execution. He should make the same allowance for his unwinding the trade, provided he picks the same time of the day. Slippage would be more important when the market gets more volatile (which is when the fund manager might find it more interesting to get involved or to unwind the position) or when the overlapping of time zones reduces the total number of market participants.

Slippage is the principal reason for leverage hedge fund traders to limit the amount of capital under management. While their overall dollar returns might increase (in the event of their being profitable), the percentage returns decline accordingly.

Ironically, slippage costs often disappear with large blocks: Many large traders can use their buying power to prop up the market in which they accumulate a position. Often the market rallies and stabilizes at the price at which the last buy trade was executed. It is in exiting the trade that slippage costs will invariably be incurred.

LIQUIDITY HOLES

■ A **liquidity hole** or a black hole is a temporary event in the market that suspends the regular mechanics of equilibrium attainment. It is an informational glitch in the mechanism of free markets, one that can cause considerable damage to firms. In practice, it can be seen when lower prices bring accelerated supply and higher prices accelerated demand.

Liquidity holes are attributable to the way information initially affects a market. Typically, liquidity holes occur when operators are aware of a major piece of information (an event, or a size order in the market), but cannot gauge its size and possible impact. Information causes anxiety, conspiracy theory, and price conflicts. Most often, operators need to interpret information. Markets are supposed to move to the extent of the difference between news and initial expectations but the latter are usually unknown and difficult to estimate precisely.

A political announcement or the release of an economic figure can create a liquidity hole by leading to disruption in the normal price determination process.

When a stop-loss is executed, as in the following example, operators freeze as they become aware of the order without further information as to its magnitude. Many suspend their trading temporarily, thus causing the market to gyrate even further.

Liquidity holes would not be very dangerous except that with the large open interest in nonlinear derivatives, some operators have large contingent orders that need to be executed regardless of the market makers' spreads.

Often barrier options (knock-in, knock-out) are to blame for the liquidity holes and the intraday volatility that results from them.

LIQUIDITY AND RISK MANAGEMENT

It cannot be stressed enough that liquidity is the most serious risk management problem. A substantial part of unforeseen losses is due either to market jumps caused by illiquidity or to liquidation costs that substantially move the markets against one's position. Liquidation costs tend to be usually underestimated since operators usually "fade" when someone is forced into a market action.

Another element to consider in the value-at-risk (see Module E) method is that most simulations exclude the liquidation costs at the stopping barrier. The market is merciless with operators who start closing down a position, particularly when the liquidating party has no choice. Since forced liquidations take place in markets under duress, one can imagine the effects of reduced liquidity on the unwiding of a portfolio.

STOP ORDERS AND THE PATH OF ILLIQUIDITY

■ **Stop-loss orders** are instructions to buy or sell a given quantity when the price prints on the screen, **unconditional** of the filling price. Buy-stop orders are generally higher than the market and sell-stop orders are lower than the market.

■ **Limit orders** are instructions to buy or sell a given quantity at a predetermined price in the market. Market rules guarantee that no price would trade "through" the order without the fill being performed.

These two basic definitions will be illustrated with examples later in the chapter.

Trying to measure the markets in accordance with their volume is a deceiving enterprise. Markets are not linear and do not reach equilibrium in an orderly way. Information can be nefarious as well as helpful. The certainty of a path should certain conditions be satisfied (a conditional path) can cause such gaps.

The mechanics of a stop-loss can shed some light on the issue of path-certainty. Stop-losses in cash products are buy or sell orders triggered by the market reaching a certain level. As such they resemble trigger options. A stop-loss in the SP500 to buy 500 lots at 624.00 will be triggered by the broker being obligated to start buying that amount at any price should there be an official print at that level. Customers usually leave a stop in the marketplace to protect profits, limit losses, or sometimes to enter the market if some magic level is attained. Most trainees are obligated to leave a stop for every open position as their bosses fear their breach of discipline.

Since stop losses guarantee an order, it becomes understandable that some operators can have an incentive to trigger the large stops. The following example shows the execution of a stop-loss in a relatively less liquid market.

Example: A large European fund manager gives a Canadian bank a stop-loss for $300 million against the Canadian dollar before going home, at noon New York time. The Canadian dollar presently trades at 1.38 against the USD and he diligently places his stop at 1.3750, a level satisfactorily far given the low volatility of the Canadian currency. The trader in possession of the order knows that should the dollar drop he might have an interesting asset in his hands.

Nothing happens for a few hours until the New York trader notices that the Canadian dollar has dropped to 1.3780. He then makes the judgment that he could push the market toward the stop, provided he runs into no real buy order anywhere. He can then sell a large block of dollars given the certainty that he can buy them back from his own order at 1.3750. He will then as clumsily as possible sell $300 million, hoping the market remains vulnerable, until the customer gets filled in his stop-loss. His aggressive selling, instead of causing more buyers to come into existence, as implied by normal market dynamics, will make operators stay on the sidelines because of the suspicion of a piece of information they do not have. Figure 4.1 depicts the liquidity hole associated with this stop-loss.

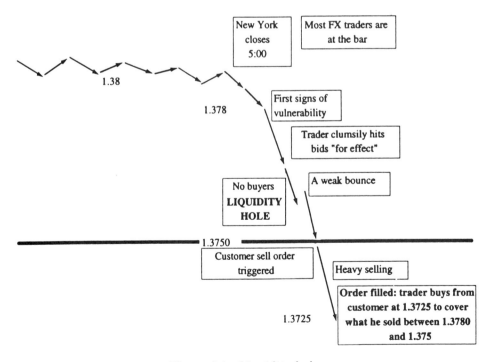

Figure 4.1 Liquidity hole.

Most traders on exchanges operate under the same principle: that of contingent forced large trades. They do not need the exact information: It is easy to sense where the stops are located from the behavior of the brokers as their levels get closer.

BARRIER OPTIONS AND THE LIQUIDITY VACUUM

Much of the recent market volatility was caused by the triggering of barrier options. As these are starting to abound, so are unexplainable gaps in the markets beginning to appear. In the previous example, we saw that a large stop was a free option. However, a stop can be canceled, or given to the trader too late for him to be able to utilize it properly. A trigger option will offer none of these mitigating features: It will be there offered to the market maker far in advance and by its nature is noncancelable.

The option trader with a knock-out on his books will place an order to unwind his deltas, conditional upon the termination of an option. He then would not mind being filled on the stop-loss, as the small casualty would be offset by terminating a liability (the short option) ahead of schedule. He would also benefit from the execution of his own stop order, if it is handled properly.

> *Example:* Sterling is trading at 1.6000 USD/GBP (one needs 1.60 dollars to buy one pound). A trader is short the 1.60 Sterling calls for a 3-month expiration with a knock-out at 1.59, in 200 million pounds (equivalent to US$320 million). He knows that should 1.5900 print and trade in one or more places on the street his option would be terminated. The option delta is 78%, and he holds 156 million British pounds against it.
>
> The option trader makes a quick judgment as to what it would take to make the currency drop to below 1.5900. The stakes for him are large and he has an incentive to trigger 1.5900. In addition to losing his option, he could make some money in the process, by playing with the stop-loss information, as in the previous example, except that the stop-loss would be his own.
>
> He faces two options. He could "sell" his order to the spot desk against .10 pips ($200,000) and ask the desk to manipulate the markets for him. He could also trigger his own stop. He would then wait to see the first down-move in sterling. Stops are more easily triggered after the Bank of England (also called the "old lady") goes home, in the New York afternoon. The best time would be after New York closes and the market rotates to Sydney, Australia, and Wellington, New Zealand. However, the sterling becomes illiquid enough for that purpose after Europe's close.
>
> The trader would sell most of his hedge as the sterling drops: 30 at 1.5945, to soften the market, then 20 at 1.5930, 25 at 1.5920, 20 at 1.5910.

The current total is 95 (out of the 156 to unwind) and he could be in trouble if the market rallies. It would perhaps be better if he put pressure on the market with the remaining 65 by aggressively offering the pounds. He would sell 30 at 1.5900 and would prefer to see 1.5890 trade to ensure that the trigger fill cannot be contested. He would then sell the balance at 1.5895 and 1.5890 by breaking them up between several counterparties to make his fill incontrovertible. Some counterparties could legally contest the trigger if there is no sufficient proof of trading. By consummating the trade with two reputable firms, he can defend himself against such allegations.

This influence on the path of the commodity reduces the Markovian component of the Brownian motion: The process now has a memory. Barriers and stops can cause the next price movement to depend on the previous one. Down moves away from 1.60 led to an acceleration.

A similar, but milder effect took place during the portfolio insurance fiasco: Locals detected a large player whose next move would depend on the past market movement and benefited from it.

ONE-WAY LIQUIDITY TRAPS

Many markets, particularly biased assets (markets subject to frequent panics), can present an asymmetrical behavior of prices. Operators experience a deceiving liquidity on the way in, and discover to their sorrow that getting out is another matter, particularly when liquidity holes occur. Traders experience such imbalance with out-of-the-money puts on biased assets that are in chronic shortage (see Chapter 15).

HOLES, BLACK-SCHOLES, AND THE ILLS OF MEMORY

The principle behind the arbitrage derivation method in modern option pricing theory is the memoryless Brownian motion, with no remembrance of where the spot came from to the last price. This assumption seems to be under the onslaught of all manner of financial theorists and traders as new theories about some form of dependence between past information and market price action seize the day.[2] Without getting into the chaos theory fad, there seem to be very respectable theories based on nonlinear dependence heretofore undetected by the conventional statistical machinery.[3] Markets may, after all, have some form of memory.

At the option trader level, market efficiency does not appear to become attainable despite the increases in the traded volume of most instruments. What is relevant is that the liquidity holes display the weakness of the Markov[4] assumption as the path followed to the last price becomes quite meaningful. *Conditional upon the market touching some level, there will be a predictable price action by some barrier option liquidator that will precipitate the market in some known direction.*

Even the most liquid markets display acute weaknesses at the most liquid of times. It is not fully explainable why a market that moves one trillion a day could be influenced by an order that represents 0.2% of the total volume. It is also unexplainable why the experience of liquidity holes has not provided immunity as the market would use the holes as known events and would adjust for their occurrence through adequate expectation.

A fact that shows why markets have memory is the noise level and frenzy activity that surrounds a new low or new high in any market, regardless of the actual volatility that led there. Markets hitting new highs and new lows start moving in gaps. Often stop-losses need to be taken care of.

LIMITS AND MARKET FAILURES

The exchanges seem to understand that free markets exhibit failures and have stepped in to suspend trading after a certain accumulation of events. The "circuit breakers" in the SP500 (the mother of all liquidity holes) stop the market for five minutes if it opens within a certain range,[5] then gradually establish wider limits of trading. The circuit breakers appear to have been effective since the 1987 stock market crash, at least as a psychological buffer and a means to allow traders to take a deep breath and gauge the available information before the resumption of trading. They have been activated routinely and appear to be a successful experiment.

REVERSE SLIPPAGE

Some traders are expert at quietly accumulating securities, causing a shortage; then noticing that the balance or the order flow has shifted to their advantage, they can cause the market to move their way. They incur positive slippage: ironically, it can be profitable to execute a large order in an illiquid market and unprofitable to execute a smaller one.

Reverse slippage takes place when the accumulation is done at continuously higher prices in the event of a buying splurge, and at lower prices in the event of a selling one. Every day, the marks-to-market of the accumulating entity will be improved during that phase. Typically, the accumulating party "digs" the market at the end of the period, by starting to buy clumsily and causing the prices to move higher in such a way as to bring stop-loss orders into play.

However, the dangers are mostly in getting out of the trade. The trader cannot engage in the same pushing of a market as he did during the position building phase. He would be causing his own collapse. In illiquid markets, particularly exchanges, the activity will be detected rapidly. Traders can tell the imprint of a source of activity no matter how well disguised. They will be merciless with a trader getting out as they have an idea of his size. An unwinding party does not have the freedom to stop midway as an accumulating one does.

Reverse slippage has been profitable for fund managers who created squeezes large enough to download a large portion of their entire inventory at one price.

LIQUIDITY AND TRIPLE WITCHING HOUR

The mechanics of stock index settlement can lead to much abuse by specialists and stock market makers who can thus induce a temporary gap in the market and create a liquidity hole to their advantage.

> *Example:* A basket arbitrageur holds cash and shorts SP500 futures as a full hedge. The contract will be cash settled (the trader gets a compensation of the difference between the previous day's settlement and the official closing price). But after the settlement, the trader will still have to close his long cash position. He will need to secure a bid not far from his settlement price for the arbitrage to be effective.
>
> The settlement terms are that the index will be computed off the official close of all the components. So the best solution for the program trader is to unwind the stocks at the "market on close" feature in the marketplace. Therefore, the tacit unspoken contract he can establish with the stock specialists is, "I do not care where I get my fill as long as that number becomes the one used to compute the price of the index."
>
> The specialists will then use their time and place advantage to move the market to where the imbalances are located. Small imbalances caused by a slight excess of sellers over buyers would bring about a "sell expiration." The specialist knows that there is no chance in the small time imparted to see a buyer come bid better than him, and he would therefore obtain the stock at a very attractive price. The entire operation takes place very quickly. What is remarkable is that it has been taking place so long without efficient markets adjusting to the pattern.

PORTFOLIO INSURANCE

A major illustration of a liquidity hole caused by forced trading is the portfolio insurance episode.[6] It illustrates the case of a panic in that a program that covered about 75 to 100 billion dollars, less than 3% of assets under management, could cause a liquidity hole of such a massive scale. That portfolio insurance caused the crash remains disputable; that it exacerbated the market movement is a certainty.

Portfolio insurance was initially marketed as a protection against adverse market movements for asset holders through a dynamic option replication technique. The absence in liquidity in long-term options justified the technique of replication in place of simple option buying. Human nature is such that a potentially free lunch appears easier to sell to a fund manager than a real option. The selling technique can reach a more generalized level as shown in the Option Wizard, *How They Fool Their Customers* (Chapter 20).

As a method of duplicating the put through delta hedging, portfolio insurance was a negative gamma trade. It could have been argued that, even if portfolio insurance had been executed through actual options, the market makers would have been short the same amount of gamma thus exacerbating the movement with their negative curvature. The answer is that the "free" feature of the option attracted capital to the asset itself thus causing people to buy the stock in larger quantities than if the program did not exist. For a discussion of the difference between a true option and its dynamically replicated equivalent see Grossman (1988).[7]

This author spent one year in the SP500 pit after the crash trying to reconstitute the episode of October 1987, as a lesson in liquidity management. To understand market-making dynamics, every trader should spend a few months in such a pit. At first, the tumultuous pace conceals the real activity. After a while, some order starts to emanate from the pit's behavior. That is when the person becomes part of this large body that is a marketplace.

My conclusion is that locals detected a pattern of forced selling as a result of lower prices in the market. It was easily detectable that the freebie called a stop-loss was available in such a manner. The traders rapidly realized that, as in a stop-loss, the decision to sell was not relieved by a lower market price. In fact, it turned out to be compounded by the lower prices. The classical "front running" of the stop-loss order was made easy because only one forum was available for the program and that most of it was concentrated among few brokers.

A sixth sense, or what locals call "pit chemistry," allows them to identify the origin of a market order without much effort. Living in the midst of a centralized marketplace, they can identify patterns and recognize the signature of every player.

It has been argued that portfolio insurance was the result of the worst possible case of market equilibrium attainment: imperfect information. A large measure of anxiety was caused by the lack of knowledge about information in the market. It is difficult for a market maker to show a bid for a future without the existence of order in the marketplace. One can also conclude that portfolio insurance became the hostage to its own initial success: smaller amounts under the program would not have caused such a snowballing effect.

LIQUIDITY AND OPTION PRICING

There has been a growing awareness in the option pricing literature about the existence of transaction costs. Several option theories have been developed in an attempt to conciliate market microstructure theories and option pricing. Leland (1985) introduced the notion of a break-even volatility incorporating an adjustment for transaction costs. Such adjustment, which he calls A, is added to the volatility entered into the risk-neutral portfolio replication of the Black-Scholes-Merton equation. The resulting break-even volatility for a short seller is the *augmented volatility:*

$$\sigma_A = \sigma\sqrt{(1 + A)}$$

where

$$A = \sqrt{\frac{2}{\pi}} \times \frac{k}{\sigma\sqrt{\delta t}}$$

σ represents the volatility (vanilla volatility), k is the round-trip transaction costs (in percentage), and δt is the time interval between successive adjustments of the portfolio.

However, the trader needs to take into account that an option book will not be monotonically long or monotonically short volatility, but that the break-even volatility will be a markup or markdown according to his position. The short premium player needs a higher volatility to break even while the long player needs a lower volatility. The short gamma pays the negative spread with stop-losses, while the long premium operator has stop-profits that could absorb some profits.

Whalley and Wilmott (1993) make the resulting break-even volatility a simple function of the sign of the gamma. As earlier, it will be $\sigma\sqrt{(1 + A)}$ when the operator is negative gamma and $\sigma\sqrt{(1 - A)}$ when the operator is positive gamma. Hence $\sigma(\Gamma) = \sigma\sqrt{(1 + A\,sign(\Gamma))}$. This creates a situation of variable volatility with the resulting complexities.

Perhaps the area in option research that will witness the largest growth will be the dynamic analysis of option risks under variable transaction costs. Replication costs for an option market maker depend on more factors than the sign of the gamma as with Whalley and Wilmott (1993).

In dealing with transaction costs, option traders have massive economies of scale because the total net gamma in their portfolio sometimes will be equal to several thousand times the aggregate gross gamma in absolute value (i.e., the sum of the gamma in absolute value for every option in the portfolio). This makes the management costs of any particular option minuscule.

Another factor, more difficult to assess, is that of the asymmetry in option costs. The option seller and the option buyer are not quite mirror images, given the difference in utility function between the two.

> ***Risk Management Rule:*** Option trader lore states that when long gamma, use limit orders. When short gamma, use stop orders.

An option trader who "sits on the bid or the offer" when short gamma is said to be penny-wise and pound-foolish. He would later have to "chase" the market. Conversely, an option trader who pays spreads when long gamma is fooling himself. "Let the market come to you" is the experienced trader's recommendation. Table 4.1 shows the characteristics of short and long gamma.

An option seller has no choice whether to hedge or not, hence all of his adjustments need to be done while incurring transaction costs, regardless of his status as a market maker. A short gamma operator needs to adjust his gamma using *stop* orders, which are triggered with the printing of a set price in the marketplace. A stop-loss with the SP500 trading at 455.00 will cause the order filler to buy at best in the marketplace once 455.00 officially trades. The stop will be filled at 455.00 plus bid/offer spread, hence transaction costs will be incurred. In addition, the bid/offer spread typically widens when the market moves, and such moves generally accompany the need to rebalance.

Table 4.1 Execution of Secondary Trades

	Long Gamma	Short Gamma
Buy Orders	Can buy when the market goes lower Posts a bid in the market that can guarantee a trade if the market goes through his level	Needs to buy when the market goes higher Leaves a stop order that becomes a market order triggered by the official printing of a given price
Sell Orders	Can sell when the market goes higher Posts an offer in the market that can guarantee a trade if the market goes through his level	Needs to sell when the market goes lower Leaves a stop order that becomes a market order triggered by the official printing of a given price

An option buyer incurs less transaction costs, if any. A seasoned long gamma player will have orders that go against the market and will know to place them in the marketplace instead of paying the spread unnecessarily. On an official exchange, the order cannot be violated by the market, which means that the market cannot trade through the order without a fill being guaranteed. It is also the case for orders put through the over-the-counter broker in currencies. Some option traders (including the author) who dislike being short gamma advocate that a skillful long premium trader will in fact earn the transaction costs, as he can become a secondary market maker in the cash market. Assume that, as in the preceding case, the SP500 trades at 449.80. The option market maker being long gamma can leave an order at 450.00. The market would not be able to trade without his order being filled. Assume that the market without him is 449.50, 450.05. By offering 450.00, he then can hope to earn part of the spread. True, the market makers would be able to match, but a certain measure of pit etiquette gives the "paper" the right to get a fill along with the market makers. In a marketplace like the Chicago pits, the brokers are powerful and can command better fills than locals. So the transaction costs are limited to the commission, a negligible cost for the large players.

At a more advanced level, every known market experiences the negative autocorrelation of prices for short-term observations, which can also be interpreted as mean reversion (see correllogram in Figure 3.3). That effect should be considered in any discussion about implicit bid-offer spread,[8] which is wider than the nominal spread as the latter can only satisfy small transactions. In some less liquid markets, such as the individual equities, the explicit spread is wider than the implicit spread since the market makers display a market wider than their intentions to trade given that their posted price represents a short option. This mean-reversion will cause the market makers to derive an "edge" and by extension allows skillful positive gamma players to profit in the execution of their hedges.

When it comes to barrier options, a skilled market maker who is short the knock-out or long the knock-in can manipulate the market to improve on his fill.

Chapter **5**

Arbitrage and the Arbitrageurs

Commerce is sordid . . . if it is a small affair in which one buys only to resell immediately what one has bought.

Cicero

A Trader's Definition[1]

■ Traders define **arbitrage** as a form of trading that makes a bet on a differential between instruments, generally with the belief that the returns will be attractive in relation to the risks incurred. Arbitrageurs believe in capturing mispricings between instruments or markets. Traders tend to ascribe the term "arbitrage" for a wide array of trading activities of varying levels of risks.[2]

In more formal academic literature arbitrage means that a linear combination of securities costing 0 can have the possibility of turning up with a positive value without ever having a negative value. Traders' definition of arbitrage is less restrictive and can be phrased as follows: arbitrage means that the expected value of a self-financing portfolio (that can be negative) is positive. The issue of risk neutrality and martingale measure (irrelevant to most traders) is relegated to Module B.

The Oxford English Dictionary (in 1971) defines it as: "The similar traffic in stocks, so as to take advantage of the difference of prices at which the same stock may be quoted at the same time in the exchange markets of distant places."

There are different levels of arbitrage as shown in Table 5.1. Some trading activities that escape the classification in Table 5.1 carry the designation "arbitrage" but do not qualify by any stretch of the imagination. "Risk arbitrage" in the equity markets has nothing to do with arbitrage; it refers to takeover where the trader buys the stock of the company being acquired and sells that of the acquiring one (thus doubling the risk).

Table 5.1 Orders of Trader Arbitrage

Degree	Definition	Examples
First Order	A strong, locked-in mechanical relationship, in same instrument	Currency triangular arbitrage Location arbitrage Conversions and reversals for European options "Crush" or "Crack"
Second Order	Different instruments, same underlying securities	Cash-future arbitrage Program trading Delivery arbitrage Distributional arbitrage (option spreading) Stripping
Second Order	Different (but related) underlying securities, same instrument	"Value" trading Bond arbitrage Forward trading Volatility trading
Third Order	Different securities, different instruments, deemed to behave in related manner (correlation-based hedging)	Bond against swaps (the asset spread) Cross-market relationships Cross-volatility plays Cross-currency yield curve arbitrage

MECHANICAL VERSUS BEHAVIORAL STABILITY

A bet on the behavioral stability of a relationship is a weaker form of arbitrage than one that attempts to capture values mechanically linked.

■ **Mechanical stability** means that two instruments have an identifiable link between them and such link is possible to reproduce artificially. **Behavioral stability** exists when one has to marshal historical records to establish the a posteriori link between two instruments.[3]

  • **Examples** of mechanical stability include locked-in cost-of-carry, a cross-currency that is the result of two components, a forward-forward box, an instrument that converges exactly into another.

  • **Examples** of behavioral stability are U.S. versus Canadian swap curves, German versus Swiss interest rates (until the Berlin Wall fell, and with it the stability of the relationship), and corporate bonds. Because there are no true, identifiable links between the commodities, it is not possible to bridge them mechanically, but history shows a remarkable price stability, to such extent that one could replace the other in a hedge. These apparent relationships provide the market with booby traps.

THE DETERMINISTIC RELATIONSHIPS

In arbitrageur's parlance, deterministic relationships are ones that can be matched entirely, creating perfect, or close to perfect arbitrages. Hedging a deterministic relationship will produce an ironclad protection that should resist all market moves and remain stable over time.

Deterministic relationships are opposed to behavioral, or stochastic relationships, where there is a correlation between instruments or some dependence but that cannot be expected to resist all kinds of eventualities.

The following are examples of deterministic relationships:

- A basket is only the sum of its components. It can therefore be replicated by buying or selling every component.
- A cross-currency, like a German mark/Japanese yen cross-currency exposure can be replicated exactly with dollar versus German mark and dollar versus Japanese yen.
- A knock-out call can be replicated with a vanilla and a knock-in call, all having the same strikes and out-strikes.

The following are examples of behavioral relationships:

- Hedging a bond exposure with a swap is taking advantage of a stable, not certain, relationship. The Italian swap market stops tracking the bond market when a crisis causes a divergence between the creditworthiness of the government and that of financial institutions. The U.S. "flight to quality" can also cause a divergence between the different issuers.
- The common practice of hedging a currency exposure with another one (e.g., "stacking" exposure to European exchange rates by concentrating the hedge in the German mark, owing to its liquidity) can sometimes bring surprises.
- Using all the value-at-risk numbers as exposure presents the same uncertainty as the preceding hedges.

PASSIVE ARBITRAGE

■ **Passive Arbitrage**[4] is the capital neutral swapping of an asset against another similar one that presents more attractive features.

Many operators can engage in arbitrage activities while carrying only one leg of the spread on their books. Investors who own a security can replace it with a similar one that commands a higher return or carries a lower risk, and thus help increase their potential earnings.

Investors who need a certain exposure to the stock market can replace their baskets with futures when the prices become more attractive. They could either carry the futures until expiration (and get back to the market by buying cash on the last day of trading at the settlement price) or switch again when the price differential flips in favor of the baskets.

Bond portfolio holders willing to maintain a set exposure can roll their positions along the yield curve to the most attractive issues. They can search for the "value" point that offers the highest yield or the fastest "roll" on the curve (see the discussion of *convergence* in Chapter 12). They can also switch back and forth between issues as the relationships switch. On-the-run, liquid issues command a higher price (lower yield), usually to compensate for their liquidity. In some bond markets like that in Italy, the difference between liquid and illiquid bonds can be significant. Such premium for liquidity should be of small relevance to the long-term holder and active switching between issues presents rewards.

Companies with a set level of financing needs can play the swap market to improve their costs without significant alteration in the level of the risks incurred.

Companies with foreign currency exposures can select the most attractive periods to establish their long-term contracts. They can also actively move their exposure up and down the curves to the optimal hedging point.

Most fund managers have their performance indexed to an industry average. The needs to beat the average force them to act like short-term traders. They can attain better value through indirect arbitrage.

Sometimes the passive arbitrageur has distinct advantages over the active one. The holder of Japanese stocks would have better luck swapping them into convertible securities when these are priced to the onerous stock borrowing costs of the marginal arbitrageur. Convertible securities would track the stock thanks to arbitrage, but if stocks are expensive to borrow, they will be discounted to compensate for the additional costs. If a fund manager needs to own Japanese stocks, however, it may be more optimal to swap his holdings into convertibles and hedge the residual interest rate risk. His expected return will therefore be enhanced by the cheapness of the warrants that the arbitrageurs are unable to capture.

Examples of such advantages abound. Expensive bonds are difficult to short when their repo cost is high. The passive arbitrageur, however, would not need to worry about the repo when he owns the bond and can replace it with one with a better yield.

An Absorbing Barrier Called the "Squeeze"

One of the pernicious aspects of arbitrage is that, while a trade could prove totally and mechanically hedged, which means that the profits will be undeniably realized on expiration regardless of what happens during delivery, operators could still go bankrupt. One example is program trading in which the short future/long stock will have to pay in cash for the losses on the future leg, without collecting anything from the paper profits on the stock side. A sharp rise would easily deplete the trader's capital: Ironically, it is the most undeniable form of arbitrage that can be the most biting. The operator, obviously, will not be alone in such a situation, and the trade will widen, making the sale of stocks against the purchase of the future unattractive. This is the case of a classical squeeze: Only the most capitalized can survive; those who have "deep pockets" can buy the inventories of the distressed smaller firms.

The same risks can affect the conversions and reversals in markets subject to the future marks-to-market rules, where profits and losses on the futures legs are immediately collected and option profits are only to be realized at expiration.

Duration of the Arbitrage

■ The **duration of arbitrage** (for a portfolio constituted of path-independent products) is the weighted average time to expiration value of the absolute amounts in a book. This number needs not to be weighted by any other factor as it discloses information that affects not necessarily the P/L risks but a spate of intangible risks, such as personnel risks.

For path dependent products it is advisable to use stopping time, as explained in Chapter 19. (It is often called first-exit time.)

This measure works well with linear products. If the operator is long the one year and short the two years in equal amounts the duration of the arbitrage is one and a half years.

The institutional structure of Wall Street and the frequency of the accounting period create a predilection for immediate profits. Guaranteed profits tomorrow against profits today would not do: The manager might lose his job or (even worse) be penalized in his compensation. Traders are not noted for their tolerance of pain. The accounting period punctuates Wall

Street's horizon. Some aggressive brokerage firms have been penalized by the market for the "proprietary trading losses" in one quarter when they were holding high-quality convergence trades (such as the Italian interest rate swaps against government paper). Two results come to mind: (1) The analysis of any payoff partakes of a larger utility framework and (2) the same arbitrage varies in attractiveness between traders owing to the differences in utility curves. There should be a constant shifting of trades between the narrow-minded and the infinitely patient.

Such predilection for short-term profits makes the efficient market frontier unenforceable as the returns for securities would have additional path-dependent restrictions put on them.

ARBITRAGE AND THE ACCOUNTING SYSTEMS

It is often easier to arbitrage one's accounting system than the market. The derivatives markets are growing faster than the systems to properly account for them. Here is a short list of examples:

- Some complex option-related products, such as index-amortizing swaps or most correlation products are not seasoned enough for the market to agree on a uniform pricing formula. The absence of market price allows firms to mark to their parameters and delude themselves in that way. Correlation (not an observable asset in the market) could be derived on a three-month historical data at one shop and one-month at another. Both would be wrong as correlation might be so unstable as not really to exist. The absence of norms would allow two traders at different houses to book different profits or losses on the same trade. Unlike listed products, there is no benchmark to use as a control figure to correct one's estimation. There is no escape from theoretical marking to market and the theory is not robust enough yet.

- Money market and swap traders often arbitrage the credit rating of their employer. They can borrow money better than they can place it at for the same maturity, and their accounting system could easily pick up the projected cash-flow differentials as profits, as few systems discount the creditworthiness of the counterpart. There are counterpart limits, but no counterpart pricing schedules in ordinary systems. The money is ultimately earned (barring bankruptcies), but it belongs to the institution's credit department, which ultimately bears the risk, not to the trader's skills.

- Traders in some houses do not pay interest on the realized losses. They earn interest, though, on the unrealized profits, under the discounting method (e.g., an option trader is long future against a long put; the profits in the puts will converge using the Exp(-r t) process while the future losses are not accounted for in the funding). Traders could, in a limited way, take advantage of the system.

- Most profits on complex options show immediately on booking the trade. A trader selling a complex note will be marked at some "fair value" that approximates the theoretical break-even point but in a frictionless market, that is, one where the subsequent adjustments to the trade took place without the costs associated with hedging (spreads and commissions). If the trader were to add up the costs of dynamic hedging the product over the life of the option, he would be surprised at the decrease in the potential profits. Trades that require the adjustments with Eurodollar futures would suffer the most. Currencies, especially the less liquid ones, require onerous costs of rebalancing in cash, rollovers, and options. Usually, the trader stays ahead by continuously booking new "profitable" trades, then pays the price on liquidation of the position or when the stream of new deals slows to a trickle (as it did in 1996).

OTHER NONMARKET FORMS OF ARBITRAGE

Many types of arbitrages, including the following, do not fall within the scope of this book because of their nonmarket orientation:

- *Credit Arbitrage.* It denotes acquiring debt in one security at a cheaper price than the debt in another. This is generally done as a passive arbitrage activity, defined earlier. It is usually difficult to short a corporate bond because of the occasional difficulties in borrowing them. However, a bonds portfolio manager can improve his expected return and maintain the overall rating in his portfolio by optimizing the mix between issues and swapping the expensive ones for better value bonds. Credit rating is not a market function, and as a trader first and last, the author recommends listening to the market rather than to the credit agencies in the definition of ranking. Such skepticism would therefore invalidate many perceived "value trades" and arbitrages.

- *Tax Arbitrage.* Many equity swaps are due to the privileged tax treatment of one party in the market. That party can then arbitrage its condition by transferring the tax to the other party for a profit. For example, German tax laws impose a dividend withholding tax on foreign, but not domestic, investors. A foreigner can replicate the position by entering in a transaction with a domestic German entity that matches the payoff of the equity swap. The German party can arbitrage the situation by buying the equities and selling the forward to foreign counterparties.

- *Legal Arbitrage.*   Some parties are disallowed by their authorities or their bylaws to engage in some specific transactions. Domestic French residents, to give an example, were banned at some point in the 1980s from buying puts or shorting their currency. Another case of legal arbitrage is the structured note market where the payoff is tied to the performance of some market, hence includes an option, but is flowering with fund managers who are not allowed to buy options. The law is skirted through the veil of the note and the fund manager is then "trapped" since he cannot deconstruct the note himself and needs to go to the bank to secure a market for the option.

ARBITRAGE AND THE VARIANCE OF RETURNS

The definition of arbitrage is becoming controversial as many forms of trading defined as arbitrage often carry a higher variance of returns than outright directional trading. This is partly because the average arbitrageur carries larger amounts on his books than the average speculative trader. It is also due to the accumulation of positions by like-minded arbitrageurs, which puts the pressure on relationships. When a security becomes perceived as expensive, there will be a rush of traders shorting it and buying a similar instrument. If the security stays so for a longer time owing to a specific buyer, the accumulation will turn too large for the arbitrage community to handle and traders will reach their limits. As the arbitrage community reaches its saturation level, pressure on the relationship between what is deemed expensive and what is deemed cheap will cause severe marks-to-market losses. Liquidation of the less capitalized arbitrageurs will ensue.

"Inefficiencies in the market will last longer than traders can remain solvent," an option trader once said.

More advanced notions of arbitrage and stochastic dominance are presented in Module F.

Chapter *6*

Volatility and Correlation

What traders and historians share is an ingrained distrust of the notion of correlation.

An option veteran

This chapter introduces the notion of volatility using minimum mathematics. The reader should try to develop a sense of where the notion of volatility can be ambiguous.

■ **Volatility** is best defined as the amount of variability in the returns of a particular asset. (As will be discussed, there are many variations in the methods of measurement):

- **Actual volatility** is the actual movement experienced by the market. It is often called historical, sometimes historical actual.

- **Implied volatility** is the volatility parameter derived from the option prices for a given maturity. Operators use the Black-Scholes-Merton formula (and its derivatives) as a benchmark. It is therefore customary to equate the option prices to their solution using the Black-Scholes-Merton method, even if one believes that it is inappropriate and faulty, rather than try to solve for a more advanced pricing formula.

■ **Correlation** refers to the least-square measured association between two random variables. It identifies the degree of certainty with which a person can predict the move in one random variable as a result of a change in the other variable. The random variables concerned are the logarithmic returns of the assets [or Log (Price Period t) − Log (Price Period $t − 1$)].

- **Actual correlation** is the amount of actual association between the moves of two markets. It is often called historical, sometimes historical actual.

- **Implied correlation** is the correlation parameter derived from option prices of the components. There will be as many implied correlations as existing maturities. (Module D includes an explanation for calculating the implied correlation using the *triangle*.)

Option Wizard: Correlation and Volatility

Traders often make the simple blunder of assuming that a 100% correlation between two assets A and B means that asset A should move by 1% in response to asset B moving up by 1% (in the same direction). This is not true: They could be correlated by 100% and asset B can move by 2% for every 1% move in asset B, if asset B has twice the volatility of asset A.

What correlation really means is the expected ratio of the moves between assets *divided* by their corresponding volatility.

The assumption behind most random walk models is that of lognormality, which is a necessary solution to the restriction that assets cannot (in theory) have a negative price. Module A describes the process of a random walk and describes correlation. The most dangerous assumption is that of a constant correlation. Traders beware: Markets have adjusted to the fact that volatility is not constant, not yet to the fact that correlation is volatile.

Figure 6.1 shows the cumulative distribution of one standard deviation over time. Assuming 15.7% annualized volatility, the market is expected to move 1% per day, 2.23% every 5 days (1% $\times$ $\sqrt{5}$), 4.47% every 20 days (1% $\times$ $\sqrt{20}$), 15.7% every 248 days—a business year (1% $\times$ $\sqrt{248}$).

Theorists have discussed at length whether the market follows a geometric Brownian motion or an arithmetic one. (See Table 6.1, Figures 6.2 and 6.3.) The difference can easily be explained as follows:

- A **geometric Brownian motion** means (roughly)[1] that the market maintains a constant expected percentage move, say 1%. This simplifies a complicated issue, and can explain why volatility in dollar

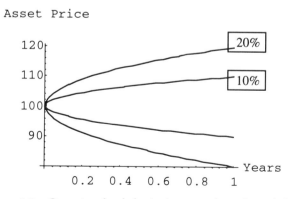

Figure 6.1 One standard deviation as a function of time.

Table 6.1   Constant Dollar and Percentage Moves

Asset S	Constant Dollar Move	Constant Percentage Move
80	19.84%	0.80
82	19.35	0.82
84	18.89	0.84
86	18.45	0.86
88	18.03	0.88
90	17.63	0.90
92	17.25	0.92
94	16.88	0.94
96	16.53	0.96
98	16.19	0.98
100	15.87	1.00
102	15.56	1.02
104	15.26	1.04
106	14.97	1.06
108	14.69	1.08
110	14.43	1.10
112	14.17	1.12
114	13.92	1.14
116	13.68	1.16
118	13.45	1.18
120	13.23	1.20

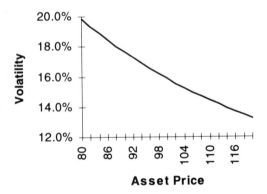

Figure 6.2   Constant dollar move 1% per business day.

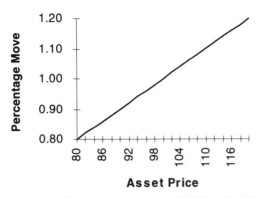

Figure 6.3   Percentage move at 15.7% volatility.

Option Wizard: "Perhaps Bachelier Was Right"

Many of the caps/floor book runners were hurt by the rally in Eurodollars (drop in yield) between 1991 and 1993. With interest rates at 9%, it was remarkable that historical volatility was close to about 9 basis points per day on average. Market markers, however, were selling out-of the money calls with the belief that "percentage" volatility would be unchanged in the rally, which means that at 4.5% Eurodollars, the "tick volatility," or "dollar volatility," would be close to 4.5 basis points. They were proven wrong as the tick volatility remained almost constant, and their positions in out-of-the-money calls made them short volatility at very low levels.

The rally in the Eurodeposits resulted in a rise in implied and historical volatility as defined by option theory (i.e., lognormal returns). Somehow the price of the at-the-money straddle in ticks remained close to the same level throughout. This prompted a famous market thinker to confide to the author: "Perhaps, after all, that man Bachelier was right." He was indicating Louis Bachelier, the French mathematician, who wrote his doctoral dissertation in 1900, 73 years before Black and Scholes, pricing options with an arithmetic Brownian motion. Bachelier was mistreated by history for a long time.*

Euroyen traders experienced considerably more trauma. As short-term interest rates in 1995 reached .10%, a 1 basis point move corresponded to 160% volatility. Volatility moved during the rally from the "social" levels (around 20%) to 200% as the Eurodeposit traders were not informed that the market needs to be lognormal. In addition, Bachelier's model seemed perfectly credible as the market started paying for 100 calls (puts struck at zero) based on the belief that the possibility of the market going negative could not be ruled out.

Moral: Traders should take theoretical dogma less seriously.

---

*See Bachelier (1900).

terms needs to be higher at higher prices. It also explains why volatility would drop as the market weakens, a dampening that would prevent the market from reaching negative levels. As the market drops from 100 to 1, 15.7%, volatility would represent .01 ticks. At .10 it would be .001 and so on.

- An **arithmetic Brownian motion** means that the market maintains constant expected dollar moves, regardless of its level. This assumption is refuted by academics because it can lead to possible negative asset prices. However, traders take it seriously as they believe that for medium-size increments, the assumption holds. In addition, money market instruments have unexpectedly flirted with negative prices throughout history.[2]

- The interesting results of a mixed process usually witnessed in financial markets—arithmetic in the short term and geometric in the long run—will be discussed later in this book.

CALCULATING HISTORICAL VOLATILITY AND CORRELATION

Centering around the Mean

For ease of calculation as well as theoretical reasons, volatility of returns for a dynamic hedger could be calculated as the square root of the sum of the squares of the *movements,* not the deviations from an average. If a market moved 1% a day every day in the same direction (say upward) for an entire month, the conventional measurement of volatility would put it at 0% since all of the moves were at the mean move. This clashes with an option trader's instinct. An option trader would still consider it to be 1% a day and in this case would prefer to buy volatility when it is offered cheaper than 16%.

Statistically, given the absence of well-pronounced trends, or trends that dominate the variance, both measures present similar results.[3]

Formulas.   Taking the return in any period for a given tradable pair in the market to be

$$x_t = Log\left(\frac{P_t}{P_{t-1}}\right)$$

The (natural) log of the two prices will correspond (roughly enough for traders) to the percentage return.

These prices need to be sampled periodically and consistently. If the frequency is every Thursday at midnight, the returns all need to correspond to such a period. Many operators use daily official close to close while others take a price during the day when all markets are very liquid.

Volatility of x for any given period is generally estimated as

$$\sigma_x = \sqrt{\frac{1}{(n-1)} \sum_{t=1}^{n} (x_t - \bar{x})^2}$$

Note that $(n-1)$ is used in place of n because of the loss of one degree of freedom in the estimation of the mean x.

$$\bar{x} = \sum_{t=1}^{n} \frac{x_t}{n}$$

Ditching the $\bar{x}$, the mean return, means there is one parameter less to estimate. It also makes the estimation of volatility closer to what would affect a trader's P/L.[4] So the volatility (nonweighted) noncentered σ' could be expressed as:

$$\sigma'_x = \sqrt{\frac{1}{n} \sum_{t=1}^{n} x_t^2}$$

To annualize and express the volatilities using the trader's conventions, multiply by the annualization factor. If the returns from calculating volatility are daily and the year is considered to be 248 days, the trader would multiply the figure by $\sqrt{248}$. If the returns are weekly, he would then multiply by $\sqrt{52}$, and so on.

Note that the trader could multiply by $\sqrt{365}$ provided he added the weekends in the data series; that would add two zeros per week to the computation and would be roughly equal with some variance for the shorter dates.

Table 6.2 provides an example of historical volatility calculation. It shows daily prices (for an imaginary pair) in succession for 22 days. This yields 21 returns. Column 3 calculates the natural logarithm of the return and Column 4 calculates the square of the $\text{Log}(S_t/S_{t-1})$. The annualized volatility is computed as the square root of the sum of Column 4 /21 multiplied by the square root of 248 = 10.73%.

The correlation between the returns x and y (both being pairs not necessarily of the same numeraire) is classically defined as:

$$\rho = \frac{1}{n-1} \frac{\sum_{t=1}^{n} (x_t - \bar{x})(y_t - \bar{y})}{\sigma_x \sigma_y}$$

but it is permissible to ignore the mean of the returns and to use:

$$\rho = \frac{1}{n} \frac{\sum_{t=1}^{n} x_t y_t}{\sigma'_x \sigma'_y}$$

Table 6.2 Computation of Historical Volatility

Day	Price	$\text{Log}(S_t/S_{t-1})$	$\{\text{Log}(S_t/S_{t-1})\}^2$
1	99.36		
2	98.73	−0.006372	0.000040608
3	98.97	0.002412	0.000005820
4	99.94	0.009795	0.000095941
5	100.20	0.002608	0.000006801
6	101.47	0.012560	0.000157765
7	102.06	0.005819	0.000033856
8	101.50	−0.005514	0.000030409
9	102.45	0.009293	0.000086363
10	102.89	0.004357	0.000018979
11	103.09	0.001886	0.000003558
12	103.71	0.006020	0.000036234
13	104.04	0.003142	0.000009873
14	105.17	0.010855	0.000117827
15	104.52	−0.006257	0.000039155
16	104.32	−0.001886	0.000003556
17	103.31	−0.009714	0.000094366
18	102.27	−0.010156	0.000103154
19	101.63	−0.006251	0.000039072
20	101.22	−0.004074	0.000016596
21	101.44	0.002185	0.000004776
22	101.04	−0.003941	
		$\sqrt{\text{Average}}$	Average
		Annualized	
		Volatility (%)	10.73

Table 6.3 provides an example of correlation calculations.

$$\sigma'_A = .006762 \text{ (using daily volatilities)}$$

$$\sigma'_B = .006363$$

$$\sum Ret_A Ret_B = .000019$$

$$\text{Correlation} = .000019/(21 \; .006363 \; .006762) = .02$$

The links between implied volatility and implied correlation will be examined later in the book.

Table 6.3   Correlation Calculations

Day	S_A	S_B	Ret_A Log (S_{At}/S_{At-1})	Ret_B Log (S_{Bt}/S_{Bt-1})	$(\text{Ret}_A)^2$	$(\text{Ret}_B)^2$	$\text{Ret}_A \, \text{Ret}_B$
1	99.36	100.32					
2	98.73	100.95	−0.006372	0.006246	0.000041	0.000039	−0.000040
3	98.97	101.40	0.002412	0.004448	0.000006	0.000020	0.000011
4	99.94	102.93	0.009795	0.014965	0.000096	0.000224	0.000147
5	100.20	102.96	0.002608	0.000281	0.000007	0.000000	0.000001
6	101.47	103.06	0.012560	0.000991	0.000158	0.000001	0.000012
7	102.06	102.83	0.005819	−0.002253	0.000034	0.000005	−0.000013
8	101.50	103.04	−0.005514	0.002091	0.000030	0.000004	−0.000012
9	102.45	103.16	0.009293	0.001113	0.000086	0.000001	0.000010
10	102.89	103.85	0.004357	0.006734	0.000019	0.000045	0.000029
11	103.09	103.36	0.001886	−0.004779	0.000004	0.000023	−0.000009
12	103.71	103.75	0.006020	0.003798	0.000036	0.000014	0.000023
13	104.04	103.76	0.003142	0.000128	0.000010	0.000000	0.000000
14	105.17	103.29	0.010855	−0.004544	0.000118	0.000021	−0.000049
15	104.52	104.93	−0.006257	0.015749	0.000039	0.000248	−0.000099
16	104.32	104.28	−0.001886	−0.006274	0.000004	0.000039	0.000012
17	103.31	103.56	−0.009714	−0.006898	0.000094	0.000048	0.000067
18	102.27	104.18	−0.010156	0.005926	0.000103	0.000035	−0.000060
19	101.63	104.85	−0.006251	0.006463	0.000039	0.000042	−0.000040
20	101.22	104.75	−0.004074	−0.000952	0.000017	0.000001	0.000004
21	101.44	105.32	0.002185	0.005442	0.000005	0.000030	0.000012
22	101.04	104.99	−0.003941	−0.003193	0.000016	0.000010	0.000013
				Σ	0.000960	0.000850	0.000019
				$\sqrt{\text{Average}}$	0.006762	0.006363	

INTRODUCING FILTERING

What volatility should be used? 10 days? 100 days? . . . There is, fortunately for traders, no straight answer, and such disagreements help create a market. Some traders with a long memory prefer to go back many years, while others are victims of some form of market amnesia.

Filtering is a simple method for taking into account that events in the past need to have uneven weightings (see Figure 6.4). The following text presents a simplified version of the Kalman filter: the exponential decay.[5]

It behooves the trader to assign importance to recent events in proportion to their distance away from the present. But the trader should be flexible enough not to take the measurement for gospel, either because he may have information about a predicted riot tomorrow that would make all past information academic, or because some structural changes took place that need to have an effect on the weighting. The last thing a trader needs to do is be scientific or play econometrician during business hours.

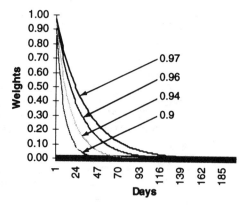

Figure 6.4   Decay factors: Volatility filtering.

Table 6.4   Computation of Volatility

Day	S1	$\text{Log}(S_t/S_{t-1})$	$\{\text{Log}(S_t/S_{t-1})\}^2$	λ^n	
1	99.36				
2	98.73	−0.006372	0.000041	0.5275	2.14E-05
3	98.97	0.002412	0.000006	0.5438	3.16E-06
4	99.94	0.009795	0.000096	0.5606	5.38E-05
5	100.20	0.002608	0.000007	0.578	3.93E-06
6	101.47	0.012560	0.000158	0.5958	9.4E-05
7	102.06	0.005819	0.000034	0.6143	2.08E-05
8	101.50	−0.005514	0.000030	0.6333	1.93E-05
9	102.45	0.009293	0.000086	0.6528	5.64E-05
10	102.89	0.004357	0.000019	0.673	1.28E-05
11	103.09	0.001886	0.000004	0.6938	2.47E-06
12	103.71	0.006020	0.000036	0.7153	2.59E-05
13	104.04	0.003142	0.000010	0.7374	7.28E-06
14	105.17	0.010855	0.000118	0.7602	8.96E-05
15	104.52	−0.006257	0.000039	0.7837	3.07E-05
16	104.32	−0.001886	0.000004	0.808	2.87E-06
17	103.31	−0.009714	0.000094	0.833	7.86E-05
18	102.27	−0.010156	0.000103	0.8587	8.86E-05
19	101.63	−0.006251	0.000039	0.8853	3.46E-05
20	101.22	−0.004074	0.000017	0.9127	1.51E-05
21	101.44	0.002185	0.000005	0.9409	4.49E-06
22	101.04	−0.003930	0.000015	0.97	1.5E-05
			SUM	15.278	

The symbol λ is used for the decay factor. It replaces the number of days to go backward in the previous regime. In place of lengthening memory, one could bring the weights closer to 1.

$$\sigma = \sqrt{\frac{1}{\Omega} \sum_{t=1}^{n} \lambda^{t} \cdot x_{t}^{2}}$$

$$\Omega = \sum_{t=1}^{n} \lambda^{t} = (\lambda + \lambda^{2} + \lambda^{3} + \ldots + \lambda^{n}) \approx \frac{1}{1 - \lambda}$$

when *n* is very large (higher than 1,000 observations as a general rule) and since λ is, by definition, less than 1.

The same decay factor could be applied to the correlation, in the same manner, to cancel the effect of recent memory.

$$\rho = \frac{1}{\Omega} \sum_{t=1}^{n} \lambda^{t} \cdot x_{t} y_{t}$$

Using the same example, Table 6.4 shows the computation of the volatility using a λ of .97.

Column 1 presents the number of days; Column 2 presents the asset moves; Column 3, the logarithmic returns (natural logs); Column 4, the square of Column 3; and Column 5 has the λ to the power of the number of days. It is apparent in moving up the columns that the weightings vanish in importance. We use λ on the first day (day 22 since we are computing volatility on day 22 or later), λ^{2} on the second day (day 21), λ^{3} on the third day (day 20), and so on.

Column 6 shows the result of multiplying Columns 5 and 4, and is the weighted squared return for the period.

The daily weighted volatility is the square root of (sum of Column 6 /21)/sum of Column 5 = .006675. The annualized percentage volatility is obtained by multiplying it by $\sqrt{248}$ = 10.51%.

The reader could try the same exercise with the weighted correlations.

THERE IS NO SUCH THING AS CONSTANT VOLATILITY AND CORRELATION

Figures 6.5 through 6.9 will show the trader to beware the notion of constant volatility and, even more, that of constant correlation.

Figure 6.5 shows implied volatility in the USD-DEM for the one-month options during a part of 1992.

Figure 6.6 shows actual two-week volatility in the SP500. The volatility of the SP500 shot up to 120% the week of the crash of October 1987, which showed a peak into the graph boundaries. Measuring the volatility of volatility would show it to be even more volatile than that of the underlying

Option Wizard: Rubber Time Explained

The notion of economic versus actual time crops up once in the while in discussions between option traders. It is a difficult matter but seems to be adjusted for properly by the markets.

Trading on the weekend does not take place too often. Markets are assumed to be open about 247 days (except for European countries with a plethora of holidays).

Traders price the process in volatility of 365 days but actually adjust back by removing holidays. For example, if they decided to price a Tuesday option on a Friday, they would use the number of business days (2) and would manipulate the formula that uses 5 days to pretend that the volatility over the next 5 days would be low enough to accommodate for the actual moves. If they assumed that volatility is supposed to be 15.7% in the market per actual number of days, it would be 1% for 1 day, 1.41% for 2 days, 15.7% for 1 year, and so on . . . The operator on a Friday would use the volatility that would give such result of the expected move of 1.41% over 4 days, namely 11.08% ($1.41\%/\sqrt{4} = .71 \times \sqrt{247} = 11.08\%$).

More advanced methods give a weight per actual day and assume that Sundays can exist as a source of volatility since nasty revolutions can take place at such idle times. Many operators count Saturday and Sundays as quarter days in the winter and even less in the summer.

Some traders actually price options "on the clock" with a real almanac of expected market moves that lower the intensity of lunchtime in Tokyo when markets go into a slumber.

The important intuition traders need to grasp is that volatility and square root of time have the same effect on the dispersion of a random walk.

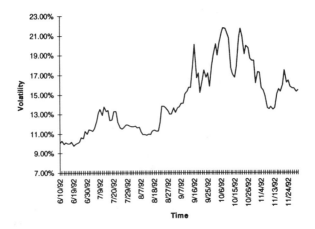

Figure 6.5   USD-DEM Implied volatility is not constant.

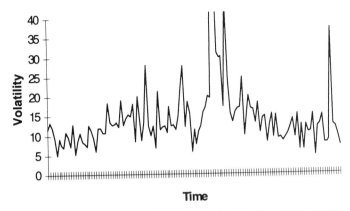

Figure 6.6 SP500 2 week historical volatility 1985–1995.

security itself, particularly if it were broken up into nonoverlapping periods of short duration.

When measuring the volatility of volatility traders should be careful to avoid running overlapping data. In addition, the length of the period matters, and it is recommended to select as short a period between sampling points as possible. Figures 6.6 and 6.7 show that historical volatility moves even more than implied.

Correlation is even more volatile than both volatility and the underlying itself. Figures 6.8 and 6.9 show the correlations of the daily moves in nonoverlapping periods of two weeks.

One does not have to be a statistician to understand that correlation moves all the time.

Chapter 15 will provide an in-depth discussion of distributions, from the vantage point of option pricing.

Figure 6.10 shows the volatility of historical volatility in nonoverlapping periods, and Figure 6.11 depicts implied volatility.

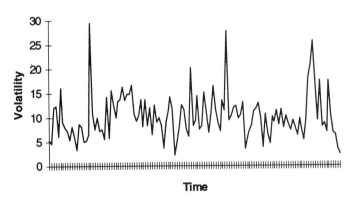

Figure 6.7 Yen 2 week historical volatility 1985–1995.

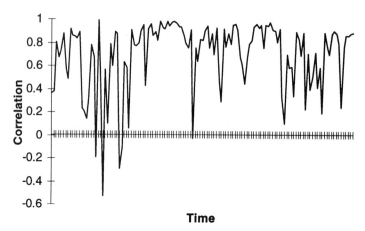

Figure 6.8 Correlation between sterling against USD and FRF against USD, 1985–1995.

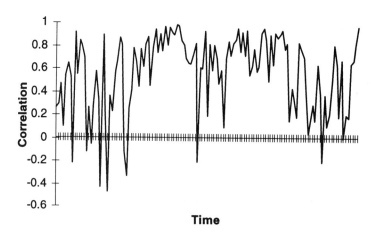

Figure 6.9 Correlation between sterling against USD and JPY against USD, 1985–1995.

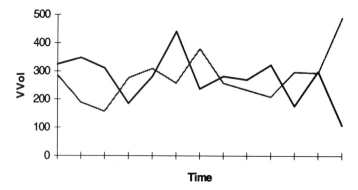

Figure 6.10 Volatility of historical volatility, 1985–1995.

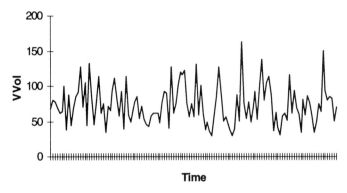

Figure 6.11   Volatility of implied volatility, 1985–1995.

THE PARKINSON NUMBER AND THE VARIANCE RATIO METHOD

Among the most significant contributions to option traders are the Parkinson number and the variance ratio method.

The Parkinson number, generated by the physicist Michael Parkinson in 1980, aims at estimating the volatility of returns for a (geometric) random walk using only the high and low in any particular period. This section will show how to use it selectively, most often in reverse, to derive the distribution of the maximum or minimum in any day knowing the historical volatility.[6] The Parkinson number will be called the P:

$$P = \sqrt{\frac{1}{(n)} \sum_{i=1}^{n} \frac{1}{4log2} \left[log \frac{S_H}{S_L} \right]^2}$$

We have S_H and S_L the close-to-close registered high and the registered low respectively in any particular time frame.

- All traders respect the integrity of the close-to-close number because of its official nature but are cautious about taking the high or low because of the misprints and manipulations attending its registration. Sometimes fictitious trades take place at one level owing to manipulation while at other times computer errors mar the data.

- In addition, there are many instances in cash over-the-counter products, such as illiquid foreign exchange markets, where a new high or a new low could escape the screens and remain the sole knowledge of the traders involved in the trade.

- Finally the Parkinson number applies to a 24-hour period assuming no closing of the market and no discontinuities (an even number of

Option Wizard: "GARCH in Their Head"

Option traders can easily understand ARCH modeling precisely because they *"have GARCH in their heads"* as said one trader to whom the concept was explained on a yellow sandwich bag. Indeed, they have a much better one than that presently available to econometricians.

Sometime in 1982, Engle* discovered heteroskedasticity (i.e., changing volatility) in times series on British inflation, and started the first attempt at modeling it. It resulted in ARCH (autoregressive conditional heteroskedasticity), which was an effort to estimate the volatility process using techniques from times series analysis called autoregressive models. It assumed that future volatility was linked to its past realizations, each realization having its own weight. Intuitively, it can be described as a process that can be forecast using past volatility data in a decreasing manner (as with the filtering technique). "Volatility begets volatility," as the saying goes. A volatile day is more likely to be followed by a volatile day and a quiet one by a quiet one. Inexpensive software packages now help the researcher in "fitting" the parameters to come up with an elaborate (but alas fragile) prediction tool.[†]

After Engle, a deluge of models started hitting the academic world, attempting to make it more potent. Bollerslev and Engel generalized it to GARCH (both autoregressive and moving average). The most interesting development came with Nelson's E-GARCH (exponential), which considered that the volatility shocks *down* (when the market drops) are the significant part in determining future volatility, a fact familiar to equity traders and Mexican peso investors.

Later more complex GARCH models were built on the realization that shocks that generally matter are those where some threshold is broken, those that depend on a regime condition, and so on. Then came N-GARCH (nonlinear), SWARCH (switching regime), and others. H-GARCH (heterogeneous) used a time scale that is similar to the concept of rubber time for an option trader. The models are getting closer to a seasoned option trader's opinion, which could be that past information about the price action impacts future volatility, but in some complex way. Subtle sets of rules in the trader's mind help him form his own opinion in a more potent way than these data-processing techniques. This might explain why ARCH and siblings (even the neural network extensions) never made an impact in the trading room: They are still at this point but a weak imitation of a veteran trader's mind. Implied volatility, basically the trader's opinion, outperforms GARCH predictions except where squeezes take place that make the implied reach abnormal proportions. Otherwise, it would be used with more success (see Taleb, 1996a).

Finally, one reason GARCH never made it is that implied volatility contains information that is not available in past prices (e.g., scheduled elections, economic releases) but that are *significant* in determining future volatility. A sudden announcement of a meeting between two trade ministers would

(Continued)

not impact the currency pair but traders know that the outcome will result in a jump (up or down, pending the nature of the agreement); such information is not contained in past prices. As a matter of fact, volatility would freeze, as the market will be numb to any information on the currency prior to the meeting. So GARCH would predict a drop in volatility.

In addition, some information that was available in past prices (e.g., jumps due to elections) does not appear to bear any significance for future volatility owing to its nonrecurring nature. A trader knows how to filter them in his volatility prediction in a way that econometricians do not. As a community, traders benefit from close to three decades of oral tradition and war stories.

The conclusion is we conclude that in the present state of the contest between the computer and the trader, the trader still has, markedly, the upper hand.

---

*See Engle (1982).

†The GARCH(1,1) can be characterized by the following process for σ_t the volatility period t.

$$\sigma_t^2 = \alpha_0 + \alpha_1 \epsilon_{t-1}^2 + \beta_1 \sigma_{t-1}^2$$

$\epsilon_t^2 = \sigma_t^2 Z_t^2$, Z_t follows a normal distribution with 0 mean and unit variance.

$\alpha_0 > 0$, (generally of the order of .01 for daily observations), $\alpha_1 + \beta_1 < 1$ (but generally very close to 1).

What is remarkable about GARCH is that both the asset price and its volatility share the same "innovation" Z_t with the difference that Z_t becomes squared for volatility.

We can see that the β_1 represents the "constant volatility" coefficient, while α_1 provides a factor of the GARCH innovation, the stochastic element. The higher the α_1 the fatter the tails of the distribution of the asset. In a way, volatility follows a Chi-square process and plotting the process generated by it shows a pronounced right tail. In short, the distribution of volatility presents a positive skew (third moment) and that of the asset presents a high kurtosis (that is the ratio of the fourth moment to the square of the second moment).

---

transactions). Otherwise, it is preferable to use the Garman and Klass (1980) estimation of volatility through the combination of close-to-close and high/low. The Garman-Klass estimator *GK* is:

$$GK = .5\left[log\ \frac{S_H}{S_L}\right]^2 - .39\left[log\ \frac{S_t}{S_{t-1}}\right]^2$$

An important use of the Parkinson number is the assessment of the distribution of prices during the day as well as a better understanding of market dynamics. Comparing the Parkinson number and the periodically sampled volatility helps traders understand the mean reversion in the market as well as the distribution of stop-losses. Some clear rules can be derived from that information.

Comparing the Parkinson number *P* with the definition of periodically sampled historical volatility gives this result:

$$P = 1.67\ \sigma'$$

It means that the volatility of the market as observed through the 24 hours or 1 week, or any stable sampling, period should be related (through the distribution of the maximum and the minimum) to the volatility as measured by the extremes.

Warning: Such measurement cannot be used to compare close-to-close volatility with intraday high/low. It can compare 24-hour high/low to data sampled every day at the same time. For markets, like most equities, which trade during the day only, it is better to use open-to-close volatility.

This estimator can give meaningful information with the following situations:

- *Pricing Barrier Options* (and the related American digital and lookback options). They get triggered through the printing of a price on the screen; therefore, the distribution of the extremes is most important. The barrier option trader needs only one information: the high or the low to see if his option was knocked-in or knocked-out. How this extreme is distributed matters more than the close-to-close or any other estimator of volatility. The Parkinson number is the sole information. If there is a bias making the P consistently higher than $1.67\ \sigma'$, the trader knows that the probability of hitting the trigger is higher. This will be discussed later in the book with reference to barrier options.

- *General Option Delta Adjustments.* The comparison between the Parkinson number and the periodically sampled volatility can reveal serious information about the mean reversion of a particular market and allow the trader to set his frequency of adjustment accordingly. If P is higher than $1.67\ \sigma'$ the trader needs to hedge a long gamma more frequently. Otherwise, he could lag the needed adjustment, a technique called "letting the gammas run."[7]

- *General Trading Strategies.* The market maker edge is strongest in cases where P is higher than $1.67\sigma'$. It is otherwise better to follow a trend. This manifests itself (see Chapter 4) in a negative short-term autocorrelation of prices.

Figure 6.12 shows the Parkinson number ratio to the volatility during the same period for the U.S. Treasury bond futures over a period spanning almost three years until May 1995. The results are strikingly convincing: There seems to be a clear bias in favor of a wider high/low range than assumed by a random walk. Additional testing by the author[8] shows the bias

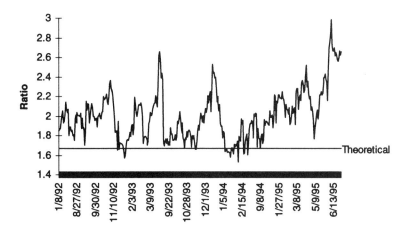

Figure 6.12   Ratio of the Parkinson statistic and open-close volatility in U.S. bond futures, 8/1992–5/1995.

to be permanent in close to the 20 markets surveyed. The reader can draw his own conclusions.

Another seminal piece of work (for traders) concerns the frequency of sampling. An interesting study for option traders is A. Lo and A. C. MacKin-ley's paper[9] on a particular application of a technique called the variance ratios. The authors intended to prove that stock prices have a memory through a simple test of variance relative to sampling frequency.[10]

Briefly, if the volatility on an hourly sampled basis turns out to be higher than the volatility on a daily sampled basis, the market can be considered as mean-reverting. On the other hand, if the market showed a higher volatility at a wider frequency between the dates then it can be concluded that there is a trend. More powerful tests were later invented[11] but this simple variance ratio is simple enough for traders to use and understand.

For example, if the market moved by 1% per day, it would be expected that over 20 business days it moved by $\sqrt{20} = 4.47\%$. Otherwise something suspicious would be deemed to be taking place, such as the market moving more often one way than the other.

What traders usually notice is the higher volatility when sampled hourly, especially in such markets as the SP500 and the Eurodollars. This happens regardless of the ratio between the volatilities for longer periods, such as 1 day and higher.

The variance ratio is well known by traders, even by those who have never heard of the method (see Figure 6.13). Often stock traders wonder why the broad market moved during 1995 by close to 35% with historical volatility close to 10%, or why the dollar lost periodically 20% of its value every year during the 1980s without volatility being any higher than the teens.[12]

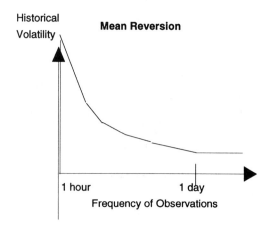

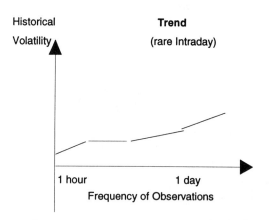

Figure 6.13   Variance ratio method.

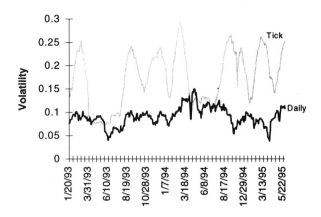

Figure 6.14   Smallest possible time increment volatility.

Figure 6.14 shows the high frequency tick data as a source of information about both the transaction cost function and the mean reversion of markets as expressed by the edge of the market maker in cash. The volatility was computed as measured by tick increments to show the reader how extreme an effect the sampling of volatility can have over the price. It shows the "instantaneous" volatility (as required by Black-Scholes-Merton for the replication of the option) as twice the daily measured one.

PART II

MEASURING OPTION RISKS

> **Risk Management Rule:** *Dynamic Hedging with Black-Scholes-Merton.*
> It is better to improve on a simple but seasoned model than operate
> with a more advanced but newer model.
>
> It is better to use a model with the smallest number of parameters to estimate.

Better models often create nightmares. Every options trader and risk manager, while reaping the benefits of the contributions of Black, Scholes, and Merton, needs to spend his time working around the assumptions that needed to be made for the model to stand.[1] Indeed, all experienced traders operate under the same model and are comfortable with it because they have learned the necessary tricks to make it work. Despite the criticisms of the formula, traders have refused alternatives because they have learned its limitations. No experienced trader would willingly trade Black-Scholes-Merton for another pricing tool.

Black-Scholes-Merton as an Almost Nonparametric Pricing System

With the model, we are able to get a unified measure of the price of an option. Traders can build from there by introducing the additional parameters as an informal tacked-on improvement, such as the jump factor, volatility of volatility, correlation between asset price and interest rates, and different statistical estimates of the underlying process. With most exotic options, the need to parametrize may be more pronounced.

Option Wizard: The Essence of Black-Scholes-Merton

The essence of the model* is risk-neutral replication of securities in a market that is said to be complete. It does not mean, however, that every security needs to be replicated by every arbitrageur, as has often been misinterpreted.

For example, with a warrant on a Japanese stock, the operators involved in such arbitrage cannot dynamically replicate it because of frequent difficulties in shorting the stock. It does not mean, however that fair value needs to be different since the replication costs hamper arbitrageurs. Black-Scholes-Merton does not require for every operator to be delta neutral in infinitesimal changes in the stock price. Some *invisible passive replicator* would trade the warrant for the stock back and forth.

Another problem, however is that an operator may need to hold a security until expiration. To reach his decision to buy the security, he will have to use a term variance that is different from the infinitesimal variance of the security.

Just as the value of some options can be thought of as *limit decomposition* of others with the full knowledge that such value would not be attainable through replication, we can consider the Black-Scholes-Merton fair price as the *limit* of the risk-neutral arbitrage.

---

*Advanced topic.

With risk management, another issue appears: that of the accuracy of the Black-Scholes-Merton predicted *changes* in price. Traders have to work around derivatives of the formula, building modifications that range from the simple rules of thumb to the more complete multifactor models.

Black-Scholes-Merton is based on five assumptions. The first two are fundamental (are philosophically of the essence of the model); the next three are parametric or distributional (can be altered without any significant change in the model):

1. *Ito Process (fundamental).* It is characterized by a random component that is independent and identically distributed (as described earlier—the Brownian motion). Its principal characteristic is that it needs to be *memoryless.* The notion of continuous prices is not as relevant as it was made out to be by early detractors of Black-Scholes-Merton: Continuous finance is a tool, not a philosophical statement.

2. *Frictionless Markets (fundamental).* There are no transaction costs, no costs of adjustment, no stamp tax, or exchange controls. This assumption added to the previous one implies that the operator can buy and sell in large quantities to adjust the delta. It leads to total

absence of the impact of utility functions. The existence of transaction costs would necessarily change the argument for a hedging policy of an isolated operator, but it would not impact fair value.

3. *Constant Volatility (parametric assumption).* It implies that the daily variations are drawn from the same distribution and that the variance is known. It leads to a constant correlation between different assets.[2]

4. *Geometric Brownian Motion (distributional assumption).* It implies (see Module B and Chapter 10) that the motion of assets is "geometric"—that the expected variance of the logarithms of the returns remains constant.

5. *Constant (and known) Drift (parametric assumption).* In trader's terms, the structure of the forwards slope is constant.

A series of corrections will be made to reduce the impact of these assumptions. First, it is necessary to gauge the cost to traders:

- *Assumption 1* needs to be lifted in cases of serious path dependency, as with liquidity holes, particularly if the manufacturing of the option might impact the path of the underlying asset (e.g., as for portfolio insurance).

- *Assumption 2,* sometimes weakened, means that option traders cannot adjust their delta every microtick change in the price of the underlying. Less frequent rebalancing of the portfolio implies less tracking of theoretical value per trade but only in the long run. Thus the operator would have to start divorcing theoretical value and dynamic replication. It means that value can be obtained from continuous time finance but the delta needs to be discretely computed.[3]

- *Assumption 3* is perhaps easiest to correct. Volatility is unstable since traders make markets in it (one can buy or sell volatility). This leads to a divorce between historical and implied volatility. The instability of volatility causes the delta to lose its quality of hedge ratio (unless properly modified), and the gamma its predictability of changes in delta. However, sometimes the trader's work will be made easy by awareness of some link between volatility changes and magnitudes of market moves. Such information is included in this text. Moreover, because the volatility is not constant, a volatility curve results and assumptions must be made about the behavior of such curve.

- *Assumption 4* will be discussed in Chapter 11. In some cases, the distribution might be considered arithmetic, as with Bachelier's early work.

Greeks and Their Shortcomings

Greek	Definition	Shortcomings	Modification
Delta	The sensitivity of a derivative price to the underlying security.	Continuous time hedging is for the textbook. The delta does not work on a portfolio of options that mixes longs and shorts. It is an extremely weak measure of risks.	Use a discrete delta with increments. *Shadow delta* adds some vegas and gammas to it.
Gamma	The rate of change or "curvature" in the delta.	It is meaningless for a portfolio of options. It does not take into account changes in volatility when the market moves.	As with a delta, use discrete increments. Examine two different numbers: Up gamma and Down gamma. *Shadow gamma* takes into account the volatility smile. *Skew gamma* measures the impact of nonlinear changes in volatility arising from an up-move or a down-move.
Theta	The sensitivity of a portfolio of options to time.	It does not take into account the changes in volatility with the shortening of expiration. It does not take into account that volatility drops when markets do not move at all.	Use a term structure of volatilities to reprice the portfolio one day hence—only when volatilities are deemed to converge. Use *shadow theta* to accelerate time decay in stable markets and reduce it in volatile conditions.
Vega	The sensitivity of an option to volatility.	It is extremely misleading in a portfolio that has calendar spreads, as different maturities do not have the same volatility of volatility.	Use a simple volatility curve model for the weightings. More advanced: Use a covariance matrix for the buckets.*

Continued

Greek	Definition	Shortcomings	Modification
Rho1	The sensitivity of an option to domestic costs of carry.	It assumes, unrealistically, parallel shifts in the curve.	Use a simple term structure model for the expected position.
Rho2	The sensitivity of an option to dividends, coupon, or the foreign rate.	Same as Rho1.	Same as Rho1.
Convexity	A general blanket term to define nonlinearity in a derivative instrument.	Convexity, a much abused term, assumes parallel shifts and moves of equal volatility.	Use a simple yield curve model (a variance-based one factor model) for the weightings.
Omega	Shortcut method to compute the expected life of an American vanilla, or the expected exit time for an American binary or a knock-out option.	It does not take into account local volatility between two points in time and space (i.e., forward volatility and skew slope).	
Alpha	Method to compute the cost of gamma.		
Correlation Vega[†]	Method to compute the sensitivity of the price of a structure in a portfolio to various correlations.		

*A bucket vega is the vega exposure between two dates.
[†]The correlation vega is covered in Chapter 22.

- *Assumption 5* has two results. The first is that indeed the rate of drift moves (interest rates are far from constant), and it is often correlated with the movement in the asset prices (in "biased" assets like Mexico the link is obvious). The second result is that the drift does not move in parallel, but in a predictable manner.

The table on pages 112–113 lists shortcomings of the Greeks and simple modifications to correct them. This will enable use of the

Option Wizard: Why Good Models Die

Most new models that attempted to correct the failings of Black-Scholes-Merton did not survive. An admirable and realistic one, Merton's jump diffusion pricing tool, is rarely implemented for the simple reason that it requires the estimation of two additional parameters, the Poisson jump size and its frequency. Stochastic volatility techniques (see Hull and White, 1987) also were undeservedly consigned to the dustbin of business school libraries because of the need to estimate two additional parameters, volatility of volatility and the correlation between the volatility and some indicator of the asset price. The same problems mar the implementation of potent yield curve models, such as those fitting the Heath-Jarrow-Morton framework; traders tend to avoid them despite the insistence of their research staff, in favor of the simple Black-Scholes-Merton that they know how to trick.

Traders are not fooled by the Black-Scholes-Merton formula: The existence of a "volatility surface" is one such adaptation. But they find it preferable to fudge a parameter, namely volatility, and make it a function of time to expiration and strike price, rather than have to precisely estimate another.

---

various derivatives of the Black-Scholes-Merton formula in the light of the previously outlined reservations.

Technical details about the Black-Scholes-Merton derivation are provided in Module G. For a very pedagogical derivation the reader should refer to Hull (1993), Cox and Rubinstein (1985), or Jarrow and Rudd (1983).

Chapter 7

Adapting Black-Scholes-Merton: The Delta

It is always preferable to be roughly hedged against a broad set of eventualities than exactly hedged against a narrow parameter.

Marty O'Connell

■ **Delta** means the sensitivity of a derivative price to the movement in the underlying asset. It is either expressed in percentages or in total amounts. A 50% delta is supposed to mean that the derivative is half as sensitive as the asset and that one needs two dollars in face value of the derivative to replicate the behavior of one dollar of the asset.

A delta is expressed as the first mathematical derivative of the product with respect to the underlying asset. It means that it is the hedge ratio of the asset *for an infinitely small move.* Somehow, when the portfolio includes more than one option, with a combination of shorts and longs, delta and hedge ratio start parting ways.

The delta is not necessarily limited to options and contingent claims. It can be used for forwards, futures, and other linear products, where its accuracy is greater. Linear means nondynamically hedged, and dynamic hedging is what makes the delta very murky. The delta for a forward would take into account the discounting of the cash flow to achieve equivalence to a cash product.

Perhaps the largest misconception in the financial markets attends the definition and meaning of the delta. Every operator instinctively knows that *hedging in continuous time will never be possible.* The difference between discrete and continuous swells when one looks at special situations such as a risk-reversal or barrier options.

Attempting to give the delta a meaning in terms of risk management is denying the dynamic interaction of parameters. It partakes of the desire by nonprofessionals to get a numerical exposure at no cost. Nothing can be schematized in dynamic markets. Delta loses in its significance when traders move from a simple option to a portfolio of longs and shorts. Many traders to this day live under a delta limit rather than a more global scenario analysis.

> ***Risk Management Rule:***   Continuous time models should be used for pricing and getting a benchmark fair value, not to hedge.

CHARACTERISTICS OF A DELTA

Figure 7.1 shows the delta for a simple strategy. The call with 100 strike price is priced at 15.7% volatility, the delta is originally 50. It appears to be the tangent to the option price, and shows the slope of the price change at the origin, 100.

In the case of Figure 7.2 it is easy to ascertain that the delta in fact is a hedge about the origin, 100, and that the hedge would need some adjustment where we see a gap between the slope and the price curve.

THE CONTINUOUS TIME DELTA IS NOT ALWAYS A HEDGE RATIO

The delta generally interpreted to mean an equivalent spot position becomes inapplicable to the management of a portfolio. Seasoned professionals ignore the current definition of the delta as both a measure of risk and an indication of a position equivalence (although their research departments and textbook-trained risk managers usually do not). For anything beyond a medium-length stable option close to the money, a delta does not reflect anything meaningful.

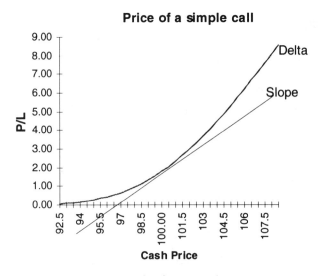

Figure 7.1   Delta for a single option.

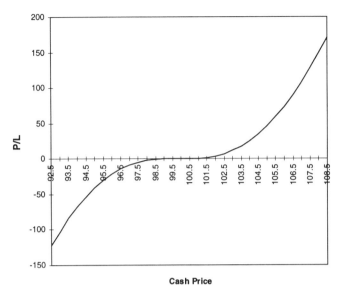

Figure 7.2   Delta and other lies.

Option Wizard: The Half Billion-Dollar Delta

The problems with the meaning of a delta are compounded with barrier options.

An interesting illustration of this microscopic change is an argument that reportedly took place (at a major institution) between a risk manager and a group of traders concerning barrier options. The risk manager (characteristically suspicious of traders' explanations) was vetoing the trade on grounds that the delta reached 10,000% at the barrier. According to his logic, it would put the position at much above any limit allowable by the firm, a $5 million trade hitting the equivalent position of half a billion! So he prevented the trader from engaging in the transaction.

The trader was infuriated by such logic. His maximum risk on the trade was less than $400,000 if everything went wrong. True, the delta jumped to abnormal proportions between 1.399999999 and 1.40 but without being branded as a heretic it was difficult to explain to the semi-mathematician-risk manager that deltas sometimes were an irrelevant waste of computer power.

According to the formula, the trader needed to buy a half billion dollars around the barrier and then sell them back at or above it to make the transition smooth. If this maneuver were feasible, it would make barrier options better instruments to trade. Leaving the trade alone, and considering it as a single bet with a positive expected return, appears to be a more conservative approach. In that light, the delta bears no true meaning. Some traders trick the delta of a barrier by changing the expiration date, as we will see in Chapter 20.

Orthodox definition of the delta:

$$\text{Delta} = \frac{\partial F}{\partial U}$$

F is the derivative $F(U,t)$
U is the underlying security.

It is the derivative of the option price to the underlying. In plain English, it would correspond to changes in the option price stemming from infinitely small changes in the underlying asset. This concept is extremely useful for mathematical derivations. From a standpoint of trading, it offers no significance, for the following reasons:

- There is no such thing as an infinitely small move in the market.
- If there were such microscopic moves they would be nobody's concern.

To make the mathematical continuous-time finance delta relevant, it needs to be accompanied by the second derivative, the gamma, and at least a third one, the DgammaDspot. In addition, because volatility tends to change when markets move, adding the vega to the exposure would be necessary.

In the real world, the **modified delta** notion appears to be a more adequate measure. It is defined as:

$$\text{Modified delta} = \frac{\Delta F}{\Delta U}$$

with the Δ as the change in option price stemming from a set change in the underlying security. If the call price picks up .05 points when the underlying asset moves from 100 to 100.1 then its delta will be $.05/.10 = .50$ or 50%.

However, moving the asset in one direction (up) is not necessarily a great approximation of the behavior of the function on the way south as well. A more powerful tool is to use the following:

$$\text{Delta} = \frac{1}{2}\left(\frac{\Delta F}{\Delta U^-} + \frac{\Delta F}{\Delta U^+}\right)$$

with ΔU^- and ΔU^+, respectively, down-moves and up-moves in the underlying asset.

One can see the results of such derivation: Delta would then depend on the magnitude of the changes in the underlying security, that is the ΔU. The increment becomes then at the discretion of the operator. It could be a function of either his utility curve or his estimation of future volatility.

The advantages of using the discrete delta is that it incorporates a little of the second and third derivatives that should complete the mathematical delta in any form of analysis.

Example. A Misleading Delta: Assume there is a flat yield curve and that the forward is equivalent to spot.
    All options are European and have a one-month maturity.

The option trader has the following position:

- He is long $1 million of the 96 calls (delta .824, total continuous delta $824,000 long).
- He is short $1 million of the 104 calls (delta .198, total continuous delta $198,000 short).
- His total continuous delta is long $626,000.
- He could hedge it by selling $626,000 of forward.

Table 7.1 shows his performance. Table 7.1 shows the delta of the position positive everywhere except around 100.
    It is apparent that the P/L on display in Figure 7.2 is similar to that of a simple long position, except around the origin—and the origin is something

Table 7.1   Inapplicability of the Continuous-Time Delta

Asset Price	P/L 000	Delta 000
92.5	−122	420
93.5	−84	349
95.5	−30	194
97	−9	90
98	−2	39
99	0	8
100	0	0
101	1	16
102	4	53
103	12	106
104	26	171
105	46	241
106	74	311
107	108	377
108.5	171	461

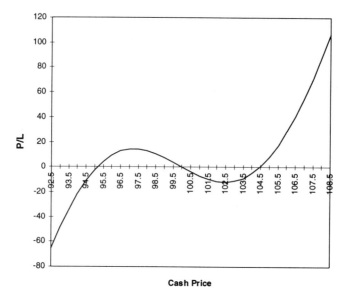

Figure 7.3 Modified delta hedge.

nobody cares about. At an option seminar, when the author asked the crowd whether they considered the graph to reflect a long, square, or short position, all the traders answered "long." Characteristically, the persons without trading experience answered "square."

The following paradox is taking shape: The trader in the example buys $550,000 cash instead of $626,000. The answers of the seminar participants who were shown Figure 7.3 were distributed between "square," "short," and a few "long":

- Those looking at the extremes (asset price 93 or 107) saw a positive P/L in a rally and a negative one in a selloff. The position in their eyes "felt long."
- Those looking at a narrow range (asset price ranging between 99 and 101) "felt short."
- Those looking at a middle range (asset price 95 or 103) "felt squarish."

It can be seen that the hedge shown in Figure 7.3 and Table 7.2 is more effective than the first one for wider variations: Maximum loss drops to −65 from −122. Maximum profit drops to 107 from 171. Using a broad set of assumptions, Position 2 is more delta neutral than Position 1 although it seems delta short. For a Δ of 2.5 points, the maximum is entirely neutral. Taking this position thus widened the neutrality increment to what appeared to be a decent margin.

Table 7.2   A Modified Delta Hedge

	P/L 000	Delta 000
92.5	−65	344
94	−22	235
95	−2	157
96	10	81
97	14	14
98	13	−37
99	7	−68
100	0	−76
101	−7	−60
102	−11	−23
103	−11	30
104	−5	95
105	8	165
106	28	235
108.5	107	385

Had the author asked the seminar participants: "How would you feel if there was a threat of a nuclear attack?" they would no doubt have answered "long." And to the question "If your time frame were six minutes?" the answer would have been "short." This leads to the following rule:

> ***Risk Management Rule:***   A delta depends on the operator's perception of future volatility and his utility, as well as his possible frequency of adjustments.
>
>   These elements matter less and less when the market gains in liquidity.

Operators are forced to define the delta as a function of increments that matter to them. The preceding position would appear square if the P/L corresponded to pennies, but it would require attention if it corresponded to millions. Somehow, operators are obligated to let the utility curve creep up into their trading.[4]

DELTA AS A MEASURE FOR RISK

Delta fails adequately to measure risks even taking a simple position. It provides the same measure to an extremely risky position and an extremely safe one.

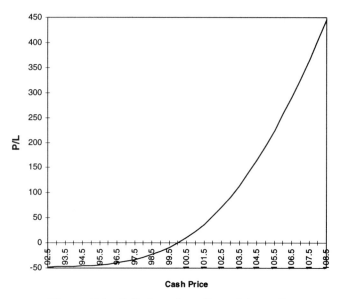

Figure 7.4   P/L for a long/low delta call.

Example: Two positions express the same view: One is long option, the other short. Initially they have the same delta.

Case 1: A trader is long 1,000 calls

Case 2: A trader is short 1,000 puts of the same delta

Figures 7.4 and 7.5 reveal the difference.

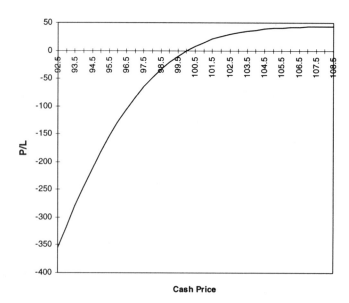

Figure 7.5   P/L for a short/low delta put.

The trades displayed in Figures 7.4 and 7.5 both have the same delta: $200,000 approximately. It is easy to see why the delta is a poor approximation of risk.

CONFUSION: DELTA BY THE CASH OR BY THE FORWARD

The delta as expressed by the Black-Scholes-Merton formula concerns the amount of cash the operator needs to execute to offset an option position. For all European options, however, the real exposure lies in the forward.

Nevertheless, operators prefer to see the cash delta as they generally hedge themselves with it. It is easier to monitor on a screen and quote in the market. When they deal with options on futures or use the futures as a hedge, they need to use a different delta fit to the exact period in the future. The difference between the two is sometimes far from trivial. Operators often must deal with questions like this one: An option that is close to the money in the forward trades at 50% delta. What is the cash delta?

The answer is to transform the potential future exposure into a cash exposure through the delta of a forward. This can be done by discounting the forward exposure using the cash-future growth rate as a discounting factor. Therefore, the delta of the cash will be the discounted value of that number. The discounting method will depend on the underlying security of the option, as will be described.

DELTA FOR LINEAR INSTRUMENTS

It is necessary to examine the deltas for linear instruments both as a hedge between futures/forward, or even futures and futures, or as a hedge for any of the two with options or vice versa.

For a view of the cash and carry arbitrage relationships, traders can read DeRosa (1992; 1996).

Delta for a Forward

A Non-Interest-Bearing Asset.   The general formula for the computation of a forward is:

$$F = e^{rt} S$$

for a non-interest-paying asset.

F is the forward, S the spot, t the time to expiration (a shortcut for $t - t_0$), r the domestic rate, rf the foreign rate, d the dividend rate.

Foreign Currency Forwards. The covered interest parity arbitrage formula is (typically the first and often only formula a trader learns—and needs):

$$F = e^{(r - rf)t} S$$

However, the forward does not immediately deliver the profits and losses. The operator has to wait until the settlement day to earn or pay the realized sum. It is easy to see that a profit on a one-year forward will turn to cash one year from now; therefore, the value of the nominal asset should be discounted like a zero-coupon bond.

Thus, the P/L generated by the forward needs to be discounted back to the cash using the usual e^{-rt}.

Therefore, using ΔS as move-in spot:

$$\text{P/L of Forward} = e^{-rt} e^{(r - rf)t} \Delta S = e^{-rf t} \Delta S$$

$$\text{Delta of a Forward} = e^{-rf t}$$

Ironically, only the foreign rate matters. Even more ironically, the delta being the discounted foreign rate, there is some relativism as far as the hedging. Two people looking at the same forward would use two different hedge ratios based on their home currency. Module C on the numeraire problem, provides a discussion of the issue.

Foreign Cross-Currency Pairs. A foreign cross-currency pair is a contract to exchange one currency for another at a determined point in the future. An example would be sterling/DM for an American citizen, or sterling/Dollar for a German citizen. Not much volume is generally transacted between these pairs, but by virtue of the multiplication of the combinations, there are too many of them. Some traders quote Drachma/Australian dollar or Lira/New Zealand dollar though not routinely so.

Example: Assume there is Currency 1 and Currency 2 with the spot expressed in units of Currency 2 per Currency 1. The forward therefore is:

$$F = e^{(r1 - r2)t} S$$

with $r1$ the rates in Currency 1 and $r2$ the rates in Currency 2.

Now the trader is confronted with the currency in which the profits and losses are computed, as they will determine how he would discount the hedge. The trader has the choice of using Currency 1 or Currency 2 as a discounting one. This difficulty arises because unrealized profits and losses from a sterling/DM trade can be either in sterling or in DM. The trader cannot translate unrealized profits and losses into his home currency without incurring a foreign exchange exposure in one of the currencies.

Discounting the hedge would give us:

$$\text{Delta of a Forward} = e^{-r(r1 - r2)t}$$

r is either $r1$ or $r2$, whichever the trader chooses as his "anchor" currency (the currency in which the profits and losses are computed).

Stock or Stock Index.   For a stock or stock index that continuously pays dividends (something that naturally does not exist but that is an assumption), the delta of a forward is the same as with the foreign currency except that the trader uses the dividend rate instead. The result is:

$$\text{Delta of Forward} = e^{-rt}\, e^{(r - d)t} = e^{-dt}$$

with d the dividend rate.

When the dividend rate is not continuous, one needs to use the exact payout to the end date.

Delta for a Forward-Forward

The forward-forward can be easily defined as an arithmetic sum of one long, one short position in the same instrument at two different dates. The complexity sometimes arises from the lack of equivalency between amounts (2 years vs. 3 years will need to be "tailed" properly to account for the present value).

> *Example:*   The delta is the difference between both individual deltas. Take $F1$ and $F2$ as two forwards with delivery $t1$ and $t2$. The forward-forward will therefore be called $F(t1,t2)$.
>
> The delta of $F(t1,t2)$ will be equal to Delta $F(t2)$ − Delta $F(t1)$.
>
> The profits to $t1$ need to be discounted at a different rate than the profits to $t2$. In addition, this gives rise to interpolation issues that will cause some difficulties in determining the exact $r1$ given $t1$ and $r2$ given $t2$.
>
> A more complex approach would be to weigh the deltas of each forward since it is not exactly the same position.

Delta for a Future

The general formula for the computation of a future is:

$$\text{Future} = e^{rt}\, \text{Spot}$$

for a non-interest, non-dividend-paying asset.

However there is a serious difference between futures and forward as the futures settle daily in cash a variation margin, which eliminates the discounting the trader applies to the forward.

- For a foreign currency, the covered interest parity arbitrage formula is:

$$\text{Future} = F \, e^{\,(r - rf)t} S,$$

$$\text{Delta of Future} = e^{\,(r - rf)\,t}$$

- For a foreign cross-currency, the same holds. Assume there is Currency 1 and Currency 2 with the spot expressed in units of Currency 2 per Currency 1. The forward therefore is:

$$\text{Delta of a Future} = e^{(r1 - r2)t}$$

- For a stock or stock index dividends, continuously paying the delta of a forward is similar to that of the foreign currency except that the dividend rate is used instead. The result is:

$$\text{Delta of Future} = e^{\,(r - d)t}, \text{ with } d \text{ the dividend rate.}$$

When the dividend rate is not continuous, the exact payout to the end date is used.

Stability of a Delta for a Linear Derivative.   The deltas of futures, forwards, swaps, and the like are stable (since they are called linear derivatives). Their second derivatives are almost equal to zero (i.e., no gamma, except for a small convexity) and they have only one meaningful first derivative, the delta. No modification is therefore necessary to compensate for the shortcomings of such approximation, except in cases of extreme convexity in very volatile markets.

DELTA AND THE BARRIER OPTIONS

Often dealers have their palms sweating when confronted with the deltas close to 10,000% when they come close to the barrier nearing expiration day. In some cases, numbers swell beyond the screen's ability to display the numbers. This issue is examined more closely in Chapters 19 and 20, but often this jump is only applicable for a small increment.

It is indeed erroneous to try to hedge according to that schedule. Getting rid of that notion makes barrier options easier to trade.

Barrier options present an extreme case of discontinuity that is very instructive for convincing anyone about the flaws of using a continuous time framework for option analysis.

Delta and the Bucketing

■ A **bucket** is the bundling of exposures by groups of neighboring maturities.

Another limitation to the delta measure is that it does not display the risks in the "basis" or the risk between buckets. The delta in the cash is sometimes insignificant when one is confronted with a volatile basis or a long time separating the cash from the future. The risk manager therefore needs to see the "bucketing." This is due to the volatility of both the volatility (it can impact back-month deltas) and the interest and carry rates.

Delta in the Value at Risk

The reader needs to review a more thorough explanation of the value at risk (VAR) concepts in Module E. A (poor) method of incorporating of the derivatives risk in the value at risk method is the following[5]:

$$\text{Equivalent position} = \text{face value} \times (\text{delta} \times \text{expected move} + .5 \text{ gamma (expected move)}^2)$$

In the case of the risk reversal in the Figure 7.1, the total exposure for such a position, according to the VAR, would then be zero. Including a gamma did not help much since the gamma is nil.

Some risk managers go the extra mile and add the vega to the analysis. Would it improve the risk measure in this example? Of course not: Despite all its hidden risks, the trade is vega neutral. In addition, the measurement needs to include the *shadow gamma* to be complete, in order to incorporate the vega of the position. At the time of this writing, current methods for assessing the risks of option portfolios resort to the repricing of an option portfolio at simulated large movements.

Delta, Volatility, and Extreme Volatility

All operators in options learn that a rise in volatility would cause the delta of an out-of-the-money call to rise and that of an in-the-money call to drop,

Option Wizard: Delta and the Probability of Being in the Money

(This issue is examined in greater detail in Chapter 17.)

The delta is the "risk-neutral" (see Module B) replication of the option. The value corresponds to the integral of the payoffs between the strike price and infinity for a call (or zero for a put) assuming the underlying process is risk-neutral. In discrete terms, it would be the sum of the payoff of every eventuality multiplied by its risk-neutral probability. The delta is the sensitivity of that value to the changes in the underlying asset.

More practically, it corresponds to the ratio of the asset the trader must carry to avoid having any instantaneous P/L from the micromoves.

The probability of ending in the money is simply the discounted probability divorced from the associated payoff. In the study of binary options, it will be shown that the delta and the probability of being in the money would be the same at very low volatility and in the absence of a skew, and would start diverging in the presence of either a skew or a high volatility (as it could cause a right-side skew, owing to lognormality, see Figure 7.7).

Barrier option traders who experience deltas in 500% magnitudes are fully aware, albeit intuitively, that delta means replicating quantity not probability. They know that the scary delta corresponds to the amounts to buy or sell to protect their book from losses and maintain their comfortable lifestyle.

We can also extend some notions from the two-country paradox: The probability of being in the money using one part of a pair as a numeraire is the delta for the party using the other side as a numeraire. So in a vanilla DEM-USD option, a delta for a USD-based person is the probability of being in the money for a DEM-based person. This striking paradox is discussed in Chapter 19 and Module C.

---

therefore bringing deltas closer to 50% (or the present value of 50%, to be precise).

In the formula, as shown here, asset S follows the geometric Brownian motion:

$$S_t = S_0 \, exp\{(\mu - .5\sigma^2) \, t + \sigma \sqrt{t} \, Z\}$$

S_0 is the price of the stock at time 0 (the present), μ the (risk-neutral) drift (interest rate differential or numeraire rates less carry), σ the volatility and t time until expiration.

Z follows a reduced centered normal distribution such as $p(z = x) = exp(-x^2/2) / \sqrt{2 \pi}$.

We have the conditional expectation $E(S_t)$ at time 0 = $S_0 \, exp(\mu \, t)$.

Table 7.3   Asset Values One Period Ahead

σ (%)	Z						
	−3	−2	−1	0	1	2	3
10.00	90.11	93.28	96.55	99.94	103.45	107.08	110.84
15.70	84.88	89.60	94.59	99.85	105.41	111.28	117.47
25.00	76.91	83.84	91.40	99.85	108.60	118.39	129.05
50.00	58.72	69.77	82.91	98.52	117.07	139.12	165.31
100.00	33.47	47.26	66.73	94.22	133.04	187.86	265.27

The rise in volatility has the tendency to increase the expected final price of the stock through compounding, while the drift would make it decrease by $.5\,\sigma^2\,t$.

Table 7.3 shows exactly what takes place when we calculate the asset price on a spreadsheet. He assumes that $t = 12\%$ of one year and plugs in .12. We also assume that $\mu = 0$ and that $S_0 = 100$. The volatility (the first column) is expressed in annualized terms (to match t, which is expressed in annualized terms as well).

The Z values share the same probability. So if the center column were at 100, in all cases the expected values of the final asset S would be higher than S_0. There is a correcting term $-.5\,\sigma^2\,t$ to satisfy the martingale property: Every cell multiplied by its probability needs to sum up to S_0. Note how $-.5\,\sigma^2\,t$ pulls down the market in the center column (Z = 0).

The compounding is caused by what is called the geometric return: Since returns compound, a higher volatility would raise such compounding and would increase the divergence between an arithmetic process (where the returns are constant) and a geometric one (where the returns depend on the level of the asset). The net effect between these two counterbalancing factors is the thickness of the right tails. This effect will be examined again in Chapters 17 and 18. Figure 7.6 shows the graph of the terminal values of S against their probability.

At a higher volatility, as shown in Figure 7.7, the distribution develops an increasing skew to the right. The mean, however, remains the same: The surfaces on each side of 100 are equal. It means that the median needs to slide left in an amount commensurate to the volatility level. This shift will have an effect on the delta.

> *Example:*   The forward trades at 100, spot at 100. Table 7.4 lists the deltas of the 110 calls, the 90 calls, and 90 puts, all with 180 days until expiration. Assume interest is at zero for simplification.

Volatility does not often rise to 180%. An nonequity option trader would see an actively liquid instrument do so only once every few years. However, these instances provide the option trader with an accelerated tutorial.

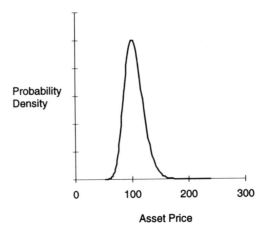

Figure 7.6   Asset distribution at medium volatility.

The following is a list of recent triple-digit volatility cases.

1987: Silver, Equity Indices, Eurodollars.

1990: Oil and related markets (Gulf War).

1992: Short sterling.

1995: Mexico (short-term options traded reportedly at 250%), Euro-yen.

1992–1993–1995: PIBOR (Paris Interbank Borrowed Rate) (French Euro-deposits experience routine panics to the point of making junior option traders extremely aware of *la lognormalité*).

This hints at a common Wall Street issue: A call on a bond can also be viewed as a put on yield. For pricing purposes, traders use a geometric

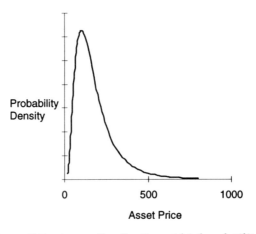

Figure 7.7   Asset distribution at high volatility.

Table 7.4 Deltas with Extreme Shifts in Volatility

VOL	90 Put Delta	110 Call Delta	90 Call Delta
10	−0.06	0.09	0.94
15	−0.15	0.20	0.85
20	−0.21	0.27	0.79
30	−0.27	0.36	0.73
40	−0.30	0.42	0.70
50	−0.32	0.46	0.68
60	−0.32	0.49	0.68
80	−0.32	0.54	0.68
100	−0.31	0.59	0.69
120	−0.29	0.62	0.71
140	−0.27	0.65	0.73
160	−0.26	0.68	0.74
180	−0.24	0.71	0.76

Brownian motion for both, which is incoherent: Both yields and prices cannot be lognormal and have a fat right tail at times of high volatility. Augmenting this contradiction is that traders often mix the same instruments in the same book. Bond futures, for example (baring the embedded outperformance option), priced on a log-Brownian price, are mixed with bonds priced on a log-Brownian yield and put together as hedges in the same book. This incorrect mixing can carry serious consequences for a large book at a high volatility, as the delta difference becomes acute.

The delta and partial-delta concepts for multivariate options will be dealt with in Chapter 22.

Chapter 8

Gamma and Shadow Gamma

One day in mid-1994, the dealing rooms in the United States were rocked with the news of the bankruptcy of a hedge fund, costing a minimum of $600 million to their investors. What worried the community was that the blown-up fund was meant to be "market neutral." Market neutrality, it had appeared, would be a great panacea in the volatile world of tightening policy and distorted relationship: In theory the fund would warehouse cheap securities, hedge them, and achieve above-average returns for the Florida residents.

One trader was asked by his manager to explain the results. He shouted: "That guy did not get the second derivative right."

SIMPLE GAMMA

■ The **gamma** is the second (mathematical) derivative of the derivative with respect to the asset price. It is easily calculated analytically with the following:

$$\frac{\partial^2 F}{\partial U^2}$$

The unevenness of the gamma in space (i.e., with time moving and the asset price remaining constant) has these effects:

- For an at-the-money option, the gamma is maximum when the option nears expiration.
- For an out-of-the-money option, the gamma is maximum when the option is far away from expiration.

This time dependence of the gamma has some consequences for calendar spreading, as shown in Figure 8.1. If a trader buys option A and sells option B, the gamma will be positive at the money (Figure 8.1 shows the A line higher than the B line), but the lines cross at some level. The best comparison is between a short-distance runner and a marathon runner. The marathon runner would win the long-distance race. The short-distance runner would win a 100-meter dash. In between, there is a race of a certain length where they would be of equal speed.

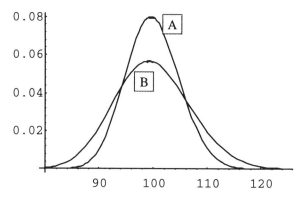

Figure 8.1 Gamma changes with time. A is a 3-month option; B is a 6-month option. Both have a 100 strike.

Figure 8.1 suggests there are important pitfalls for option replication and portfolio stabilization: Often operators hedge their gamma with an option trade that takes care of their immediate need (defined in a narrow region around the origin) but does not provide long-term stability to the position. They look at their gamma reports and buy the exact, necessary protection; such protection might be short-lived in a bursting market.

> ***Risk Management Rule:*** A range needs to be associated with every gamma measurement.

GAMMA IMPERFECTIONS FOR A BOOK

More even so than the delta, the gamma measure is often too narrow to display the results of the actual move in a logical increment. For a book, this measure loses in accuracy because the multiplication of options causes the gamma to increase in "locality"—to depend more and more on a particular spot range. A gamma could be long at 100, short at 101.65, long again higher and so forth, according to which structure dominates at a given spot point.

A practically sound way to measure the gamma is to vary the underlying price and calculate the actual change in hedge ratio over the increment. The operation needs to be performed twice:

1. To display the "up-gamma" by moving the price north and computing the change in delta.
2. To display the "down-gamma" by moving the price south and computing the change in delta.

Option Wizard: More Pitfalls for Risk Managers

Risk managers without market experience commonly blame traders for incorporating the third derivative in the analysis. However, traders need to use as powerful a measure at all stages of the game even if their designation of "gamma" could embrace more than its theoretical scope. Traders call delta something that has a little gamma in it and gamma something that has a little Ddelta-Dvol in it.

Table 8.1 Up-Gamma and Down-Gamma

	Delta	Up-Gamma	Down-Gamma
93.5	−36	0	0
94	−35	1	0
94.5	−35	1	0
95	−35	1	1
95.5	−34	2	1
96	−33	3	1
96.5	−32	4	2
97	−30	5	3
97.5	−28	7	4
98	−25	9	5
98.5	−21	12	7
99	−16	16	9
99.5	−9	20	12
100.0	0	25	16
100.5	11	30	20
101	25	37	25
101.5	42	44	30
102	62	52	37
102.5	86	61	44
103	114	71	52
103.5	147	81	61
104	185	91	71
104.5	228	101	81
105	276	111	91
105.5	329	121	101
106	387	131	111
106.5	450	139	121
107	518	146	131
107.5	589	152	139

■ The **up-gamma** (or right gamma) is the discretely computed change in delta should the asset price move higher by some defined increment. The **down-gamma** (or left gamma) is the same with the asset moving lower.

Averaging both and coming up with a total aggregate is deceiving. In a risk reversal (see following definition) situation, the gamma will be positive one way and negative the other. Netting the two would show the gamma to be deceivingly square. Using the up-gamma and down-gamma would display the third-order risk.

■ **Risk reversal** is any position that has an up-gamma over some increment of a different sign than the down-gamma.

Example. A Regular Option: The trade is long \$2,000M of the 110 calls with 1 month to go. The initial delta is \$36M and the trader goes delta neutral (a small 1.8%). Volatility is 15.7%. Table 8.1 shows the up-gamma and down-gamma changes. Anyone looking at Figure 8.2 can see the instability of the rate of change of the delta. This is manifested for every point by a difference between an up-gamma and a down-gamma.

Example. Case (Risk Reversal):   The classical example shown in Figure 8.3 shows that the gamma needs to be measured with respect to the origin (Table 8.2).

Figure 8.2   An unstable delta for a single option.

Table 8.2 Up-Gamma and Down-Gamma for a Risk Reversal

	Delta	Up-Gamma	Down-Gamma
93.5	449	−140	−165
94	375	−126	−153
94.5	309	−112	−140
95	249	−98	−126
95.5	197	−84	−112
96	151	−71	−98
96.5	113	−59	−84
97	80	−47	−71
97.5	54	−36	−59
98	33	−26	−47
98.5	18	−16	−36
99	7	−7	−26
99.5	2	2	−16
100.0	0	11	−7
100.5	3	20	2
101	11	29	11
101.5	23	38	20
102	40	48	29
102.5	61	58	38
103	87	68	48
103.5	119	79	58
104	156	90	68
104.5	198	100	79
105	245	111	90
105.5	298	121	100
106	356	130	111
106.5	419	139	121
107	486	146	130
107.5	558	152	139

CORRECTION FOR THE GAMMA OF THE BACK MONTH

Often the calendar spreading gives rise to two different levels of gamma: a long gamma in one maturity against a short gamma in another one. This may be stable except that the two maturities might not have the same variance, since the "basis," or the difference between cash and futures might be positively correlated to the cash, which would lead to unequal moves between forwards. In that case, the static analysis of the gamma would be misleading.

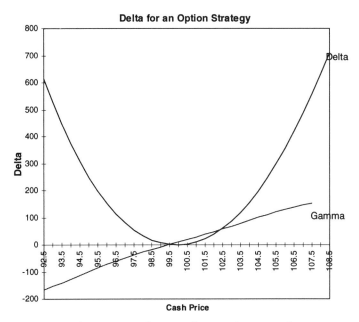

Figure 8.3   Gamma for a risk reversal.

A correction is necessary because the Black-Scholes-Merton does not allow for the rates moving. The following simplified example shows such adjustment.

Example: This is a simple calendar spread between two different maturities in the SP500 contracts on the Chicago Mercantile Exchange (CME):

	Position	Delta	Gamma	True Gamma (in front contract equivalent)
Sep (90 days)	Long 2000 contracts	1030	100	100
March (270 days)	Short 2000 contracts	(1054)	(58)	(65)

First Adjustment

The back month could have a lower or higher volatility exposure than the front owing to the present valuing. When the future curve trades at a discount (i.e., the back month is lower than the front), one unit of the commodity in 6-month maturity would be less than one unit of the commodity in

3-month maturity; one contract in 6 months' worth of exposure becomes smaller than the 3-month one. When the future trades at a premium, the opposite effect is expected. However, such effect is weak and swamped by other factors affecting the volatility of the back-month contract.

Second Adjustment

The back month can also have a higher or lower gamma owing to the stability of the basis (the cash-future relationship).

There are multiple methods to check the volatility of the back month relative to the front:

- Single-factor method: It consists in using the relative volatilities of every month. The 6-month can be more or less volatile than the 1-month and the trader would discount the gamma accordingly.

- Another method, more complicated, can be derived by construction. It involves the use of a covariance matrix of the forward curve. Its basic methodology is covered in Chapter 12.

In the preceding example, the operator discovered empirically that March had 12% more volatility than September. It means that whenever September moved by 1 point, March moved by 1.12 points. The operator needed to be hedged for such discrepancy. He therefore computed the gamma by multiplying it by 1.12 to get 65 gammas instead of 58.

> *Risk Management Rule:* Gammas of different maturities cannot be compared without proper adjustment.

This point will be discussed further in Chapter 12.

Shadow Gamma[1]

Often the gamma itself means nothing as the position is sensitive to volatility changes (or skew prices) and requires richer analysis techniques. This necessitates the embedding of the expected effect on other factors determined by the move (such as volatility or sometimes interest rates).

Most practitioners commit the basic mistake of running their positions without taking into account that moves in the underlying asset are linked to changes in other elements in the market. Jumps in the market invariably lead to jumps in volatility. A gamma number that does not factor this element would be meaningless.

> ***Risk Management Rule:*** Whatever can be predicted with confidence needs to be incorporated in the risk analysis. Ignoring them would make the Greek measures an entirely theoretical workout.

This does not conflict with the desire to keep Black-Scholes-Merton. Predicting, not modeling, is recommended since predicting allows the trader to change his mind while modeling freezes the opinion into an inextricable apparatus of estimators.

■ **Shadow gamma** is the computation of the forecast changes in delta taking into account the changes in volatility and its impact on the position (Figure 8.4, Table 8.3). The position is then reevaluated using new volatility parameters.

Example: A trader is long the wings (i.e., long out of money options). He estimates that volatility should rise if the market moves away drastically, in any direction. (For simplification, assume that the asset is parallel and that up-moves in the underlying would cause the same changes in parameters as down-moves.) He would like to capitalize on that effect when the option markets are closed by trading the gamma overnight.

Make the initial assumption that at 98 or 102 the volatility will be one point higher.

At 98.00 overnight in the future, the trader can buy 731 units of underlying instead of 645. At 102 overnight, he can sell 698 units of the underlying instead of 612.

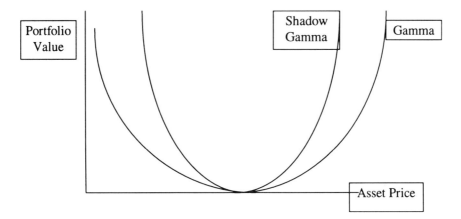

Figure 8.4 Comparing P/L from gamma and shadow gamma.

Table 8.3   Shadow Gamma

Asset	P/L Unchanged Volatility	P/L Higher Volatility (100 b.p)	Delta Unchanged Volatility	Delta Higher Volatility (100 b.p)	Delta Difference
96	279	352	−1,605	−1,730	−126
96.5	206	273	−1,323	−1,445	−122
97	146	207	−1,071	−1,185	−114
97.5	99	154	−846	−947	−102
98	61	112	−645	−731	−86
98.5	34	81	−464	−532	−67
99	15	59	−300	−346	−47
99.5	4	46	−146	−171	−25
100	0	39	0	−1	−2
100.5	4	46	145	167	22
101	15	58	292	337	44
101.5	33	80	447	513	66
102	59	110	612	698	86
102.5	94	150	793	896	103
103	139	200	991	1,109	118
103.5	194	261	1,209	1,339	130
104	260	334	1,450	1,588	137

So the trader can sell more futures in the rally, buy more in the sell-off. The real gamma is stronger than in a one-factor matrix. While the conventional matrix shows an up-gamma of 292, the shadow gamma is 337. While the conventional down-gamma is 300, the shadow down-gamma is 346.

The shadow gamma works both ways: By sticking to a tighter future re-balancing, the short gamma hedger can thus more accurately hedge the changes in the P/L.

For a change $x\%$ in the underlying[2] if it is assumed that volatility picks up by $Sig(x)$ (without complicating matters any further by drawing a poly-nomial).

At point x_0 with $v' < x_0 < v$

Shadow up-gamma $(x_0) = (Delta\ (x, V + Sig(x)) - Delta\ (x_0, V))/(x - v0)$

Shadow down-gamma $(x_0) = (Delta\ (x_0, V) - Delta\ (x', V + Sig(x')))/(x_0 - v')$

A more advanced shadow gamma (see Table 8.3) consists in using an exact association between the forwards and the cash and project more ac-centuated cash moves.

Example (advanced). Grid of Expected Volatility/Spot Dependence: The seasoned option trader can look into his memory and assess the impact on volatility of a market move. The result is the volatility map (Table 8.4). Although this is nothing but a forecast, it is generally better than the common methods of looking at moves with constant volatility.

It is undeniable that large moves, especially when they take place after a quiet period, result in a higher volatility. It is also undeniable that volatility behavior could be predicted for a "biased" asset (asymmetrical assets that cause anxiety during price drops) as the violent moves down cause an inconsiderable measure of panic. The trader, therefore, should recompute his P/L at those prices and try to cover with the delta and the gamma positions that satisfy his risk appetite.

Note. The preceding map linking expected volatility to various asset prices could be derived from option prices in the market with the skew and smile analysis techniques. The market cannot be fooled for too long, and it discovered that large moves are generally accompanied with jumps in volatility. It also believes that some moves (typically rallies in stock indices) generally take place with excruciating slowness and will indicate that behavior through option prices.[3]

Table 8.4   Map of Volatility at Different Price Levels

Starting Price	Price One Day Hence	Resulting Volatility Change (3 Month Options)
	105	1
	104	0.5
	103	unch*
	102	−0.5
	101	−0.2
100	100	unch
	99	unch
	98	0.5
	97	1
	96	2
	95	3
	94	4
	93	7 (panic)
	92	10
	91	10
	90	10

*Unchanged.

Threshold Shadow Gamma is a variation of the shadow gamma method. It corresponds to the belief that the expected change in volatility is not a linear function of the move and requires the use of schedules of moves. (Instead of using mathematical methods, it is always recommended to ask traders to draw scenario analyses.)

Shadow Gamma and the Skew

With *biased assets* (see Chapter 15) the gamma needs to take into account the behavior of volatility and the movement along the "skew curve." If there is an asymmetry in option volatilities between the upside and downside strikes, the gamma needs to take into account that the volatility of an at-the-money option may increase or decrease. An indication of future volatility can be drawn from where the out-of-the-money calls and puts are presently trading.

Skew gamma is also called "asymmetrical shadow gamma."

GARCH Gamma

ARCH is a volatility modeling method that traders avoid talking about. It corresponds to the realization by econometricians that volatility moves in clusters. A large move would cause another large move, and a quiet day is likely to be followed by a quiet day. To traders, there was nothing remarkable about such insights. However, ARCH provided the framework for heteroskedastic thinking in academia.

GARCH gamma by Engle and Rosenberg (1995) is the first academic discovery of shadow gamma. As the markets move, so will the future volatility, and this information needs to be incorporated into the future delta. The difference between present and future delta is called GARCH gamma.

Superficially, GARCH gamma sounds like shadow gamma. However, shadow gamma does not make any statement as to the behavior of the future market's actual volatility, whereas GARCH gamma predicts both future historical and implied volatility. Shadow gamma is a simple heuristically obtained forecast of the price of options as a deterministic function of the path taken by the underlying securities.

Advanced Shadow Gamma

■ **Advanced shadow gamma** takes into account the trader's expected volatility and interest (or carry) rate moves that accompany the changes in the asset price. In addition, both volatility and interest rate curves are expected to shift in a nonparallel way.

Advanced shadow gamma could be easily used in a commodity that has both its price change and its volatility correlated to the interest rates. Currency pairs in which there is a "weak" side often present such difficulties. The Mexican peso hardly sells off against the OECD[4] currencies without a corresponding defensive rise in interest rates and the corresponding increase in volatility. The same applies to the currencies in a "band" (e.g., the former ERM)[5] where the weak parties need to be defended with prohibitively high interest rates to deter the speculators and other scourges of central banks. This leads to the necessity of running the forward using more complex factors. The analysis would take place as follows.

If the cash currency drops by 10% in a "biased" asset, in addition to the rise in the volatility the operator needs to forecast some increase in the interest rate differential. That widening in the differential would cause the back month to move further than the front month. Such imbalance creates additional gamma that could be interpreted as higher or lower.

Should the currency experience the (unlikely) rally in the asset price, the interest rate differential would narrow but not in the same amount.

> *Example:* Assume the existence of the imaginary currency of Syldavia. SYL-USD is the symbol for the currency pair.

$$US \text{ Dollar Rd (one year)} = 6\%.$$

$$Syldavian \text{ currency Rf} = 20\%.$$

$$Spot \text{ price} = 100.$$

The one-year forward price, satisfying the covered interest rate parity formula ($100 \times \text{Exp}(.06 - .20)$), would trade at 86.93.

In a crisis, the currency drops to 90. Such a drop would cause the interest rates in the Syldavian capital to rise by 2000 basis points (in the one-year) (Figure 8.5). As a result, the forward is now at $90 \times \text{Exp}(.06 - .40) = 62.79$. So while the spot fell by 10 points (10%), the one-year forward took a hit by 24.14 points (27.75%).

The assumption in Table 8.5 is that the trader had only one position in his portfolio, one-year options.

More precision could be brought into the model by repeating the exercise for every expiration (e.g., the 6-month and the 2-years), making the same forecast then assessing the total impact on the portfolio.

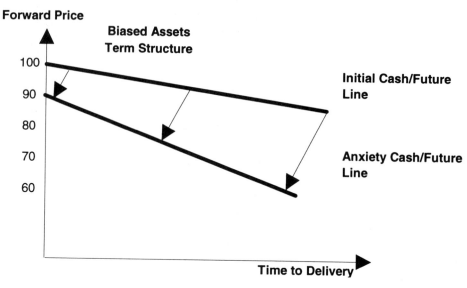

Figure 8.5 Behavior of the yield curve at times of stress.

Table 8.5 **Map of Volatility and Interest Rate Differentials at Different Price Levels**

Starting Price	Price One Day Hence	Resulting Volatility Change (1 Year Option) (3 Month Options)	Resulting Interest Rate Differential (1 Year Forward) (3 Month Differential)[†]
	105	1	
	104	0.5	−.75%
	103	unch*	−.5
	102	−0.5	−.5
	101	−0.2	0
100	100	unch	0
	98	unch	0
	96	0.5	2
	94	1	4
	92	2 (panic)	10
	90	3	20
	88	?	?
	86	?	?

* Unchanged.
[†] Trader unable to forecast.

CASE STUDY IN SHADOW GAMMA: THE SYLDAVIAN ELECTIONS

Syldavia is a country that faces decisive elections as it will be choosing between an anarchist regime or a Western style capitalist one. Six months before the elections were announced, when Syldavia was a quiet country, volatility was at a boring 14% for all maturities. It is expected to return to that level should the anarchists lose. For some reason, financial markets tend to prefer Western capitalism and dislike the anarchists.

The volatility is presently at 20% in the one-month options, declining all the way to 16% in the one-year.

To simplify the case study, the position assumed will be exclusively in one-month options. The trader has in his book a mixture of strikes, as shown in Table 8.6. The results of the ballots are due in one hour and the trader, trusting no polls, imparts no true probability to each event. The Syldavian currency presently trades at 100 to the dollar with interest rates at 14% against 6% for the USD.

The trader met with his peers and came up with a road map concerning the outcome of the elections (Figure 8.6). Using this road map, the trader will have to ignore the conventional Greeks and limit himself to the analysis

Table 8.6 Risk Matrix and the Outcomes of the Syldavian Elections

Asset	P/L V = 14.7%	P/L V = 20%	P/L V = 29%	Delta V = 14.7%	Delta V = 20%	Delta V = 29%
93	14	−86	−225	334	383	462
			−181			
94	40	−52	Scenario A	189	282	406
95	52	−29	−143	65	193	357
96	54	−13	−110	−32	118	317
97	47	−5	−80	−104	60	287
98	34	−1	−52	−150	20	267
99	18	0	−26	−173	1	258
		0			0	
100	−8	Starting Point	15	−175	Starting Point	260
101	−17	1	26	−156	19	272
102	−31	4	55	−118	55	293
103	−40	12	85	−57	108	324
104	−41	26	120	25	174	362
105	−34	48	158	127	252	407
	−15				339	457
106	Scenario B	77	201	247		
107	16	116	250	379	431	510

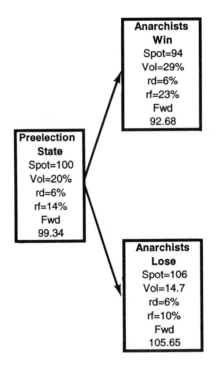

Figure 8.6 Outcomes of Syldavian elections.

of his P/L should either of the two states occur. The markets will go from the preelection state to either of the two outcomes without any trading in between so the idea of delta rebalancing will have to be forgotten for now.

Table 8.6 allows the trader to look at the conventional delta/gamma matrix and compare it with the "true" distribution.

According to the conventional theoretical Black-Scholes-Merton delta notion, the trader starts with neutrality at 20%. The delta shows accordingly 0 at the delta column that corresponds to the combination of 100 in the asset price and 20% in the volatility.

There is no possible trading in between the states so the trader will have to derive the shadow deltas and gammas from the exercise. Scenario A corresponds to the expected P/L should the Anarchists win and Scenario B to that if the Anarchists lose. Scenario A presents a high volatility lower security price while scenario B presents lower volatility higher security price.

The first discovery traders can make about the position is that although it presents a Black-Scholes-Merton gamma that is flat (mildly positive in the rally and negative in the selloff), it is short shadow gamma. A rally causes a loss of 15 and a selloff a loss of 181.

A more advanced series of assumptions for option trading will be covered in Chapter 16.

Chapter **9**

Vega and the Volatility Surface

A loud Italian option trader was known to start singing "volare, volare," an Italian popular song, every time the market experienced a panic, to the great annoyance of his peers. When asked for the reason (by the angry author) he explained that volatility came from the Latin volare, *which means "to fly."*

For reasons of convenience, this chapter will cover all issues relating to the evolution in the volatility curves and forward volatility as well as the forward-start and other non-time-homogeneous options. The best way to study a forward-start option is by understanding the sensitivity to forward or local volatility of any structure.

Vega and Modified Vega

■ The **vega** (also called zeta, kappa by nontraders) is the sensitivity of an option to the changes in the implied volatility for a maturity equal to its stopping time. A nonvanilla option will be more precisely sensitive to the forward volatility in the market between its inception and its stopping time. Any convex structure will have a vega.

This section of the chapter will focus on the simple vega of a European option of known maturity.

It is expressed as:

$$\text{Vega} = \frac{\partial F}{\partial \sigma}$$

σ is the implied volatility for the maturity matching that of the option, F is the derivative security. The best way to ascertain it numerically is by repricing the instrument at different levels of volatilities.

Usually the vega is expressed as a discrete measure (i.e., for a discrete move in the volatility). In addition, many multiply it by the level of volatility to make it correspond to a set percentage move in volatility level. For example, if volatility is 18% and the vega is .5, the option (or the structure) will pick up 50 cents when the volatility rises by one percentage point to 19% (and so on . . .).

Some people would derive the vega for 1.8 moves in implied volatility (10%) so they can compare their position risks across instruments by assuming that other markets had a 10% vega move as well. Their vega will then be 1.8 times .5 = .90.

Most vegas decrease with time except that of a lookback and reverse knock-out whose vegas increase with time under some conditions.

As with the gamma and the theta, it is easy to see that the vega follows a bell shape, with the maximum reached when the option is at the money (by the forward) (see Figure 9.1).

Figure 9.2 shows how the rise in volatility would lengthen the tails. It also gives a hint on the convexity: The vega of at-the-money options stays the same when volatility rises but the vega of the options away from the money rises.

Risk Management Rule: The vega of at-the money options is stable to volatility. Options that are away from the money (in-the-money or out-of-the-money) are convex with respect to volatility for the owner and concave for the seller.

The rule is easy to verify: The second derivative of an option price with respect to volatility equals 0 when the strike price equals the forward and becomes increasingly positive when the strike price is away from it.

Warning: The raw vega may be relevant for an individual option but means little for the risks of an option book. That effect will be explored in great depth with the study of the term structure of volatility.

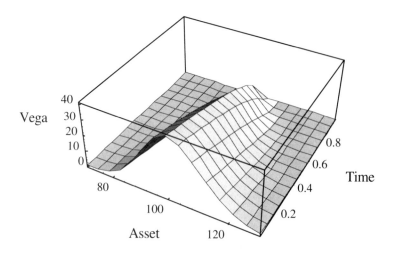

Figure 9.1 Vega with time.

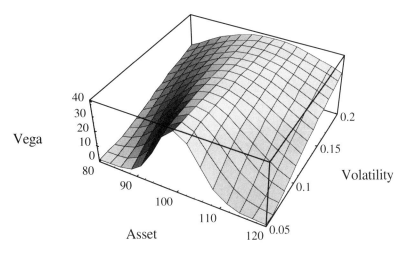

Figure 9.2 Vega and volatility.

The reader should by now be familiar with this book's leitmotiv: what works for one single option will not work for a book. The conventional training of people, which consists of toying with the conventional derivatives of the Black-Scholes formula, has a negative effect on their operating style. Trading an option bears little relevance to trading a book.

In mathematical terms, the book, neutral in its lower moments (see Chapter 11), can easily lose its stability in the higher moments. An option book, we will see, is not as "compact" as mathematicians believe. It will generally be neutral in the lower moments and exposed to various risks in the higher moments. A simple option, though, loses exposure in higher moments.

Vega and the Gamma

Vega is related to the gamma in a strange way since they seem to evolve in different ways. The vega is the integral of the gamma profits (i.e., expected gamma rebalancing P/L) over the duration of the option at one volatility minus the same integral at a different volatility. Intuitively, the vega P/L that results from the volatility going higher for a long option holder should be equal to the expected sum of the gamma profits over the period should the market go his way. It is precisely that difference for a gamma hedger that should correspond to a higher P/L.

Example: A straddle owner sees his 3-month straddle increase by $100,000 owing to the volatility in the market moving from 15% to 16%. This means, precisely, that if the new, higher volatility prevailed, his gamma profits should yield over the next period the same exact $100,000—barring slippage.

Mathematically, it is:

$$\text{Vega} = \sigma\, t\, S^2\, \text{Gamma}$$

with S the asset price, t the time left to expiration, and σ the volatility.

The Modified Vega

> ***Risk Management Rule:*** One should not compare, net, or add the vegas of two options of two different maturities without any weighting in the measure.

This concept will be explained later in the chapter.

■ The **modified vega** is a simplified one-factor model using the variance of the volatilities broken up by maturities as an indicator of hedging precision.

The modified vega, while a more potent indicator of risk than the unweighted vega, is not recommended as strongly the more advanced *modified forward vega*, which will also be described. The reader will be able to choose between the two methods.

Since all maturities do not react the same way to changes in the perception of future volatility, there is a need to correct the vega both for hedging and risk management purposes.

To intuitively understand why the vega exposure for a book needs to be weighted, consider a position long one-month options for an equivalent $100,000 vegas and short two-year options for the same vega amount (which means that the book has a smaller number of two-year options). Assume that a shock hits the market. Would it be unreasonable to assume that the volatility of the one-month option would increase more than the back (unless information on structural changes indicates that the volatility spurt would be sustained)?

In other words, if the stock market were to crash tomorrow, one-month options would be expected to rise considerably but such volatility would not be expected to be sustained for an entire year, and one-year options would rise in volatility, but less than shorter term options. The market is expected to settle down after a while and a longer term option would only be affected in its early phase. On the other hand, should the market stay dormant for a brief period, it would be foolish to believe that the structure of volatility changed so that the market lost all of its vigor.

The modified vega[1] corresponds to the sensitivity of the options portfolio to nonparallel changes in the general level of volatility. Shorter maturities are usually more sensitive to volatility barring temporal information. But operators need to be open-minded: Should they discover that for some reason the vegas act in reverse, they should calibrate their weightings accordingly.

$$\text{Modified vega} = \sum_{i=1}^{n} V_i F_i$$

with V_i the vega for the maturity bucket, F_i the volatility weight. The complications in computing a bucket vega are discussed later in the chapter.

The convention is to use a volatility factor pillared around the 3-month, a medium-term horizon that is liquid enough to satisfy a risk manager. All options would be compared with that maturity in their sensitivity.

How to Compute the Simple Weightings

The most important step in volatility risk management is the awareness of the existence of some weights. Most methods used by operators, despite different levels of complexity, yield similar results.

"Theoretical" Weighting.   Volatility weightings by the square root of the respective nominal duration of every maturity are often called "theoretical" by traders. It means that long-term volatility is constant and that options revert back to that known long-term level at the speed of the inverse of the square root of time ($1/\sqrt{t}$). Such thinking is grounded on the awareness of a constant long-term volatility as reflected by the price of the longest option on the board. Operators are often proved wrong in markets because the volatility of the SP100 and the SP500 indices has been undergoing constant dampening.

Calculation Method.   The operator selects a pillar, say the 3-month options (generally the most liquid maturity) and weighs the exposures in the other months using a factor of duration $\sqrt{(90/\text{days to expiration})}$:

> *Example:*   An exposure in 1-month option will have $\sqrt{(90/30)} = 1.73$ times the importance of a vega in the 3-month option. An exposure in the 1-year will have $\sqrt{(90/365)} = .50$ times the vega in the 3-month. It means that $100,000 in vega exposure in the 1-month is equivalent to $173,000 exposure in the 3-month and $346,000 in the 1-year.

Empirical Weightings.   Volatility weightings that are derived from the observed behavior of prices in the market are called empirical.

Calculation Method.   The operator selects a pillar, say the 3-month options and weighs the exposures in the other months using the relative volatility of each period. Typical relative volatility can be obtained by taking the following ratio:

$$\frac{\text{Sum of the absolute changes in one period}}{\text{Sum of the absolute changes in the other period}}$$

Measurements by the two methods tend to be similar, with a hitch: the weightings can exhibit considerable instability. There is some nonlinearity to take into account. At times of shock, the front options tend to overreact and lead: The back-month options usually wait to see if there are structural changes or if the change in volatility was a simple blip. Smaller shocks can cause the opposite effect.

Table 9.1 lists some results of a study performed by the author[2] that processed one-day changes in volatility (1988–1994, 1400 observations), using over-the-counter closing data. The study computed the ratio of the move in the period's implied volatility to that of the 3-month.

Using 10-day nonoverlapping changes (1988–1994, 1390 observations), the results shown in Table 9.2 were obtained (in the shape of the ratio of the move in the period's implied volatility to that of the 3-month) (Figure 9.3).

So the unbelievable appeared to be true: There is such a strong mean reversion that the long-term mean seems to drop after a large move upward and vice versa, as betrayed by the relative stability of the one-year options.

Using currencies in the studies presented some significant advantages over other financial instruments. There is in the major currencies a developed liquid over-the-counter currency option market where instruments are quoted in rolling periods of one month, two months, and so on. In addition currency options are quoted in implied volatility parameters for an at-the-money European option, which reduces the risk of a "bad print." A "bad print" is a wrong settlement price for an option that distorts the implied volatility calculations. Listed markets tend to have fixed expirations that complicate the study because it is arduous to follow a constant date. So on some days, the "front"-listed option would have 15 days until expiration, whereas on others it would be 33 days, a matter that can hinder the study.

Table 9.1   Volatility Weightings (Daily Observations)

Period	DM	JY	Square Root
1 month	1.84	1.75	1.73
2 months	1.30	1.31	1.22
3 months	1.00	1.00	1.00
6 months	0.60	0.64	0.71
1 year	0.36	0.39	0.50

Table 9.2   Cumulative (10-Day) Volatility Weightings

Period	DM	JY	Square Root
1 month	1.68	1.73	1.73
2 months	1.26	1.29	1.22
3 months	1.00	1.00	1.00
6 months	0.65	0.66	0.71
1 year	0.37	0.44	0.50

Warning: While this weighting scheme is applicable to swaptions and bond options, operators should take proper care in the measurement of vegas for forward-forward options such as Euros (EuroMarks, Eurodollars, Eurolira, etc.). The buckets correspond to different underlying instruments with their own volatility and their own volatility regimes.

A shortcoming is that the weightings may not be stable enough for the trader to consider them "square." This leads to a numerical exposure that would take into account the tracking fluctuations between maturities.

Advanced Method: The Covariance Bucket Vega

A more modern method to assess the vega risks consists in studying the covariance matrix of the nonoverlapping forward buckets. Prior to starting the analysis, it is necessary to define the forward volatility.

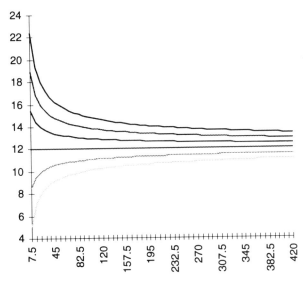

Figure 9.3   Volatility cone at long-term volatility 12%.

Forward Implied Volatilities

■ A **forward** (also called forward-forward) **implied volatility** between two dates (t1 and t2) represents the expected volatility between the two periods inferred from option prices.

We will discuss further down the generalization of forward implied to the Dupire "local" volatility.

Risk Management Rule: It is imperative for traders involved in path-dependent or deferred-start options to examine their vega risks in forward buckets.

Computing Forward Implied Volatility

We start by decomposing time in non-overlapping slices that correspond to traded dates in the market (Figure 9.4).

We define the earliest possible starting date as t_0, which, when it is the present moment, becomes 0. We define $\sigma_{t1,t2}$ as the volatility between two points t_1 and t_2. So the volatility between t_0 and t_n would be that conventionally quoted in the market as the volatility for the period. Accordingly, the volatility of a 90-day option would then be expressed as $\sigma_{0,90} \cdot \sigma^2_{(t0,tn)}$ would then be the variance.

If we used equal time slices:

$$\sigma^2_{t0,tn} = \sigma^2_{t0,t1} + \sigma^2_{t1,t2} + \ldots + \sigma^2_{tn-1,tn}$$

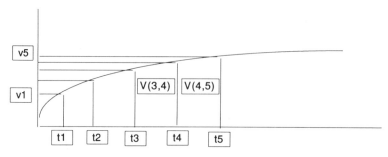

Figure 9.4 Time slices. V(3,4) would be the forward volatility between three months and four months.

Or using unequal time slices n_1 through n_n (more adequate since the markets price narrow buckets for very short dates and wider ones for longer dates):

$$\sigma^2_{t0,tn} = \frac{1}{t_n - t_0}((t_1 - t_0)\sigma^2_{t0,t1} + (t_2 - t_1)\sigma^2_{t1,t2} + \ldots + (t_n - t_{n-1})\sigma^2_{tn-1,tn}$$

With $\sigma^2_{tn-1,tn}$ the annualized variance between t_{n-1} and t_n. The difference between two points could be months or simply minutes. One can even consider the frame where $t_3 - t_2$ is one hour and $t_4 - t_3$ is one month.

It is therefore possible to infer the "local" volatility between two points t_1 and t_2 while knowing the volatility between 0 and t_1 and that between t_0 and t_2.

$$\sigma^2_{t0,t2} = \frac{1}{t_2 - t_0} ((t_1 - t_0)\sigma^2_{t0,t1} + (t_2 - t_1)\sigma^2_{t1,t2})$$

Hence, choosing periods $t_{n-\alpha}$ and t_n such that there are prices for options expiring on these dates available in the market, the following can be derived:

$$\sigma_{tn-\alpha,tn} = \sqrt{\frac{\sigma^2_{t0,tn}(t_n - t_0) - \sigma^2_{t0,tn-\alpha}(t_{n-\alpha} - t_0)}{(t_n - t_{n-\alpha})}}$$

which traders call forward volatility (or sometimes "forward-forward volatility") between $t_{n-\alpha}$ and t_n.

Example 1:   Derivation of a forward curve.

$t_0 = 0$ (the present moment)

$t_n = 180$ days

$\alpha = 90$ so $t_{n-\alpha} = 90$ days

The volatilities 90 days and 180 days in the market are 17% and 15.5%, respectively. The notation would use $\sigma_{90} = .17$ and $\sigma_{180} = .155$ which leads to:

$$\sigma_{90,180} = \sqrt{\frac{.155^2(180) - .17^2(90)}{90}} = .1384$$

The market is pricing a 13.84% volatility for the period between 3 months and six months.

Table 9.3   Forward Curve

Days	DM Vols (0, days)	Forward Volatility between Buckets
30	16.00	16.00
60	15.30	14.57
90	14.70	13.42
180	13.60	12.40
360	12.85	12.05
720	12.20	11.51

Example 2. Generation of a Forward Volatility Curve: Starting with a spot volatility curve as in Table 9.3, one can compute the forward volatility. Figures 9.5 and 9.6 show the contrast between spot and forward curves.

Sometimes the existence of arbitrage is revealed by a significantly lower or higher forward volatility for a given bucket: Because options are traded in spot volatility terms rather than forward volatility, it is more difficult to spot arbitrages and easier for markets to get out of line.

Warning: The forward volatility method is only applicable to options on fungible assets, such as foreign exchange or equities. Eurodollar options, for example, are non-overlapping instruments and the use of the preceding method of analysis on vegas emanating from a Eurodollar book could distort the risks.

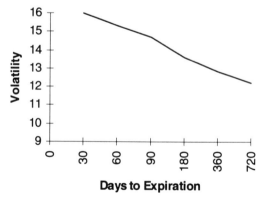

Figure 9.5   Spot volatility curve.

Forward Curve

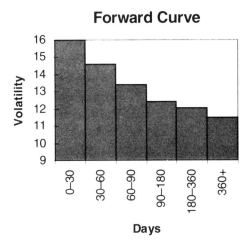

Figure 9.6 Forward volatility curve.

A bucket vega is a more potent risk management tool for vanilla options. However, *with path-dependent options, it is the only possible way of analyzing exposures.* As will be discussed, vanilla options present a linear bucket sensitivity to variance whereas path-dependent options present uneven exposures in the time buckets. Some of them, like knock-out options, could be long vega one bucket and short in another.

Example. How to Translate Regular Vegas into Forward Buckets: *Note:* This technique is only applicable to vanilla products.

Assume the following exposure in the DEM options, read from a "straight" bucket.

Maturities	Exposure
0–30	100
0–60	– 148
0–90	17
0–180	167
0–360	–233
Total	–97

The preceding numbers resemble those that come out of commercially available risk management systems. Should the trader buy a 3-month option, the entire position vega would show in the bucket that ends with the 3-month, in the case above the 0–90.

The operator needs, however, to correct them in some rapid manner. Assume that path-independent options have exposures that are linearly distributed through time (e.g., a 3-month option would have a third of its exposure to vega in the first 0–30 bucket, one third in the second 30–60 bucket, and one third in the 60–90 bucket).

This can easily be theoretically proven. It suffices to say that the gamma is strongest at the end but that the odds of being at the strongest point are slim, while the gamma is more even, but weaker, at the beginning. It can also be viewed that the expectation of gamma profit and loss does not vary with the period, that the difference in integrals at two different levels of volatility would correspond to the vega.

The operator must take into account the unevenness of the buckets. Since he has decided to present narrower slices at the beginning and wider ones at the end, a one-year option will have:

- 50% of its exposure in the 180–360 bucket.
- 25% of its exposure in the 90–180 bucket.
- 8.33% of its exposure in each of the 0–30, 30–60 and 60–90 buckets.

Table 9.4 decomposes the exposure.

Multifactor Vega

This advanced vega method includes the establishment of a forward volatility correlation matrix. It could be done on a spot volatility exposure provided the position does not include path-dependent or deferred-start components.

Without elaborating on the method (it is described at length in Chapter 12), it is possible to establish the notion of expected risk based on normal behavior of the buckets.

Step 1.   The operator builds a correlation matrix of the percentage moves between forward-forward buckets, say by slicing time into 0–30, 30–60, 60–90,

Table 9.4   Decomposition Steps for Conventional Buckets Exposure

(000)	0–30	0–60	0–90	0–180	0–360	
Exposure	100	−148	17	167	−233	

	Break-even 0–30	Break-even 30–60	Break-even 60–90	Break-even 90–180	Break-even 180–360	Total Exposure
0–30	100	−74	5.67	27.83	−19.42	40.00
30–60		−74	5.67	27.83	−19.42	−60.00
60–90			5.67	27.83	−19.42	14.00
90–180				83.50	−58.25	25.00
180–360					−116.50	−116.50

Table 9.5   Correlation Matrix for Volatility Buckets, DEM Options 1994–1995 (284 business days)

Bucket	0–30	30–60	60–90	90–180	180–360
0–30	1	0.33	0.25	0.174	0.098
30–60		1	−0.33	0.16	0.154
60–90			1	−0.14	−0.057
90–180				1	−0.19
180–360					1

90–180, 180–270, 270–365, 365–730, and so on. Using historical analysis, the operator then fills in the correlations between the relative periods (see Tables 9.5 and 9.6).

Statistical issues will appear, as with any correlation matrix of the sort. The principal one relates to how far back the operator must go to get a matrix that carries any significance. A lengthy sampling period probably would include periods so far back that the behavior of volatility might have been entirely different from the present. A shorter one incurs the risk of missing statistical significance. Another difficulty relates to the choice of linear methods of statistical association (i.e., correlation) in markets that may not be tractable with the least-square models.

Step 2.   The final exposure is computed with the aid of some simple matrix[3] algebra, yielding one single number. Such an analysis would disclose, in addition to the vega weightings, the stability of the exposures. Neighboring buckets would present a stronger compatibility so the exposures between them would cancel out more thoroughly than exposures in remotely spaced buckets.

Table 9.6   Annualized Volatility of Changes (per bucket), 1994–1995

Bucket	Annualized Volatility of Volatility (%)	Daily Volatility of Volatility (%)
0–30	48.80	3.07
30–60	38.74	2.44
60–90	40.47	2.55
90–180	18.65	1.17
180–360	13.53	0.85

Formulas. Traders do not need to be daunted by the matrix computations as these are usually provided by spreadsheet packages. It will be helpful to set down the formulas prior to using an example that fits the previous matrix.

The volatilities of the forward buckets are:

$$
\mathbf{V} \text{ (daily volatilities)} =
\begin{bmatrix}
V1 = Vol(0\text{–}30) \\
V2 = Vol(30\text{–}60) \\
V3 = Vol(60\text{–}90) \\
V4 = Vol(90\text{–}180) \\
V5 = Vol(180\text{–}360) \\
V6 = Vol(360\text{–}730)
\end{bmatrix}
$$

The trader then builds the exposure vector, using for input the vegas for 10 percent change in volatility (i.e., P/L resulting from volatility moving from 15% to 16.5%) and multiplying every one by 10 times the corresponding V (daily volatility). Owing to the nonlinearity of the effect of volatility on a book, the exposure can be better approximated by using a local band, here 10%, rather than move volatility to zero and obtain a "face value vega" that would be grossly distorted.

$$
\mathbf{E} =
\begin{bmatrix}
E1 = Exp(0\text{–}30) \\
E2 = Exp(30\text{–}60) \\
E3 = Exp(60\text{–}90) \\
E4 = Exp(90\text{–}180) \\
E5 = Exp(180\text{–}360) \\
E6 = Exp(360\text{–}730)
\end{bmatrix}
$$

The operator then builds the forward volatility correlation matrix: The unit used for the variance corresponds to the percentage changes in volatility, using the differences of the natural logarithms of the periods:

$$
\mathbf{M} =
\begin{bmatrix}
1 & Corr12 & Corr16 \\
Corr12 & 1 & \\
& & \ddots & \\
Corr16 & & 1
\end{bmatrix}
$$

The transpose of E is multiplied by V, and the result is multiplied by E. The resulting number would express the net P/L that is expected from a move of one standard deviation in the general volatility levels.

Table 9.7   Bucket Exposure

Bucket	Vega Exposure	Daily Bucket Volatility (%)
0–30	40,000	3.07
30–60	−60,000	2.44
60–90	14,000	2.55
90–180	25,000	1.17
180–360	−116,500	0.85

Example: Take the previous exposure, as shown in Table 9.7.

The exposure, using the one-factor "weighted" volatility framework, would show the position to be flat. (See Table 9.8.) The trader can analyze the position using the conventional method by reconstituting the "raw" buckets. Thus vega(0,90) can be reconstituted with the intermediate buckets:

$$Vega(0,90) = Vega(0,30) + Vega(30,60) + Vega(60,90)$$

The same position presents a value at risk of $21,000. So, using accurate historical data, such a position is supposed to move by an average of $21,000 per day in spite of being square.

An even more interesting approach is to incorporate, in addition to the time buckets, possible skew shifts.

Table 9.8   One Factor Bucket Exposure

Bucket	Vega	Weightings	"Weighted" Exposure
0–30	100,000	1.73	173,000
0–60	−148,000	1.21	−179,080
0–90	17,000	1	17,000
0–180	167,000	.71	118,570
0–360	−233,000	.55	−128,150
		Total Weighted	1,340

Option Wizard: Curve and Surface Shifts

Any curve (volatility, interest rate, forward prices) can experience the shifts shown in the following charts:

First Order: Parallel Shift

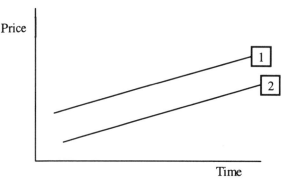

Second Order: Rotation

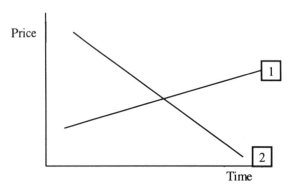

Third Order: Convexity Changes

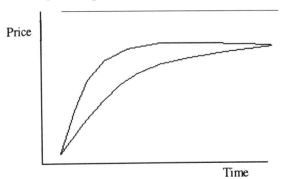

A curve therefore can experience any combination of the preceding factors. The same notions can apply to a volatility surface:

First Order: Parallel Shift

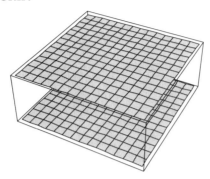

Second Order: Rotation

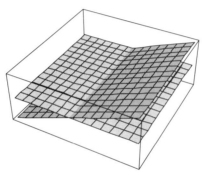

A Combination

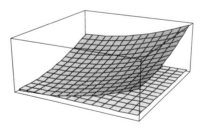

Higher Order: More interesting deformations are experienced, some of which can be quite ludicrous—but not impossible—as shown in the following chart:

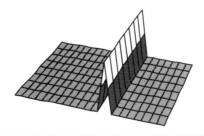

Volatility Surface

■ **Volatility surface** (also called a Dupire-Derman-Kani Surface by traders) is the representation of the values of implied volatility in the market represented in function of the time to expiration (horizontally[4]) and the strike price (vertically). It is used to derive:

- A spot curve displaying the volatility from 0 to time *t*.
- A "local" volatility curve showing the instantaneous volatility at different possible asset price levels at different points in the future.[5]

It is easily seen that the local volatility is to forward volatility what a diagonal spread is to a calendar. The local volatility is the generalization by Dupire, Derman, and Kani of the forward volatility between two points.[6]

The Table 9.9 shows the implied volatility as a function of the number of days to expiration and the strike price of the listed SP500 options as shown on the Chicago Mercantile Exchange. To prevent the chronic inaccuracies associated with the settlement price system, these were provided by a market maker who drew an accurate snapshot of where options were quoted in the pit at the most liquid times.

Needless to say that put/call parity is respected since puts and calls typically trade at the same volatility. The American feature is "weak" (see Chapter 1) and market makers typically use the out-of-the-money leg of any strike as a benchmark. If the put is out of the money, its volatility will be used, not that of the corresponding call.

Instead of using the raw strike, it is more meaningful to use the "percentage of moniness," usually defined as the log (asset/strike).[7]

The first future trades at 585 in this table.

Figure 9.7 shows the volatility surface. It is called the spot surface, not the forward volatility surface, as described earlier in the chapter.

Figure 9.8 corresponds to a function estimating the volatility as a function of strike and time to expiration.[8]

The Method of Squares for Risk Management

The same method used to compute the multifactor vegas with the aid of a volatility matrix by isolating the exposures in buckets and testing the stability of the hedges can be applied by cutting the position in squares of strikes and time to expiration. The advantage of such a method is that it discloses the sensitivity of the position to various deformations, such as the skew stability (Figure 9.9).

The method of squares consists of cutting the position into units composed of small squares and estimating the vega per square. Such a method

Table 9.9   Implied Volatility Surface

SKEW	SP500 Skew 11/15/95					
		Days to Expiration	December 30	January 67	February 121	March 219
	Strike	Log(S/K)	30	67	121	219
	525	0.11	21.5	18.45	17.43	17.22
	530	0.10	20.7	17.95	16.95	16.92
	535	0.09	19.7	17.45	16.6	16.60
	540	0.08	18.9	16.95	16.05	16.35
	545	0.07	18.15	16.45	16.1	16.00
	550	0.06	17.25	15.85	15.75	15.8
	555	0.05	16.4	15.45	15.4	15.5
	560	0.04	15.55	14.95	15	15.25
	565	0.03	14.7	14.45	14.5	14.97
	570	0.03	14.05	13.95	14.25	14.7
	575	0.02	13.45	13.45	13.9	14.42
	580	0.01	12.85	13	13.55	14.15
	585	0.00	12.35	12.6	13.2	13.92
	590	−0.01	11.85	12.2	12.9	13.7
	595	−0.02	11.35	11.8	12.6	13.4
	600	−0.03	10.85	11.45	12.3	13.25
	605	−0.03	10.45	11.15	12.05	13.05
	610	−0.04	10.05	10.9	11.8	12.85
	615	−0.05	9.86	10.55	11.5	12.65
	620	−0.06	9.86	10.3	11	12.45
	625	−0.07	9.86	10.15	11	12.45
	630	−0.07	9.86	10	11	12.45

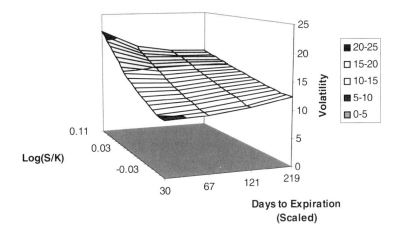

Figure 9.7   Volatility surface.

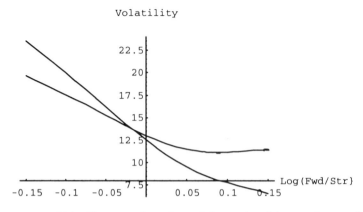

Figure 9.8 Volatility as a function of the ratio of forward to strike.

is required in "skewed" markets such as the equity indices or the beastly Euro-Yen where the risks of the shape of the skew are often superior to those of volatility.

The trader would next run the correlation matrix between the implied volatilities of the different squares to obtain a clear picture of the risks. This method is not necessary in well-behaved markets but imperative in skew products. In the DEM-USD pair, for example, the square s17 is very correlated with the square s57 or any other in the t7 bucket. This is not the case of the SP where skew shifts can cause some rotation of the volatility surface.

The final vega exposure can be obtained by drawing a giant matrix and repeating the exercise of the multifactor vega described earlier in this chapter.

Strike

	t1	t2	t3	t4	t5	t6	t7	t8
115	s11	s12	s13	s14	s15	s16	s17	s18
110	s21	s22	s23	s24	s25	s26	s27	s28
105	s31	s32	s33	s34	s35	s36	s37	s38
100	s41	s42	s43	s44	s45	s46	s47	s48
95	s51	s52	s53	s54	s55	s56	s57	s58
90	s61	s62	s63	s64	s65	s66	s67	s68
85	s71	s72	s73	s74	s75	s76	s77	s78
80	s81	s82	s83	s84	s85	s86	s87	s88
	s91	s92	s93	s94	s95	s96	s97	s98

Time

Figure 9.9 Decomposition of the vega by squares.

Chapter **10**

Theta and Minor Greeks

Almost one century ago, a young French mathematician named Gaston Bachelier had the insight (among other surprising intuitions) to write, in his doctoral thesis, see Bachelier (1900), that the expected price tomorrow of a call value was today's. He gave the right answer to what most option beginners fail to understand: that time decay is not the expected P/L from an option. If the option is priced at the right volatility (assuming interest rates are 0), time decay will be expected to be 0.

THETA AND THE MODIFIED THETA

■ The **theta** is a loss in time value of an option portfolio that results from the passage of time.

Theta is called rent by traders. Some traders never go home paying theta: Many former option traders incur time decay phobia.

The pricing is straightforward: The trader can use the difference between the price of an option today and the same on the next day, keeping everything else constant.

One way to look at the representation of theta is that it goes hand in hand with gamma. The alpha (gamma per theta ratio) will be the same regardless of the number of days to expiration, and so on. Selling very short-term options, a sport that is periodically practiced by newcomers, would be an attractive breadwinner except that the risks are exactly the same as selling longer options, unless the trader sells an expensive strike.

Figures 10.1 and 10.2 show the time decay for an at-the-money and an out-of-the-money option.

Modifying the Theta

Theta corresponds to the repricing of a portfolio with one day less to expiration and checking the difference between the two prices. However, what if the volatility and other parameters for period $t+1$ were different than those of period t?

167

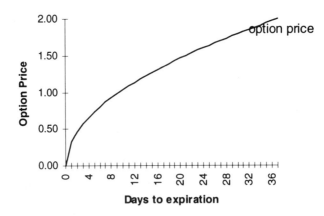

Figure 10.1 Changes in at-the-money option price with time.

Example: Thirty-day options trade at 16%; 29-day options trade at 15.8%. Should the trader assume that a position in a 30-day option would "converge" to 15.8% volatility tomorrow when the position will have 29 days of shelf life? Or should he assume that the 29-day implied volatility tomorrow will be at 16%?

There is always the question of whether, like interest rates, forward volatility is a predictor of future volatility or whether a volatility curve exists for structural reasons. Should the reader believe that the term structure of volatility reflects future volatility, that there is valuable information embedded in the curve, there is no reason to modify the theta. In many cases, however, it makes sense to do so. Sometimes, information about a meeting causes the curve to price at a higher volatility in the days

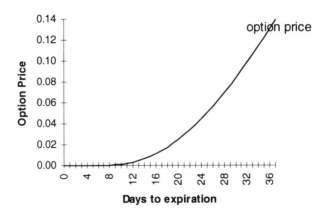

Figure 10.2 Changes in out-of-the-money option price with time.

immediately following the event and the predictive powers of the volatility curve become incontrovertible. Most times, there is no reason for such a curve other than the belief in the mean reversion of volatility. In those cases, modification of the theta should be entirely subjective and left to the discretion of the trader.

■ **Modified theta** is the price of an option today using current volatility less the price of the same option tomorrow using the volatility of one day shorter option.

It is usually interpolated using a square root of time method, to take into account the possible drop on the volatility curve.

Theta for a Bet

As markets come close to the barrier, theta can be overwhelming (see Chapters 17 and 18).

Theta, Interest Carry, and Self-Financing Strategies

Traders eliminate the interest costs of holding the premium to compute the theta because the carry of an option should be neutral to a trader who funds himself. In other words, if the trader incurs carry costs, the price of the theta will be increased by the interest paid on the premium, making it totally neutral. Thus, if interest rates are 20%, theta will be lower by 20% of the total premium (the option will have a lower price because of the present-value effect) but the carry costs of holding the option will offset these savings. It is assumed that the trader has borrowed the money to buy the option and that he would pay the difference in higher interest.

Many traders erroneously factor the premium costs in the theta computation.

As a convention, in this book, theta includes no premium costs.

In the derivation of an option value through a self-financing strategy, the seller of the option is supposed to buy an interest-yielding instrument. This is equivalent to the option trader funding himself from his firm by paying for negative balances and earning interest on positive ones.

More controversial is the notion of the forward. When the trader moves the portfolio up one day for reevaluation, should he move up the spot to the forward, considering that the expected spot is the forward price? Many traders do not do so, as it matters little. However, in markets where the cash-future line is steep, this makes a considerable difference. It seems best to deal with this issue using the trader's expectation. If the trader feels that the expectations built into the forward are erroneous, he needs to analyze the delta with such belief in mind.

The expectation of an asset S, period t, at period 0 was:

$$E_0(S_t) = S_0(e^{\mu t})$$

This issue will be dealt with at length in Chapter 12.

Shadow Theta

Losses from theta are generally worse than predicted, as premium buyers become the victims of additional marks-to-market losses. This is often because losses from theta, caused by quiet markets, are compounded by losses from the drop in implied volatility that accompanies quiet markets (as markets stop moving, the expectation of future movement declines). This is not always applicable to structures and needs to be measured using appropriate care and subjective judgment. A quiet market ahead of a political announcement or a refunding session can lead to situations of "reverse decay." Also, option prices are sometimes so undervalued that the forecast of the quiet period is built in.

> *Example:* Thirty-day options trade at a volatility of 16%. It is conceivable that, 7 days from now, if nothing happens, the 23-day option would be priced at 14%. The shadow theta is the regular theta plus the price impact of the expected decline in volatility.

Theta is a number that, taken on its own, has little meaning. It theoretically assumes that nothing else but time moves (volatility and asset price constant). Traders, however, may have information about the behavior of volatility if the spot does not move, and the changes in volatility should spot moves.

Theta becomes much lower when the markets move. This is the same reasoning as the one used in the shadow gamma analysis. Again, it relies on an entirely subjective perception of the behavior of implied volatility under a certain set of conditions.

> *Risk Management Rule:* If the trader believes that volatility may drop should the market remain frozen such information needs to be included in the time decay.

Figure 10.3 shows the phenomenon, with the two curves, both producing the profits and losses at some point in the future. The first curve ("unchanged volatility") shows the regular theta. The second curve ("variable volatility") shows the shadow theta and a combination between shadow

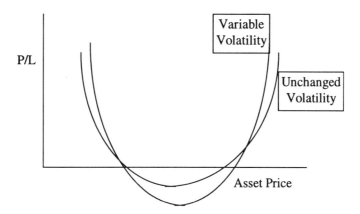

Figure 10.3   Theta and shadow theta.

theta and shadow gamma as it is generally accepted that volatility changes when the market moves.

In the past, the author has tried to measure this effect with some success. It helps in determining the optimal gamma hedges when the market whipsaws between levels and thus allows for better capturing of the gamma. Tighter rebalancing always helps mitigate the accelerated time decay.

Weakness of the Theta Measure

The major weakness of theta is that it is a path-independent measure. No true measure of time decay between period t and period $t + 1$ (i.e., t plus 1 day) can forecast the effect of the "whipsaw," the path where the market snaps away from its origin then returns to it during the time interval. Such an event is theoretically improbable but rather frequent in reality.

MINOR GREEKS

Rho, Modified Rho

■   The **rho** is the sensitivity of an option position to the interest rates in the numeraire currency as well as the rate determining the cash/future relationship.

The most misunderstood option risk is the rho. Most of the confusion occurs because it assumes a parallel shift in the curve, and parallel shifts generally take place exclusively in the imagination of rookie risk managers.

The rho needs to be broken up into its components: the rhop, the rho1, and the rho2.

Yield curves are not given in the market as one simple continuous line. The securities from which the curve is derived correspond to fixed and known maturities. Maturities that fall in between, for mark-to-market purposes in dealer's inventories need to be interpolated in some way or another.

The way "broken dates" are interpolated is a matter of significance, particularly for nonyield-curve option instruments that depend on some interest rate for input. A currency option requires the risk-neutral yield curves for both sides of the currency pair. An equity option requires, in addition to the numeraire currency yield curve, the curve for the dividend payout (something so difficult that equity option traders prefer not to talk about it).

This book will not discuss the techniques of interpolation as they have been the subject of Byzantine hairsplitting polemics between quants with free time on their hands and some patience for details.

The first principle used for interpolation is **eliminate jaggedness.** Visualize an extreme case of a seesaw yield curve as in the chart on the left:

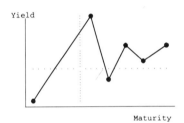

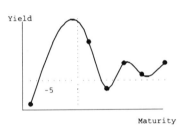

Interpolating straight-line on the yield curve in this chart causes some sharp local peaks. True, the yield curve might be irrational but there are significant reasons to smooth out the peak: The market cannot be expected to experience such drops between two dates (except, of course, if there is some information in between).

One method, among many others, used to smooth out the curve is called *cubic spline.* It is used by road-building engineers to make sure that their roads do not experience very sharp turns anywhere and cause accidents.* Applying such technique would result in the curve on the right, more pleasant to the eye.

The second curve appears smoother but may present some unsatisfactory peaks that the trader can then correct again. There are mixtures of techniques that the research assistant would gladly explain at length.

This leads us to the second principle: **Adapt to the market.** If the market happens to use some irrational technique for interpolation the trader needs to conform to it for pricing, though not for the decision-making process.

---

*The method simply consists of fitting cubic polynomials between nodal points by making sure that the derivative of each polynomial is equal, at each node, to that of the derivatives of both the preceding and the following polynomial.

- The **rhop** corresponds to the risks associated with the financing of the premium of the option.

- The **rho1** corresponds to the sensitivity of a portfolio of options to the base currency interest rates in which the P/L is computed. For a dollar-denominated equity option, it is the USD rate. For a yen-demoninated equity option, it is the yen rate. In a currency option pair, it is the base currency or, if the pair is in two different currencies, say DEM-JPY, the rho1 is calculated for the currency in which the unrealized P/L is initially accounted.

Rhop is included in rho1.

- The **rho2** corresponds to the sensitivity of the portfolio to the risk-neutral rate of return of the underlying asset.[1] For an equity, it is the dividend payout. For a currency, it is the foreign interest rate, or "counter rate."

The yield curve moves in parallel only by accident. It could undergo moves that change its shape in addition to the moves in the market prices. Typically, yield curve models are built to ascertain the speed of variation of the relative maturities. Simple models take into account the slope of the curve as a indicator of future relative speed of movement, while more complex ones take into account the deformations of the curve (in higher and higher degrees of deformation). Because this text is not about primary yield curve risks (it is principally concerned with volatility, not the underlying process) but has a focus on secondary yield curve risks (the risks are incidental to the position), simpler methods of calculating the true rho can be used without much loss of precision. The section on stacking in Chapter 12 shows more sophisticated risk measurement techniques.

- The **modified rho** is the application of any simple one-factor yield curve model, (the relative variance of each maturity) to calculate the true sensitivity of an option book to the interest rates in the market.

A brief examination of interest rates would show that the shorter rates are often more volatile than the longer ones. While a purblind person could see that moves are generally higher in the front than in the back, a more thorough analysis is required to find the factors determining the relative exposure of one contract compared with another. Yield curve models generally use some assumptions about the "reversion," itself a function of the shape of the curve.

The modification of the Rho should take into account the relative volatility of the underlying instruments and their correlations.

As with volatility weightings, there are several methods for computing such behavior, ranking from the very simple to those inspired by the richer Heath Jarrow Morton (1987) general framework of models. Like the vega modification, a simple method of relative weightings outperforms the un-weighted rho by a large measure.

Simple weightings are calculated by measuring the average move of one maturity compared with another.

> *Reminder:* A benchmark is required. The benchmark is a liquid maturity to which the rest of the curve exposures are equated. Traders generally use the 3-month as the benchmark. The rho and modified rho of the benchmark are equal.

> *Example:* In computing a simplified modified rho, select the simplest method of finding "weightings" to each maturity.

Step 1: Breaking up the exposure in "buckets."

Step 2: Repricing the portfolio with higher interest rates.[2] The exposure is in dollars per rise of 100 basis points in interest rates.

Benchmark: 3-month.

	0–3 months	3–6 months	6–9 months	9–12 months	12–18 months	18–24 months	24–48 months
Rho1 (raw)	$100,000	$300,000	$400,000	$600,000	−$750,000	$420,000	− $1,000,000
Modification (weights)	1.22	1.22	1	.94	.91	.82	.75
Modified Rho	$120,000	$366,000	$400,000	$564,000	− $682,500	$344,400	− $750,000

Total Rho1 (raw): $70,000

Total Rho1 (modified): $362,000. Quite a difference.

Omega (Option Duration) [3]

■ The **option duration**, also called omega, is the expected life of a soft path-dependent option. For a barrier option and American binary structure, the option duration is generally called **first exit,** or **stopping, time.**

The option duration is conceptually different for an American option than for a barrier, because the barrier is an exit price known in advance, whereas an American option does not provide for a predetermined exercise price or time.

American options have an expected life that is equal to or shorter than that of an equivalent European option of the same maturity. So do barrier options as these instruments can be terminated earlier than the end date.

This aspect of American options is particularly meaningful when one has recourse to a steeply rising or a steeply declining volatility term structure. The exercise of an American option depends on the two following decision rules (see Chapter 1):

- **The Soft Rule:** A comparison of the premium over intrinsic value (determined by the time value of the option) and the earnings from the reinvested premium in a money market instrument. If the option premium costs $2 in financing until the final expiration date and the extra premium of the option is only $1, it becomes optimal to exercise the option.

- **The Hard Rule:** A comparison of the premium over intrinsic value and the costs of maintaining the underlying delta until expiration. The position in the underlying asset can have a "negative carry" (i.e., the currency pair one is short has one currency, the short, yielding a higher interest rate than the long leg, or a stock paying an extremely high dividend, much higher than the financing rates in the market). For example, being long USD-MXP (long dollars against short the Mexican peso) with the annual interest rates in Mexico for the term at 50% and those in the United States at 6%, will cost 44% per annum in carry. A deep in-the-money call on Mexico would force the operator into the following choice:

  Sell Mexico against the deep in-the-money call and incur the costs of borrowing the currency at 50% and lending dollars at 6%.

  Abandon the option as the game isn't worth the costs. It is more advantageous to forgo the returns from the possible future volatility.

As shown earlier, the rules of premature exercise depend on two parameters that can vary: volatility and carry. While testing the premium versus carry rules, operators need to keep in mind that the game can change and the optimal decision reversed should one of the two undergo changes. This makes a more complex method of decision making necessary when either interest rates are volatile or the yield curve presents a steep slope. A nested binomial (or trinomial) tree is one such best technique, although some operators resort to the heavier Monte Carlo methods.

The strength of a binomial tree is that it can include within itself some information on future volatility and interest rates, through both the forward price and its process. The volatility does not need to be constant between

Option Wizard: Discrete States of the Parameters on Trees*

There are two levels of methods involving "local" volatility: the basic and the stochastic parameter binomial/trinomial.

The **basic binomial tree** prices options using information available from the market and applies it to the growth between nodes. Such information could be the forward volatility, the interest rates forwards, the skew, and so on.

The following chart shows that the parameters used correspond to both forward volatility and forward interest rates rather than spot rates. Each state between S(0) and S(3) depends on a forward volatility for the magnitude of the u or d moves (the size of the steps) and the carry rd-d (interest rate differential or dividend net of financial carry). Forward volatility affects the absolute size of both u and d while the carry determines the ratio u/d.

See also Module B.

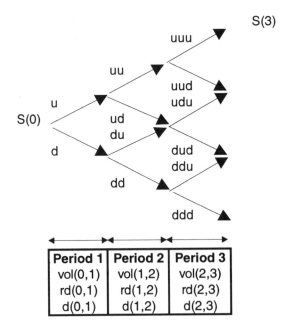

Period 1	Period 2	Period 3
vol(0,1)	vol(1,2)	vol(2,3)
rd(0,1)	rd(1,2)	rd(2,3)
d(0,1)	d(1,2)	d(2,3)

For reasons beyond the scope of this book, a trinomial tree is more adaptable to the processes of forward-forward parameters. The trinomial presents the advantages of allowing for changes in volatility through the middle node (binomial trees often do not recombine when operators try to include a "smile").

The **stochastic parameter tree** is an adaptation of the preceding tree with another branching for volatility and/or interest rates at every node.

The following figure shows a simplified state of the volatility curve at node 1. We can define Vu as volatility going up and assign a term structure to

(Continued)

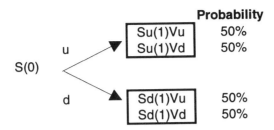

the state, as well as a probability of each move,[†] with Vu and Vd states in the term structure of volatility. The intuition of the evolution can be visualized with the following chart of the spot curve (a forward curve is generally derived from it at every node):

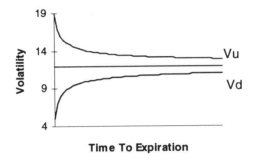

Time To Expiration

This methodology has been applied to interest rates yield curve evolution but can easily be applied to the volatility curve.

---

[*] The reader unfamiliar with binomial trees would gain from reading an introductory text on binomial option pricing, such as Cox and Rubinstein (1985) or Hull (1993).

[†] Most traders who discussed the point with the author throughout the years showed a marked preference for simulating and modeling a "skewed" process: higher probability of declining volatility and lower probability of rising volatility, both states having equal expected payoffs (higher up-moves).

---

nodes. The operator can thus defer the early exercise if the tree disclosed that he would have to regret it should the following day bring a higher volatility.

Another way to view it is that the American option needs all kind of possible information between time zero and the expiration. A closed form formula would not carry such information: The Black-Scholes-Merton method only requires operators to plug into their computer the market parameters on the expiration date without more information in between.

A shortcut method used by the author is the "Rho fudge." Its purpose is to find the right duration (i.e., expected time to termination) for an American option. Knowing the right maturity allows for:

- The use of the right parameter for the pricing of the option (i.e., volatility and term interest and carry rates).
- A better test for early exercise.

It involves deriving the sensitivity to interest rates of the path-dependent option by assuming that the expected life of the option would match that of the synthetic interest rate instrument thus derived.

$$\text{Omega} = \text{Nominal duration} \times \left(\frac{\text{Rho2 of an American option}}{\text{Rho2 of a European option}} \right)$$

The reason Rho2 (it corresponds to the foreign rate or the dividend payout) is used instead of Rho1 is because it excludes the financing cost of the premium. The trader also can compute the Rho2 from the delta by assuming that the delta is a zero-coupon bond of the nominal maturity provided.

Example: Assume that the 1-year American option is equivalent to a European one (zero probability of early exercise): The omega should then be one year.

Rho2 of a 1-year option = delta × 1 (i.e., a rise in 100 basis points in the foreign rate or the dividend payout would correspond to a 100 basis points rise in the option price).

$$\text{Omega} = \frac{\text{Delta} \times 1}{\text{Delta}} = 1 \text{ (years).}$$

Now assume that the structure reacts only by .73

$$\text{Omega} = \frac{\text{Delta} \times .73}{\text{Delta}} = .73 \text{ years.}$$

This method, while far from thorough, provides a rapid tool to compute the expected life of a knock-out or any American binary option.

Alpha

■ The **alpha** (also called gamma rent) is the theta per gamma ratio for an option position.

It reflects the gamma quality in terms of the "rent" and thus is the best indicator of the quality of the earnings from gamma for one dollar risked overnight. A high alpha means that the premium owner is not adequately compensated for the costs of the time decay. A low alpha means that the trader is risking little theta for the gamma.

The premium seller who does not collect enough premium for the risks taken will not survive for long. Typically, spreading options (see Chapter 16) helps achieve a better alpha (that is a lower one for the longs and a higher one for the shorts), through the purchase of a cheap option and the sale of an expensive one.

It is computed as follows:

$$\text{Alpha} = \text{Decay/Gamma}$$

A more advanced computation of the alpha would use the modified theta, instead of the analytical theta, as a rate of decay.

The modified theta takes into account the slide on the curve. It can be computed as:

$$\text{Alpha} = \text{Modified decay/Gamma}$$

Gamma is also more accurate when discretely computed. It is always preferable to calculate the *shadow gamma* when deriving the alpha, to get the full picture of both the risks and the returns.

The fair value alpha according to a schedule of volatility levels is presented in Table 10.1. Assuming interest rates are zero (or that the premium account would be eventually charged back to the trader in his cash account)[4]

$$\text{Theta} = \text{½ Gamma} \times (\text{Volatility})^2 (\text{Asset price})^2$$

Hence

$$\text{Alpha} = \frac{\text{Theta}}{\text{Gamma}} = \frac{1}{2}\sigma^2 S^2$$

which is insensitive to time to expiration (at constant volatility, or flat volatility term structure). Most beginning option traders (and some unskilled veterans) think that by selling short-term options they may be capturing more time decay for the risks involved. The gamma of a longer option is lower than that of the front but so is time decay.

The alpha could be dependent on time to expiration if the volatility level depended on the number of days to go. If the volatility of the 3-month traded lower than the 6-month, then the alpha of the 6-month would be different from the alpha of the 3-month. Otherwise, it would be the same.

Eliminating the interest carry from the equation, as explained earlier in this chapter, allows the trader to get a pure theta number untainted with interest rates.

Table 10.1 Fair Value Alpha for a Given Volatility and No Interest Rates Effect

Volatility	Alpha
2.0	56
4.0	225
6.0	506
8.0	899
9.0	1138
10.0	1405
11.0	1700
12.0	2023
14.0	2754
16.0	3596
18.0	4551
20.0	5618
22.0	6796
24.0	8086
26.0	9488
28.0	11002
30.0	12627
32.0	14363
34.0	16210
36.0	18168
38.0	20237
40.0	22416
42.0	24706
44.0	27105

Risk Management Rule: An alpha that is lower than the fair value alpha for a short gamma position or higher than a fair value alpha for a long gamma position will result in long-term losses (by the law of large numbers).[5]

Table 10.1 shows that at 10% volatility, a gamma should cost $1,405 regardless of the expiration.

Example: The alpha for a portfolio could yield unexpected results. In a calendar spread where the 1-month trades at 11% annualized volatility and the 3-month trades at 12%, the trader buys $100 million 1-month at-the-money calls at 11 vols: total 13.5 positive gammas, at a cost of $22,950 per day.

He sells $100 million 3-month at-the-money calls: total 7.5 negative gammas for a total cost of $15,172 per day.

The net position will be long 6 gammas at a cost of $7,780 per day.

The alpha is therefore $1,297 per gamma. According to the scale in Table 10.1, the trader's costs are such that he will break even at close to 9.5 volatility, which represents an average of .6% moves per day.

TABLE OF GREEKS

The calculations shown in Tables 10.2 and 10.3 are usually memorized by market makers. They can thus rapidly compare options without using calculators.

For simplification, no interest rates are assumed. The reader should present value the vega using e^{-rt}, t being the period in fraction of years.

Weights: Derived using the ratios of the square root of time of the period. These are the weights for those who believe that volatility mean-reverts at a $\sqrt{t}$ speed.

Vega: Classical unmodified at-the-money vega. The reader can multiply the period length by his own factor to get the modified vega.

Table 10.2   Vega, Gamma, and Theta

Days	Maturity	Weights	Face = 1 million Vega	$r = 0\%$ Gamma	Vol 15 Theta
3	3d		0.36	2.93	−1297
7	1w	361%	0.55	1.92	−668
14	2w	255	0.78	1.36	−443
21	3w	208	0.96	1.11	−355
30	1m	174	1.14	0.93	−293
61	2m	122	1.60	0.65	−203
91	3m	100	2.00	0.53	−165
182	6m	71	2.83	0.46	−143
373	9m	58	3.46	0.41	−128
365	12m	50	3.98	0.38	−116
456	15m	45	4.46	0.35	−108
547	18m	41	4.88	0.33	−101
730	2 year	35	5.63	0.31	−95

Table 10.3   Vega Ratios for Out-of-the-Money Options

Forward Delta	Vega Ratio %
50	100
45	98
40	95
35	91
30	85
25	77
20	68
15	57
10	43
5	25

Gamma: Computed for a volatility at 15%. For a different volatility, use the inverse ratio: gamma is inversely proportional to the volatility level.

Gamma at 10% = Gamma at 15% × (15/10) = 1.5 × Gamma at 15%

Theta: Classical unmodified theta, for a volatility at 15%. To compute theta for a different volatility, one should use the ratio of the volatilities:

Theta at 10% = Theta at 15% × (10/15) = .667 × Theta at 15%

Vega Ratio: Table 10.3 shows the vega relationship to the at-the-money option (by the forward). The vega of a 3-month at-the-money option is known from the vega column in Table 10.2. The reader can thus derive the vega of an out-of-the-money option provided he knows the delta.

For a deep in-the-money option, the vega ratio is 100 minus the delta of the out-of-the-money corresponding instrument of the same strike. Put-call parity allows for vegas of European options and all the second derivatives to be the same for puts and calls of the same strike.

Because interest rates of zero are assumed, it becomes necessary to be careful with the relationship when interest rates rise: The difference between forward delta and cash deltas increases. Unfortunately, most option traders measure their deltas initially in the cash.

Stealth and Health

These simplified measures are used by barrier option traders.[6] Both measures have their limitations as they do not take into account the volatility of the underlying asset.[7]

■ **Stealth** corresponds to the percentage difference between the strike and the trigger. **Health** is the percentage difference between the current spot (not the forward, as will be explained) and the trigger.

Stealth is used as an indicator of how much the option resembles a vanilla. The higher the stealth, the closer the option to a regular option in both price and risk profile:

- The market trades at 100. The 100 call with a knock-out at .00001 will in all respects be similar to a 100 call plain vanilla. The 100 call with a knock-out at 300 (the nasty reverse knock-out) also will be priced like a regular call: Its difference will not appear until close to 300.

- The 100 call knock-in at .01 will be priced like no option. Likewise, a 100 call knock-in at 300 will not behave like much.

Health is an indicator of the execution risk. Because options traders need to unwind their hedges at the barrier (and need to come as close to that point as possible), it is a necessary risk management tool that makes them aware of the proximity of the execution. Typically, a warning flag comes up when that number drops below 1 standard deviation. Some people mistake the health for the difference between the trigger and the forward: The options do not knock out at the forward. This would only be applicable to the rare forward knock-out/ins.

A much more potent measure than both is to use the expected stopping time (also called expected time of arrival or first exit time, as described in Chapter 18).

Convexity, Modified Convexity[8]

Convexity, also called curvature, is examined here in a conventional framework in an effort to incorporate the idea of a general yield curve behavior in the measurement. Traders will learn here that:

- Convexity needs to be associated with the volatility of the parameter concerned.
- *Convexity exists everywhere,* alas for the dynamic hedger.

■ **Convexity** for an instrument describes the nonlinearity of the payoff of the instrument with respect to a parallel move in one parameter. The instrument is then called convex with respect to that parameter.

Although convexity originally referred to bonds, it was discovered that the concept needed to be applied to all financial instruments and to their sensitivity with respect to more than one parameter. The convexity of derivative securities—since their pricing depends on many parameters—will be defined as their second partial derivative relative to a particular parameter. The convexity of an option vis-à-vis spot is its gamma. Out-of-the-money options will present a convexity relative to volatility and interest rates.

Convexity of a Bond to Interest Rates (Simplified)

y is the annual yield expressed in continuously compounded rate equivalent.

t is the unit period (1 year in this case).

i is the number of years.

C_i is the cash flow of the period i.

B is the Bond price (the discounted coupons or payments).

$$B = \sum_{i=1}^{n} C_i \, e^{-yt_i}$$

Convexity is $\dfrac{\partial^2 B}{\partial y^2} = \sum_{i=1}^{n} C_i \, t_i^2 e^{-yt_i}$

Convexity of an Option to the Underlying Asset.   The gamma is $\partial^2 V/\partial S^2$ for a derivative security. The measure will depend on the structure with V the derivative price and S the underlying asset.

Vega Convexity.   The vega convexity is $\partial^2 V/\partial \sigma^2$ with σ the implied volatility in the market.

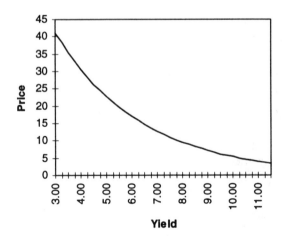

Figure 10.4   Convexity for a fixed income instrument (zero coupon 30-year bond).

Table 10.4   Case of an Exactly at-the-Money Call

	Value	Vega
1	0.28	0.28
2	0.56	0.28
3	0.84	0.28
4	1.12	0.28
5	1.40	0.28
6	1.68	0.28
7	1.96	0.28
8	2.24	0.28
9	2.52	0.28
10	2.80	0.28
11	3.08	0.28
12	3.36	0.28
13	3.64	0.28
14	3.92	0.28
15	4.20	0.28
16	4.48	0.28
17	4.76	0.28
18	5.04	0.28
19	5.32	0.28
20	5.60	0.28
21	5.88	0.28
22	6.16	0.28

Convexity in Figure 10.4 is the effect of a nonlinear change in payoff resulting from the changes in yield. It is magnified in this example by the use of a 30-year maturity and no coupon.

Convexity for a Nonlinear Derivative.   Table 10.4 is an example of a case of an exactly at-the-money call. It is European and exactly at the money by the forward. We can see in Figure 10.5 that its vega is linear. Tables 10.5, 10.6, and Figure 10.6 show the vega convexity for an option that is away from the

Option Wizard: Middlebrow Convexity versus Modified Convexity

Middlebrow convexity is a measure of the sensitivity of a structure to a parameter. The technique is erroneous for comparative purposes as the convexity of a 2-year bond (with respect to yield) could hardly be compared with that of a 10-year bond since the two rates exhibit different volatilities.

Modified convexity is an attempt to rectify that by rescaling to the relative volatilities.

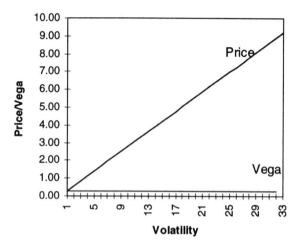

Figure 10.5   Volatility sensitivity for an at-the-money option.

Table 10.5   Case of a 180 Day 15% Out-of-the-Money Call (or 15% In-the-Money Put)

	Value	Vega
5	0.00	0.00
6	0.00	0.00
7	0.00	0.01
8	0.01	0.02
9	0.03	0.03
10	0.07	0.05
11	0.12	0.07
12	0.18	0.08
13	0.27	0.10
14	0.37	0.12
15	0.49	0.13
16	0.62	0.14
17	0.76	0.16
18	0.92	0.17
19	1.09	0.18
20	1.26	0.19
21	1.45	0.20
22	1.65	0.20
23	1.85	0.21
24	2.06	0.22
25	2.27	0.22
26	2.49	0.23
27	2.72	0.23
28	2.95	0.23
29	3.18	0.24
30	3.42	0.24

Table 10.6   A Simplified Modified Convexity

Maturity	Factor	Convexity	Modified Convexity
2	1.23	0.04	0.05
3	1.2	0.09	0.11
4	1.16	0.15	0.17
5	1.13	0.22	0.25
6	1.1	0.30	0.33
7	1.08	0.38	0.42
8	1.05	0.48	0.50
9	1.03	0.58	0.60
10	1	0.69	0.69
15	0.91	1.27	1.15
20	0.85	1.87	1.59
30	0.84	2.98	2.50

money. Chapter 15 provides a discussion for the impact of vega convexity on option pricing.

Note. When volatility rises excessively, all options become concave with respect to volatility because every option is capped at the price of the underlying asset. If the underlying asset is worth 100, an option price cannot exceed 100 or rational traders (there are a few) would resort to buying the asset instead of the call.

Viewed differently, at a very high volatility, an asset becomes a call on itself since it can rise infinitely but only go down in a limited way. Therefore, there will be a convergence between the price of the asset and that of the call option.

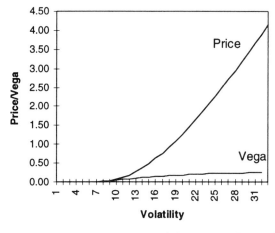

Figure 10.6   Volatility convexity for an out-of-the-money (or in-the-money) option.

Modified Interest Rate Convexity. While most instruments that offer convexity will command a premium for the extra kicker, traders should carefully measure the behavior of the underlying parameters. Many bond traders find that instruments with the highest convexity, the long-term low-coupon bonds, become positioned on the yield curve at the least volatile point, thus making the benefits of their convexity smaller than expected. It becomes erroneous to compare the convexity of a 5-year with that of a 30-year bond without the use of factors similar to the volatility weightings.

The same applies to options. Often the highest convexity is found in back month out-of-the-money options with the most stable implied volatility.

Information about convexity multiplied in the middlebrow literature of the 1980s and early 1990s. Assuming parallel moves the number is generally useless. Using a trader's intuition is more helpful than computing indicators that are misleading to the public. What is remarkable is that these methods ignored the academic developments pioneered by Vasicek (1977), Cox-Ingersoll-Ross (1985a) and others who developed methods of gauging the changes in the shapes of the yield curve.

Much of the convexity-based hedging implemented by the middlebrow fund managers was therefore based on faulty assumptions.

The easiest way to modify convexity is to take into account relative volatility.

Example: A one-factor model used to correct convexity.

Data: May 1993–May 1995

Maturity	2y	5y	10y	30y
Sensitivity	1.231335	1.144669	1	0.839248

Sensitivity is the relative sensitivity of the yield curve (expressed in yield) to that of a 10-year Treasury bond. A one-factor model, in essence, selects one instrument as a "pillar" and assumes a 100 percent correlation with others.

Using a polynomial interpolation, it is possible to construct the quick-and-dirty approximated function[9] (Table 10.6).

The convexity used in this example is defined as a dollar difference between the absolute change from a 100 basis points move up and a 100 basis points move down, for an instrument trading at par with interest rates at 6%, which is close to the general yield curve in June 1995. This quick-and-dirty method could be refined further by measuring exact duration.

Example. Eurodollars Are Convex: This example illustrates the difference between forwards and futures where there is a correlation between the price of the instrument and its rate of financing. Its simplicity allows for easier understanding of the notion. It illustrates the risk management rule on convexity and concavity of futures that was discussed in Chapter 1.

The "boost" (not to be confused with the name of a double-barrier linked product) is an implicit convexity to being short Eurodollar futures because one can reinvest profits at a higher rate and can finance losses at a lower rate.

Eurodollar futures are of the marked-to-market category; operators receive the variation margin at the closing of a profitable day and need to pay it after a losing one. There is a connection between financing costs and profitability: When the market goes down, the short Eurodollar futures position earns money. The money is wired to the investor and can thus be invested at high rate (since the Eurodollars went down). Conversely, the trader incurs losses when the market goes up, but these losses can be financed at a lower rate.

Assume that the position shown in Table 10.7 is short 400 Eurodollar contracts on the Chicago Mercantile Exchange for a contract that expires in one year. In addition, assume for pedagogical reasons that the yield

Table 10.7 Illustration of the Boost

Future	Rate	Profit	Reinvestment	Total
88	0.12	6,000,000	720,000	6,720,000
88.5	0.115	5,500,000	632,500	6,132,500
89	0.11	5,000,000	550,000	5,550,000
89.5	0.105	4,500,000	472,500	4,972,500
90	0.1	4,000,000	400,000	4,400,000
90.5	0.095	3,500,000	332,500	3,832,500
91	0.09	3,000,000	270,000	3,270,000
91.5	0.085	2,500,000	212,500	2,712,500
92	0.08	2,000,000	160,000	2,160,000
92.5	0.075	1,500,000	112,500	1,612,500
93	0.07	1,000,000	70,000	1,070,000
93.5	0.065	500,000	32,500	532,500
94	0.06	—	—	—
94.5	0.055	(500,000)	(27,500)	(527,500)
95	0.05	(1,000,000)	(50,000)	(1,050,000)
95.5	0.045	(1,500,000)	(67,500)	(1,567,500)
96	0.04	(2,000,000)	(80,000)	(2,080,000)
96.5	0.035	(2,500,000)	(87,500)	(2,587,500)
97	0.03	(3,000,000)	(90,000)	(3,090,000)
97.5	0.025	(3,500,000)	(87,500)	(3,587,500)
98	0.02	(4,000,000)	(80,000)	(4,080,000)
98.5	0.015	(4,500,000)	(67,500)	(4,567,500)

curve is flat and moves in parallel (a 100% correlation between the financing of the position and its profitability).

When the Eurodollars go to 9300, the trader is able to reinvest his positive variation margin at 7%, thus earning $70,000 over the year until expiration. When Eurodollars go to 9500, however, the trader incurring a loss will only finance it for $50,000. This difference of $20,000 represents a minute convexity differential, but needs to be taken into account by traders.

A boost becomes significant when dealing with back months, since profits in 5-year Eurodollars will be reinvested over the next 5 years. So the boost increases when maturities lengthen.

The boost accelerates when rates are high, as the reinvestment rate is higher.[10]

The "Double Bubble"

An interesting aspect of the boost is that being short a Eurodollar strip presents a positive convexity. This would not be remarkable except that being short Eurodollar strips presents a remarkable hedge to being long zero coupons. Since zero coupons are convex as well, the trade would offer double convexity, or what one famous arbitrageur dubs "the double bubble."

Chapter *11*

The Greeks and Their Behavior

Time is elastic.
Marcel Proust

Using a dynamic framework, this chapter presents an analysis of the changes of the Greeks in time and space (the relation between the asset and the strike). Only these two dimensions are necessary because time and volatility exert the same effect on the first and second derivatives, though not on the value of the portfolio. Volatility and time are one and the same element in a Brownian motion, since variance (the square of the volatility) is exactly a proportion of time. Where the time exerts its own independent effect is on the e^{rt} and e^{dt} (carry rate and discount rate), which generally do not carry any undue significance.

The analysis will consider the following effects:

- The various changes of Greeks with time that traders typically call the *bleed* (the metaphor is that of a slow loss of vital blood—option traders dislike decay).
- The various changes of parameters with space that traders call the speed or the "D": DdeltaDspot, DgammaDspot, DvegaDspot. For a mathematician they are various third derivatives.

THE BLEED: GAMMA AND DELTA BLEED
(HOLDING VOLATILITY CONSTANT)

■ The **bleed** is the change in the delta and the gamma of an option position with the passage of time.

The delta bleed and gamma bleed are computed by repricing the portfolio one day shorter and measuring the difference.

$$\text{Delta bleed} = \text{Delta today} - \text{Delta next period}$$

$$\text{Gamma bleed} = \text{Gamma today} - \text{Gamma next period}$$

Option Wizard: The Difficult Boss (Another War Story)

One option trader recounts that he was given a limit by the management in the form of a certain amount of maximum allowable delta, vega, and theta exposures for his position. So he knew he needed to leave a wide margin between his exposures and the position limit.

One day, he was long out-of-the-money options and the market exploded higher, taking him late in the day into an area where his long vega increased owing to the position of his out-of-the-money options. He was then called into his boss's office to be informed that the fine-tuning clerk whose job consisted in measuring the trader's compliance with the sacrosanct limits had detected a trespassing of some gravity. So the following dialogue took place:

Boss: You are outside the limit.

Trader: I know, but the market moved rapidly late in the day. Anyway, my delta was computed off a lower volatility so I'm protected.

Boss: You mean you agree that you are outside the limit.

Trader: I repeat, the dynamics of the position took me there. When the option markets closed, I was inside the limit.

Boss: So you tried to cheat by being outside the limit after the close of the market.

Trader: If I knew what the market was going to do, I would have taken a straight position. I had a strong convexity to my vega that made it increase at a higher volatility. You have to look at both third derivatives with respect to spot and with respect to volatility.

(silence . . .)

Boss: Ummph. This time, I will sign off on the sheet. Next time, don't cheat again.

Every option trader has such war stories. The most ludicrous ones involve a limit in the shape of a delta restriction.

Time pushes all the out-of-the-money options further out-of-the-money, therefore reducing their deltas. Time also pushes all the in-the-money options further in-the-money, therefore increasing their deltas. Although this seems trivial, traders should not overlook the following confusion: Gamma is said to increase with time, but for an out-of-the-money option being pushed further, out-of-the-money would cause some gamma loss. The results are therefore mixed.

Book runners are always miffed at the alterations brought about by time. Because portfolios of book runners always include a mixture of strikes, with strong concentration away from the money, a meaningful daily bleed is guaranteed.

Risk Management Rule: An option position that is long up-gamma (see definition, Chapter 8) and short down-gamma will bleed into shorter delta over time, and vice versa.

The rule is simple to understand: (1) Such a position is long out-of-the-money calls short out-of-the-money puts. The calls will decrease in deltas (shorter delta) since the delta of out-of-the-money options decreases with time and the puts will decrease in deltas for the same reason (longer deltas); (2) the same position can be constructed (put/call parity) with deep-in-the-money calls and puts. The same result can be proven by the put-call parity rules (see the discussion on option equivalence in Chapter 1).

Example: For simplification, assume that the book has two trades:

Short $1,000,000 in face value of a 100 call expiring in 60 days (OPT1 in Table 11.1).

Long $5,040,000 in face value of a 106 call expiring in 30 days (OPT2 in Table 11.1).

Option Wizard: Thank God It's Friday

The bleed is always accentuated for traders ahead of a weekend when, after Friday lunch, they start examining their Monday exposures, not always without a shock. The endless dialogues between traders as to when to set the clock usually take place then: whether to use Monday "sheets," Friday sheets, or somewhere in between (sheets are printed reports showing the price of the option at different levels of asset price and volatility).

Traders commonly use risk management systems with discrete time. Options are not usually priced on a continuous clock. Time to expiration is not updated every second, but in 24 hour increments. Most operate on a 7-day-week basis, 365 days a year. While this jump function is of small consequence during the week, it becomes an endless source of confusion when, on Friday, the traders issue portfolio simulations with a Monday date.

When pit traders perform "covered" trades on a Friday afternoon, where they trade the option covered with the delta, disagreements occur as to the amount of deltas to swap. It is then easy to see that one part of the pit uses Friday deltas, another one Saturday, another one Sunday, and so on.

Implied volatility as usual is at 15.7% annualized (for both options) and the market is initially at 100.

The trade starts delta neutral as both legs match each other.

Table 11.1 shows that the deltas (delta 1 column) of the at-the-money 100 calls (OPT1) remains constant (almost, except for a total loss rounded to 2 deltas) while the 106 calls (OPT2) lose their deltas (delta 2 column) rapidly (from to 512 to 175). They "bleed" fast.

The table shows the acceleration of gammas for the 100 calls offset ("positive gamma bleed") by a deceleration for the 106 calls, with an important effect on the overall gamma of the portfolio.

The graphs in Figure 11.1 (A) and (B) show that the delta bleed is topical (it depends on the location of the spot). It reverses above the strike that caused the bleed. This analysis leads to the fourth derivative: how the bleed behaves with respect to spot. Most nonoption traders, particularly those with an engineering education, believe that fourth derivatives are of small importance in practical life. They are trained to cut everything beyond the second derivative, which, for options, would be a gamma. This attitude is incompatible with the trading of a portfolio of options where the risks change abruptly between levels. Many option traders report disagreements with Taylor-expansion-minded semimathematicians who deride their attempt at looking at the heart of the position with fourth (and higher) derivatives.

Table 11.1 Effect of Time over the Deltas and Gammas

Days Hence	OPT1	Delta1	Gamma1	OPT2	Delta2	Gamma2	Total Delta	Total Gamma
0	2.54	−513	−63	0.21	512	199	0	136
1	2.52	−513	−63	0.20	493	197	−20	133
2	2.50	−512	−64	0.19	472	194	−40	130
3	2.47	−512	−64	0.17	452	191	−61	127
4	2.45	−512	−65	0.16	430	188	−82	123
5	2.43	−512	−65	0.15	409	184	−103	119
6	2.41	−512	−66	0.14	387	180	−125	114
7	2.39	−512	−67	0.12	364	176	−147	109
8	2.36	−512	−67	0.11	342	171	−170	104
9	2.34	−512	−68	0.10	319	166	−193	98
10	2.32	−512	−69	0.09	295	160	−217	92
11	2.29	−511	−69	0.08	271	154	−240	85
12	2.27	−511	−70	0.07	247	147	−264	77
13	2.25	−511	−71	0.06	223	139	−288	68
14	2.22	−511	−72	0.05	199	131	−312	59
15	2.20	−511	−72	0.04	175	122	−336	49

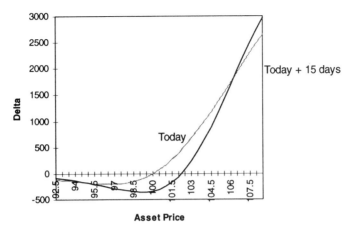

A. Delta change over time for a ratio diagonal

B. P/L change over time for a ratio diagonal

Figure 11.1   Effects of time over a ratio diagonal spread.

Fourth derivatives will not be explored in any depth here, except to warn traders of the effect of change in bleed at different levels.

Bleed with Changes in Volatility

Changes in implied volatility do not overly complicate the bleed. Volatility shifts can operate like a time acceleration, with an effect that is linked to the length of the option (more exactly the square of the volatility shift is proportional to the length of the option). Every option beginner knows that the shorter the option, the greater the effect of time on the structure. A longer dated option, say a one-year call with 20 deltas, would lose, at 16%

volatility, .04 deltas (the delta would go from 20% to 19.96%). A change in volatility from 16% to 15% would move the delta from 20% to 18.2%.

> *Warning:* The barrier options trader needs to be aware of the two-way bleed (see Option Wizard, *Forward and Backward Bleed*). A rise in volatility can initially lengthen the delta, while a further rise could decrease it. Barrier options are thus considered extremely topical: What works on one point of the possible map does not necessarily work on others. The third, fourth, fifth, and sixth moments (see definition later in this chapter) are always there to confuse operators.

Going into the Expiration of a Vanilla Option

Bleed moving into an expiration is so rapid that handling it properly requires a great deal of experience. That is where the difference between the experience of listed traders with discrete expirations and that of over-the-counter operators with almost continuous ones becomes most apparent. Bleed then becomes so fast that volatility changes cannot carry too large an effect on it.

Many operators start trading an expiration as a binary one, with all the bleed taken on the report generated the previous day. At 5 o'clock the previous day, they generate a run with the deltas of the option in binary form: zero if the option is out of the money and 100% if it is in the money. However, it does not mean that they will adjust their position in a binary way. Most still trade it in a smooth manner, with progressive adjustments. Others use more sophisticated devices and trade "on the clock," with their risk management system adjusting the delta by repricing the portfolio continuously.

> *Example. An Expiration Day Report:* Assume that the market trades at 100 and that the operator is short the 101 calls expiring in the over-the-counter market at 10:00 A.M. the same day.

Figures 11.2 and 11.3 show the option delta and price the day before expiration. Figures 11.4 and 11.5 show the same elements on the following day.

So the operator needs to flip between Report I (Figures 11.2 and 11.3) and Report II (Figures 11.4 and 11.5) by making sure that the convergence takes place in a smooth manner. Ideally, the following would occur: The operator would subscribe to the smoothness rule by ascertaining that the transition between two points does not take place abruptly. So Report I would hold at all times but with a continuous rescaling in accordance to the passage of time.

One day before expiration, the trader would look at Report I. Then he would need to try to maintain the same smooth profile between two points by narrowing down the scale, as by a microscope in which the magnifying power is gradually increased.

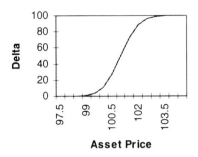

Figure 11.2   Report I: Single option delta 1 day before expiration.

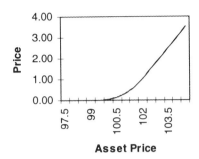

Figure 11.3   Report I: Single option price 1 day before expiration.

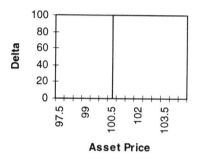

Figure 11.4   Report II: Single option delta at expiration.

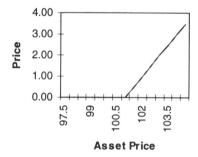

Figure 11.5   Report II: Single option price at expiration.

If the trader has no transaction costs, expirations would be completely smooth, as by the Black-Scholes-Merton formula. However, traders need to restrict their trading to a number of discrete interventions. It does not mean that they need to adjust their delta on expiration in a binary form. They must remember the golden rule that hedging is smoothing. Depending on the traders' perception of their own risks, they could narrow the scale in a continuous way, as follows:

1. Day Before		2. Half a Day to Go		3. 1 Hour to Go	
Delta	Asset	Delta	Asset	Delta	Asset
1	98	1	98.84	1	100.37
25	100.44	25	100.61	25	100.89
50	101.00	50	101.00	50	101.00
75	101.65	75	101.40	75	101.11
99	102.95	99	102.38	99	101.40

Option Wizard (Advanced): A Modicum of Ito Calculus

When the author was being interviewed for his first job, a senior foreign exchange trader showed him the following scheme on a tomato-sauce-stained restaurant napkin:

One should sell a call option on USD-DEM for the hefty premium it then commanded. Then he would leave a stop-loss to buy the full amount at the strike price. If the spot recrossed, then he would do the reverse. Given this brilliant strategy, the premium in the market appeared unjustified.

The author tried to register some doubt about this plan but could not quite explain stochastic integration to a head option trader (besides this was 1983 and option traders concealed any degree other than an MBA to avoid the "nerd-discrimination" that prevailed at the time).

Most option traders report that they have had to explain to a boss why they do not follow such a strategy. The reason is as follows:

> **Local time*** never becomes zero, owing to the non-differentiability of the Brownian motion. We know from the spreadsheet exercise that the Brownian motion never becomes smooth. Making the time intervals smaller does not make it more differentiable; otherwise, there would be a rebalancing strategy that would outperform others. If traders rebalanced at the interval where the function became smooth, they would keep the entire premium and there would be no need for this book.

The frequency of rebalancing does not affect the fair value of the option. Assume that traders operate in the Black-Scholes-Merton world of no transaction costs. The rebalancing P/L does not depend on the rebalancing frequency. It does not matter whether they rebalance over the time interval Δt at the increment Δt or at increments $\Delta t/2$ or $\Delta t/4$ or $\Delta t/n$, with corresponding spot moves ΔS, $\Delta S/2$, and so on. The expected P/L would be more precise the smaller the adjustment period, but it certainly would not vary.

The key to understanding Ito's calculus is knowing that there is a lag between the decision to rebalance and the final execution price and such lag is never eradicated.

In fact, the costs of hedging are $\sqrt{2/\pi} \sqrt{(\Delta S)^2}$ times the amount of time spent swinging between S and $S + \Delta S$, the resulting volatility, since the trader hedges himself after the move ΔS and thus loses the absolute value of ΔS times the face value.

This figure illustrates the rebalancing strategy issue. In practical terms, the amount of times, he would have to pay the transaction costs of one tick between 1.5000 and 1.5001 in USD-DEM is equal to the amount of time he would pay the transaction costs of 100 ticks between 1.5000 and 1.5100. For the market will snap more often between 1.5000 and 1.5001 in a compensating way.

(Continued)

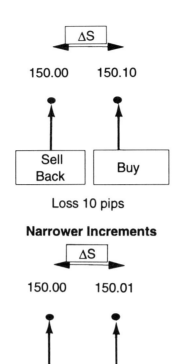

Intuitively, the trader can truly derive an option price as the expected rebalancing at the strike. An out-of-the-money option is less likely to whip around the strike because the strike is away from the center of the distribution.

First Conclusion: The costs of replicating an option (assuming no transaction costs) by buying the entire face value at the strike or by continuously rebalancing the delta are expected to be the same. They will correspond to the Black-Scholes-Merton value.

Second Conclusion (food for thought): In some cases, the wrinkles of the market favor the strategy of hedging with discrete increments and executing the full face value. Markets supported by central banks will cross the intervention level and not return. Likewise, in serially correlated markets, some chartists and voodoo traders enjoy being short delta below some level and long above it.

---

*See Karatzas and Shreve (1991).

Ddeltadvol (Stability Ratio)

■ **Ddeltadvol** corresponds to the changes in deltas resulting from changes in volatility levels.

The reader can decide whether weighted or unweighted volatility needs to be used. The concept is similar to that of the bleed except that it can move in two directions. Volatility moving up exerts the effect of the reversing of time on an option portfolio. Likewise volatility moving down causes the time to shorten and carries exactly the same effect as the bleed. The effect of the moves in volatility over the portfolio is called the **forward and backward bleed.** At a more advanced level; a portfolio, made up of spreads cannot be projected through time without the testing of the effect of both the bleed and the Ddeltadvol. The trader can thus only run a scenario of a series of paths with changes in implied volatility and reprice the portfolio as if he remained risk neutral in hewing to a delta-neutral strategy. Because the delta neutrality will depend on the volatility at the rebalancing point, the exercise is called a path-dependent portfolio testing.

Test 1 of Stability

The trader should raise the volatility and examine the first derivatives, particularly the delta. An increase in the deltas means that the position becomes increasingly longer vegas in a rally and shorter in a sell-off. It is called a positive Ddeltadvol. It means that the book is net short options below the money and net long option above the money. A negative Ddeltadvol means the reverse.

> *Example:* A simple vertical spread is the most likely candidate for instability, curiously. If the operator is long a 100 call and short a 110 call, the deltas will shorten with Test 1. Higher volatility would raise the deltas of the out-of-the-money calls and keep the at-the-money calls constant.

Option Wizard: Forward and Backward Bleed

The *forward bleed* is the effect of time with the expiration becoming shorter. It consists in moving the portfolio one day hence.

The *backward bleed* is the effect of time in reverse, as if the book went back in time. It is similar to the notion of reverse time decay. The increase in volatility exerts such an effect on the non-interest component of an option price.

This test needs to be run routinely on books in emerging market currencies, the *biased assets* and other products where it not advisable to be short volatility when the market decreases. It presents the benefit of being simpler to perform than those tests that require matrices. The reader should note that this test tells little about the gamma; it can only explain the sensitivity of the vega to the skew.

Test 2 of Stability: The Asymptotic Vega Test

Repeating the preceding test at different levels of the underlying asset could show the different exposures at various levels of the topography. Sometimes the vega "flips" when the market rallies above or drops below a cutting point. Such reversal is usually caused by the clustering of options in one location dominating a particular area. That cluster, in turn would be dominated by another one further away from the money. Figure 11.6 shows such behavior.

> *Example:* One is long the 110 calls in $100 million, short the 130 calls in 300 million. When the volatility is sufficiently low and the market re-mains between 100 and 115, the book would exhibit long vegas. This would appear in a positive Ddeltadvol Test. At higher volatility levels, however, the test would reverse and show a negative Ddeltadvol.

In the preceding example, the vegas appear jagged. An abrupt rise in volatility, however, would turn the vegas to monotonously short across the entire spectrum. This is called the asymptotic vega test, which is only per-formed for stress testing as it gives way out-of-the-money options undue importance.

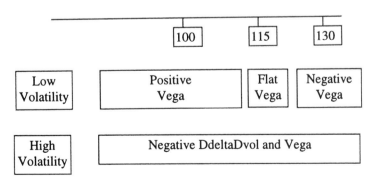

Figure 11.6 Option clusters.

MOMENTS OF AN OPTION POSITION

Moments for a distribution are ways mathematicians characterize some of its higher order behavior. What the author calls moments for a position corresponds to the sensitivity of an option book to the higher moments of the distribution. The modern financial approach of relying on a normal distribution allows theoreticians to ignore its higher moments. The reason is that the normal distribution is entirely characterized by its first two moments—the mean and volatility. A **compact distribution** is defined (see Ingersoll, 1986) as a distribution the higher moments of which become increasingly small in relation to the second moment. "Compact support" can be seen in the tails of the bell curve that come rapidly close to 0. Therefore, in theory, an option trader will only be exposed to the market direction (via the delta) and the market volatility (through the gamma). Higher derivatives should not truly matter.

Too bad. Given that the true world distributions do not entirely look *normal* (except by accident) we need to worry about fat tails, positive and negative skew, jumps, and other annoying matters. We will therefore stretch the mathematical language by using the designation moment for a position instead of a distribution.

The moments of an option position[1] represent the sensitivity to some order of change in the underlying security. The more information about the higher moments, the more able the trader would be to track the position and predict the changes over a wider range of prices.

The way operators look at the moments in their framework of analysis concerns the orders of move in the asset price with time kept constant. So the method of moments reveals little about the vega and its changes and the sensitivity to time.

- *First Moment.* The delta, which indicates an exposure to mean of the distribution.
- *Second Moment.* The delta of the delta, the gamma.
- *Third Moment.* The delta of the gamma, which is called the skew. It is the gamma exposure in function of the asset price and becomes naturally the level of asymmetry between them. If the gamma becomes more positive in the rally and more negative in the sell-off, the third moment will be positive. It will be otherwise negative. (It becomes apparent that odd moments are indicators of symmetry while even moments are indicators of convexity.)
- *Fourth Moment.* The tails. It corresponds to the gamma of the gamma as it is the second moment of the second moment. When the fourth moment is positive, the position is convex and therefore can allow some sleep at night. In practical terms, it means that the

gamma increases when the market moves away from the center and decreases when volatility moves down.

Probabilists usually ignore higher moments since those vanish very rapidly. However, option traders, surprisingly, do not. It is their business to deal with the fine tuning of the option position at higher moments. So one probabilist choked at a mathematical finance conference while listening to two option traders argue during lunch about the seventh moment of a distribution (indeed a true story).

An option book being spread out between items at all the possible time and space points of the distribution will become very sensitive to the moments of moments, and endlessly so, even without adding the beastly compound option structures. This is because traders tend to maintain a delta-neutral, gamma-neutral book with thousand of strikes netting out. Canceling the lower moments (locally) is rather easy (one phone call to take care of the first two moments). Canceling the next 5,000 moments, however, would necessitate closing down the book. Going down the risk management positions shows why option traders make good probability experts:

- *The Fifth Moment.* It becomes the asymmetry sensitivity of the fourth moment. A portfolio solely containing a short American barrier option hedged with a short vanilla option will therefore be extremely sensitive to the fifth moment. It will increase in concavity as the market comes closer to the barrier and will act more linear as the market moves away from it.

- *The Sixth Moment.* Except for compound options, even moments do not seem to be very beastly.

- *The Seventh Moment.* It is the sign of the convexity changes as the underlying asset moves up or down. Typically, convexity positions constructed with higher order out-of-the-money options one side of the market (only out-of-the-money calls on calls) against at-the-money options of an inferior order (e.g., a vanilla at-the-money) will have a seventh moment that is very pronounced. In the call on calls case versus at-the-money, the convexity will slide down and hit zero. Where someone buys out-of-the-money calls on calls and sells out-of-the-money puts on calls (delta neutral, of course), the seventh moment will be very scary.

With compound options, traders can thus reach seriously higher orders of moments. An installment option (a fifth-order compound option), we will see, requires an analysis that takes into account at least nine moments for hedging stability.

> ***Risk Management Rule:*** Positions that seem neutral in the lower moments and have an increasing exposure in the higher moments will present trading difficulties.

For example, a delta-neutral risk reversal will appear to be harmless for anyone stopping at the delta and gamma. However, the skew can have a drastic effect on the P/L. The skew can be more volatile than the second moment, and this is also true for fourth moment positions.

Ignoring Higher Greeks: The Lock Delta

Stress-testing a portfolio is a must in risk management. Although it is a casual, uncomplicated method, it proves effective for micromanagement of the risks when one looks into only a single asset in an independent portfolio of options.

■ The **lock delta,** or asymptotic delta method is a measurement of the risks in a derivatives portfolio at extreme boundaries, generally, zero or the infinite. The principal use of the asymptotic delta is to display the structure of the position that is hidden by scenario analysis.

Option Wizard: Parametric and Nonparametric Tests

The market parameters being considerably unstable, it is always necessary to perform tests that are independent of the distribution. The Lebanese lira, for example, is pegged to the dollar most of the time and often jumps after some political mishap. Even the notions of fat tails and skew are hardly applicable owing to the extreme non-normality of the market. Using Greeks such as gamma represent dangers. The tests performed on a portfolio containing such assets need to be entirely street-smart, with simple scenarios (e.g., If the currency moves down to such a level, what is my P/L?).

A nonparametric test is defined as one where no assumptions are made about the distribution (and its parameters). There is an entire branch of statistics called "robust" that deals with such issues. Stress tests fall into the nonparametric category.

It is necessary in poorly behaved instruments like emerging market debt where the distribution and its parameters (especially volatility) are so unstable as to make the conventional risk management tools inadequate.

Other partial derivatives than the delta are by definition zero at these boundaries: The portfolio then ceases to behave like a derivatives portfolio. As such, its sensitivity to volatility will be nil: Its gamma and vega will be zero. In that respect, calling the measure a delta can be an exaggeration. The measure is the netting of the underlying if all options were exercised. It can literally be done on a napkin for positions that do not include exotic options and correlation products. One can count the net number of calls, add them to the cash and futures, present value them, and translate the number into asymptotic maximum up-deltas. Conversely, one can do the same with puts and come up with the maximum down-deltas.

Risk Management Rule: The firms that survive large shocks in the market (and the breakdown of convential associations between instruments) are the ones lucky enough not to have "scientific" risk managers among their staff.

Experienced risk managers do not take the heavy models too seriously. The key for survival resides in distinguishing between risk managers who believe in models, and those confident enough not to.

Example 1. Lock Delta for a Covered Write: In all examples, the market trades at 100.

A portfolio is long 100 futures, short 100 3-month calls struck at 110. The upside asymptotic delta is zero delta. The downside asymptotic delta is 100 long deltas as shown in Figure 11.7.

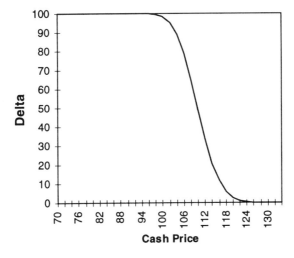

Figure 11.7   Lock delta for a covered write.

Example 2. Lock Delta for a Strangle Write: A portfolio is short 100 out-of-the-money calls struck at 104 and short 100 out-of-the-money puts struck at 96 (a 96–104 strangle). The upside asymptotic delta is 100 short deltas. The downside asymptotic delta is 100 long deltas as shown in Figure 11.8.

Example 3. Lock Delta for a Ratio Write: A portfolio is long 100 calls struck at 100, short 200 calls struck at 104 (a ratio write). The upside asymptotic delta is short 100 deltas, the downside asymptotic delta is zero as shown in Figure 11.9.

Before option market makers discovered the simulation matrices, the system was principally asymptotic delta-related: The clearing firm measured the net difference between upside and downside risk and charged the customer a margin in accordance with the net residual exposure, which is that of the asymptotic delta. A covered writer was absolved of margin, but the sale of an additional call (a one-by-two covered write) caused the margin to become that of a naked call. The clearing firms then were not interested in the mathematics of option pricing and did not concern themselves, to their protection, with Greek derivatives.

The mentality of nonmathematical equity option traders was then entirely pragmatic: Stocks used to experience sudden harrowing jumps on takeover rumors and experienced unstable volatility, with brief discontinuous movements following company news and announcements. Survival instinct prevented the early participants from putting much trust in formulas

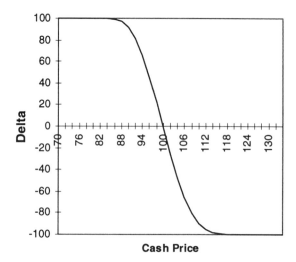

Figure 11.8 Lock delta for a strangle write.

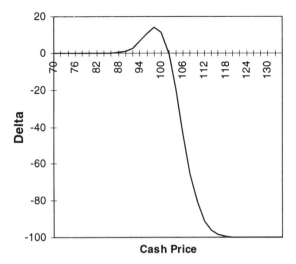

Figure 11.9   Lock delta for a ratio write.

and volatility-based measurements when the distribution displayed acute fat tails.

Over-the-counter (OTC) dealers and institutions not being subjected to margins on their OTC portfolio use the regular parametric scenario analysis for the management of the exposures. They therefore do not have the watchdog protection of a narrow-minded exchange to protect them from the nonstatistical risks.

The asymptotic delta risk loses its significance in the case of dynamic hedging, as it does not take into account the hedging of the position between points. Conversely, the asymptotic delta risk measurement does not reveal the risk of *whipsaw* that could range far in excess of the amounts disclosed. In brief, it only discloses the risk from events where the trader *does not have time* to hedge.

Chapter *12*

Fungibility, Convergence, and Stacking

Find me an arbitrage in commodities and I will show you a squeeze.
An option proverb

FUNGIBILITY

■ **Fungibility** refers to the degree of specificity required for the satisfaction of the deliverability obligation. A highly fungible commodity is an abstract one and could be created electronically (like a swap). A non-fungible one is specific and cannot be created at will, such as livestock that requires the delivery of a cow at a specific place at a specific time.

From the vantage point of financial theory, fungibility reflects the feasibility of risk-neutral replication of a derivative security.

Fungibility of a commodity represents the degree of dependence on time and space for the delivery process. This issue prevents theoreticians from reaching a generalized derivatives-pricing model, as it shows how deep differences between products could be. Some commodities are totally theoretical and intangible (an inflation index), others are palpable and specific.

Whenever there are two instruments in the same category, the market for the more fungible one will be considerably larger and more liquid. Bond futures seem to be more interesting than cash bonds because the operators do not have the specificity of a particular bond to borrow (despite the conversion optionality). Likewise, swaps are better arbitraged than bonds.

Example: A contract specifying for the deliverability of calves of some detailed species becomes subjected to the dynamics of supply and demand for that particular specification. Sometimes open interest exceeds the number of animals *alive* of that specification, causing an imbalance between longs and shorts. The owners of the underlying asset, typically seasoned traders with a vast experience of the squeezing process, will accumulate the physical and force delivery of the underlying. Within the narrow time window available, it becomes impossible to create animals from scratch, regardless of the money available. The owners of the physical typically know it and would not fail to benefit from it. The squeeze will last until open interest numbers drop to the physical ceiling.

Ranking of Fungibility

Commodities can be classified between two extremes: totally fungible and delivery specific.

- An extremely fungible commodity is a currency that a bank can create electronically and wire anywhere in the world. The only restriction becomes exchange control, the establishment of hindrances to convertibility, something no longer common with the currencies of the industrialized world. Being able to wire currency instantaneously without any restriction removes it from the time or place restrictions. This has a momentous effect on the term structure of prices.

- At the other extreme lies a physical commodity that needs to be delivered at one specific location. The location specificity subjects arbitrage to shipping considerations. It is therefore possible to see the same commodity with the same grade trading at two different prices at two different locations at the same moment because of the shipment costs and time. Spot oil can trade for 18.23 for 3-day delivery in the New York harbor and 18.75 for the same delivery date of the grade in Rotterdam. Since moving inventory at an acceptable price within the deadline of the delivery is impossible, a certain margin between securities will be allowed. For the right price, however, someone would charter a Concorde and fly any shipment anywhere.

  Nonfungibility makes elements of one grade trade at a different price than those of another grade. Time and place restrictions operate in more than one way. Storage can involve such costs that those holding a product in the ground would dictate the marginal carry of the commodity.

Example: Oil in the ground does not really cause the owner to incur any direct physical carrying cost. If the owner is a government that is not chartered to sell a chunk of the homeland, no financial carry is usually taken into consideration. On the other hand an individual who owns the land could always make a comparison between its future market value and the investment of the proceeds in some treasury bill. Someone with no marks-to-market has no real financing cost to take into consideration.

So there is no true force to prop up the price of the forward, except, of course, the behavior of the real users who can buy long dated forwards to lock in the price of future needs, which, for trading purposes, can be deemed at best negligible. The forward price can therefore trade at a much lower price than cash, and the difference between the cash and the future can fluctuate wildly without any trader having the guts to confront the market.

Example: Often the commodity can escape all rules when it comes to a perishable or live animal. No financial power can electronically create a live animal (not yet given the state of genetic engineering) or extend its life beyond term to make a long-term forward delivery.

Fungibility and the Term Structure of Prices: The Cash-and-Carry Line

> *Risk Management Rule:*   A calendar spread in options on cash assets in less fungible commodities needs to be decomposed into its different components and analyzed separately.

The prices follow the following curve: If a commodity one year hence becomes too expensive relative to the spot, an arbitrageur can buy the cash, compute proper carrying costs (both financial and physical storage), then sell the future to lock in a profit. This puts an upper boundary on the future costs, provided the commodities do not go through deterioration through time. This upper boundary is called the *maximum contango* (see Figure 12.1).

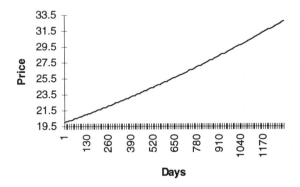

Figure 12.1   Boundary for a commodity's forward prices: Maximum contango.

Example: A commodity is trading at $20.00 per unit, incurring storage (and insurance) costs of 8% annualized and fixed. The maximum contango line will espouse the shape of the yield curve for interest rates plus the storage costs. It is not possible for a commodity to exceed the line, but the yield curve can take any shape underneath it (see Figure 12.1).

So commodities are split into:

- Those that can only be arbitraged one-way on the time line, like most physical commodities.
- Those that can be arbitraged two-way, like currencies and liquid equities and fixed income instruments.
- Those that are not arbitrageable on the time line, like all perishable products.

Table 12.1 classifies commodities according to their fungibility.

Table 12.1 Classifications of Products by Their Degree of Fungibility

Commodity	Fungibility	Stability of Term—Structure of Volatility
Currencies, gold	High in the absence of exchange controls	High
Cash bonds (United States, Germany)	Medium except for "tight" issues (that are difficult to borrow in the repo market)	Medium
Euro (Eurodollars, Euromarks, etc. . . .)	None, since the contracts do not overlap	Low for the front contracts, higher for the back months
Stocks	High in most liquid U.S. issues Low in Japan and Germany	High even in case of unstable borrowing
Agricultural commodities	Impossible when the back months trade at a discount, or when the products are highly perishable Low in cases of cash-and-carry	None

Fungibility and Option Arbitrage

Option arbitrage consists principally in synthetically moving the liquidity of one instrument against another, that is trading between the liquidity of the products. A fungible product will subscribe to the line $F(t) = F(0) + Carry$, with most Greeks of the forward fungible with those of the cash, plus or minus a variance. The initial Greeks such as delta and gamma can be used for the cash or the future interchangeably.

Another way is to consider the structure of correlation between the products. A high correlation matrix will lead to a spreadable volatility curve. A low correlation matrix requires the bucketing of expirations as semiindependent products.

The stability of second derivatives will be higher than first ones, and so on, as one goes into higher order differentials. This means that if the deltas of the 9-month does not properly hedge that of the 3-month, the gamma hedges will be more stable. The DgammaDspot will be even more stable and so forth. A trader should initially square up his delta in each expiration, then concentrate on the gammas, and so on.

A trader who is long a 1-year call and short a 2-year call in oil should first do a 1-year/2-year swap or its equivalent. He will end up with residual delta in the rallies as he will get longer the 1-year forward and short the 2-year. He then will have to square up the incremental deltas back and forth.

This leads to the following rule:

Risk Management Rule: Option arbitrage cannot be performed in markets that do not have a risk-neutral forward market. The forward needs to be perfectly arbitrageable for the option operator to feel confident about his activities there.

Changes in the Rules of the Game

Currencies appear to be arbitrageable on both sides of the forward line. At times of crisis, however, a currency under siege can command high interest rates or might turn out to be unobtainable. An operator will still be able to deliver it and incur a liability but covering that liability by borrowing the currency overnight could prove onerous. The Irish punt commanded 4000% overnight interest rates during the 1992 financial crisis. The central bank's stated objective was to make it as difficult as possible to borrow, "to give the speculators a lesson." The Spanish peseta after a weakening against the other European currencies will become tight as many short sellers need to

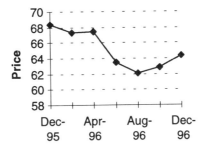

Figure 12.2   Live cattle prices on Friday October 27, 1995, Chicago Mercantile Exchange.

borrow it to cover. Sometimes the central banks create a wedge between the domestic and the offshore (or Euro) markets.

> *Example. Live Cattle:*   Figure 12.2 represents the curve of cattle prices. As expected, the curve does not exhibit any smoothness: It is difficult to transfer a live animal into December 1996, when the animal could become sick.
>
> The volatility is difficult to gauge owing to the illiquidity of the back month. Whereas it is the rule for a fungible product that the price of a back month at-the-money (forward) straddle to be at least that of the price of a straddle of a shorter expiration (minus financing), such a restriction does not apply to such instruments. The straddle in the back month could trade at a lower price than that in the front without any possible arbitrage.

CONVERGENCE

■ **Convergence trading**[1] is any form of speculative position taking based on the belief that the (risk-adjusted) term structure of a security or its derivatives (interest rate yields, volatility, gamma costs, etc.) does not represent *a completely* unbiased predictor of the future.

Securities are supposed to include some bias in proportion to their risk (in the form of covariance with the market or liquidity constraints). Typically, financial market equilibrium would, according to theory, represent a balance between the drift of a security and its risk premium. However, Wall Street does not hold a coherent and stable belief in risk premiums and would therefore consider a carry to be whatever disagrees with their vision of the future price.

Example: An imaginary commodity future with an extremely high drift:

Spot price: 100.
1-month price: 110
2-month price: 125
3-month price: 145

The structure of the financial markets indicates that (assuming no risk premium for the commodity) the price of the instrument should pick up 10 cents in the next month. This is called the "ride up" on the curve. It implies that the expected price 1 month from now is 110, 2 months from now 125, and so on.

- *First-Order Convergence.* An operator who shorts the one-month future can expect that if the security does not drop by $10.00 a month, .33 a day, he will benefit from the positive convergence of his trade. This operation is called first-order convergence, as it seems risky.

- *Second-Order Convergence.* The operator who prefers not to incur the risks of a naked short position would engage in a spread. He would buy the 1-month forward at 110 and sell the 2-month at 125. That way he can consider that he reduced his directional risk (assuming the two instruments are highly correlated).

- *Butterfly Convergence.* A shrewder operator, provided he can access markets without incurring high transaction costs, would look at the previous trade and consider the trader rather naïve. The trade leaves the person exposed to the shifts in the curve generally resulting from imperfect correlation between instruments. So he adds a twist: a butterfly.

  He buys the second month twice and sells the first and third month against them, thus achieving some relative safety from moves in the marketplace. This is called two-factor immunization: The first one is the direction, the second one is the slope of the curve. The operator leaves himself only exposed to the convexity in the shape of the curve.

There is a Wall Street continuous dilemma between those who believe that the future converges to spot and those who believe that the spot "deconverges" to the future. In other words, the question is whether the curve corresponds to some utility function, some structural condition, or to market expectations. Many operators make different judgments at different times depending on the information available in the market. They may believe in convergence at some times, say in the absence of a central bank policy and subscribe to the expectation belief at other times.

Option Wizard: Carry versus Convergence

One should not confuse carry and convergence. Convergence includes carry. Carry corresponds to the cash flow differential between instruments or the difference between an instrument and the cost of holding it (or the "risk-free" rate according to financial theory). Convergence is calculated by repricing the instrument with a decrease on the term structure in addition to the carry.

Most sophisticated convergence calculations take into account seasonal factors, such as year-end liquidity.

Mapping Convergence

For a Fixed-Income Instrument.   Dollar convergence is equivalent to:

Carry + Drop on the curve in basis points

The drop on the curve should be computed in by breaking down the cash flows of every instrument and repricing them on the zero-curve with one day shorter to go.

For a Eurodollar Future.   There is no carry. The drop on the curve can be more easily computed in two ways:

1. The easy way is by interpolating the straight line difference between contracts and repricing the instrument as if it were one day shorter.
2. The more accurate method is to use the polynomial approximation for the time function or the spline in order to avoid abrupt changes in convergence. The price of the securities would be replaced by the seasonal adjusted one. The December future, for example, would be purged of the liquidity premium. (Year-end interest rates are often higher because of balance sheet requirements. Operators need to take such effect into account.)

For a Currency Cash Position.   For a currency cash position, carry is the convergence. It is estimated by checking the overnight interest rate differential.

For a Currency Forward.   A currency forward is only a currency spot position plus two fixed income zero-coupon positions, one long and the other short.

The convergence would be priced as the spot carry plus the difference in the effects in the drop on the curve in each of the two instruments.

Convergence and Convexity

Often time decay can be mistaken for convergence. Instruments that present a high convexity will often have a theta built into them.

The bond future includes an option to choose between a variety of deliverables. Estimating its convergence would require some adjustment to take into account the "time decay" of the embedded option.

Securities of the Government National Mortgage Association (GNMAs) need to be priced on an option-adjusted basis. The owner of the structure has a high level of negative convexity in his books.

Levels of Convergence Trading

- *First-Order Convergence Trading.*   The positive carry trade. Owning a bond because of its carry.
- *Second-Order Convergence Trading.*   The forward-forward. Playing the carry differential between two maturities.
- *Third-Order Convergence Trading.*   Butterflies, barbells.
- *Fourth-Order Convergence Trading.*   Double butterflying, running a minimum variance stacking program. (See next section.)

Volatility and Convergence

Many speculators (called "carry hogs") are attracted by "positive carry" instruments. Typically, these instruments will exhibit a skew behavior with a strong volatility in the event of a sell-off. Often the holder's premium is only a compensation for the holding risks.

Convergence and Biased Assets

There was a corny theory on Wall Street that assets, particularly those of foreign countries that carried a high return were attractive on a risk-adjusted basis. True, these assets were deemed risky, but they presented a better than average risk/return. Returns were deemed to be convergence. Risks were interpreted as their historical volatility. Traders who traded in that manner were in their own eyes sellers of expensive insurance. The method extended to diversification techniques where uncorrelated high-yielding products were bundled in a package that would present what appeared to be abnormal returns.

Needless to say, those traders disappeared. The use of the sacrosanct correlation methods caused the buildup of positions in currency pairs that appeared to be highly correlated but presented a very high carry/convergence. Speculators flocked to funds that did the following trades:

- They bought the Italian lira, which commanded a high interest rate, and borrowed Dmarks, which carried a low interest rate, and were lulled by the protection of the European Monetary System.
- They bought the Scandinavian currencies against the DM for the same reasons. Historical volatility appeared to be low.
- They invested in Mexican fixed income assets comforted by some "pacto" where the Mexican government committed to stabilize the currency within a band.

These assets proved to be heteroskedastic (i.e., had a changing volatility structure: 3-month historical moved from 2% to 50%) and presented a skewed behavior in the bargain. Massive losses ensued, both in September 1992 and in the Mexican debacle of 1995. Except for brief periods, however, the fund managers and traders presented outstanding "Sharpe ratios," a measure that is useless with skew and fat tails.

The traders collected fees and bonuses during their previous years thanks to the optionality of their payoff.

STACKING TECHNIQUES

Stacking is a short-term hedging technique that aims at minimizing the execution of a multiple leg hedge by concentrating on a few liquid instruments that track the position best.

Stacking is best used as a transitory hedge. It is used by cap/floor and swap traders who can thus hedge the residual deltas stemming from a market move (the secondary, gamma-related hedges). It is also prized by market makers unwilling to commit time to the fine tuning of a position they may not carry on the books for long. It is also practiced in basket trading. The risks of stacking increase with time: Relationships and hedge ratios change. The technique of stacking is not meant to be a permanent hedge, only a temporary maneuver around the liquidity of a market. Stacking a position permanently can cause serious troubles. It is to be remembered that Metalgessellshaft, the large German concern that experienced a ten-digit loss from an oil hedge gone awry, was *market neutral* but had stacked all its exposure in the front future.[2]

Example. The Quick-and-Dirty Hedge: A trader needs to rapidly hedge a two year *strip* in the Eurodollar markets, by selling the equivalent of 95 of each of the first expiration (for the purpose of simplification, assume that the hedge ratio is equal in each maturity). Given the volatility of the Eurodollar markets, he may need to do it quickly.

Table 12.2 Simple Stack

	Position	Hedge 1	Net Exposure
Euro1	−95		−95
Euro2	−95		−95
Euro3	−95		−95
Euro4	−95		−95
Euro5	−95	760	665
Euro6	−95		−95
Euro7	−95		−95
Euro8	−95		−95
Unweighted Total	−760	760	0

- *A Market-Neutral Stack.* An easy method would be to compute the amount of total exposure, that is 760 contracts, and then sell them all in one expiration to ensure market neutrality. The trader would pick the fourth or the fifth expiration and sell 760 contracts.

- *A Butterflying Stack.* A stack that would offer some protection for the shifts in the shape in the yield curves.

In Table 12.2, the net exposure corresponds to the risks the trader has on the books after stacking.

Traders need to hedge as an emergency. Working eight orders at the same time can cause confusion, partial fills, and headaches as no broker can concentrate on all the expirations at once. Even when there is a market for a strip as a spread, bid/offer are wider than every individual leg.

The trader needs to hedge the primary risk as rapidly as possible, then fine-tune the resulting mismatch by working spreads (Table 12.3).

The trader could further lower the risks by putting spread orders in the market and waiting for fills to come at more attractive prices than if he executed it as a strip (or less unattractive price, as is usually the case). It could be done the following way: Trader can buy 95 Euro1 against Euro3, buy 95 Euro5 against Euro7, and so on, thus reducing every leg until the position becomes entirely flat.

Example. Minimum Variance Stacking: As some securities do not closely track each other, there are methods of optimizing a hedge. The correlation matrix can be used to search for the best combinations or the most appropriate stack.

In the preceding example, the front Eurodollar future does not track the market very well. The back-month futures, on the other hand, are almost interchangeable.

Table 12.3   Butterfly Stack

	Position	Hedge 2	Net Exposure
Euro1	−95		−95
Euro2	−95		−95
Euro3	−95	380	285
Euro4	−95		−95
Euro5	−95	0	−95
Euro6	−95		−95
Euro7	−95	380	285
Euro8	−95		−95
Unweighted Total	−760	760	0

The computations in Table 12.4 are based on one year of data as of May 15, 1995. ED1 is the perpetual front-month Eurodollar contract, ED2 the perpetual second, and so on.

Volatility is the annualized standard deviation based on daily log-returns.

A single stack, as shown in Table 12.6, reduces the position to 28% of the initial risks.

A butterfly stack (Table 12.7) reduces the risks to 14% of the initial position.

A stack taking advantage of the full power of the correlation between periods reduced the risks to 5% of the initial position with three trades only: The trader bought 95 ED1, 285 ED3, and 380 ED4. (See Table 12.8.) Eliminating the first month, as it does not correlate to the rest and does not have a similar variance, corresponds to the bulk of the reduction. Because

Table 12.4   Eurodollar Correlation Matrix*

	ED1	ED2	ED3	ED4	ED5	ED6	ED7	ED8
ED1	1.00	0.90	0.84	0.78	0.76	0.74	0.72	0.70
ED2	0.90	1.00	0.97	0.93	0.90	0.88	0.86	0.84
ED3	0.84	0.97	1.00	0.97	0.96	0.94	0.92	0.90
ED4	0.78	0.93	0.97	1.00	0.98	0.97	0.95	0.94
ED5	0.76	0.90	0.96	0.98	1.00	0.99	0.98	0.97
ED6	0.74	0.88	0.94	0.97	0.99	1.00	0.99	0.99
ED7	0.72	0.86	0.92	0.95	0.98	0.99	1.00	1.00
ED8	0.70	0.84	0.904	0.94	0.97	0.99	1.00	1.00
Vol%	10.96	15.90	18.50	18.90	18.23	17.10	16.00	15.30

*Eurodeposit's correlation matrices show the same general pattern. Eurolira, Euroyen, Short Sterling, PIBOR, and so on, show the same high correlation in the back more and higher relative independence of the front contract.

Table 12.5   Initial Position

Contract	Standard Deviation (%)	Net Exposure
ED1	10.96	−95
ED2	15.88	−95
ED3	18.50	−95
ED4	18.85	−95
ED5	18.23	−95
ED6	17.13	−95
ED7	16.16	−95
ED8	15.32	−95
		NET VAR(000)*
		112.99

*NET value at risk is defined as the expected profit or loss for 1 standard deviation in the market. The formula for its computation is provided in Module E.

we found the combination that minimized the variance (to the close-to-optimal level), such method is called *minimum variance stacking*.

Other Stacking Applications

- *Basket Trading.* When trading the SP500 cash-future arbitrage, *program traders* can create sub-portfolios of liquid instruments to concentrate their hedges. Hedging a short future with all of the 500 stocks will not be feasible immediately. It may not be necessary given the

Table 12.6   Single Stack

	Vol. (%)	Pos (Mil)
ED1	10.96	−95
ED2	15.88	−95
ED3	18.50	−95
ED4	18.85	−95
ED5	18.23	665
ED6	17.13	−95
ED7	16.16	−95
ED8	15.32	−95
		NET VAR(000)
		32.16

Table 12.7 Butterfly Stack

	Vol (%)	Pos (Mil)
ED1	10.96	−95
ED2	15.88	−95
ED3	18.50	283
ED4	18.85	−95
ED5	18.23	−95
ED6	17.13	−95
ED7	16.16	288
ED8	15.32	−95
		NET
		VAR(000)
		17.76

Table 12.8 The "Smart Stack"

	Vol (%)	Pos (Mil)
ED1	10.96	0
ED2	15.88	−95
ED3	18.50	190
ED4	18.85	−95
ED5	18.23	−95
ED6	17.13	−95
ED7	16.16	285
ED8	15.32	−95
		0
		NET
		VAR(000)
		7.36

speed with which index arbitrageurs reverse their basket position. They identify beforehand a number of liquid stocks and stack their position in a subbasket. In a trending bull market, as basket traders find themselves chronically short the future, they can perform "pairs trading" to reduce the risks.

- *Index Replication.* Traders short USD-ECU rapidly replicate the position by stacking USD-DM (United States dollar against the Deutsche Mark). They will later cross the position from the USD-DEM into other components by hedging the less volatile crosses such as DEM-Drachma, DEM-Guilder, DEM-FRF (French Franc).

Chapter *13*

Some Wrinkles of Option Markets

Sell [volatility] on Thursday and buy on Friday.
An old option proverb (about volatility selling prior to a weekend)

Expiration Pin Risks

■ The **expiration pin risk** is the expiration variance for an options position. It results from the absence of timely information about the outcome of the option assignment lottery.

There is a lag between the close of an option market and the notification to the parties short options about whether or not they were assigned. The lag is necessary for processing reasons, but when the option is too close to the money, there could be a great deal of uncertainty about the outcome. The pin prolongs the uncertainty and thus the life of the option, but sometimes creates a contingent claim that is not rewarded for.

> *Risk Management Rule:* Put/Call parity does not hold for non-cash-settled listed options (both European and American).

The expiration pin risk could be significant when the operator is involved in a conversion or a reversal. The notification of the exercises is due at least 24 hours before the answer about the results of the assignment process.

Example: A market on a listed exchange is closing at 100 exactly. The trader is short the 100 calls, long 100 puts and long the underlying future—what a text book would call a perfect hedge (the so-called conversion). The trader does not know whether to exercise or not. Should he exercise all his puts and deliver the futures, he would hope that the calls get entirely abandoned. Should he abandon the puts, he would wish to see all his calls exercised so he can deliver his futures. The party on the other side will be in the same quandary.

What makes matters even more complicated is that a closing price on a future is not a real indication as to where the market will be at the times of exercise. The future closing does not usually terminate the option: There is a gap of a few hours in which information can still hit the markets with operators guessing the general effect of such information without more precision.

In the preceding example, assume that the future closes at 101 but that after the close news of a government scandal hits the market. The operator may wonder what to do with the 100 puts, officially out-of-the-money. He knows with some certainty that the market would be lower if it were open to trade. His risks are that he may abandon the puts and not be assigned on the calls with the market opening markedly lower. The other risks are that he may exercise the puts and still be assigned on his calls, with the market unchanged if the news is subsequently denied after the deadline. Often some of the counterparties with a large open interest can manipulate the markets and turn the uncertainty in their favor, as when they become in possession of a large sell order and decide to exercise options deemed out-of-the-money.

Some solutions have been offered by exchanges to reduce pin risks, none of them satisfactory. One of them is to allow conversion-reversals to be netted provided one can find a counterparty that has exactly opposite sides.

The only markets where a conversion or a reversal is a pure arbitrage is where the underlying is a cash-settled future that expires at the same time as the option. Examples: Eurodollars, Euromarks, Pibor (the quarterly options), SP500 (quarterly[1]).

Warning: Traders, like poets, often give the same designation to two different items. "Pin risk" is also used to refer to the P/L swing at the barrier for a portfolio containing barrier options.

STICKY STRIKES

■ **Sticky strikes** are over-the-counter or listed strikes in which the buildup of a large open interest alters the behavior of the market around the strike price near expiration.

Sticky strikes are usually magnified by the concentration of the long or short open interest in the hands of one or more parties that do not delta hedge. The pressure on the underlying occurs because the option traders' behavior will diverge from that of the customer.

For example, if a large coverered writer is short the SP100 450 calls, option traders burdened with long gamma will tend to buy and sell around the strike, creating to their detriment some stability around their worst-case-scenario price. There will be bids underneath the strike and offers above. Meanwhile, the party short the largest portion remains indifferent to the market being only interested in the terminal state of in-the-moneyness or out-of-the-moneyness.

The concentration in the hands of a nondelta hedger will cause such stickiness. As expiration nears, locals will need to buy all their deltas below and sell all of them above and the underlying will tend to stick around the strike until some fresh supply or demand pushes it away. If the same open interest were distributed in the hands of market makers, the stickiness would be greatly reduced as there would be two-way orders by long matching short gamma.

Typically when such a strike is reached on expiration day (and there are high odds of having a strike crossed), it acts as an absorbing state for the market. There will be large sellers above it if approached from below and large buyers underneath it if approached from above.

These conditions where the option's open interest determines the path of the underlying are starting to emerge as many customers are picking derivatives in place of the primary securities. Warrant traders are most subjected to that effect as the ratio of secondary delta hedgers to total traders there is greatest.

Note: Cash traders complain that it is often the case of the tail wagging the dog. Very little research has been done to ascertain the impact of expirations on the behavior of the spot.

There is a saying in currency options markets, where daily expirations tend to affect the behavior of the spot, that one always has to gain from selling a cheap overnight option or buying an expensive one. When overnight options are cheap, the market will be stabilized by the traders sucked into it. The market at 10:00 A.M. New York will converge to the strike should spot be in the vicinity. Conversely, the market will whip when options are expensive.

Risk Management Rule: When dynamic hedgers are long a strike (and consequently, static hedgers short it) the strike will be sticky. It will whip otherwise.

MARKET BARRIERS

■ A **market barrier** is a level that is supposed to cause some stickiness because of institutional constraints.[2]

Market barriers should not be confused with barrier options. The following are examples of market barriers:

- A currency band where central banks limit the market from trading through some level by intervention.

- A floor for the price of an agricultural commodity guaranteed by the government.

Market limits that, when reached, cause the exchange to shut down represent a weaker form of market barrier.

A Currency Band: Is It a Barrier?

Some economists consider that market barriers should cause the volatility to be dampened in their proximity. Somehow the claim in the literature that a target zone is heteroskedastic proved to be true, but exactly in reverse.[3]

Figure 13.1 shows the "rubber trees" shrinking as the market comes close to the barrier. Obviously, a market at, say, 20 pips from a limit cannot go up more than that. To compensate for that fact (assuming constant skew), it should be limited to a move down by 20 pips, and so on. The volatility drops as one comes close to the barrier, and the asset starts "pasting" around it.

A more complex analysis would increase the skew, by saying that the market on the way down would be able to drop by more than 20 cents but that the probability attached to it should be low to satisfy the following "fair" game (assuming for simplification that interest rates are negligible):

$$pu = (1 - p)d$$

with p the probability for the market to go up, u the size of the up-move, $(1 - p)$ the probability for the market to go down and d the size of the down-move.

Traders do not buy the argument: The volatility of the forward should increase dramatically as one comes close to the band. Every time the markets approach such a band, some warfare erupts between speculators and central banks. In addition, as by some phenomenon physicists call *hysteresis,* the markets have a tendency to snap through the barrier with a vengeance.

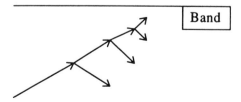

Figure 13.1   The rubber tree around the band.

The Absent Barrier

Practitioners discovered (at great expense) that the reflecting/absorbing barriers set as boundaries in the analysis of currency bands turned out to be optical illusions. Before the explosion of the European Rate Mechanism, there was a great deal of literature on the topic.

Somehow when a currency reaches a band in the spot, which is the only observable portion of the trading, the forward continues to trade unfettered. What appears to be extreme interest rate volatility is nothing but the volatility of the currency being translated in interest rate terms.

Spot is not necessarily what is visible on the screen. Spot for delivery in a week is a sum of spot + forward "points," themselves function of the interest rate differential. The trader buys or sells spot and then buys or sell the forward points. There is no real market for nonsynthetic forward outright. The method of calculation is as follows:

$$S = F \times e^{(r2 - r1)t}$$

S is the spot, F the forward.

If one freezes S, F will continue trading. For S to remain constant, $(r2 - r1)$ will adjust. Generally, it is the currency's interest rate, here $r2$ that will take the brunt of the adjustment.[4]

The impact on an option's position is that a European option, or one that is not for cash delivery, will trade off the forward, totally unconcerned with spot. Notice that 99% of vanilla currency options are European.[5] Such an option will go through the barrier like a knife in warm butter. Its price will adjust to the final F. In pricing these instruments, it is therefore necessary to eliminate the idea of a barrier.

Risk Management Rule: A currency band, even when fully enforced, does not represent a flawless barrier for a European option unless interest rates for both elements of the pair are banded as well.

WHAT FLAT MEANS

A flat position is a position that does not present any market risk. For cash and short-term products, a flat position is a matched position. A derivatives position is presented as flat only vis-à-vis a particular mathematical partial derivative. One could be flat delta (i.e., the first derivative function of spot) but not gamma or vega. Flat gamma is local and one could be exposed to the

Option Wizard: An EMS War Story

A trader who survived the EMS (European Monetary System) breakup of 1992 recounts the following. In the events leading up to the turmoil of September 1992, he had to execute a large option order in sterling versus German marks for a customer. He needed to buy quantities of out-of-the-money puts on the sterling, calls on the mark, struck 10% outside the official government band. The customer was a conspiracy theorist fund manager who believed in the imminent breakup of the monetary order. He belonged to the small coterie of traders who took on the Bank of England later that month.

The trader, being risk averse, decided to do what most of his headache-free peers do: call a large market maker, add on a margin, and earn the difference. He called two of the largest option dealers in the world asking for their selling price and received the following answers:

1. W., based in the United States, and a former CME pit trader, told him that they were reluctant to show a price "because the strike is outside the band" and the options were "too risky." They would accommodate him if necessary, but at very expensive implied volatility and only for a moderate amount.

2. B., based in Europe, literally laughed at him. "But Zey are outside the band, if I am not mistaken," he was told. "How many do you vant? I can sell you all you need. You should give your money to charity instead."

W. was a former pit trader surrounded by former pit traders. He is now the head of worldwide foreign exchange for a large bank. The second dealer, B., was a graduate of a prestigious European school of engineering. He is now back to engineering and other precise activities after his desk was decimated by disastrous losses in September 1992. After all, in the physical world, barriers are barriers, bridges are bridges, and horses are horses.

---

third derivative of the security price to spot, usually the indicator of the risk reversal, commonly called DdeltaDspot, and so on.

The need to understand the relativity of the flat concept needs to be stressed for noninitiated managers of derivatives traders, or users of the product who, unable to exactly offset a position for lack of liquidity, start running trades to reduce the risk. Running trades against a book to offset a Greek (i.e., a first-order or second-order partial derivative) causes complications for the non-market maker.

Path-dependent and barrier options are never flat with respect to partial derivatives for long. The pin risk for barriers makes them only hedgeable dynamically. Binary options are never flat.

Primary and Secondary Exposures

A primary exposure for an option trader is one that is caused by the initial trade. A market maker selling a cap has as an initial exposure the delta equivalents in the FRAs or Eurodollar futures. A foreign exchange option trader has to hedge both his initial delta and forward exposure.

A secondary exposure is the one that results from changes in one or more parameters that determine the price of the derivative. It can come from the convexity of the book with respect to volatility or the underlying. The trader may have to fight the market if he is long gamma and would have to chase the market otherwise. He may have to adjust the volatility exposure as the curve shifts and causes both the shorts and the longs to be weighted again.

Secondary exposures can also stem from the *bleed,* the overnight changes in the deltas, gammas, rho1, and rho2.

Chapter 14

Bucketing and Topography

Never hire a very well dressed option trader.

T.G.

This chapter will cover common methods of risk management as used by institutions. They tie in with some of the analyses discussed in Chapter 9 on vega. These should be mandatory reading for persons who understand options but have never examined the risks of a book taken as a whole.

STATIC STRAIGHT BUCKETING

■ **Bucketing** represents the breaking down of the risks of the position with respect to a particular parameter in time intervals. Operators thus obtain the delta buckets, vega buckets, gamma buckets, and so on.

It is a static risk management method because the markets are assumed to be constant. No convexity truly shows; Vega and rho, for example, can vary in some combination of instruments with the asset level or, sometimes, may increase or decrease as the parameter changes. The effect is assumed to be beastly with compound, barrier, and other exotic options.

It can already be detected that the bucketing does not show higher moments of the sensitivity of the portfolio to the asset price.

■ **Straight bucketing** is a simple method that shows the exposure between cash and the expiration time t. It is only applicable to products that have a known and certain expiration date and start immediately.

Example. A Bucketing Method for a European Option: Start with a currency position in GBP-USD (Great Britain pound against the United States dollar).

Spot is 1.6050.

The trader buys a 6-month call (183 days) in the amount of GBP 100 mil. The price is 4.578% and the trader pays $4,578,000 for it. Its hedge is 50 deltas. The following parameters hold:

183-day USD rate 5.8438% (basis 360 days)

GBP rate 6.915% (basis 360 days)

$$\text{The forward} = \text{Spot} \times \frac{[1 + (183/360 \times .058438)]}{[1 + (183/360 \times .06915)]} = 1.5973$$

Table 14.1 shows deltas, gammas, vegas, Rho1, and Rho2 (all in USD). All measures are unweighted. The bucketing is called "straight" because the exposure in the 6-month corresponds to an exposure starting at time 0 and ending in 6 months. It is easy to see that the delta as shown in Table 14.1 corresponds to the present value of the forward delta. Thus the spot delta is equal (in 000) to (82656) / [1 + (1.83/360 × .06915)] = (79850).

All the other elements are straightforward.

The **gamma** of GBP 8,355,000 means that the position should increase by such amount should the market rally 1% and decrease likewise in a sell-off. This is an approximation: The position will not actually pick up such an amount in a rally owing to the third derivative (it is now at maximum gamma being at-the-money).

The **vega** is straightforward: $438,000 for a rise of 1 volatility percentage point.

The **rho** domestic corresponds to the sensitivity of the option to a change of 100 basis points in the U.S. rates. The Rho2 foreign corresponds to the same with the foreign rate. However, the Rho1 is lower because it also is sensitive to the discounting of the premium the other way. The methods for calculating rho1 and rho2 are as follows:

- *Foreign Rho2.* The procedure to obtain rho2 is to multiply the delta by the rate and interpolate for 183 days. It is (183/360) × 82656 × 100 bp = $420,168. The present value of that using the U.S. rate is 408,000 (assuming no convexity).

- *Domestic Rho1.* It is the same number minus the exposure to the financing of the premium. The premium was $4.57M. The effect of the

Table 14.1 Buckets

(000)	All	1w	1m	2m	3m	6m	9m	1y	2y	5y+
Delta	(79850)					(82656)				
Gamma	8355					8355				
Vega	438					438				
Rho1	385					385				
Rho2	(408)					(408)				

rise of the U.S. rates would be to cost him more in the daily financing of his premium, by $4.57 \times 183/360 = \$23,200$. Roughly, the net Rho1 is $408,000 - 23,200 = 384,800$.

Note: The effect of convexity over this position would be to lower the negative P/L stemming from a rise in foreign rates and increase the positive P/L stemming from a drop, and vice versa for domestic rates.

American and Path-Dependent Options

The bucketing method works in general better for European options because the buckets are only partially unstable. They could be increased or decreased (through the gain or loss of gamma or vega when the option moves in on out of the money), but it is not possible for the exposure of one particular option to change buckets.

With American and path-dependent options, the exact duration of the exposure is uncertain. This makes the bucketing method often inappropriate. A barrier that increases in probability of becoming extinguished will move in vega, gamma, and Greeks closer to the short-term buckets. Likewise when the market moves away from the strike, American and path-dependent options start resembling a European option and would have an exposure closer to the nominal maturity.

Volatility shifts would also exert the same effect on the barrier maturity. A higher volatility shortens the duration of a barrier knock-out option. Paradoxically, it would lengthen that of an American option.

Some options like the knock-in structures or deferred strike options are impossible to fit in a straight bucket because their exposure starts at one point and ends at another, therefore making them dependent on a forward-forward bucket. They depend more on events that take place during some time segments than in others. Worse, some structures (like barriers) are calendar spreads in disguise. The trader can be seriously misled by the net bucket exposure disclosed by the straight system.

The only way to see the risks of these instruments is to engage in dynamic bucketing, which requires the trader to review the position at various states of the underlying at volatilities and try to match the risks accordingly.

Advanced Topic: The Forward or "Forward-Forward" Bucket

Although rarely implemented, owing to the computational complications, the need to see a forward-forward option risk appears to be essential with path-dependent options, options on products such as knock-in options, and non-time-homogeneous structures such as variable bets. The building of such a bucketing system obsessed the author for a long time, until the most recent accretions in numerical techniques.

Table 14.2   A Forward-Forward Bucket

(000)	0–1w	1w–1m	1m–2m	2m–3m	3m–6m
Delta	82	82	82	82	82
Gamma	8	8	8	8	8
Vega	.4	.4	.4	.4	.4
Rho1	.4	.4	.4	.4	.4
Rho2	(.4)	(.4)	(.4)	(.4)	(.4)

The forward-forward bucketing would appear as shown in Table 14.2.

The computer's method for filling the cells is quite complicated when the portfolio includes path-dependent options. As there are no analytical methods for that, it needs to move the cells in such a way as to leave the parameters affecting the other parts constant.

The forward-forward bucketing needs to be constructed by breaking up the exposures in distinct volatility periods and running the following simulation on the total position:

- Volatility is raised for one particular bucket but not others. The binomial tree is run with the new higher volatility between the nodes for that period but is maintained constant for other periods. The difference in price stemming from that would be the vega.

- If the portfolio consisted only of European options, it could be assumed that the volatility does not depend on the location of the shock but on the general effect over the entire portfolio. Every bucket would therefore share an equal portion of the total gamma.

- The vega and the gamma will be bucket dependent for non-European instruments.

This method is reviewed extensively in Chapter 9.

TOPOGRAPHY

■ **Position Topography** for an options book is a risk management method that displays the distribution of the exposures of the portfolio across time and possible asset prices.

- There are two kind of topography reports: strike (or static) topography and gamma (or dynamic) topography.

- Topography has considerable advantages as it allows for transcending the Greeks as shown in Table 14.3.

Table 14.3 Old Days Strike Topography

Strike	March P	March C	June P	June C
65	26			
70	−20			
75	−20			
80	21			
85	5	1		
90	11	2		
95	−5	−19	11	−2
100	−72	−71		
105	2	70		
110	1	23		11
115		−9		
120				
125				

Strike Topography (or Static Topography)

■ **Static Topography** is a two-dimensional map of the position displaying the distribution of the exposure in face value horizontally (across expirations) and vertically (across strikes).

When option trading was still at a primitive state and option traders were dealing with only one or, at the most, two expirations, they used to maintain their open positions on a card provided by the clearing house so they could rapidly see what they had in their inventory. The clearing houses handed out the cards without charge. Table 14.3 depicts a sample card.

The trader could thus examine the position beyond the deltas and gammas and trade his position instead of trading his Greeks. Such a method, indeed, has an admirable tutorial value as it forces the trader to learn the intricacies of option trading without having recourse to pseudo-mathematical methods like the Greek reports. Instead of waking up at night with cold sweats and shouting the abstract, "I do not enjoy my being short 22.23 gammas and 71 weighted vegas," the trader would phrase his worries about the position in more precise terms such as, "I am short so many of the 105 calls that I need serious protection."

Modern book runners, however, do not have such luxury. As there are no set expiration dates and no set strikes, the card in Table 14.2 would need a few thousand lines and columns to reflect the topography of a large over-the-counter portfolio. In addition, it does not allow for any option structure beyond the vanilla.

So over-the-counter books need a design that allows traders to bundle the exposures in time and space points and examine their concentration risks. The strike topography is generally designed as shown in Table 14.4.

The over-the-counter strike topography displays the face value exposure per bidimensional bucket. The report shows horizontally (strike-wise) the net of the face value exposures between midpoints on the grid and vertically (time periods) the net of face value between points. So the 1W/100 bucket displays the net of all the trades between two days and one week and every option struck between 99 and 101.

The strike topography should deliberately exclude most nonvanilla options, which can be remedied in a separate report. American options, in addition should be handled with care, because their nominal expiration is not exactly the expected one. Only soft American instruments should be included on the matrix. A more thorough treatment of American options corresponds to shifting their nominal maturity into the "omega" or real time to expiration.

An application of the topography method is the method of squares, explained in Chapter 9.

Adding Correlated Instruments. It is possible to incorporate more than one similar commodity by summing them up, that is assuming 100% correlation. Such a method aims only at examining the strike concentration or the origin of gammas and vegas and can thus simplify without deluding the trader about his position. For example, if one thinks that it would be necessary to examine the risks of the French franc and the German mark in one report for topography purposes only, then all the USD-FRF strikes would be converted into USD-DEM. The real improvement, however,

Table 14.4 Over-the-Counter Strike Topography

Spot	80−	85	90	93	96	98	100	102	104	107	110	115	120+
1d	−83	86	−12	−33	−41	−10	−9	90	97	16	−49	56	15
2d	47	9	18	68	−15	−73	20	54	13	−54	−67	−24	−4
1w	−33	66	−18	−25	45	66	−35	50	−71	18	27	23	−58
2w	−38	34	12	44	55	54	−53	−41	47	64	−28	−9	37
1m	35	−17	−55	34	3	52	43	7	−8	−15	30	−27	13
2m	12	45	2	−25	33	38	−20	15	5	−21	1	−26	−34
3m	−14	−27	21	13	−28	−5	22	−6	−35	13	−24	39	6
6m	−9	−11	1	23	20	−28	28	6	−11	−29	29	−15	−18
9m	−2	−14	−1	8	−6	−6	0	−17	5	1	3	1	3
1y	6	−7	−6	2	1	−3	−2	5	9	1	10	9	5
2y	2	5	−2	4	−1	2	4	−1	−2	5	−2	−4	3
3y	−4	3	1	0	−5	−2	0	−2	−3	−5	3	−4	5
5y+	−1	4	0	1	−5	−4	0	4	−2	−4	−5	−4	−2

would come from the hardly practicable three-dimensional map that allows for the slopes of the correlation.

Scaled Strike Topography.   Since the difference between strikes that are close to the money is more meaningful for short-term options than for back-month structures, it is necessary to scale. For all intents and purposes the "gap" between the 100 and the 101 strikes is insignificant for a 5-year option and very annoying for an overnight structure. The method as shown in Table 14.5 used to account for the risk difference is the scaling method that, in place of strikes, examines standard deviations. At 15.7 volatility, a 1 standard deviation difference between strikes is 1 percentage point, that is, between 100 and 101. In one year, it is the square root of 252 (252 days of business), namely 15.7. So the equivalent to an overnight gap of 1 point is the one-year gap of 15.7 points. Hence, assuming the spot traded at 100 (and no drift), the report would put in the same column the 101 overnight strike and the 115.7 one-year strike.

Dynamic Topography (Local Volatility Exposure)

Dynamic topography is a potent method of analysis as it can reveal the stability of a position through time. It consists in keeping the position constant and running simulation one day ahead, two days ahead, one week ahead, and so on, and disclosing the map of the resulting Greeks.

The needs for the dynamic topography are accentuated in an environment where the positions change rapidly and frequently. A conventional gamma or vega matrix can obscure the real position if strong changes take place through time. For example, if the position is long one-week options and short two-week options in large quantities, the position report would mask the real issues, which is the risk one week from today for one entire week.

Computation Technique.   The report is not concerned with the deltas but simply with the gammas. The operator starts by running today's gammas for different asset price levels. Then he would block the options expiring on the following day and run the gammas one day hence for all of these levels, and so on. Moving the calendar one day hence means running the global position as if the calendar date was one day forward.

Table 14.5   Scaled Strike Topography

Standard Deviations	−4	−3	−2	−1.5	−1	−.5	0	.5	1	1.5	2	3	4
1d							100	−150	50				
2d													

The following report would not perform very well for exotic options since their path dependency makes every report conditional. In other words, the exposure on a 100 call 103 knock-out depends on whether or not the market traded through 103 the previous day.

The map shown in Table 14.6 would result. It may appear similar to the previous ones but is truly a different animal, as it eliminates the positions that expire as time goes by.

The preceding topography technique could be further improved with the use of correlations. The operator would need to run the reports using the possible changes through time of the correlations between markets.

Shortcomings. There is no known way to derive from the dynamic topography the exposures to path-dependent options. A trader might look at the gamma of the book should the market reach 102 in one month. Whatever number he looked at would not be accurate if the position included knock-out options. Say that he had a structure that knocked out at 104.5. Because the market ended at 102 does not necessarily mean that it did not transit through 104.5, in which case the gamma exposure would be markedly different. The same applies to a lookback: A pulldown from a high level would result in a lower gamma than a situation where the market trades at its extremum (its maximum or minimum).

The complications of path dependence are that many more possible paths are available than end points and there is no rapid way to visualize the position taking those into account.

Table 14.6   Gamma Topography (Dynamic)

Spot	80−	85	90	93	96	98	100	102	104	107	110	115	120+
1d	−83	86	−12	−33	−41	−10	−9	90	97	16	−49	56	15
2d	47	9	18	68	−15	−73	20	54	13	−54	−67	−24	−4
1w	−33	66	−18	−25	45	66	−35	50	−71	18	27	23	−58
2w	−38	34	12	44	55	54	−53	−41	47	64	−28	−9	37
1m	35	−17	−55	34	3	52	43	7	−8	−15	30	−27	13
2m	12	45	2	−25	33	38	−20	15	5	−21	1	−26	−34
3m	−14	−27	21	13	−28	−5	22	−6	−35	13	−24	39	6
6m	−9	−11	1	23	20	−28	28	6	−11	−29	29	−15	−18
9m	−2	−14	−1	8	−6	−6	0	−17	5	1	3	1	3
1y	6	−7	−6	2	1	−3	−2	5	9	1	10	9	5
2y	2	5	−2	4	−1	2	4	−1	−2	5	−2	−4	3
3y	−4	3	1	0	−5	−2	0	−2	−3	−5	3	−4	5
5y+	−1	4	0	1	−5	−4	0	4	−2	−4	−5	−4	−2

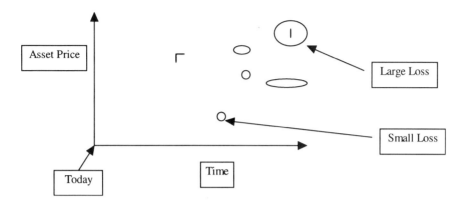

Figure 14.1   Payoff topography.

Barrier Payoff Topography

A payoff topography is a map showing where a large sum of money could be lost on a "pin," a worst-case scenario for a bet option or a reverse knock-out (see Chapters 17–20). Somehow, the pin risks, which can be massive, do not show far in advance. Moreover, no true expiration date is attached to the pin, which makes the expected stopping time a fuzzy function of volatility, rates, and so on.

There is, however, the need to see the worst-case scenario. This disclosure is greatly simplified because the worst possible case for a barrier lies on the strike at expiration. So it would suffice to establish the map of the nominal maturity of the payoffs to prevent the trader from adding to a negative "zone." Figure 14.1 shows such a map.

Chapter *15*

Beware the Distribution

I prefer the judgment of a 55-year old trader to that of a 25-year old mathematician.

Alan Greenspan

■ Take one maturity and measure the implied volatility differential between the at-the-money options and the out-of-the-money "wings" priced off the Black-Scholes model. The **tails** will represent the general pricing of the wings while the implied **skew** will measure the degree of asymmetry of the distribution.

This notion has already been discussed relative to the volatility surface. This chapter focuses on the reasons for the existence of the tails and the skew.

Risk Management Rule: Option traders are likely to get the "bad" distribution through their market making. Somehow, the anxiety of markets gets reflected in their position. Economists call this phenomenon *adverse selection.*

THE TAILS

While the "skew" is an evasive issue to most traders, the "tails" are easily explained. The tails are the volatility of the out-of-the-money options relative to those at the money using the conventional Black-Scholes formula.

Random Volatility

The prime reason for the higher price of in-the-money and out-of-the-money options than the Black-Scholes value, is the phenomenon traders call the "volatility of volatility," or vvol. It is related to the fourth moment, or kurtosis.[1] There are other related reasons, like the convexity of the vega. In the old days, however, traders used to disbelieve the phenomenon and attribute the inflated prices of out-of-the-money options to the "lottery effect," which meant that investors were ready to spend small sums to get a large payoff and that such attraction of the large payoff would blind them to real value. The lottery effect, in the long run, seemed to have favored the investors owing to the convexity for which they paid so little.

The following simple explanation of option pricing uses an adaptation of the Black-Scholes-Merton formula for a variable volatility inspired from the Hull and White model.[2]

Assume that volatility follows a process like that of the asset itself, without any drift. This is a simplifying method aimed at assessing the damage from variable volatility rather than hoping to model volatility itself. Most techniques of volatility modeling have, at the time of writing, led to little if any convincing results. The model is further explained in Module G.

Table 15.1 shows the impact of actual volatility swings on a 90-day at-the-money option priced at 15.7% volatility. Three cases are considered. Case 1, with vvol = 0.25, means that volatility changes on average about 0.16 per day (i.e., between 15.7 and 15.86), randomly, just like the asset itself. Case 2, with vvol = 0.5, means that volatility changes twice as much. Vvol = 0 corresponds to the conventional Black-Scholes case, in which volatility remains constant and the entire sample is drawn from the same volatility of 15.7%.

Each case leads to different option prices. It is easily seen that an at-the-money option is entirely unaffected by volatility shifts, and that out-of-the-money options benefit the most from it. The last three columns show the Black-Scholes implied volatility using the conventional method of practitioners, which shifts from a particular price to the implied volatility equivalent. The trader can thus confirm that the Black-Scholes values are identical to the vvol = 0 case.

The stochastic volatility model used for Figure 15.1 gives the results of fat tails in proportion to the volatility of volatility. Since the volatility of volatility is not known and can hardly be estimated, the reader should retain from the exercise a set of rules rather than a modeling framework.

The results show an increase in values where there is convexity to volatility (i.e., away from the money). At-the-money options imperceptibly lose in volatility owing to their minuscule concavity (a call is capped at the price of the asset).

If the trader were to include correlation in the model between asset price (or its changes) and volatility (or its changes), he would have significant results: The smile would tilt left or right, with the following characteristics:

> The smile would not change in its convex shape but would pivot to accommodate asymmetry between upside and downside. A negative correlation between $\Delta S/S$ (changes in asset) and $\Delta\sigma/\sigma$ (changes in volatility) would result in upside option prices that are cheaper than downside strikes and

Table 15.1   The Impact of Volatility of Volatility

Strike	Case 1 vvol 0.25	Case 2 vvol 0.5	Case 3 vvol 0	Delta (Black-Scholes-Merton)	Implied Using Black-Scholes-Merton 1	2	3
86	0.13	0.26	0.08	0.03	17.3	20.1	15.0
87	0.17	0.31	0.11	0.04	17.1	19.7	15.7
88	0.22	0.38	0.16	0.05	16.9	19.2	15.7
89	0.29	0.45	0.23	0.07	16.7	18.8	15.7
90	0.37	0.53	0.31	0.09	16.6	18.4	15.7
91	0.48	0.64	0.42	0.12	16.5	18.0	15.7
92	0.61	0.76	0.56	0.15	16.3	17.6	15.7
93	0.78	0.91	0.73	0.19	16.2	17.3	15.7
94	0.98	1.09	0.93	0.23	16.1	16.9	15.7
95	1.21	1.31	1.19	0.27	16.0	16.6	15.7
96	1.50	1.56	1.47	0.31	15.9	16.3	15.7
97	1.83	1.87	1.82	0.36	15.9	16.1	15.7
98	2.21	2.23	2.20	0.41	15.8	15.9	15.7
99	2.64	2.65	2.64	0.46	15.8	15.8	15.7
100	3.13	3.13	3.13	0.52	15.8	15.8	15.7
101	2.67	2.68	2.67	0.57	15.8	15.9	15.7
102	2.27	2.29	2.27	0.62	15.8	15.9	15.7
103	1.91	1.95	1.90	0.66	15.9	16.1	15.7
104	1.60	1.67	1.58	0.71	15.9	16.3	15.7
105	1.34	1.43	1.33	0.75	16.0	16.5	15.7
106	1.11	1.23	1.07	0.78	16.1	16.8	15.7
107	0.92	1.06	0.88	0.82	16.2	17.1	15.7
108	0.76	0.92	0.70	0.85	16.2	17.4	15.7
109	0.63	0.79	0.57	0.87	16.4	17.7	15.7
110	0.52	0.69	0.46	0.90	16.5	18.0	15.7
111	0.42	0.60	0.35	0.92	16.6	18.4	15.7
112	0.35	0.53	0.28	0.93	16.7	18.7	15.7
113	0.28	0.46	0.21	0.95	16.8	19.0	15.7
114	0.23	0.41	0.16	0.96	17.0	19.3	15.7
115	0.19	0.36	0.13	0.97	17.1	19.7	15.7
116	0.16	0.32	0.09	0.97	17.2	20.0	15.7
117	0.13	0.28	0.07	0.98	17.4	20.3	15.7
118	0.10	0.25	0.05	0.98	17.5	20.6	15.7
119	0.08	0.22	0.04	0.99	17.7	21.0	15.7
120	0.07	0.20	0.03	0.99	17.8	21.3	15.7

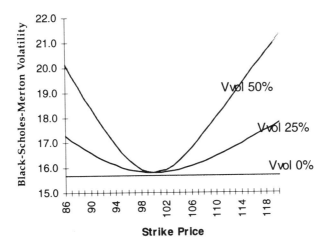

Figure 15.1   Smile effect, 90-day option, stochastic volatility model.

could explain the skew. A positive correlation between them would lead to positive skew.

Warning: It is difficult to establish a dependence between asset price and volatility. To show the behavior of asset prices in a skewed environment this exercise should be appropriately altered for the following reasons:

1. Asset returns and volatility may be correlated, but in a nonlinear way. Typically, the correlation holds from small moves but may reverse for a large one. A clear example is the SP500 futures: Volatility drops after a small rally but increases after a large one.

2. It is clear to traders who have studied data that the volatility, if anything, is *correlated* (or, more appropriately, *associated*) to the *range* in asset prices, not the asset price or its variation. It is not surprising to see that the behavior is marked by "thresholds." The market drops would not increase volatility if they were to take place within the confines of a known range, particularly after a rally. Such a relationship is not easy to model (in spite of all the ARCH-style attempts).

A frequent question is, Why does a variable volatility cause fat tails?[3]

- The primary explanation is that of likelihood of asset prices conditional on states of volatility. Assume random volatility and random asset prices. It is easy to understand that, conditional on being in the tails, the most likely state is one of high volatility. High volatility can more easily take the market to the tails than a lower one. Thus the tails will have the thickness of the higher volatility.

- The lower volatility is more likely to keep the market in the middle, the "peak." Thus the distribution, when in the middle (i.e., no meaningful changes in the market prices), is more likely to take the shape of a lower volatility.

The concept is even easier to understand graphically. Figure 15.2 shows two distributions, one of which has four times the volatility of the other. The higher volatility distribution has fatter tails than the lower one. The lower volatility distribution has a higher peak than the higher one. It becomes conceivable that in mixing the two distributions, the higher volatility would dominate the tails, the lower one would dominate the body.

Histograms from the Markets

- A **histogram** shows the relative frequency of a certain magnitude of the returns (or more frequently the logarithms of the price changes) during a certain time interval. Typically, a histogram shows daily changes. Frequency is obtained by bucketing the moves and counting the percentage (or total number) of occurrences in every bucket.

Figures 15.3 through 15.6 show the actual distribution of the following assets: the Japanese yen, SP500 and the 30-year U.S. government bond yields, and the Euromark futures. The first three cover 10 years and the last one 3 years. They show the histograms of the frequency of the differences of logs of prices (the returns) plotted against a normal distribution of the same overall volatility. All of the figures display the high peak syndrome.

The astute reader might observe "high peaks" in place of "fat tails." In fact, traders betting against the fat tails typically make bets against the peak: They try to make some profits when nothing happens rather than during extreme moves.

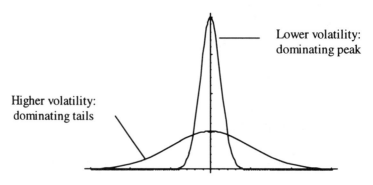

Figure 15.2   Mixing normal distributions.

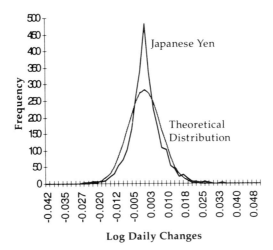

Figure 15.3 Japanese yen, sampling of 2,703 returns from January 1985 to June 1995.

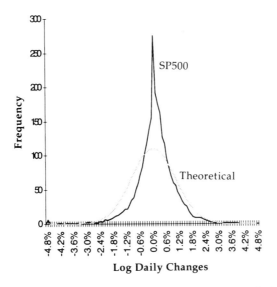

Figure 15.4 Standard & Poor's 500 cash index. The series include all returns from January 1985 to June 1995.

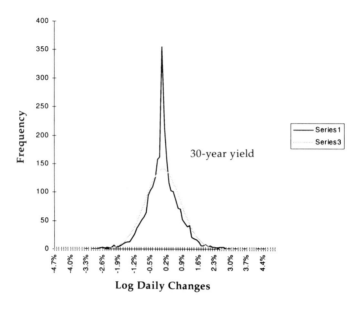

Figure 15.5 U.S. government 30-year yield. Distribution of the natural logarithms of the yields on a perpetual 30-year bond (new issue rolled in), from January 1985 to June 1995.

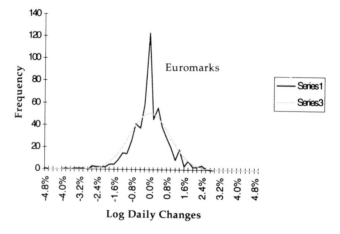

Figure 15.6 EuroMark futures, 1992–1995. The constant first contract was used.

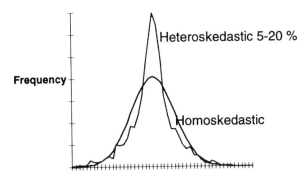

Figure 15.7   Changing volatility regimes histogram.

Example. A Tailor-Made fat-Tailed Distribution: For amusement (on a summer day that qualifies as "high peak"), the author conceived the following distribution: three regimes in the market, each one of which carries a different volatility. The regimes are as follows:

s1: Volatility is 15% (normal market conditions).

s2: Volatility is 5% (holiday mood and summer slumber).

s3: Volatility is 20% (anxiety).

Each regime is equally probable.

The Monte Carlo simulator, sampling between them, produced the histogram shown in Figure 15.7.

THE SKEW AND BIASED ASSETS

■ The **skew** is the assymetry in the distribution. Take a daily move $x_t = \text{Log}(S_t/S_{t-1})$, with σ' its noncentered volatility (assuming mean return of 0 as explained in Chapter 6). The (noncentered) skew will be:

$$\frac{1}{n} \sum_{t=1}^{n} \frac{x_t^3}{\sigma'}$$

which will be positive if there is a positive correlation between x_t and x_t^2 and negative if there is a negative correlation. Intuitively the skew expresses the correlation between the move of a random variable (x_t) and its volatility (x_t^2).

Many traders hear about the Pareto-Levy family of stable distributions. This is a broad class of distributions said to be "stable" because they can be shifted. The trader needs to know no further than that the bell-shaped distribution is but one particular case of this large and unhappy family. A description follows.

The characteristic function of the Pareto-Levy distribution:

$$\text{Log } f(t) = i\delta t - \gamma|t|^{\alpha} (1 + i\beta(t/|t|) \tan(\alpha\pi/2))$$

where i is the imaginary number $\sqrt{-1}$. When $\alpha = 2$, it becomes the Fourier transform of the normal distribution (with also $\beta = 0$, $\gamma = 1$, $\delta = 1$), exp $(-t^2)$.

The function has no second moment (that is no variance) when $\alpha < 2$ and no first moment (that is no mean) for $\alpha < 1$. It means that the function has an infinite variance, an implication that is scary for anyone involved in the markets. Physically, the left and right tail never come close to the origin. No more compact support.

As shown in the following chart, the inverse characteristic function (i.e., the density function stemming from it) would have the following shape: As α goes down from 2 toward 0, the tails get thicker and the convergence of the density toward the zero probability mark gets slower. As α gets smaller, a wider and wider graph is needed to show the distribution. That illustrates the notion of infinite volatility: It is impossible to fit the graph into the confines of a visual frame.[†]

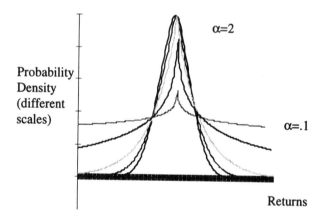

Even scarier: When the distribution has no mean, no peak is visible, but lines go up to the ceiling without ever meeting.

Many *chaos* theorists have complained of the misuse of the Pareto-Levy class of distributions in the common down-market literature.

It is easier for traders to think of fat tails as a result of changing volatility than the product of some blowing-out variance. In fact, Pareto-Levy is the fruit of very high volatility of volatility on a very small volatility.

---

*This option wizard can be skipped at first reading.
[†]Feller II (1971) provides a trick to numerically invert the Fourier transform and derive the density function.

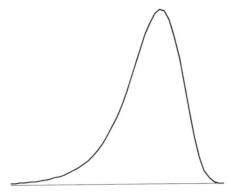

Figure 15.8   A highly skewed distribution.

Figures 15.8 and 15.9 show two different degrees of skewness in the distribution. The skew is not easy to translate into skewed volatility surface. The linear skew measure presented above is too weak a statistic to properly explain the true dependence between volatility and asset prices. There are many cases where a dynamic hedger would make money owning expensive puts and shorting cheap calls in spite of a close to symmetric histogram.

A histogram does not show the path. Suppose that the Syldavian currency initially goes up and down symmetrically by 1%. As it goes down, however, three days in a row the volatility increases. Such increase in volatility is likely to push it down further but can as well bring it back to the origin. The histogram would look almost balanced. In reality, it would show a slightly bulging left tail, but nothing serious enough to be detected. What the histogram shows well is the classical scenario of a market that only goes down by, say, $4 (with 20% probability) and goes up by $1 (with 80% probability). It does not very well show the correlation between asset price and volatility, only the correlation between asset changes and volatility changes.

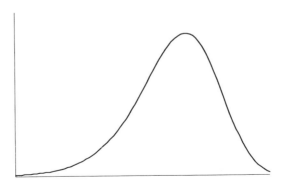

Figure 15.9   A medium skewed distribution.

> ***Risk Management Rule:*** The histogram does not appropriately show the dependence between price **level** and market volatility.

How this dependence is to be translated into the distribution of implied volatility between strike prices is uncertain. The customary method has been to look at the final histogram, derive a probability distribution and try to compare it with that implied by option prices. The trader can generate a density from an option price by taking the second derivative of the option with respect to the strike price. (See Breeden and Liechtenberger, 1978.) As a trader, the author is extremely suspicious of this technique as it ignores the path dependency that arises from changes in volatility. As explained with the greater fool theory (Chapter 3), the behavior of implied volatility is a determining factor in option trading. Out-of-the-money puts therefore become great assets not only because the market might drop violently, but mostly because the behavior of the market at lower levels might benefit their owner. This leads to the following rule:

> ***Risk Management Rule:*** **Path Dependence.** The value of the skew for a dynamic hedger resides more in the behavior of implied volatility along the path leading to a terminal value than in the probability of the asset ending up on such terminal value.

Biased Assets

The old trader's adage, *"Up the escalator, down the chute,"* seems to describe the behavior of a variety of assets.

- **Biased assets** are assets with an asymmetrical distribution, characterized with an increased volatility in the sell-off and, to a lesser extent, a diminished volatility in the rally.

The structure of their market is such that a sell-off causes anxiety while rallies cause euphoria. Such anxiety would cause severe volatility on the way down while euphoria generally leads to orderly markets on the way up. An example that easily comes to mind is the Mexican currency. Table 15.2 presents a simplified world composed of two poles of extreme regimes for biased assets. There are naturally shades in between as well as transitional periods between states.

There are many explanations for biased assets, some of which will be described in the following sections.

Table 15.2   A Simplified Two-Regime World for Biased Assets

Characteristic	Type 1 Regime	Type 2 Regime
Market condition	A severe break in a market following a protracted rally (or a quiet period)	A normal condition where the market offers high returns through high "carry" or positive "trend"
Historical volatility	Increases	Generally low
Implied volatility	Increases markedly, often overshoots historical	Low, generally close to historical. Out-of-the-money calls trade usually lower than recent historical
Skew	Flatter skew but higher volatility	High skew at lower volatility generally from call selling. The lower the volatility, the higher the skew.
Serial correlation	Often negative autocorrelation, "whipping" markets	Positive autocorrelation, a slow, "quiet trend"
Correlation with other assets	Total breakdown of correlations. Low correlations increase. High correlations decrease	Medium, stable correlation with similar assets.

Nonparallel Accounting

That some assets have owners but no one is consciously short them is one of the miracles of modern finance. In other words, there is an accounting discrepancy between the owner who is subjected to some rules and the seller who does not have any marks to market.

Bonds issued by the government of Italy are marked to market by the owners who show a measure of happiness when the prices go up (i.e., yield comes down). Paradoxically, the government of Italy too will exhibit happiness when the prices go up because their financing costs in the future will be lower. While the owner's wealth increased in the move, that of the Italian Republic did not decrease. If the government of Italy had a P/L showing that they issued bonds at 100, now trading at 105, and that they would lose a few trillion lires should they buy back their issues, the matter would be altogether different.

Stocks are issued by corporations. At the end of a day when the stocks are up, the wealth of the country increases by the jump in capitalization. Wealth was created out of nothing. But corporations who issued the stocks should not begrudge the value created at their expense: The owners can issue even more stock, manager's stock options have improved, employees now are richer in their retirement plan, and so on. This is a miracle where barring a few exceptions, just about every person in the world benefits from a rally. The unhappy minority is composed of (1) those who do not own stocks and see their neighbor driving away in a new car (they could be considered the true shorts)—only rarely do these become the majority; (2) the uncovered short, the commodity traders, the hedge funds hoping to make a killing in the next market crash.

Value Linked to Price

A stock price that goes up often brings stability to the company because it can now have access to easier financing. When the market value of a company goes up, the debt-to-equity ratio improves from both an accounting and economic standpoint.[4] From an accounting point of view, the company can raise cash and retire debt thus increasing the left-hand side of the balance sheet. From an economic one, the total capitalization increases. Such increase can lead to a better credit rating and ensure a wider (and cheaper) ability to borrow. Likewise a drop in price makes it riskier, therefore more volatile. The same applies to governments. When an emerging country has higher asset prices, the government can easily fulfill its debt obligations by issuing debt. But when the asset prices are trashed, governments might find it increasingly difficult to borrow, thus precipitating a vicious cycle and creating more uncertainty.

Currencies as Assets

Veteran option traders can easily detect if the currency pair is biased. Typically, currencies that are "parallel" exhibit a symmetrical behavior between sell-off and rallies. They are the ones where the trading of the currency pair is dominated by flows based on the commercial exchange of products. On the other hand, the currencies that act as investment assets vis-à-vis one another are going to behave in an asymmetrical manner. The German mark against the Italian lira, the Spanish peseta, or the Greek drachma represents such behavior.

The following are some rules to remember:

- Generally, currencies that act as assets present a strong correlation between their price and their interest rates. Interest rates are raised either to "defend" the currency or because of the capital flights in a sell-off.

- Currencies that are trade vehicles will have an independence between their price and interest rate.

Reverse Assets

Some assets like gold, and to a lesser extent the Swiss franc, the German mark, and the yen, will exhibit the mirror image of others, often when they behave exactly as the opposite of a regular asset. They become the recipient of the capital flights away from regular investment currencies and equities.

Volatility Regimes

The high volatility for a short span of time followed by a low volatility for a long period shows a "fat tailed" histogram of the distribution. Many applications of the Poisson arrival time have shown consistent results with the actual histograms, with such methods as the jump diffusion process.

Typically, the histogram will also show a "skew"; the distribution will be asymmetrical with fat tails on the left and thin tails to the right. As described earlier, however, the histogram conceals the sequence of events. The conditional skew (conditional on the previous regime being Type 2) is very high.

These facts can appear rather well in a histogram once one isolates the Type 1 from Type 2 regimes.

Figure 15.10 shows regime Type 1 including the first move down in the markets that ensures the passage into a Type 2 market.

For a Type 1 regime plus transition, a trading strategy should be set up to benefit from the following scenarios:

	Rally	Sell-Off
Slow	Likely	Unlikely
Fast	Unlikely	Likely

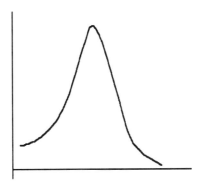

Figure 15.10   Regime type 1 including a transitional buffer.

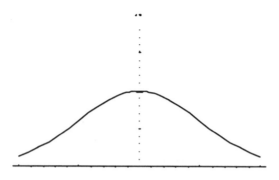

Figure 15.11   Type 2 regime (after the crash).

Correlation between Interest Rates and Carry

The major feature of biased assets is the strong correlation between interest rates and the carry. More of it is explained in Chapter 8, which is the chapter devoted to gamma and shadow gamma.

MORE ADVANCED PUT-CALL PARITY RULES

In general, for European and soft American options, the delta-neutral call will replicate the risk profile of a delta-neutral put. For that reason, the volatility of an in-the-money call needs to be exactly the same as that of the offsetting out-of-the-money put. Hence when mentioning trades "for a credit" or for a "debit," the trader examines the transaction by stripping every intrinsic portion (adjusted for present value) out of the total costs.

Therefore, the contrast between in-the-money and out-of-the-money becomes nonexistent (except for delta differences) since both have an equivalent time value and each can replicate the other synthetically using a deterministic instrument. The difference becomes at the level of the "moniness": how far in distance between the strike and the asset price.

Accordingly, this analysis will consider options as far as their "upside moniness" (how far the strike is above the current asset price), and their "downside moniness" (how far the strike is below it).

Barrier Products.   A short regular knock-out option long the vanilla will replicate the long knock-in option, both of the same strike and outstrike.

$$-KO + V = KI$$

$$\text{hence: } KI - V = -KO$$

For example, a 102 *KO* call with a 98 outstrike can be replicated by buying a 102 call knock-in at 98 and selling a vanilla 102 call. At the barrier, both options will be square.

This applies to reverse knock-out options as well.

American Binary Options.   These can synthetically be constructed using *KO* with rebates corresponding to the size of the bet. Synthetically, a binary "call" bet (if touched) at 104 with a payoff of $2 is a 104 knock-out call with both strikes and outstrikes of 104 (the option will never be in the money) and a rebate of $2. The rebate can be interpreted as an American binary, with some possible complications attending the time value on the payment date.

European Binary Products.   These have the same put/call parity rules as regular options, but with a twist: A long call is the mirror of a short put, in vegas and all, unlike a regular option that has a rule of long call + delta = long put + deltas. This is called the reversibility rule and can be constructed as follows:

> At the limit, a binary is a spread. Establish first the equivalence of spreads by taking two theoretical strikes 96 and 94:
>
> Long a 96 P short a 94 P long a net .13 deltas will replicate the short 94 C long a 96 C but long .13 deltas, surprisingly. Unlike a simple option, the replication of a spread is done through deltas of the same side and the same magnitude.
>
> By extension, a long binary 95 puts long .13 deltas (in the forward) is equivalent to a short binary 95 calls long .13 deltas.

Rainbow Options (Dual or Multiple Strike).   The put-call parity rules do not fully hold. For example, a put on IBM or Microsoft cannot be replicated with a call on IBM or Microsoft and the underlying assets. Traders are just thankful that the financial markets do not present too many of these. Most traders hate these instruments because of their deception.

Compound Options.   Put-call parity rules hold at the second option order level. A long (European) call option on a call can be replicated with a long put option on a call and long the call, all of the same strike and outstrike. A short put option on a put can be replicated by shorting the call on the same option and shorting the option, and so on. Even third-order options, like a call on a compound option can be hedged by using a put on the same order and the option one order below it.

The breakdown of the put-call parity rules for an American option leads to the notion of omega, the expected life of the option (different from the nominal duration). It is therefore preferable to consider that American

Option Wizard: A Vexed Question

There was a middlebrow swaps head trader at a famous institution who gave the fear-shaken MBAs he interviewed the following question:

"The Eurodollars are capped at 100.00, and cannot trade any higher. When the market goes to 100.00 what is the price of the 100 strike calls?"

"Zero," the interviewee would answer (proudly).

"Right. This is a good answer. How about the put?"

". . ." (silence, a lengthy silence).

"Well" the swaps trader would announce, "you failed my test, the put should trade for zero. Don't you understand put-call parity rules? Perhaps you should get a job in manufacturing or in the accounting department of some corporation."

One day, the swaps trader met his match in the person of a friend of the author, a veteran quantitative trader (quite a rare breed). The swaps trader started his usual bullying, and the veteran answered:

"Your question makes no sense. If your axiom is that the Eurodollar market cannot possibly go to 100 (rates go to zero), then there is an incoherence in the reasoning. The market could approach 0, but the volatility would be such that it would take eternity to get there.

"Second, there is a worse conclusion: A market that reaches 100 *(assuming it is bounded there)* would be dead and offer no volatility whatsoever.

"There are many explanations for that. An explanation in trader's terms is that a market that goes to 100 would be in itself a free option. So traders can sell at 100.00 knowing that it would be free money: They can partake of a sell-off without a possible rally! Knowing that if the market has any volatility in it, traders would sell it at 99.99 thus paying a tick for the perpetual option, and so forth. The market then would settle at a price where your call would be worth more than zero.

"In mathematical language, a market trading at 100 would be degenerate, which then would make your question about puts and calls superfluous."

The quantitative trader did not get the job (to his great luck). One result of the conversation, however, is that the swaps head trader stopped asking his question.

options need to be priced on a term structure of volatility that is shorter than the nominal European one. At all times, an option on one strike will be close to the European (the out-of-the-money one with longer expected life) while the counter option will be priced as an American.

At a more advanced level, one needs to examine the skew effect. Put-call parity being suspended, the deep in-the-money option would obey the early exercise rules, which would translate, in addition to the term structure effect, into a different skew.

Chapter *16*

Option Trading Concepts

Hiring a trader is like selling volatility. If he does very well or very poorly, you are out of a job.

An old option proverb

This chapter provides the necessary definitions of option trading concepts covered elsewhere in the book.

■ Officially, **option replication** corresponds to a self-financing method to replicate the payoffs of an option instrument with some other instruments (Figure 16.1). In practice, option replication is a broader concept that covers all operations done through options.

■ **Static replication** is a risk management strategy that consists in finding a match for an option position that does not require continuous rebalancing. Static replication aims at both reducing the P/L variance from the trade and minimizing the transaction costs.

The first and easiest static replication is the put-call-asset arbitrage where a call is synthetically made into a put and so on.

The reader should be warned against the static replication of instruments that have a *stopping time* (i.e., an unstable duration) with instruments that have a constant duration. This topic will be covered in the discussion of binary and barrier options.

Finally, there is the need to distinguish between *decomposition* and replication. Many trades require operators to decompose them as a value discovery method and a hedging orientation. Decomposition can reveal the skew risks, for example. In most cases, however, the replication will be impractical.

Static replication via the rolling back of the risks on a binomial tree (Derman's method)[1] consists in taking the final payoff of the security, constructing a binomial tree around it, and trying to replicate the payoff at almost every node of the tree. Such a method can be helpful in hedging the risks of some barrier options. We will show an adaptation to such method where, in place of the payoff, both the payoffs and the Greeks are matched.

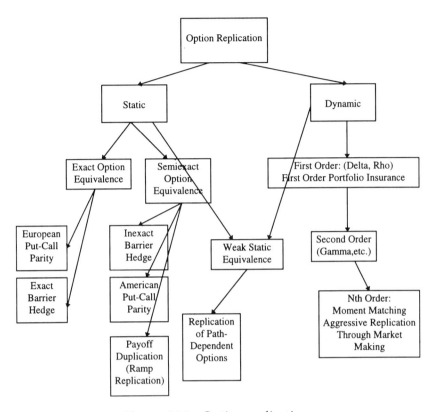

Figure 16.1 Option replication.

The recursive option replication method used by the author with a great measure of success consists in taking a series of *states* for the structure and finding trades that minimize the exposure to the *states* (see Figure 16.2). A state is defined as a possible asset price in the future.

Greeks to Match on Every State

Delta.

Modified Gamma.

Modified Vega.

Theta.

Modified Rho (Rho1, Rho2).

Bleed.

Correlation delta (if any).

The best static hedge is the one that matches the Greeks on every state across all the nodes.[2] A shortcoming is that often operators need to spend a

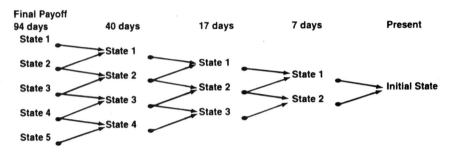

Figure 16.2 Recursive option replication.

great deal of the income from the trade paying bid/offer spreads to matching the Greeks as it may require such a combination of trades in oft-illiquid markets. The answer is very often dynamic hedging.

■ **Dynamic hedging** implies sticking to a minimum Greek exposure and rebalancing continuously to achieve a certain neutrality. It is opposed to static hedging where the trade is looked on as one combination with some expiration outcome.

The difference with the operation in Figure 16.2 is that a dynamic hedger does not look for trades that completely neutralize the tree.

Dynamic hedging concerns all the Greeks in the book. It starts with the rebalancing of the deltas (as the market moves or as the delta bleeds with time). As gammas change, it involves the adjustment through options to reduce or increase gammas and the consequent time decay. As markets move, Rho1 and Rho2 need to be adjusted and so on.

One matter worthy of mentioning concerning dynamic hedging: It makes every option become path dependent.

■ **Neutral spreading** is an option trading technique that consists in buying a certain quantity of options against selling another, all of different strikes and expiration. It is a form of dynamic hedging that allows for some Greek risk provided there is proper compensation for it.

In floor trading lore, a spreader is someone who matches the "red" tickets with the "blue" ones (originally on the exchanges red tickets were sales and blue tickets were buys).

While there are varying degrees of neutral spreading, it is generally assumed that if someone buys an option and sells another, provided their strikes and expirations are sufficiently near one another, the ability to capture "value" is greatly enhanced. The study of biased assets will show that the spreader needs some additional constraints in some markets where the skew makes "downside" strikes remarkably dissimilar to "upside" ones.

Most successful option trading firms were started by spreaders, and, to this day, the most successful one ever, Swiss Bank Corporation (in its association with O'Connor and Company, originally a successful Chicago Board Options Exchange [CBOE] market maker firm), requires floor experience from its traders to hone their spreading skills.

Sophistication in spreading is usually obtained only by dint of experience. How some instruments marry with each other can certainly be determined theoretically, but as with most games, only thorough practice would allow the person to be able to match an option with another.

Classical spreading techniques can be easily extended to the exotic options arena: Many of the rules are common. However, the distance between strikes and expirations becomes more difficult to assess.

The value of spreading as a market-making technique is greatly appreciated by the exchanges and the financial backers, since such traders commonly have easy access to capital and the exchanges allow them great leverage.

The advantages of spreading include:

- *Capturing of Central Limit.* The market maker can reduce the variance (read luck) and maximize the drift (read skills). The notion is described in Chapter 3.

- *Insulation from the Risks of the Formula.* Generally, trading options against options is a serious way to be protected from the imperfections of Black-Scholes-Merton (or others). Assume that, with the market trading at 100, the at-the-money options puts and calls struck at 100 show an implied Black-Scholes-Merton volatility of 15.7%. Regardless of the effect of the formula and the distribution, put-call parity arbitrage will make puts and calls of the same strike and expiration trade at the same time value (hence the same volatility).

  Suppose that the market for the 104 calls shows a volatility of 16.2 and that the market of the 104.5 calls shows a volatility of 15.5. Selling the 104 calls and buying the 104.5 calls while adjusting the amounts to satisfy a low residual gamma and delta neutrality seems to be a good idea. Should one discover (as many did) that Black-Scholes-Merton underprices out-of-the-money options, there will be no material effect on the trade: Both options would be affected. Conversely, should one discover that Black-Scholes-Merton overprices the upside (which would be true in biased assets), the same will be true. The strikes are sufficiently close together for the spread to be impervious to the formula.

- *Realization of Theoretical Edge.* Trading options against options proves to be a safe way to hedge against the host of second, third derivatives, and so on that plague the trader:

    First Level: Delta neutrality (including the rho1, rho2).

    Second Level: Gamma neutrality.

    Third Level: Vega neutrality.

■ **Theoretical edge** is the difference between the trading price of one instrument and some defined fair value.

It is safe to see how a spread sometimes confers such a theoretical edge:

1. **Insulation from the Broad Set of Parameters.** There was a market maker on the floor of the CBOE who attributes his survival to the fact that he only traded calls.

2. **An Effectual Market-Making Device.** Options are generally individually illiquid while the general market is very liquid. That is the reason, as mentioned earlier, that the active market makers can secure easy financing. The more active the trader, the more profitable he will be at the end if he keeps transacting "above" or "below" theoretical value.[3] Some market maker firms impose a volume requirement on their traders to force them into activity. By forcing them to trade actively under severe gamma and theta constraints, they can ensure that the traders are satisfying some budget requirements.

Initiation to Volatility Trading: Vega versus Gamma

> *Risk Management Rule:* "Long" or "short" volatility carries no true risk management meaning. One needs to qualify the gammas (with a range) and the vegas.

The expression "long and short volatility" is not an expression that can be used by a dynamic hedger. In the early 1980s, it was difficult for traders to explain to the bleary-eyed bosses the difference between gamma and vega. Typically for one option, the position would be straightforward since it will be long or short both.

X once worked (briefly) for a boss who attributed his expertise in option trading to the fact that he had been extremely profitable once (accidentally) on an option position. X was short calendars and was asked whether X was long or short volatility. X was short volatility but that he wanted the

Option Wizard: Basic Forms of Option Strategies

Simple trades with simple products:

>Straddles, strangles, butterflies, volatility bets.

Complex trades with simple products:

>Long leptokurtosis (fourth moment bet).
>
>Playing the volatility term structure.
>
>Calendar/diagonal spreading.
>
>Long vega convexity.
>
>Long the Eurodollar "dampening" effect.
>
>Distributional arbitrage: skew trading.

Simple trades with complex products:

>Playing the variance ratio with barrier options.
>
>Bets and the reflecting barriers.

Complex trades with complex products:

>Distributional arbitrage through contingent premium options.
>
>Playing the second order convergence with barriers: arbitraging the slope of the curve.
>
>Playing the reverse knock-out convexity against ramp options.
>
>Arbitraging higher moments of the distribution with a combination of bet and compound options.

---

market to move. It was immediately easy to see the confusion in the boss's eyes. It was difficult for X to explain that he was long gamma and short vega, and after he ran out of breath trying to explain the theory of option pricing to him, he resolved never to work for a bad listener.

In a two-option book, the following structures are used (Table 16.1):

- Option A is a short term at-the-money option.
- Option B is a medium term at-the-money option.

Risk Management Rule: Long or short gamma needs to be qualified with a range (as shown in Chapter 8). A trader needs to explain if he is continuously long gamma, long up-gamma, down-gamma, or if the gamma flips somewhere.

A calendar spread has a gamma that reverses away from the money. The reason is that a calendar seller can only hope to make a limited sum of money from the calendar (generally the credit for an at-the-money calendar). An operator willing to bet against the wings has several options: Either play the out-of-the-money options against the at-the-money, or, more easily play the calendar.

By applying a ratio to the time spread, the operator can achieve a gamma that would remain neutral to mildly short at-the-money but that becomes rapidly very positive in the wings.

SOFT VERSUS HARD DELTAS

■ A **soft delta** execution is a delta hedge done through an option, that, accordingly, vanishes asymptotically (to the asset price). A **hard delta** does not vanish at the limit of the move in the underlying asset.

Soft deltas are generally used to cover secondary deltas (i.e., deltas arising from market moves) that cannot be hedged with a hard delta without increasing the risks in the extremes.

Example: The trader has the following position on the books: long at-the-money option and short larger quantities of out-of-the-money calls:

Asset	100	102	104	106	108	110	112	114
Delta	0	10	15	17	15	12	−10	−50
Gamma	Long	Long	Long	Square	Short	Short	Very Short	Very Short

At 106, the trader has some profits stemming from the long deltas. Selling hard deltas would cause his negative gamma to turn worse in the tails:

Asset	100	102	104	106	108	110	112	114
Delta	−17	−7	−2	0	−2	−5	−27	−67

By selling deltas through options, with the purchase of a put for example, or a put spread, the following would be achieved:

Asset	100	102	104	106	108	110	112	114
Delta	−2	−1	−8	0	2	0	−10	−50

Sometimes the best way to sell deltas is by shifting strikes (i.e., moving the center of the gamma closer to the short zone). At the beginning, the clumps of long gamma were centered around 100 and the short gamma around 112. The rally should give the trader the opportunity to shift the center from 100 to 106, thus stabilizing the position. The best possible hedge in this case is a soft delta (buying options struck in the 106 zone) added to a selling options struck in the 100 zone. The next step, should the rally continue, would be to move the longs into the 112 zone by repeating the operation.

Recommendation. In the rebalancing of an option position, the trader needs to perform the following test: Does the gamma flip the other way? If the long gamma flips into a negative gamma, it will be very dangerous to sell "hard" deltas (i.e., cash or futures) because the P/L would then turn out to be worse in the tails of the matrix.

VOLATILITY BETTING

These trades can involve more than one option. All options considered in this section are vanilla.

- A **first-order volatility trade** using vanilla options is a trade that satisfies the following conditions:

  - It is monotonically long or short volatility though without necessarily having a constant gamma.
  - Its vegas and gammas are on the same side of the market.
  - It is intended to be delta neutral.

These characteristics apply to simple option trades: long straddles, long strangles, and so on. Any form of trading where all options are long or short would satisfy such rules (Table 16.1).

First-order volatility trades present the advantages of being tractable, with a P/L that is easy to forecast (Figure 16.3). They represent positions with a smaller degree of complexity.

Table 16.1 The Volatility Rules

	Long Vega	Short Vega
Long Gamma	Long A, Long B Long A, Long B	Long A, Short B
Short Gamma	Short A, Long B	Short A, Short B Short A, Short B

Weightings are not used in this introductory framework.
Option B has longer time to expiration than option A.

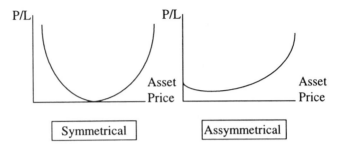

Figure 16.3 First-order volatility trade.

■ A **second-order volatility trade** is an option trade that includes long and short options of different strikes or different maturities but within the confines of one product. It is characterized by the following:

• The gamma always flip from positive to negative on the map.

• Its raw vega can change sign somewhere along the lines (this is not an essential condition).

• Its weighted vega always reverses somewhere on the map.

• Owing to its complexity, graphical representation in two dimensions often becomes irrelevant and of weak revealing powers.

A call spread (one by one), such as buying the 102 calls selling the 106 calls in equal amounts, will exhibit the characteristics of a single call when the market is at 100. Should the market rally to 104, however, it will then have the zero-gamma, positive down-gamma, negative up-gamma that characterizes a risk reversal.

A ratio spread where the operator buys the 102 calls and sells twice as much of the 106 calls will present opposite characteristics.

Higher Moment Bets

■ A **third moment bet** is a form of distribution arbitrage where a bet is made on the correlation between the volatility of a particular market and the asset price.

■ A **fourth moment bet** is long or short the volatility of volatility. It could be achieved either with out-of-the-money options or with calendars.

Example: A ratio "backspread" or reverse spread is a method that includes the buying of out-of-the-money options in large amounts and the selling of smaller amounts of at-the-money but making sure the trade satisfies the "credit" rule (i.e., the trade initially generates a positive cash flow). The credit rule is more difficult to interpret when one uses in-the-money options. In that case, one should deduct the present value of the intrinsic part of every option using the put-call parity rule to equate them with out-of-the-money.

The trade shown in Figure 16.4 was accomplished with the purchase of both out-of-the-money puts and out-of-the-money calls and the selling of smaller amounts of at-the-money straddles of the same maturity.

Figure 16.5 shows the second method, which entails the buying of 60-day options in some amount and selling 20-day options on 80% of the amount.

Both trades show the position benefiting from the fat tails and the high peaks. Both trades, however, will have different vega sensitivities, but close to flat *modified* vega.

Case Study: Path Dependence of a Regular Option

The following illustrates the degree to which option replication could be path dependent.

This case study uses a string of returns[4], including a beginning price and the end price, and its volatility. With these numbers, it is possible to reshuffle a high number of sequences while the beginning price, the end price, and the volatility remain the same.

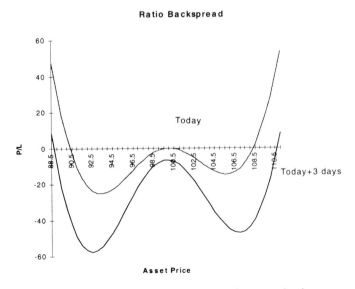

Figure 16.4   Trading the wings, first method.

Calendar Spread

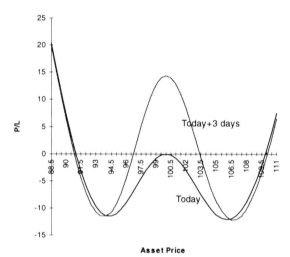

Figure 16.5 Trading the wings, second method.

To show how to create the price movement, a sequence of percentage returns is taken, say, 1%, 5%, −1%, −5%. A security starts at 100. The next price is 100 (1 + .01) = 101. The next price is 101 × (1 + .05) = 1.0605. The next price is 106.05 × (1 − .01) = 1.0499. The next price is 1.0499 × (1 − .05) = 99.74 (the final price). The price sequence is then 100, 101, 1.0605, 1.0499, 99.74. Mix the preceding returns, and get 5%, −5%, −1%, 1%. The price sequence will therefore be 100, 105, 99.75, 98.75, 99.74, quite a different path.

In the following example, the goal is to replicate 252 trading days by taking an arbitrary distribution with a 15.6% volatility (average movement 1% per business day) and reshuffle it into 106 different paths.

All the prices start at 100 and end at 98.6. Figure 16.6 shows eight sample paths and illustrates the discrepancy in the paths that can result: One path shows a high of 127, the other shows a high of 105. It is again counterintuitive that both have the same mean and the same volatility. Indeed, some of the shuffled results have a yearly range of 10% while others have a yearly range of 60%.

Figure 16.6 shows only eight of the paths used in the analysis for the sake of clarity.

The trader buys $10 million of a one-year European call option struck at 100 and rebalances the delta daily. European options are said to be path independent, therefore only the final outcome matters for them. Table 16.2 shows the profit and loss from a strategy that would buy volatility at the exact 15.6% and hedge, without transaction costs, at the close of every day.

This author once, for his amusement, posed the problem to three categories of people: the junior trader, the experienced trader, and the trading

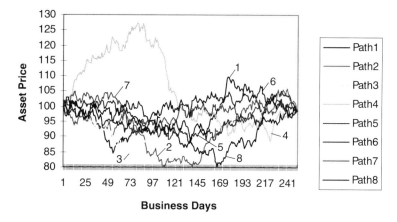

Figure 16.6   Eight paths of the same volatility and same final return.

manager. Most junior traders and trading managers rehashed what they knew from the training packages that volatility was volatility and the order of events did not matter. Experienced traders explained that we were dealing with a discrete, not continuous time world and that there would be a variance that would be a function of transaction frequency. The interesting result is that all of the experienced traders got the answer right and all the trading managers got it wrong. The financial community is still largely unaware of the poor tracking of the risks through dynamic hedging.

Most experienced traders explained that it was preferable, when long gamma, to have the large moves when gamma is at the maximum and the small moves when the market is furthest away from the strike.

Table 16.2   Results of the Dynamic Hedge

P/L	Frequency	P/L	Frequency	P/L	Frequency
−72000	1	−20000	1	32000	6
−68000	0	−16000	12	36000	4
−64000	1	−12000	13	40000	4
−60000	0	−8000	4	44000	4
−56000	0	−4000	2	48000	3
−52000	0	0	6	52000	1
−48000	0	4000	5	56000	1
−44000	1	8000	7	60000	0
−40000	0	12000	2	64000	0
−36000	1	16000	6	68000	2
−32000	1	20000	5	72000 +	1
−28000	2	24000	7	Total	106
−24000	1	28000	2		

Table 16.3   Extreme Path Dependence: A Risk Reversal

P/L	Frequency	P/L	Frequency	P/L	Frequency
−600,000	2	−150,000	8	300,000	7
−550,000	0	−100,000	5	350,000	7
−500,000	0	−50,000	11	400,000	0
−450,000	1	0	8	450,000	0
−400,000	2	50,000	9	500,000	1
−350,000	0	100,000	6	550,000	1
−300,000	4	150,000	9	600,000	0
−250,000	4	200,000	7	650,000	2
−200,000	3	250,000	9		

The results show how path dependent the world can be for a dynamic hedger. The preceding example shows a simple position that is monotonically long gamma. The next position is initially close to flat gamma but presents mixed features.

Table 16.3 represents the following risk reversal: Long $100 million of the 90 call, short $100 million of the 110 call and delta neutral. The delta, as before, is rebalanced daily. The results are quite unsettling.

The distribution that caused such P/L had no skew; generally there was no difference between down-volatility and up-volatility. There was also no correlation between the volatility of the market and the level of the underlying asset. In short, a clean distribution, extremely theoretical.

This suggests the following trade-off: The only way to reduce path dependence is to increase the transaction frequency. Such increase in the transaction frequency will raise the costs of trading. The impact can be further compounded because a negative gamma trader incurs higher such costs than a positive gamma counterpart.

Many heads of trading rooms, underestimating the impact of the path, will issue comments such as, "On balance, in the long run, I will eventually capture the 'edge' in the market." Most of them are unaware of the following rule: In options, variance of P/L is usually underestimated. One needs more diversification. One of the rules of diversification, which is diversification through time, does not properly work owing to the leverage and the fact that traders are continuously monitored by a nonstatistical person breathing down their neck. Moreover, the life of a trader is too short for adequate time diversification.

In the real market, the results will certainly be worse, for the following reasons:

- The trader usually will hedge himself, when short gamma, with stop losses, which increase the costs and causes a higher incidence of whipsaws.

- Most markets exhibit some form of a skew.

- Traders have some form of absorbing barrier in their P/L. Many of the 106 runs had losses in excess of the final worst-case apparent result of $600,000. If we stopped a trader at $300,000, we would have many more negative runs.

- Perhaps the element that would make the preceding spread widest is implied volatility. It is assumed that the trade is only adjusted with the asset, not with options. Seeing the P/L of every path and analyzing the P/L volatility would show that some of them are scary.

Table 16.4   The Nasty Path

Days to Expiration	Asset Price	Option Price	Option Delta	P/L Option	P/L Future	Cum P/L ($000)
30	100.00	0.02	26			
29	100.13	0.02	28	1.4	−3	−2.0
28	100.26	0.02	30	1.5	−4	−4.1
27	100.39	0.02	32	1.6	−4	−6.4
26	100.50	0.03	34	1.0	−4	−9.0
25	100.65	0.03	38	2.5	−5	−11.6
24	100.78	0.03	41	1.9	−5	−14.6
23	100.91	0.03	44	2.1	−5	−17.8
22	101.04	0.03	47	2.2	−6	−21.3
21	101.17	0.04	51	2.3	−6	−25.1
20	101.30	0.04	55	2.5	−7	−29.3
19	101.43	0.04	60	2.6	−7	−33.8
18	101.56	0.04	64	2.8	−8	−38.8
17	101.69	0.05	70	2.9	−8	−44.3
16	101.82	0.05	75	3.1	−9	−50.2
15	101.95	0.05	81	3.2	−10	−56.7
14	102.08	0.06	88	3.4	−11	−63.9
13	102.21	0.06	96	3.5	−11	−71.9
12	102.34	0.06	104	3.7	−12	−80.6
11	102.47	0.07	112	3.8	−13	−90.3
10	102.60	0.07	122	3.8	−15	−101.1
9	102.73	0.08	133	3.8	−16	−113.1
8	102.86	0.08	145	3.7	−17	−126.7
7	102.99	0.08	158	3.5	−19	−142.0
6	103.12	0.09	173	3.1	−21	−159.5
5	103.25	0.09	190	2.3	−22	−179.7
4	103.38	0.09	208	0.9	−25	−203.5
3	103.51	0.09	229	−1.6	−27	−232.1
2	103.64	0.08	253	−6.3	−30	−268.2
1	103.77	0.06	273	−17.2	−33	−318.2
0	103.98	0.00	0	−63.8	−57	−439.4

The preceding position becomes long or short vega at some level, and adjustments would worsen the final spread.

The following basic example was designed by the author in his formative years to satisfy a bet with one of his colleagues.

SIMPLE CASE STUDY: THE "WORST CASE" SCENARIO

Inexperienced risk managers typically describe an option risk as being the premium when one is long and conversely when one is short. This does not apply for a dynamic hedger. This case study, with a simple example will show how a premium seller can earn more than the initial premium collected and a premium buyer can lose more than the expenditure.

An out-of-the-money call has a 20% delta.

Asset price: 100.[5]

Strike price: 104.

Days to expiration: 30.

Price: .19.

Amount: $10,000,000.

Initial premium: $190,000.

It would appear that a buyer of the call would only lose the premium, $190,000, not more.

It is apparently a very safe trade. Look at the worst-case scenario for a delta hedger: Initial delta: $280,000. The hedger sells the entire amount.

Look at the P/L table over the next 30 days: The path followed by the underlying is particularly vicious as it rallies daily (see Table 16.4).

It is easy to see that dynamic hedging got our man in trouble, causing losses of $440,000 where they should have been limited to $190,000. Such events are rather common (though rarely to such an extreme) with trends where out-of-the-money options on the side of the trend decay mercilessly and delta hedgers end up losing on both the option and the delta hedge.

PART *III*

TRADING AND HEDGING
EXOTIC OPTIONS

In Part III of this book, the focus is on the risks of the major exotic options from the standpoint of the dynamic hedger (and the informed customer). In place of an anecdotal enumeration of all the possible instruments, the discussion will concentrate on the hedging techniques through decomposition of the blocks of risks.

Risk managers who never traded before will learn that:

- The risk of any soft path-dependent option can only be understood through thorough grounding in American binary options and stopping times. Typically, they commit the tragic mistake of loading their minds with peripheral notions, most of which are related to pricing.

- Understanding multi-asset options needs to come from the notion of matrix analysis and cross-gammas by *intuitively looking at the covariance matrix as one volatility.* In addition, every structure can become multi-assets through correlation hedging.

- Understanding non-time-homogeneous risks needs to come from the grounding in calendar spreading and the learning about the notions of forward volatility, not through the dissection of *deferred* options and other minor varieties.

In this text, Asian options and lookbacks are subjects of minor importance. Asian options are simply an application of a basket methodology (the basket is in *time*), and lookbacks can be thought of as a simple footnote on barrier options.

Finally it is necessary to stress that training in exotic options is often better performed with a good basic and structured education in vanilla puts and calls. Conventional option trading provides a good training in the failings of the distributions. This refers to what has been described as complex trading with simple instruments as opposed to simple trading with complex instruments.

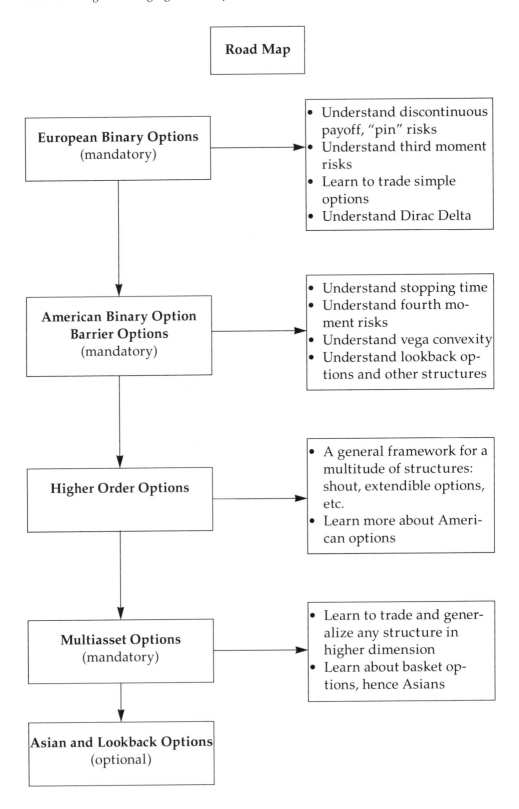

Chapter **17**

Binary Options: European Style

Options that are trivial to price (like binary options) are difficult to hedge. Options that are difficult to price (like Asian options) are trivial to hedge.

Howard Savery, Exotic Options Trader

The next two chapters are devoted to the trading issues related to bet options. The reader needs to complete these chapters before attempting to understand barrier options. To make the progression easier, the discussion will start with European binary options, as the concept of the "pin" needs to be well understood before proceeding with American binary options, which add the complexity of an unknown and highly unstable "duration," or stopping time.

The concept of the pin is so central to understanding both option theory and practice that this author started originally writing the book with that topic in mind and had to compose all the previous chapters to provide the reader with the tools to master the risks of the barrier structure. For a hard-working person, however, a thorough knowledge of barriers and digitals provides appropriate training in handling the risks of what exotic traders call the "junior stuff."

Binary options are perhaps the best training ground for a trader as they can teach more about advanced book management. At the heart of most exotic structure and every bet resides a binary. It also provides an advanced test of the skills of any risk manager: Many experienced risk managers who fail the binary exam should perhaps consider some serious retraining.

Barrier options are also difficult to comprehend for risk managers with a superficial knowledge of options. Ironically, traders with shallow experience commonly misunderstand these options even though they dabble in them; whereas the often-more-qualified trainees master the barrier options. They invariably allowed the author to distinguish between the true experienced risk manager and those who needed further training.

EUROPEAN BINARY OPTIONS

These options are also called digital derivatives, bet options, and gap puts and calls.

■ A **binary option** pays a single sum upon the satisfaction of the obligation. It is called binary because, like 0 or 1, it either pays the full amount or zero, with nothing in between.

This discontinuous payoff makes binary options particularly hard to hedge using regular structures that present a continuous payoff.

The opposite of a binary or gap payoff is a ramp, or conventional option. Binary options can be either American or European.

■ A **European binary option** is a bet on the asset being higher or lower than a certain level at expiration. American bets are "if touched" types that will terminate the bet upon an event at any moment between inception and expiration and are thus more difficult to hedge.

Some variations that can be both American and European will be examined. European binaries can thus have only one strike, unlike American ones that can be of the either-or type. There are no double bets per se, as a European double bet can be constructed as the sum of two independent bets.

Binary options are present in many structures, as a European or American type. Contingent premium options are a simple construction of European vanilla options plus a bet that pays the initial premium if the option is in the money.

Common trading beliefs hold that a European bet is easy to hedge except close to expiration, where the delta becomes explosive as spot enters the neighborhood of the strike. It will be shown that it is difficult to hedge in both circumstances. As a matter of fact, much money was unwittingly lost in the daily management of a digital with a long time to its expiration.

One reason traders get an accelerated training with bet options is that their delta imitate the gamma of a regular option.

Often European bet options exhibit parameter linearity problems that make hedging their vega particularly difficult for a dynamic hedger.

Figure 17.1 shows that a binary option is short gamma and earning theta (but moderately) when it is in the money and long gamma and paying time decay when it is out of the money. Exactly at the money, it loses all its optionality and acts like a future. This risk-reversal feature for a barrier appears to facilitate their hedging with a few skewed instruments. It will be shown that the appropriate hedge for a barrier is a narrow spread, done in such a size as to compound the skew effect. Most of all, barriers need to be priced with the skew structure of the market in mind. In a commodity that becomes volatile after a sell-off and loses steam after a rally, such a structure can indeed be very favorable unless the price of the barrier includes a compensation for such imbalance (with the volatility differential we call the skew).

Look carefully in the microscope at the part that is long gamma (the left side of the figure).

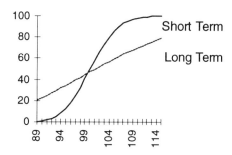

Figure 17.1 Mixed convexity of a European binary.

What causes the long gamma is the local convexity. A binary will present a positive leverage when it is out of the money (the trader is risking less to make more) and negative leverage otherwise (the trader is risking more to make less). If the bet pays one dollar at expiration and is currently worth one penny, it will present very large convexity features. It can thus pick up 99 cents and lose 1 only. This would look like a long gamma structure.

Figure 17.2 shows no true difficulty in protecting the vega and gamma of the binary using ordinary vanilla options. As expiration nears, however, the profile would start sliding toward the pin exposure. Figure 17.3 shows the price sensitivity nearing expiration. The graph will become more and more vertical for a narrow segment and flat otherwise.

Hedging with a Vanilla

Look at the shape of Figure 17.3 and try to find the profile of a structure that would imitate such a payoff. The first option to come to mind is the call spread.

Option Wizard: Risk Reversal (revisited)

A risk reversal, as defined in this book, corresponds to situations where the gamma and/or vegas flip from positive to negative across one point.

Initially, a risk reversal corresponded to fences (out-of-the-money call purchase financed with the sale of a put) but rapidly option traders started referring to it as a description of asymmetric risk in an option position. It became the **third moment.**

A risk reversal for a book manager is the switch in risk across one point. The best description of a risk reversal to date*: "It is like buying drought insurance and financing it with flood insurance."

---

*Lenny Dendunnen.

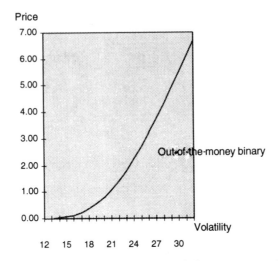

Figure 17.2 Price of a 30-day, 15 percent out-of-the-money option and its sensitivity to volatility.

Figure 17.4 presents a call spread where the operator is long the 100.00 strike and short the 100.01.

The difference between Figure 17.3 and Figure 17.4 lies in the scale. The shapes are very similar. This shows that the binary is really a call spread in disguise. It presents all such features: long gamma where the proximity of the long leg makes it dominate (below the long) and short gamma where the proximity of the short leg makes it dominate (above the short). So the microscopic call spread is long gamma below 100 and short gamma above. Like a conventional option, the gamma weakens away from the strike, and the combination peaks at a certain spot. In between, it looks like a risk reversal.

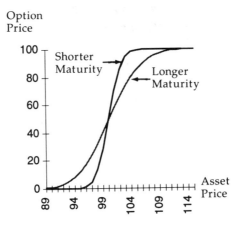

Figure 17.3 Binary option nearing expiration.

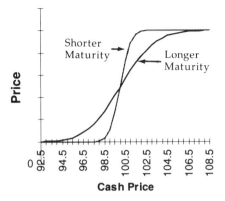

Figure 17.4   A call spread nearing expiration.

One additional piece of information, critical to understand the similarity between the two positions: They are both European, path-independent, and share a common expiration date. As the difference resides merely in the scale, the increase in the size of one should perfectly replicate the other.

The next step is to compute the face value of the call spread that is fit to hedge the barrier.

Assume the payoff of the barrier is $100 per unit if the bet is satisfied and none if the bet is not satisfied. So the amount of the call spread should be such that one tick represents $100. So the trader would need the miserly amount of 10,000 units of the call spread. Such replication, however, only becomes effective *everywhere on the map of risk-neutral possible outcomes* if there is no zone in which it fails to track the other leg. In this example, the trader selected a market that moved in indivisible "ticks" of .01. Should the market trade in discrete increments of .05, his task would be made easier as the replicating amounts could thus be smaller (2,000 units).

Option Wizard: Dividing a Tick

The exchanges make it illegal to shave a "tick" into smaller increments.

Traders could otherwise trade in smaller units by dividing the trade. Imagine that the market moved in minimum increments of .01. Buying 50 lots at 100.00 and 50 lots at 100.01 from the same person would accomplish a "ginzy," as the average would be 100.005.

The exchanges did not make buying at two different prices illegal, they made the trading with the intention of breaking up the tick into smaller prices an illegal operation. What is illegal is telling a trader: "I will buy some from you at 100.01 if you also will sell me some at 100.00."

In continuous time finance, the replicating trade would need to be done in infinitely large amounts for an infinitely small difference between strikes to properly hedge the book. But markets do not trade continuously, be it only for the sake of convention, as there is a set minimum price increment called the "tick." Such an increment is formal on exchanges as trading in smaller fractions is disallowed (see Option Wizard, *Dividing a Tick*). It is the product of etiquette and convention in over-the-counter markets, as most screens and systems are not set up to handle any number smaller than a set fraction. Traders in some markets consider it downright impolite to display a price in too precise an increment (more than 1/100).

Definition of the Bet: Forward and Spot Bets

It is important to see if the bet contract defines satisfaction as "higher" or "at least" the bet strike price, which, in mathematical symbol, is $>$ or $\geq$. The difference is minor but affects our replication. If the bet terms specify "I pay if the asset is 100 or higher" then the call spread needs to be defined as long 99.99 short 100. If the bet says "higher than 100" then the replication would necessitate the long 100 short 100.01.

Another important feature concerns the timing of payment. Some bets, particularly when they are out of the money, are sold as options where the "buyer" pays some premium immediately and gets some payment if the asset satisfies the bet at expiration. Others are denominated as a bet where the party that loses pays the money. The only difference between the two lies in the discounting of the premium.

■ A **spot bet** is where one of the parties outlays the premium initially and would receive payment if the conditions of the bet are satisfied.

A forward bet is one where the parties agree to exchange payments at the end. Thus, the party paying the initial premium would be considered the "buyer," arbitrarily. The following are examples:

- A bet where one of the parties pays $50 if the spot is higher than 100 on the Friday after Thanksgiving and would receive $50 is a forward bet.
- A bet on the outcome of a tennis game is typically a forward bet.
- A note that may pay 6% interest if Mexico stays above a range and 5% otherwise is a spot bet. The owner of the note, through the reduced coupon, is paying in advance for the bet.
- A contract where one pays 10 cents and may receive $1 if the fed eases on the next meeting is a spot bet.

So there is no trick worthy of analysis other than:

- The forward bet is forward valued.
- The spot bet has one leg present valued (the initial payment) and one leg forward valued (the payment received).

This book tries to minimize dwelling on simple interest rate arithmetic. So the reader should assume that interest rates are zero (for a while) and get on with bigger and better things.

By convention, a call bet is the term used for the agreement where a party is betting that the price will be higher than the strike on expiration date. A call bet for one party is a put bet for another.

By convention also, the bet is quoted in percentage of the total at stake. If the final payment is $1 then the bet priced at 25 cents corresponds to a spot or forward expenditure of 25 cents. If the bet payment is $500, then it becomes $125.

PRICING WITH THE SKEW

Assuming replication is important to probe the structure of an option and get a feel for its theoretical value. Replicating, however, is rather impractical if one takes into account the slightest amount of transaction costs. This author has never seen anyone replicate a binary option with narrow spreads.

As the skew exists in most markets and since the binary is sensitive to the skew, proper allowance should be made in the pricing. If the minimum tick size is .01, the option will be sensitive to the difference in skew between the 100 and the 100.01. This is not a joke: If there is a microscopic skew volatility difference between the strikes owing to the large amounts involved on the spread, such skew will bear a meaningful effect on its theoretical value.

The way to price the skew effect is to look at the wider replicating portfolio and the amounts involved. Assume that there is a difference of .5 volatility points between the 99.5 and the 100.5 strikes of the same maturity as the binary. The skew effect on the structure should be equal to the dollar effect of the skew on the replicating portfolio. It is computed as follows:

Assume that the trader has a 3-month bet paying $100 if the market is higher than 100 (for simplicity, assume that interest rates are nil and that volatility is 15.7). The Black-Scholes-Merton value is 49.6. The 99.50/100.50 replicating spread will be approximately 100 times the bet if, in this make-believe schematic world, the market moves in very large increments of 1 point. This assumption is necessary to eliminate the possibility of the market settling between 99.50 and 100.50, in which case the replicating portfolio would not match the binary option. Taking the Black-Scholes-Merton values of the call spread, the value of the bet should be close to 49.6 (this discussion will not get into the notion of the small risk-neutral difference between the values of both instruments). So in this world of only one-dollar moves, the trader appears to be hedged.

But there is the skew in the market, as can be seen in an exaggerated example:

Assume that the call spread trades for .69 because the 99.5 call trades one volatility point higher than the 100.50. This means that the binary option needs to be more expensive, and must trade at $69 (as opposed to $49.6 using Black-Scholes-Merton) to make up for the skew. Would anyone bet so much that the spot would be higher on expiration? The numbers show how exaggerated the skew effect can be on the barrier.

Now the conflict: A bet trades at the probability of the asset price ending up higher than the bet level. The difference between the delta and the bet will be explained later; it is important to note that the skew—any skew—makes the two elements diverge. That divergence will lead to the more complicated notion of the skew paradox.

In practice, however, the skew would not be as pronounced as in the preceding example except perhaps in biased assets or SP100 options after an anxiety attack. The normal skew ranges (in well-behaved assets) between .5 and 3 volatility points for the difference between a .25 delta call and .25 delta put (i.e., between a 75 delta call and a 25 delta call). Interpolating a 2-point skew, a 3-month option shows about .12 skew at 15.7 volatility for the difference between 99.5 and 100.5 (since the difference is .06 deltas and .5 deltas command a 2-point skew). The price effect of the .12 skew is .025 on

Option Wizard: The Replication Map

Two path-independent trades should be equal in price if they present the same payoff everywhere on the map of possible prices (by the rule of stochatic dominance).

Path-independent means that they could be treated by looking at expiration only. That statement was qualified earlier with the explanation that path-independent options become path dependent when hedged dynamically. The present case involves static, not dynamic, hedges.

Replicating a binary with a call spread makes it necessary to look at *limiting cases*. The call spread will work *outside* the strikes, but *not inside*. The narrower the call spread, therefore, the most perfect the replication.

The call spread, as a limit decomposition of the binary, will always be higher in price, by a small amount that vanishes as the increments narrow.

the call spread, making the difference between strikes .524 instead of .49. So through the replicating portfolio, the price of the bet is found to be worth approximately $52.4 instead of $49.6. This is still meaningful enough to alert traders about potential mispricing.

> **Verification:** Widening the increments to cover a spread that would be 50 deltas apart (i.e., the one quoted by equivalence with the 25 delta risk reversal) would reveal the following strikes: 95.70 and 105.4 that is 9.7 points apart. It would then be necessary to execute 9.52 spreads on the hedge to make $100 if the bet is satisfied (if the market settled above 105.4) and lose the premium paid for the spread if the market settles below 95.70. Priced on the skew, the value of the vanilla call spread would be $52.30, whereas the same one, Black-Scholes-Merton-priced (using the same volatility on both legs), would yield $49, similar to the fair value of the bet without the skew.

A Formal Pricing on the Skew

Intuitively, the price of the binary can be defined as the risk-neutral probability (i.e., taking the mean of the asset returns out of the equation thanks to delta neutrality) of ending up in the money. If one takes the earlier argument of the perfect replication through the call spread, the following equation results, using the call price C, the strike price of the binary K, and h the difference between the strikes of the replicating call spread:

$$\text{Binary call} = \lim \frac{C(K + h) - C(K)}{h} \text{ when } h \to 0$$

Thus it resembles the derivative of the call with respect to the strike.[1]

Furthermore, if the trader determined that the volatility of the call was a function of the h, he would therefore create a skew function and establish a pricing mechanism.

Taking the skew as a function of K, that is $\sigma(K)$, and the skew slope at point K the derivative of the volatility with respect to the strike as shown in Figure 17.5. The bet value becomes $\delta C/\delta K + \delta C/\delta\sigma \times \delta\sigma/\delta K =$ Bet (no skew) + vega of the vanilla call of the same strike × "skew slope."[2]

> *Example:* Spot trades at 100. Zero interest rates are assumed, for pedagogical reasons. Consider the 3-month 100 bet call. The skew for a 3-month maturity increases by .5 volatility between 99.50 and 100.50; the skew slope would then be .5/1 = .5. The vega of the at-the-money call for the 3-month maturity is .190 per vol point. The value of the bet is therefore .496 (the Black-Scholes-Merton value at 15.7% volatility) + .19 × .5 = .591 for one unit paid at expiration in case the bet is satisfied.

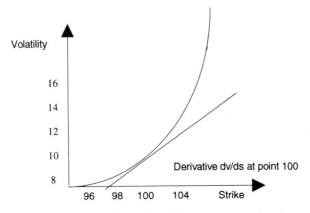

Figure 17.5   The skew slope for a given expiration.

The Skew Paradox

Quiz: The reader is told that a market went up on any day only by steps of $1 and went down by steps of $9, with no other possible price change. Such process is shown in Figure 17.6. Out of 10 steps, 9 will be up and 1 down. What would be the reader pay for a one-day at-the-money call bet paying $1 if the market closes tomorrow higher than the present level?

The answer is $.90 The key is that the bet does not depend on the expected return but on the expected number of times the spot would be higher. That the market drops in large amounts is irrelevant. The payoff of a bet option is the same whether the market drops by $1 or by $50.

Either by put-call parity rules or by use of the same argument, one arrives at a value of .1 for the put. This is an intuitive explanation for the skew. It also shows the difference between the bet and the delta: The delta, unlike the bet, is concerned with the magnitude of the moves since the trader needs to be protected for such eventuality.

Graphically, it could be represented as shown in Figure 17.7. The area A needs to be equal to area B. Financial markets impose the constraint on every security that the left integral be equal to the right one plus the risk-neutral drift, which results in a mean of the risk-neutral drift, m.

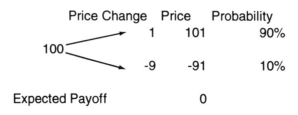

Figure 17.6

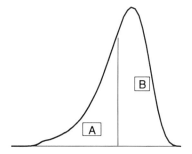

Figure 17.7 A skewed distribution.

Hence *m* is set in such a way that

$$\int_{-\infty}^{m} f(x)p(x)dx = \int_{m}^{\infty} f(x)p(x)dx + \text{risk-neutral drift}$$

with $f(x)$ the payoff and $p(x)$ the probability attached to it.

This does not mean that an *equal number of observations* should fall on both sides of the fence. A bet is only concerned with the number of observations, not the expected value of each.

Therefore the bet that x exceeds m on a certain date is simply

$$\int_{m}^{\infty} p(x)dx.$$

The skew by increasing the potential payoff on the left integral needs to be compensated with a shift of the mean to the right to prevent the markets from giving the short seller any higher expected return than the long holder (this is what is called the fair dice argument) (Figure 17.8).

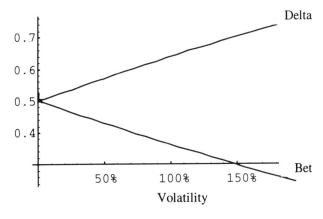

Figure 17.8 Delta and bet with volatility rising.

Difference between the Binary and the Delta: The Delta Paradox Revisited

Why isn't the delta the probability of exercise?

Simply because the delta takes into account the payoff.

In the graph of the skewed distribution (Figure 17.7), the delta is simply the right integral for a call and the left one for a put. The probability of being in the money is, to put it bluntly, the binary option.

The difference is subtle. In dealing with a geometric Brownian motion, the distribution is shifted to the right (the compounding effect of lognormality was discussed earlier in Chapter 7), and the higher the volatility the higher the shift as the asset grows in constant percentage. The higher the volatility the bigger the shift to the right. This results in the increase of the delta as a hedging protection.

This increase in the volatility is accompanied with an increase in the right side of the distribution. The distribution at higher volatility will exhibit a bulging right side that would illustrate the lognormality effect. According to the preceding principle, this will result in an increase in the risk-neutral frequency of observations to the left to maintain the fair dice condition in the environment (see Module B). Such increase in observations

---

Option Wizard: Pricing the European Bet

$d1 = (\text{Log}[S\ e^{-rft}/K\ e^{-rt}] + rt + \sigma^2 t/2)/(\sigma \sqrt{t})$

$d2 = (\text{Log}[S\ e^{-rft}/K\ e^{-rt}] + rt - \sigma^2 t/2)/(\sigma \sqrt{t})$

A vanilla call $= x\ N[d1] - k\ \text{Exp}[-rt]\ N[d2]$

Delta $= N[d1]$

Binary cash "call" $= e^{-rt}\ N[d2]$

Binary cash "put" $= e^{-rt}\ (1 - N[d2])$

Binary forward "call" $= N[d2]$

Binary forward "put" $= (1 - N[d2])$

S is the underlying.

r is the interest rate of the numeraire currency.

rf is the return of the asset concerned (foreign currency rate or dividend payout).

K is the strike price.

t is time to expiration.

Option Wizard (Advanced): The Dirac Delta

The Dirac delta is commonly used for the impulse function. It could be easy for traders to visualize the behavior of volatility at one point in time surrounding a special announcement. The daily volatility could still remain at, say, 16% but the forward-forward volatility for that second would be immensely high (in the hundreds or thousands), which would make it very difficult to measure.

The delta function can be simplified as follows: Take *e*, a small number, the smallest possible unit that can be imagined. Then the rectangle defined by the sides 1/*e* and *e* would have an area of 1 while all the areas surrounding it would have a measure of 0.

A simplified definition: $\delta(t) = 1/e$ for $0 < t < e$ and $\delta(t) = 0$ elsewhere.

Dirac Delta Simplified

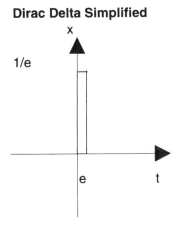

The Dirac delta is often used for the gamma at expiration: The cumulative gamma would be the delta, but it is seemingly very large at the very narrowly defined expiration instant. It also applies to the delta of a binary option close to extinction.

---

is needed to compensate for the difference between the payoff to the right and the payoff to the left. The value of the bet will therefore drop.

The delta is there to account for both the possible payoffs and their frequency while the binary option only accounts for the frequency.

Mathematical Note: A feature of the two-currency paradox is that the delta for one party is the binary of the other and vice versa. This is due to the Jensen's inequality: The expectation of $\frac{1}{x}$ (the inverted price) is not the inverse of the expectation of *x*, as discussed in Module C. Also, for one particular strike, the delta of the put is equal to the price of the binary call and vice versa. This can lead to the binary paradox—an incredible situation:

- A bet in dollars for a dollar-based person on USD-DEM is different in price from the translation into German marks of a bet in German marks on USD-DEM of the same strike and expiration. Such a difference will increase through both time to expiration and an increase in volatility.

- The reason is straightforward: Define $N(d2)$ as the price of a bet for a dollar-based person. $N(d1)$ will be the price of the bet for the person based in DEM, by the numeraire inversion.

- The extension of the paradox is a little unsettling: Two positions on two different continents cannot be marked at the same price. Furthermore, two traders performing a trade on opposite sides of the fence would thus both show a profit or a loss on the same leg.

First Hedging Consequences

- Bets need to be priced with the skew of the market taken into account using the preceding method.

- The trader should not be deceived by the apparent lack of gamma and vegas at the origin.

- The best replication for a digital is a wide risk reversal (that would include any protection against skew). There will be a trade-off between transaction costs and optimal hedges. The trader needs to shrink the difference between the strikes as time progresses until expiration, at a gradual pace. As such an optimal approach consumes transaction costs, there is a need for infrequent hedging.

- When the bet option is away from expiration, the real risks are the skew. As it nears expiration, the risks transfer to the pin. In practice, the skew is hedgeable, the pin is not.

The Delta Is a Dirac Delta

As shown in Figure 17.9, the delta for a bet looks similar to the gamma of a regular option. In addition, it will behave and "bleed" like the gamma of an option. This is because a delta is almost a bet (in the risk-neutral universe, to be correct). The delta of the bet will therefore be the gamma.

A familiarity with the Dirac delta function is helpful in understanding the way the delta moves. The Dirac delta is an interesting function that has zero value everywhere except for one point, but with the integral over the map equal to 1. Likewise the delta at expiration is zero everywhere, but the integral of the delta over the possible moves will equal the bet's face value.

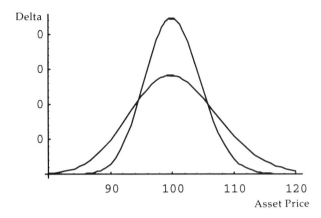

Figure 17.9   Delta of a bet (strike 100): Three months and six months to expiration.

The gamma of a vanilla option follows a Dirac delta on expiration second; however, few traders take expiration gamma seriously, because it is only the derivative of the exposure. With binary options, however, the awkward delta is of some concern because many traders hedge it with cash when the market is liquid enough for them to do so.

A delta can be viewed as the quantity that is necessary to purchase to break even over a certain move by the cash. Because the trader knows how much money he needs to make over one particular move, the notion becomes almost trivial. However, in coming closer and closer to expiration, the quantity that needs to be purchased will be close to nil in areas that do not cross the "strike" of the bet. The delta for the bet, however, will become close to infinite in one very narrow point close to the strike point. In practice, the example of the perfect replication holds: If the market were allowed to move by only one-tick increments, between say 100.00 and 100.01, then the delta between 100.00 and 100.01 would be 100 times the bet payout size (if the trade is of the at *least* variety; otherwise the trader would have to hedge between 99.99 and 100.00). A trader betting $100 would have to get a position of a face value of 100/.01 = $10,000 to satisfy his risk.

Figure 17.9 shows how the delta concentrates around the strike as the option nears expiration. Figure 17.10 show the "step function" of the bet price very close to expiration time. Figure 17.11 show the Dirac delta, the derivative of the function shown in Figure 17.10.

Gamma for a Bet

Because the delta of a bet resembles the gamma of an option, it becomes conceivable that the gamma of a bet would resemble the DgammaDspot, or third

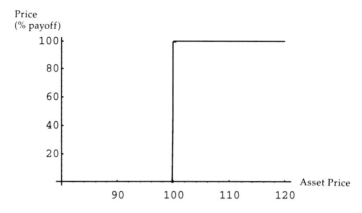

Figure 17.10   Price jump on expiration day.

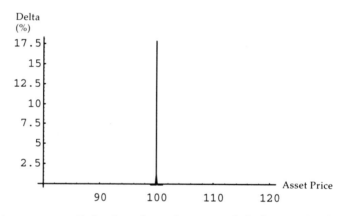

Figure 17.11   Delta for a bet a few seconds before expiration.

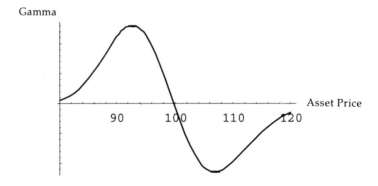

Figure 17.12   Gamma of a bet.

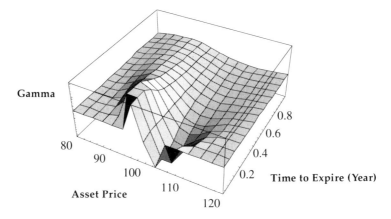

Figure 17.13 Gamma in time and space.

derivative with respect to spot. It is interesting to see how trading exotic options can help a person learn about the behavior of regular instruments.

Like a vanilla option, the gamma of the bet is flatter and more stable when the option has longer until expiration (Figures 17.12 and 17.13).

Conclusion: Statistical Trading versus Dynamic Hedging

In summary, we deemed that it was extremely difficult to hedge a binary with an option that has a continuous payoff owing to the onerous transaction costs. Even where there are minimum tick increments, a static hedge exists that perfectly matches a binary payout but is impractical and impossible to execute. So it is best to leave the hedging to structures that are likely to bite, especially as they come closer to expiration.

Hedging the bet with deltas only would be easier and sometimes the variance of the P/L could be reduced, but by no means could it be eliminated. In some cases, it might be increased. However, it is easy to be "shooting" the delta, that is overhedging it, in zones where the trader would be exposed to losses beyond his risk appetite. So if the 102 bet causes him some headaches, he could buy more deltas at 101 and take the risks of having the market drop back down. Buying way ahead of the barrier would then give him some extra P/L at 102 that could be spent in transaction costs whipping around the bet strike. "Shooting" deltas neither increases nor decreases the total return. It only smoothes the P/L around the barrier at the expense of slightly worsening it away from it.

Banks are sometimes best left to run some of the binary options like bets, much as insurance companies can live with a certain amount of local risk that

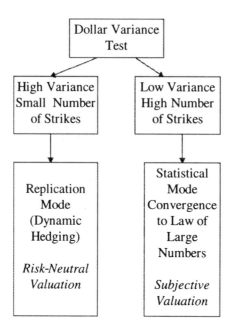

Figure 17.14 Dollar variance test.

is possible to diversify away. The good news about binary options is that their worst-case scenarios are bounded and diversifiable. Their vega vanishes as they become close to the money presenting a meaningful protection. A hitch is that in such cases, because of the absence of delta neutrality, traders need to value the bets using their own subjective distribution, not the risk-neutral one. Figure 17.14 shows the different hedging and valuation policies available to institutions.

Many of the nonfinancial bets, like bets on political events, are of a binary nature and leave no choice: They do not lend themselves to continuous hedging. Many banks issue notes with a payoff linked to a political event or the determination of federal reserve policy (e.g., a note that bets on a discount rate cut). Precisely because binary options have a discontinuous payoff, they can be easily adapted to such nonfinancial and nontradable bets.

So the trader can assume the pin risk when the amounts at stake are not life-threatening. The object is to have enough of them to become "statistical," that is, let the variance be dominated by the number of bets. Otherwise, the trader should be less statistical and more replicating.

CASE STUDY IN BINARY PACKAGES— CONTINGENT PREMIUM OPTIONS

This combination is being covered despite being a simple construction to illustrate the use of binary options in packages.

■ **Contingent premium options** are vanilla options where the option buyer only pays the price of the option in the event of it being in the money.

These options can thus be constructed with simple options plus a forward bet for the premium amount.

This sounds pretty much like a free lunch except for the hitch: It creates an area of negative profitability around the strike as shown in Figure 17.15. The owner of the option will still have to pay the premium of his option if it is slightly in the money, and such amount is, if the option is initially at the money, twice what he would have paid for a regular option. In other words, the only way to lose money on such a trade is to be slightly right.

Mechanically, it is generally composed of a regular option plus a binary where the face value of the bet corresponds to the initial premium.

Recommended Use: Potential Devaluations

A generally good use of a contingent premium option is in distributional arbitrage. The trader can have the contingent option struck at a price where he believes there is a reflecting barrier, like a currency band, or an officially defended limit to the move of an asset. The idea is that, should the price break through such a level, the market will no longer be supported by the authorities and a devaluation will cause the option to be clearly in the money.

Figure 17.16 shows a market mapping through an intervention level with a vengeance.

Another interesting use is with strongly biased assets where down moves are rare but accentuated. The trader can structure a position to

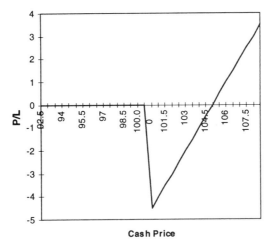

Figure 17.15   Expiration P/L for a contingent premium option.

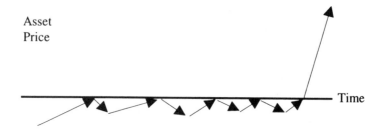

Figure 17.16 Bouncing against the intervention level.

benefit if the market precipitously falls with an at-the-money contingent premium put.

A final use for such structure is in markets with the "fat tails" where moves in either direction are accentuated, making intermediate moves quite rare.

CASE STUDY: THE BETSPREADS

Betspreads are simple binary call or put spreads. There is no mystery to them as they are obtained by construction. A betspread is a structure that collects a certain amount if the share price ends up between strike 1 and strike 2 and collects nothing elsewhere.

From a trading standpoint, they resemble butterflies and condors (a butterfly with 4 strikes) in the sense that if a binary bet resembles a call spread, a betspread resembles a condor.

While this book is not concerned with single strategies, betspreads merit some attention. The study of betspreads can enlighten the trader in the management of a pure binary options book. Because a binary option is by construction a risk reversal, a betspread is therefore a double risk reversal. This is encouraging as the position risk can be shifted down by one moment of the distribution, as shown in the following analysis.

A six-month betspread paying $1 if the asset ends up between 100 and 105 would look as depicted in Figure 17.17.

With time, the price of the betspread would naturally converge to the final payoff, and the risk would become topical. Figures 17.18 and 17.19 illustrate the effect of the passage of time on the price of the structure.

From that, it becomes easy to conclude that perhaps the best hedge for a binary option is a similar binary option.

Examine the gammas. Figure 17.20 shows the gamma of a betspread. Compare it with Figure 17.12 (gamma of a bet). The risk reversal (third moment) aspect seems to be replaced by a fifth moment instability, which is, in this case, preferable.

Spread

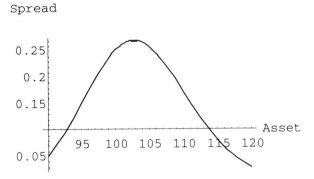

Figure 17.17   Price of the betspread.

Spread

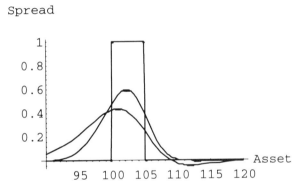

Figure 17.18   Betspread one month to one minute to expiration.

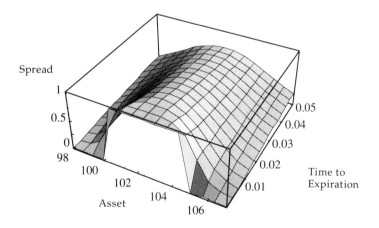

Figure 17.19   The effect of time on price.

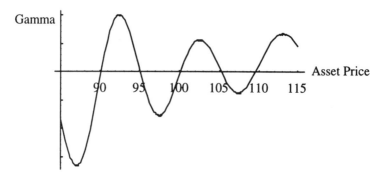

Figure 17.20 Gamma of a betspread.

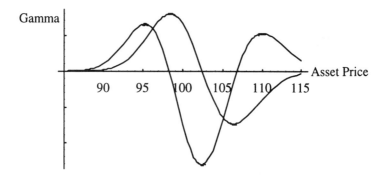

Figure 17.21 Gammas of a series of betspreads.

The accordion shown in Figure 17.21 is a series of betspreads.

Conclusion: the bets are easier to hedge than regular options as the asymmetry of the vegas can be reduced with the trading of another bet.

Advanced Case Study: Multiasset Bets

A bet that pays if either of the two commodities ends up higher or lower than a certain level at expiration is called a multiasset bet.

The reader can, as an exercise, study the exposure to the correlation of a structure that presents two bets, of the either-or variety, using the preceding methodology and that presented in Chapter 22. To price it intuitively, he can imagine the value of the limit decomposition of a rainbow call spread.

Chapter 18

Binary Options: American Style

Adam K., one of the greatest option traders of all times (and one of the fastest minds the author ever met) called the author with the following request:

"I hear you are giving a 4-day seminar on hedging exotic options. Can you give it to me during lunch time tomorrow? All I need is the beef. You see, I don't have patience for details."

AMERICAN SINGLE BINARY OPTIONS

■ **American binary** (or digital) option is a common bet option with the difference that it pays when the price is "touched" rather than if the price settles above or below a certain price.

As defined, the American binary is path dependent (Figure 18.1). A trader cannot go on an extended trekking vacation and come back on expiration day to satisfy the bet obligation. The bet can thus reach expiration any time before.

The first noticeable difference between the American and the European bet is the price. Because the option has at least equal chances of being knocked out, it is therefore a larger outlay than the European one for the "buyer" at all times (generally twice).[1] The buyer is defined as the person who receives the payment if the price is touched. The American bet will thus be more expensive with the consequence that the risk of the lack of satisfaction for the seller will be much larger.

Option Wizard: The Contamination Principle and Barrier Options

If there is a point, namely the barrier, that can create some positive P/L (the termination of the bet is positive for the buyer), then the position will be long gamma in smoothly decreasing amounts in areas surrounding it. It will therefore be long vega from that position.

If, for reasons of carry (see Girsanov), the bet termination results in negative P/L, then, again the areas close to such point will carry a negative gamma.

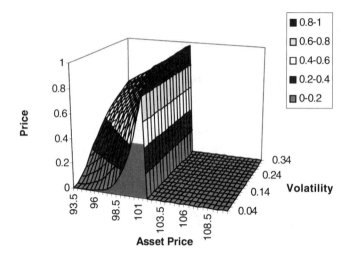

Figure 18.1 American digital.

Example: Spot trades at 100. Assume volatility at 15.7%. A European bet that spot will be higher than 105 at expiration 100 days hence will be worth 26% of the face value. An American bet will be worth 51% of the face value of the payoff.

Another difference is that because, unlike the European, it is not possible to cross the fence (i.e., move "in" the money), the American bet will always be long volatility for the seller. Intuitively, it is easier to sense that, unlike another structure, the movement would benefit the seller if it takes the option closer to the money. If movement one way can translate into higher profits, by the contamination principle the movement should help in the other direction.

It was established in Chapter 17 that the European binary is a risk reversal. The American binary is generally monotonic in gamma, though not always (Figure 18.2).

> *Risk Management Rule:* With no drift (forward trades at flat with cash), the American binary never changes in the sign of the vegas and gammas: It remains a pocket of localized long vega.

The issue of interest rates will be tackled in Chapters 19 and 20. A positive curve can lead to negative gamma near the bet price for an American binary and positive gamma away from it. The rule is as follows:

> ***Risk Management Rule:***   The American binary will be positive gamma everywhere (for the "owner," the person who earns the pay-off when the barrier is hit) when the delta hedge against the option incurs a negative carry.

For a definition of negative carry in an asset, traders can easily use the following rule: forward price for the period $t + 1$ is higher than the forward price for period t (the spot).

> ***Risk Management Rule:***   The profile of the American binary will look like that of a risk reversal (i.e., a third position moment different from 0) if the delta hedge of the owner earns a positive carry superior to the time decay of the same binary on the same asset without drift.

A peculiar aspect of the American binary that leads to the notion of stopping time is that the distribution of the expected time to extinction is what matters. In a way, an American binary is a bet on time.

The expected exit time has been around for a while in probability theory. Module G provides technical details and references. The issue also will be discussed further in Chapter 19.

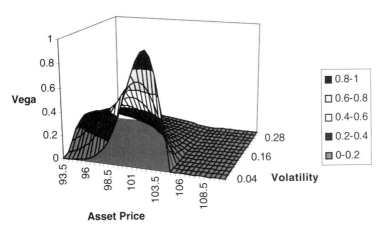

Figure 18.2   Volatility sensitivity of an American digital.

Hedging an American Binary: Fooled by the Greeks

This section provides a simplified tutorial for the management of the vega risk of any nonvanilla structure with a concave vega.

Case Study: National Vega Bank

This case study describes the attempt to hedge the following option: a 105 "if touched" bet paying $1 on termination per unit. The trader at National Vega Bank becomes, due to an ugly structure that is otherwise stripped and hedged, long the 105 American bet in $10,000,000. Spot is at 100 and, as usual, the forward trades at flat. Volatility, as in most examples, is at 15.7% which corresponds to 1% a day move 252 days a year. The bet expires exactly 100 days from now. "Fair" value (better called unfair value) is 54.7% (i.e., $5,470,000).

Table 18.1 P/L of the Three Legs of the Trade

Price	Price	Option P/L	Hedge P/L	Total P/L
94.8	0.21119	−3353	4160	807
95.2	0.23034	−3162	3840	678
95.6	0.2506	−2959	3520	561
96.0	0.27201	−2745	3200	455
96.4	0.29455	−2520	2880	360
96.8	0.31823	−2283	2560	277
97.2	0.34304	−2035	2240	205
97.6	0.36896	−1775	1920	145
98.0	0.39598	−1505	1600	95
98.4	0.42407	−1224	1280	56
98.8	0.45321	−933	960	27
99.2	0.48335	−631	640	9
99.6	0.51447	−320	320	0
100.0	0.5465	0	0	0
100.4	0.57941	329	−320	9
100.8	0.61313	666	−640	26
101.2	0.64761	1011	−960	51
101.6	0.68279	1363	−1280	83
102.0	0.7186	1721	−1600	121
102.4	0.75497	2085	−1920	165
102.8	0.79184	2453	−2240	213
103.2	0.82911	2826	−2560	266
103.6	0.86673	3202	−2880	322
104.0	0.90462	3581	−3200	381
104.4	0.9427	3962	−3520	442
104.8	0.98089	4344	−3840	504
105.2	0	Closed	Closed	504

By "buying," the trader has a similar position as being long a call-spread, which is long delta. In addition, as he is betting on the spot moving, he will be long volatility.

The first thing that comes to mind is the delta. The trader will hedge it by selling the equivalent of 8% of the face value of the security, namely $800,000.

Table 18.1 and Figure 18.3 show the resulting three legs of the trade: The P/L for the binary, that from the delta, and the final net. As can be seen in Figure 18.3, the position is mildly long gamma. However, the gamma disappears beyond the barrier. In addition, the trader would need to rapidly unwind his position. As shown in Figure 18.3 and discussed in the Option Wizard, *The Gap Delta*, there is a discontinued payoff. Should the trader avoid catching the market on time, the hedge would be off by a slippage factor.

Figure 18.4 shows the effect of time at 2 asset price levels. The gamma would increase, as time flows, near the barrier and decrease everywhere else. The slope of the decay at 103, 2 points away from the barrier, is considerably steeper than the slope at 100, 5 points way. As decay and gamma go in pair, the reader can infer an increase in the gamma near the barrier with the passage of time.

The Ravages of Time

Figure 18.5 depicts the initial position with fewer days to go, showing the effect of time. Needless to say, the position would increase in gamma as

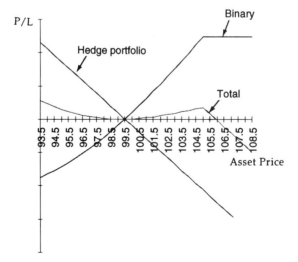

Figure 18.3 Gamma position: P/L of the three legs of the trade.

Option Wizard: The Gap Delta (I)

The gap delta is the difference in deltas near a particular barrier. The trader needs to unwind a certain amount of deltas that were used to hedge a barrier structure by dumping that amount in the market at a given price.

The trader has no guarantee of getting the exact target price, owing to liquidity matters. Trying to execute ahead of the barrier is equally dangerous as it raises the dangers of the "fake trigger," a situation where the market trades near the barrier then pulls back without hitting it.

The difference between the price the unwinding was executed at and the barrier is called the **slippage** (as defined in Chapter 4). Many traders get negative surprises as markets near the barrier. Illiquid markets can be vicious as they undergo **liquidity holes** (as defined in Chapter 4) near a particular barrier.

The gap delta receives extensive treatment in other parts of the book, as it deserves as much attention as possible.

---

time comes closer to expiration. As time goes by, the following problem takes place: the stakes get bigger close to the barrier.

The P/L cannot be read between two different dates on the graph on Figure 18.5. It corresponds to the recentering of the position at 100 the day of the run. The P/L lines are all made to be zero at 100, which prevents the user from comparing two dates, but allows visualizing the P/L within one date. Such an issue of noncomparability is explained in the Option Wizard, *Looking at a Graph through Time.*

Note. It is assumed that the trader did not unwind his delta in the market after the barrier is hit. This shows the precipitous drop in P/L as the binary, being terminated ceases to accumulate positive P/L while the delta continues to build a negative P/L.

From Figure 18.5, it is evident that the delta becomes larger close to the strike next to expiration. So the trader needs to sell the asset in the rally.

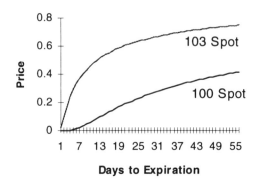

Figure 18.4 American binary 105 calls: Over time.

Option Wizard: Looking at a Graph through Time

Unlike many functions that one can easily project through time, an option position needs to be analyzed while keeping in mind that markets are not just frozen between periods and that traders are not stuffed birds. The positions will change and traders react accordingly.

A graph representing the same position one month later would not correctly forecast the P/L as it does not include the appropriate adjustments an option position continuously undergoes.

However, the following takes place: These deltas present as many potential problems to deal with, as the knocking-off of the binary would necessitate unwinding larger and larger amounts of money. The trader would need to buy back what he sold. The higher the delta, the more he would need to sell, the more he would have to buy back. From whom? Most probably from those he initially sold to.

In addition, look at the potential danger: What if the binary were not knocked off? The P/L accumulated on the buildup of time value in the binary would deflate rapidly, causing considerable time decay.

Look then at the same graph without recentering it (Figure 18.6). It is easy to infer that the position increases in gamma through time and, consequently, in time decay. As can be seen, the time decay becomes a serious matter close to the end. The P/L should be interpreted from the origin of 100 to the next point. It assumes delta hedging at the date and at the price of 100 without subsequent hedging until the barrier is hit. So the 10-day position was made delta neutral on the delta of the tenth day, considerably lower

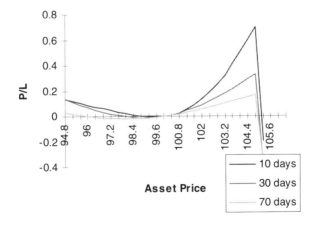

Figure 18.5 Binary option: 70 days through 10 days.

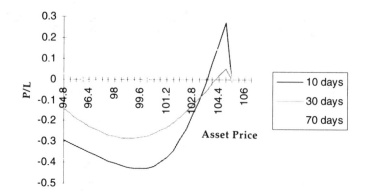

Figure 18.6 P/L through time.

than that of the seventieth day. Otherwise, the price of the bet would exhibit different features.

Another piece of information can be gathered from the same graph but without delta hedging.

There is a subtle difference between Figures 18.5 and 18.6. In the previous one, the 30-day line came below both the 10-day and the 70-day, owing to the delta neutrality at 100.

Figure 18.7 provides the intuition of the true risks. The longer the time to expiration, the more horizontal the slope of the asset price to the option value, the lower the risks. With little time left on the clock, the trade is safe away from the strike and risky near it. Figure 18.8 shows the corresponding gamma.

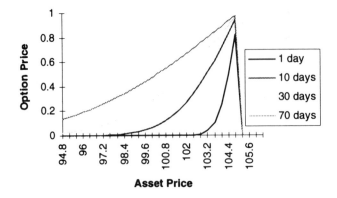

Figure 18.7 American binary option: Price through time.

Gamma

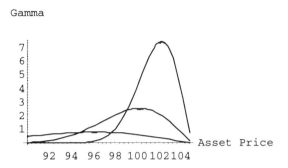

Figure 18.8 Gamma as near expiration.

Understanding the Vega Convexity

In Figure 18.9 the first noticeable effect is that the difference becomes thinner at the extremes. While every option trader knows than an option's vega diminishes away from the strike, this seems to be quite exaggerated. In addition, the vega vanishes completely at the barrier.

This effect is not trivial. It raises the problem of how to hedge the vega of an American binary option with instruments *that do not vanish at the barrier.* Many attempts at the so-called static option replication have been made without much success at finding a structure that can imitate the payoff everywhere and cancel the pin risk.

The notion of vega convexity is best demonstrated by creating a portfolio that is long vega through the binary and short vega with other instruments in the market that present a linear sensitivity to implied volatility.

First, look at the effect of volatility changes on one structure, as shown in Figure 18.10.

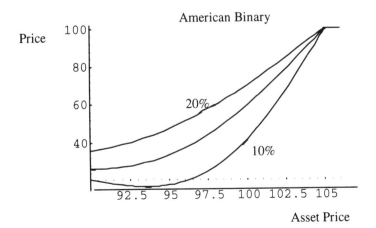

Figure 18.9 Volatility effect.

Price

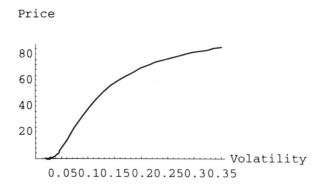

Figure 18.10 Sensitivity of an American digital to volatility.

The reader can see that the function is concave. Higher volatility causes the price to increase, but at a decreasing rate. It means that should the trader go vega neutral against the structure, he will end up short volatility of volatility, or to use a different language, short the fourth moment. From a trader's experience, the worst moment to be short is the fourth moment because, unlike the third moment (the skew), there is generally no clear compensation for the risks incurred. The prices in the market, using constant volatility models, do not factor such exposure.

Starting at 15.7 volatility, the trader decides to hedge the vega using an instrument of the same official duration. So he sells enough volatility to be "vega neutral," that is for small moves in volatility.

Figure 18.11 shows the volatility concavity. This concavity is mostly due to the shortening of the first exit time as volatility rises. The vega sensitivity shrinks as the trader comes near the trigger. Such concavity would change according to the position of the market relative to the barrier. Figure 18.12 shows the concavity close to the barrier which is more pronounced than the one shown in Figure 18.11.

P/L

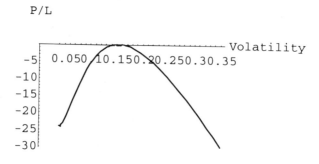

Figure 18.11 Volatility concavity of an American binary.

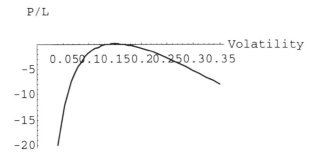

Figure 18.12 Concavity close to the barrier.

So far, the following risks have been shown:

- *Duration Risks.* The barrier is a bet on duration. Vanillas do not hedge in a shifting volatility curve against the shifts, lengthening, and shortening of the structure. So much for static option replication.
- *Gap Risks.* The risk of having to pay up to unwind the deltas close to the bet level.
- *Vega Risk* (after the barrier). Vega hedges need to take into account that the exposure vanishes past the bet price. It means that whatever hedge the trader performs should shrink accordingly past that level. Good luck in finding one.
- *Vega Concavity* (for the owner). Whatever structure is used as a hedge needs to have a positive fourth moment (i.e., long volatility of volatility) to be able to offset the risks of the structure.

These risks, inherent to the American binary, are present in some shape or another in all barrier options.

Trading Methods

American binary options are truly options on time rather than options on the asset. As such, they can only be hedgeable with instruments that are similarly options on time. These instruments are necessarily other barriers, with similar payoff, at some trigger point not too far removed from the bet itself.

Hedging a long position in American bets with European vanilla options is a true losing proposition, except in cases where one prices the fourth moment risk into the structure. Hedging them with binary options of the European variety creates an illusion of a hedge: The European bet is altogether another instrument, except on expiration minute.

The greatest danger traders face in their activity comes from the reading of the risk on a computer sheet. Vegas stemming from a European vanilla with its clear and well-defined duration are more reliable than those arising from the American binary options with unknown duration and unstable moments. So traders who navigate with the Greeks are going to be subjected to serious dangers. "Non-Greek" traders (i.e., nonparametric traders) who absorb as much information about their strikes fare better. That is why it is best recommended to divorce a barrier book from a vanilla position to better see the strikes and navigate without the superficial information about the lower Greeks.

Case Study: At-Settlement American Binary Options

Some binary options, as if the American binary feature was not deleterious enough, present the additional difficulty of a conditional feature. Besides the "if touched" variety, there is the "if settled" type that makes the regular American binary seem easy to trade by comparison.

An if settled binary only pays the bet value if the underlying asset officially **settles** through the trigger. This means that the asset price needs to settle higher than the trigger if the bet is a call and lower than the trigger if the asset is a put.

Many traders believe that such a feature comes into play on the last day. But the last day for an American binary is going to be every possible day.

This feature acts on the price of the binary in a strange way: It creates a negative gamma hole around the price of the barrier. Earlier, it was seen that the important feature of an American binary bet is that (except for some cases of a high carry on the delta), it remains long gamma for the "owner" until termination. This feature is attributable to the fact that the position could remain only on one side of the barrier and could not cross it at all without termination, which would make the vega and gamma dimension mute.

An American if settled binary would therefore act like a European binary during the day and like an American between days as shown in Figure 18.13. This causes serious complications with the unwinding of the gap delta.

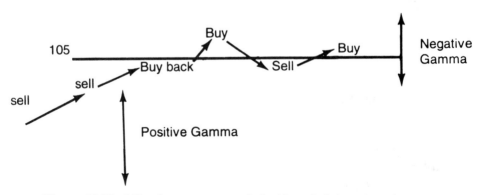

Figure 18.13   Mixed gamma around the if settled American barrier.

Example: A 105 Call if settled American bet pays $1 on termination. The trader sells deltas against the position. As the market rallies, he would need to sell more to benefit from the probability of cashing in on the bet. However, he would have to buy everything back if the strike is crossed. Should the market cross the gap early in the day, the uncertainty would last the longest. The trader has no way of knowing whether he would remain in the terminating zone or if he would cross again to reenter the opposite area. What if the market moved back down and settled on the "negative" side of the bet? This constitutes a negative gamma position around the barrier that vanishes in the extremes, high above or low below, as depicted in Figures 18.13 and 18.14.

Other Greeks

Studying the behavior of other Greeks such as the rho is generally futile because of the instability of the measure. Having established that the gamma was unusual, there is no need to go into secondary, less significant Greeks.

AMERICAN DOUBLE BINARY OPTIONS

■ An **American double bet** is a bet whose condition is satisfied if the market touches *either* of two levels during the life of the option. These levels are generally called high barrier and low barrier.

A particularity of American double bets is that they are not the sum of two bets. A European double bet is SDF decomposable, which means that one could add two European binary options and get the resulting European double bet, which needs not be examined here for that reason. An American double bet is a structure that terminates whenever **one of** the legs is touched, which is a serious difference. The SDF is explained in the Option Wizard, *Smallest Decomposable Fragment,* in Chapter 2.

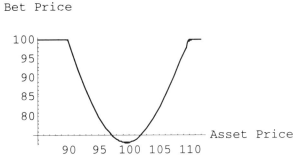

Figure 18.14   American bet.

One feature to remember about the American double bets is that, counterintuitively, they will trade at a very narrow discount of the bet value (it is usually expressed in percentages; a bet priced at 96% pays 100 for every 96 dollars invested in it). Prices such as 98% or 99% are common for options that are a few weeks away with barriers straddling the market by only 2 or 3 daily standard deviations.

An interesting feature of American bets is how short their expected exit time may be. A double bet trading at 80% of face value implies, roughly, assuming no drift and no interest rates, that it has about 20% of the nominal time to live.

The double bet feature is often present in the so-called range notes where the investor is sold financial assets and notes that pay their coupons according to whether the market remains within some range or not. In that case, the assumption is that the coupon is the face value of the bet. Figure 18.15 shows the profile of the double binary with time.

Vegas of the Double Binary

The barrier reacts to an increase in volatility by shortening its expected time of arrival. This presents a very concave way of being long vega. For that reason, even hedging by selling other concave vegas (like a single barrier) might not be sufficient. The instrument trading at 80 or 90 can only reach 100 as volatility increases, which limits its vega power. The concavity, as a rule of thumb, can be ascertained from the following: As the amounts to possibly lose from a trade become considerably higher than the amounts to possibly earn, the concavity feature intensifies.

It is easy to see that above an implied volatility of 20% the bet reaches a price close to 100%.

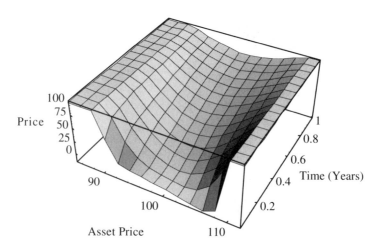

Figure 18.15 American double binary.

Table 18.2 shows the trade of a double bet at 16% volatility (Figures 18.16 and 18.17) and an attempt to hedge the vega exposure with a linear vega. The amounts are expressed per unit of a 1% bet.

Other Applications of American Barriers

Amortizing Interest Rate Securities

■ The maturity, coupon, or in some structures, the principal, of **amortizing interest rate securities,** varies according to whether some predefined rate was reached in the market. They can be defined in any possible manner but those that are path dependent can irreversibly decline in coupon payments or principal if some interest rate level is reached.

As such, it is safe to assume that the amortizing swap is a zero coupon instrument plus a series of forward American bets on every coupon payment, each bet being a specific level in the market. This assumption requires no special feature like requirements for the market to remain under some level for a prolonged period.

They can be forward bets because each bet is timed like the payment of a regular coupon. Again every structure varies from pricing purposes but the trading intuition remains that of a sum of American bets.

Amortizing swaps represent another situation where the traders were long American digital options and discovered themselves to be long gamma *until* the barrier. The traders sold options to flatten out their gamma and rapidly discovered the notions of vega convexity and that of a vanishing leg of a hedge. As these securities were fashionable for a brief period, the build up in inventory caused a few spectacular losses when the dealers rushed to buy back their gamma.

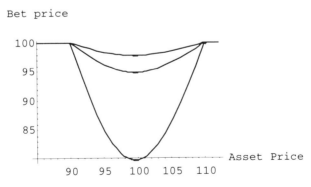

Figure 18.16 Volatility effect of 12, 16, and 18% on a one-year 90/110 American bet.

Table 18.2   A Vega Hedge for a Double Binary Option

Volatility (%)	Price (%)	P/L	Hedge P/L	Total
6	24.4	−70.5	23.71	−46.81
7	35.2	−59.7	21.34	−38.38
8	46.0	−48.9	18.96	−29.92
9	56.2	−38.7	16.59	−22.12
10	65.3	−29.6	14.22	−15.38
11	73.2	−21.7	11.85	−9.86
12	79.8	−15.1	9.48	−5.63
13	85.1	−9.8	7.11	−2.66
14	89.3	−5.6	4.74	−0.83
15	92.5	−2.4	2.37	0.00
16	94.9	0.0	0.00	0.00
17	96.6	1.7	−2.37	−0.66
18	97.8	2.9	−4.74	−1.84
19	98.6	3.7	−7.11	−3.40
20	99.1	4.2	−9.48	−5.23
21	99.5	4.6	−11.85	−7.26
22	99.7	4.8	−14.22	−9.41
23	99.8	4.9	−16.59	−11.65
24	99.9	5.0	−18.96	−13.95
25	99.9	5.1	−21.34	−16.28
26	100.0	5.1	−23.71	−18.63
27	100.0	5.1	−26.08	−21.00
28	100.0	5.1	−28.45	−23.37
29	100.0	5.1	−30.82	−25.69

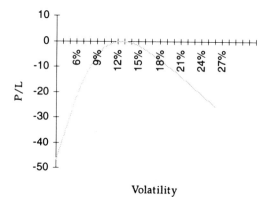

Figure 18.17   Nasty vega neutrality.

Option Wizard: Too Much Hedging Is Bad for You

This chapter will end with the following war story: An aggressive derivatives house lost a considerable amount of money on a trade where they managed to buy "cheap" volatility with a series of knock-out options using rebates, in fact obtaining a strip of American binary options. They had a considerable "margin" in the trade, which means that the trader went home with some theoretical marks-to-market profits and thought highly of himself.

The trader was asked by his boss to manage the risk and reduce the exposure. "Cash-in on the money," he was told. This was a reference to the money they believed they had earned off the customer. So the trader examined the Greeks and sold the vega, to perfect the vega neutrality in a manner that would befit such a sophisticated house as his.

A few weeks later, the trader was out of a job. Volatility exploded and he lost considerable money due to the difference in convexity between the vegas he owned and the vegas he so massively sold. His boss, not very recipient about notions of fourth moments and other nerdy matters, fired him on grounds that the trader did not properly offset the exposure. Actually, the trader, hedging a double barrier with out-of-the-money options, was even short the sixth moment.

The trader, like most derivatives traders who lose their jobs, landed himself a better position (he had gained valuable experience) and concluded with the following wisdom: ***Hedging increases your risks.***

Risk Management Rule: It is necessary to avoid hedging a discontinuous exposure with continuous one.

Credit Risk

Assume that a trader buys a USD denominated Mongolian government note. As the note will trade at an interest rate differential with the default-free USD rate, it is convenient to view the payment differential as a form of forward American bet on the default by the Mongolian government. Again, the American bet is a general framework: One could estimate that the face value of the bet is the total paper minus some recovery value.

Chapter 19

Barrier Options (I)

A true trader is a human being endowed with the rare gift of a positively sloping learning curve.

This chapter opens with a discussion of knock-in and knock-out options (of the regular variety that knock in or out when they are out-of-the-money).[1] These options represent the simplest forms of barrier trading and hedging. Reverse barrier options will be covered in Chapter 20. The terminology "reverse" indicates the unusual nature of the transaction, as well as the hedging difficulties incurred in its management. Table 19.1 shows the different barrier categories and rates their trading complexity.

With reverse barriers, the payoff at the barrier is significant. The trader needs familiarity and experience with regular knock-outs before muddling in the waters of reverse barriers. Prior understanding of American binary options is a must.

Rebates will be covered in the next chapter, as those make a barrier option closer to an American binary. The next chapter will also discuss double barriers as well as the major possible variations around the barrier theme.

Unless otherwise mentioned, the underlying options concerned are European style.

BARRIER OPTIONS (REGULAR)

Regular barrier options include calls down and out, puts up and out, calls down and in, puts up and in. This section is required to understand all other barrier structures.

Knock-Out Options

■ A **knock-out option** is a regular option with a second strike price, called "trigger," "outstrike," or "barrier." The option is considered expired when the second strike, the barrier, is crossed.

The terminology varies (as with most new products), but knock-outs are defined as having the trigger placed in such a way that the option dies

Table 19.1 Categories of Single Barrier Options

	Category	Description	Trading Difficulty and Risks
Down and out call	Regular knock-out call	The option dies out-of-the-money	Low
Down and out put	Reverse knock-out put	The option dies in-the-money	High
Up and out call	Reverse knock-out call	The option dies in-the-money	High
Up and out put	Regular knock-out put	The option dies out-of-the-money	Low
Down and in call	Regular knock-in call	The option is born out-of-the-money	Low
Down and in put	Reverse knock-in put	The option is born in-the-money	High
Up and in call	Reverse knock-in call	The option is born in-the-money	High
Up and in put	Regular knock-in put	The option is born out-of-the-money	Low

when it is out-of-the-money. The trigger will be below the current spot if the latter is below the strike. It will be above the current spot if the latter is out-of-the-money. Otherwise, the option is called a reverse knock-out. Reverse knock-out structures are more difficult to trade than knock-outs because the option vanishes when it holds a large intrinsic value, a difficulty that causes traders to call a regular knock-out a vanilla by comparison.

Knock-out options are often unaccommodating to trade because of the discontinuity in the deltas as the option crosses the trigger. Slippage is greatest with them, particularly when gaps occur and the trader who needs to unwind his hedge at some price ends up doing so at a markedly less attractive level. This is one reason that dynamic hedging is said to be costly. When in possession of a large enough size to impact the market, however, some traders are known to create considerable profits out of their structures. These are the cases that create *liquidity holes,* much to the consternation of the financial community, whose members see the knock-outs as a source of large volatility.

Example: If the underlying security trades at 100, assuming no forward curve, a one-month at-the-money option would trade at 1.80% of face value.

The same at-the-money call but knocking out 2% below the present strike would trade for 1.34% (plus a higher commission owing to its wider bid/offer spread).

From the customer point of view, if the market should rally immediately, the knock-out will be equivalent to a regular call obtained cheaper. In a break, the worst-case scenario will be the same. The knock-out would fare worse if the market went down prior to the rally, a scenario that tends to occur somewhat more often than the theory would suggest (Figure 19.1).

Customer Demand for Knock-Out Options.   Many customers prefer to use barrier options for the simple reason that they come cheaper. In addition, many users of an option prefer to rid themselves of it when it is no longer needed.

The major users are as follows:

- Funds managers holding a large stock market exposure, in order to lower their hedging expenditure. Funds managers owning stocks always prefer to own puts as protection. They generally feel, however, that 5% above the market they no longer need such protection as they would normally flatten themselves up in such conditions. Such a profile is similar to that of a *risk reversal* (or collar) except that they would not necessarily lose their stocks in a violent rally.

- Speculators who believe strongly in *trends and serial correlation* (or dependence) in a market. A fund manager prefers to be long as long as the market does not sell below a certain point. He can thus buy an out-of-the-money call that knocks out at a certain price if he is wrong. The knock-out agrees with the psychology of trend followers. Its path dependency conforms to their beliefs in the shape of the

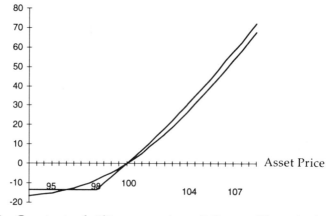

Figure 19.1   Constant volatility comparison, P/L a vanilla and a knock-out call.

distribution. They believe that the world is going to behave differently than a random walk and that they can translate their beliefs into option trades. Most frequently, the barrier would be placed close to a chart point or some level that chartists consider critical for the market direction. When chartists lose faith in a trend, they do not mind canceling their bet.

- Corporates who have a contingent exposure but who believe that they could square it up should the market move their way.

Discontinuity at the Barrier.   The delta of a knock-out shows discontinuity at the barrier. In the earlier example of 100 calls/KO 98 (pronounced 100 calls knock-out 98 in the vernacular), it moves from .66 to zero. The seller of the option can either jump up in joy for having lost a liability or jump up in anger at having lost considerable money by being filled at worse than the stop level he set at 98.00.

Figure 19.2 shows the behavior of the delta of the KO at different asset price levels. In this example, the trader who is short the knock-out call needs to buy more contracts than if he were short a vanilla. While the vanilla has the at-the-money delta close to 50%, the knock-out option has a delta of about 68%. This is to compensate for the fact that in the rally the knock-out and the vanilla will be equivalent in price, whereas the trader sold the knock-out at a lower price than the vanilla. As the market goes higher, however, the deltas and prices converge.

Should the market jump down by 2 points immediately, the 68% deltas would generate close to $1.36 per unit sold. To be exact, $1.34 because the final delta in the example is 66%, causing the structure to be hedged at an average delta of .67 (owing to the small gamma effect of the move). The trader sold the option at 1.34. But he needs more than 1.34 to cover the transaction costs of liquidation at the barrier.

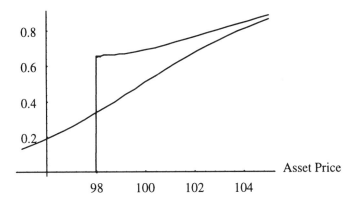

Figure 19.2   Delta comparison between a vanilla and a knock-out.

> *Trading Rule:* The transaction costs of unwinding the hedge should be taken into account when selling a barrier.

Let us say that some panic choked the market and that the execution slippage at the barrier turned out to be .10. This translates into a final price for the barrier of at least $.1 \times .66 = 0.066$ more than the initial 1.34 should the option terminate. Therefore the minimum fair value for the operator will be 1.34 plus .066 times the probability of hitting the barrier (which corresponds to the value of an American binary paying .066 at 98 and expiring at the same time as the barrier option). It will be roughly 1.39. That is the minimum, as more costs will crop up to affect the structure.

As the market approaches the barrier, the deltas of the knock-out and the vanillas start to diverge: The trader needs to accumulate more and more delta to make up for the fact that he might lose the option soon and be freed of an obligation. When the asset becomes close to the barrier, however, he needs to unwind the deltas as they become superfluous. It is a double-edged sword. Hitting the barrier is a blessing because the trader loses a liability (the option), but the way the barrier is touched is significant. Should the market gap through the barrier (it often does so), the hedge would be unwound at a worse level than expected and the trader would wish he had not hit the barrier. The slippage around the barrier is meaningful.

Figure 19.3 shows the 100 call/90. The option price and deltas start resembling the vanilla when the difference widens. It becomes conceivable that less is at stake when the difference between the strike and the trigger widens.

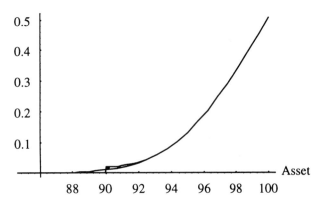

Figure 19.3   Delta for a 1m out-of-the-money knock-out and a vanilla.

Knock-In Options

The knock-in option is an option that comes into existence when a particular price is hit in the market. A regular knock-in comes into existence as it is out-of-the-money which simplifies its trigger conditions. A reverse knock-in comes into the world with intrinsic value (by the forward), which complicates its existence.

Studying knock-in options as their own instrument must be limited because they are, by construction, nothing but a combination of a vanilla and a knock-out. This will be shown later in the section.

Customer Demand for Knock-In Options.   For the same reason knock-out options are a device for a trend follower, knock-in options are a device designed for a mean-reverting mentality. They are inherently options that come alive against the market direction.

The knock-out options can be used in structures. But perhaps the most important thing for a dynamic hedger is not to focus too much on the uses of the product and concentrate instead on their hedging techniques.

> *Example:*   Using a similar example as before—a one-month 100 call knocking in at 98—Figure 19.4 shows an interesting graph. The first time traders encounter the plot of the price with respect to the underlying security, they know they are confronted with two piecewise options of opposing deltas.

This can be confirmed by looking at the delta (see Figure 19.5).

In spite of its scary complexity, the knock-in call presents exactly the same features as a knock-out: The jump in deltas is of equal magnitude,

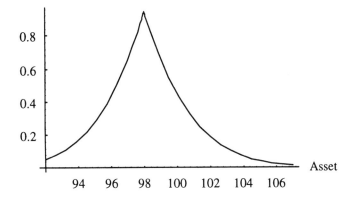

Figure 19.4   Price of a knock-in call.

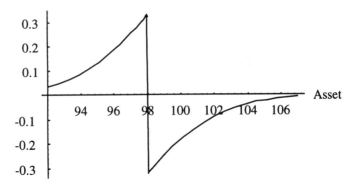

Figure 19.5   Delta of a knock-in call.

although its move is in the opposite sign. This means that the knock-in could complement the knock-out of same maturity and strike to create a vanilla. If the reader took Figure 19.5 and subtracted Figure 19.2, he would see the same graph.

At the barrier, the delta of the knock-in moves *up* from −.32 to .33, which means that the operator has a gap delta of .65 to make up for. A knock-out call, likewise, has a gap delta of a jump *down* of .65, which means that the operator long one and long the other would have nothing to do. This is the basis for the rule of the short barrier.

■ **Long the barrier** means that the operator benefits from the hitting of the trigger, either by the decrease in liability (a knock-out) or by an increase in wealth (a knock-in).

A short knock-out is long the barrier. A long knock-in is long the barrier. A short knock-out benefits when the market hits the trigger as the contingent liability extinguishes. A long knock-in benefits in the same manner, as the triggering moves it from a conditional asset (the underlying option) to an unconditional one.

By extension, the long knock-in and long knock-out are flat the barrier and have exposure to the underlying option, hence the arbitrage relationship:

$$\text{Knock-in } (K, t, H) + \text{Knock-out } (K, t, H) = \text{Vanilla } (K, t)$$

Where K is the strike price, t time to expiration, and H the barrier level. A long knock-in of one strike plus long knock-out of the same strike and maturity are equal to a long vanilla. Look at the one-month 100 calls KO 98, 100 calls KI 98, and the 100 calls (Figure 19.6). Below the 98 point, the knock-in exhibits the same behavior of the vanilla (for a good reason: It is now a

Option Price

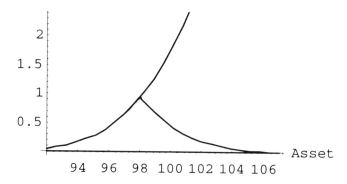

Figure 19.6   Vanilla, knock-in, and knock-out.

vanilla). The knock-out will then be dead. Above 98, the knock-out behaves like a vanilla, while the knock-in increasingly divorces itself from it.

Effects of Volatility

Figure 19.7 shows the price sensitivity of a knock-out to volatility levels. To the right, as volatility increases, the barrier gets flat vega while the vanilla retains its effect. This is due to the barrier becoming closer in a nonlinear way as volatility rises. Volatility remains linear for a vanilla. Eventually, the barrier would dominate: As the barrier nears, by the sheer effect of volatility becoming higher, the option has a shorter and shorter time to live.

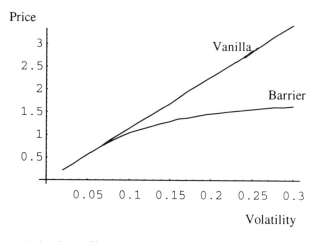

Figure 19.7   Volatility effect on a 1m 100/98 knock-out and a vanilla call.

Option Price

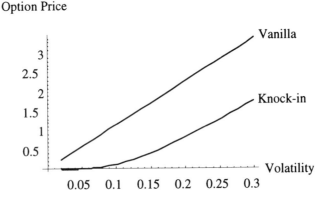

Figure 19.8   Knock-in and a vanilla.

Figure 19.8 shows the opposite effect for a knock-in. The knock-in will have a convex vega while the knock-out will have a concave one. This is meaningful for hedging purposes.

Trading Rule: Volatility brings the barrier closer in a nonlinear way. This occurs because volatility is always non-linear for events that are away from the center of the distribution (they affect the out-of-the-money and in-the-money options).

Close to the barrier, the options have different vegas since the barrier loses in convexity. Far from the barrier (the "other side"), the options would start converging in behavior, including their sensitivity to volatility. It is understandable that when the barrier is away from the asset price, the barrier option converges in price to that of the vanilla. Operators thus test barrier pricing systems by placing the barrier at 0 (or .00001) for a knock-out call and a very high number for a knock-out put and verifying that the price becomes that of a vanilla.

This leads to the vega linearity rule.

Trading Rule: The vegas emanating from the barrier part of a barrier option are concave for the seller. The combination barrier vega + vanilla vega will result in a concave vega for the long barrier (see definition) and a convex vega for the short barrier.

The extension of the rule is that the concavity/convexity would start vanishing as the trader moves away from the barrier into areas where the vanilla dominates. Figures 19.9 and 19.10 show the vegas of the two instruments.

Vega

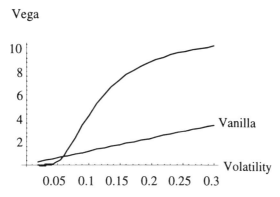

Figure 19.9 Vega of a down and in and a vanilla.

A more thorough analysis will involve changing the example into an out-of-the-money option struck at 105 with the same trigger at 98. The maturity is lengthened to take a 6-month option; volatility remains at 15.7%.

Figure 19.11 shows the shifts in vega from changing the asset price. As the market moves away from the barrier, the vegas of the knock-out call start resembling those of a vanilla.

Likewise, the vega of the knock-in call will start resembling those of the vanilla the closer the trader is to the trigger (see Figure 19.12).

Adding the Drift: Complexity of the Forward Line

> ***Risk Management Rule:*** A regular knock-out (i.e., triggered when it is out of the money) will never have a delta higher than one if the cash-forward line is flat. In an upward sloping forward curve, the delta of the calls can be higher than one. In a downward sloping curve, that of the put would be, too.

Vega

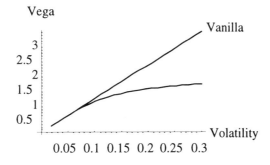

Figure 19.10 Vega of a down and out and a vanilla.

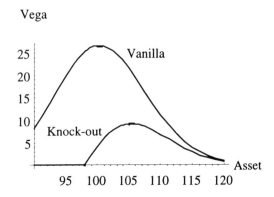

Figure 19.11   Vegas for a knock-out and a vanilla (6 months to expiration, 100 calls, 98 barrier).

Extensions of the rule are:

- Near the barrier, options will retain a high value when the delta is higher.
- Any delta higher than one will lead to a negative gamma somewhere in the map. As this rise in delta is to compensate for a strong barrier payoff, the move into an area where the underlying option dominates would bring back the option into normal proportion.

Figure 19.13 shows the effects of a rise in interest rates on the deltas. Figure 19.14 shows the corresponding gammas. The gammas in Figure 19.14 are so extreme that there is no way to fit the trough in a conventional graph. In the event of high interest rates, the position starts exhibiting an increase in the third moment. Taking interest rates out permits a simpler analysis; they will be incorporated again later.

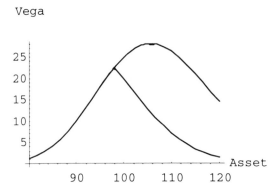

Figure 19.12   Vegas of a knock-in and a vanilla.

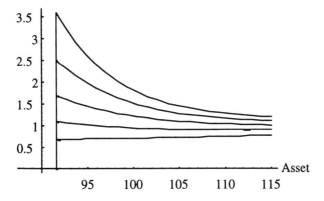

Figure 19.13 Rising interest rates' effect on the delta (strike 98.50, volatility 15.7%, time to expiration 2 years, barrier 91.50).

Risk Reversals

Comparing the vegas of the knock-in and knock-out with those of risk reversals would reveal some striking similarities: a vega that increases in one direction and fades in the other. This prompted a rich literature of option replication through risk reversals.

Put/Call Symmetry and the Hedging of Barrier Options

This section examines the technique of hedging the barrier option by symmetry as exposed in the common literature before warning the trader about some of the pitfalls of the blind execution of the concept. The exact derivation and reasoning behind the formula is provided later in the section "The Reflection Principle."

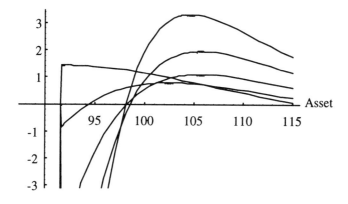

Figure 19.14 The gammas corresponding to Figure 19.13.

Every European option has a symmetrical equivalent pair that matches its risk. The symmetry is established vis-à-vis the forward, not the cash. That amount is called "distance." Assuming no skew (i.e., symmetrical volatility on both sides of the forward), the distance between puts and calls is computed as follows:

K is one strike price and F the forward. The symmetrical K' (a put if K is a call and a call if K is a put) assumes the equality.*

$$\text{Log}\left(\frac{K}{F}\right) = \text{Log}\left(\frac{F}{K'}\right)$$

hence

$$K' = \frac{F^2}{K}$$

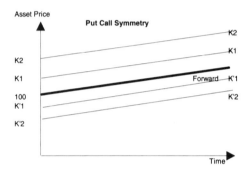

The second, symmetrical strike is set in a way to make the forward become the geometric average of the two strikes. The preceding chart shows the strikes $K1$ and $K2$ and their corresponding symmetrical $K'1$ and $K'2$.

In the absence of a skew, the strikes will be set so that the ratio of price between put and calls will be the square root of the ratio of the strikes:

$$\frac{\text{Put}(K')}{\text{Call}(K)} = \frac{\sqrt{K'}}{\sqrt{K}}$$

The reader could, solely for entertainment, test the equality during a moment of (severe) boredom.

The symmetry should present the following attributes: A long one short the other in proper ratio (of square root of strikes) should offer a zero gamma zero vega. So the put-call symmetry in a delta-neutral structure should be neutral moments until the third moment.

Experienced dynamic hedgers consider the notion of symmetry unstable. There is an extreme difference between "upside" and "downside" strikes, extreme to the point of causing meaningful behavioral differences if the market rallies or sells.

---

*While put/call symmetry has been practiced by traders for a few decades, the first formal treatment of the subject can be found in Carr (1994).

This method has been deemed questionable by the author. Its value is pedagogical as it gives some insight on the risks of barrier structures.

Assuming no drift, the barrier could be somewhat replicated using the risk reversal. Assume further that a call knock-out is a call but not quite so. So it could be a long call mitigated with a short out-of-the-money put. The strike of the out-of-the-money put should be selected to be entirely symmetrical to the call at the barrier—in such a way and in such amounts that the structure would be worth exactly 0 when the market reaches the barrier level. Assume the trader is dealing with a 105 call KO 98 for 6 months. There is a structure, such as an out-of-the-money put that, combined with the 105 call, should be able to replicate the barrier option everywhere except on termination, in which case the barrier needs to be unwound in the market. Such a structure is only effective if the volatility does not change at all during the operation.

Case 1: Knock-Out Call

Assuming the market trades at 100 and volatility at 15.7%.

Price of 6-month vanilla 105 Strike call: 2.35

Price of the 6-month KO (105/98) call: 1.06. The notation KO (strike, outstrike) is used in the examples.

The symmetrical put should be of a strike price that, multiplied by the strike of the call (i.e., 105), satisfies the geometric average 98. It will be such that $K \times 105 = 98^2$. $K = 91.47$

Price of the put symmetrical to the KO with strike 91.47: 1.20

The ratio of puts to calls should be $\sqrt{(105/91.47)} = 1.0714$ puts for 1 call.

The trader should verify that at the barrier (i.e., 98.00), the risk reversal should be worth 0.

One additional constraint on the replication: The risk reversal needs to be closed in the market after the barrier is hit. However, the restriction needs not to be stringent: A simple execution of a delta neutrality would do immediately after the trigger is hit. The trader would then have ample time to close the risk reversal. Table 19.2 plots the risk reversal prices.

The thinking goes: The barrier is nothing but some form of risk reversal. It should then react, in its vega, like the risk reversal. The reader should retain the major benefits of this methodology while remaining cautious about its pitfalls. An important result is that the barrier call should be sold cheaper when there is a downside skew than when there is a flat skew.

Table 19.2 The Method of Barrier Replication

Asset Price	KO	Call	Put	Risk Reversal (long 1 call short 1.0714 puts)
		Ratio: 1.0714		
91	0.00	0.48	4.07	
92	0.00	0.59	3.62	
93	0.00	0.73	3.20	
94	0.00	0.88	2.82	
95	0.00	1.06	2.47	
96	0.00	1.26	2.16	
97	0.00	1.49	1.88	
98	0.00	1.74	1.63	0
99	0.53	2.03	1.40	0.53
100	1.06	2.35	1.21	1.06
101	1.59	2.70	1.03	1.59
102	2.14	3.08	0.88	2.14
103	2.69	3.49	0.75	2.69
104	3.27	3.94	0.63	3.27
105	3.85	4.42	0.53	3.85
106	4.46	4.93	0.45	4.46
107	5.08	5.48	0.37	5.08
108	5.72	6.05	0.31	5.72
109	6.39	6.66	0.26	6.39
110	7.07	7.30	0.21	7.07

Extending it to knock-in options should be straightforward because KI call (105/98) + KO call (105/98) = Vanilla call (105). It follows that KI(105/98) = Vanilla call (105) − KO(105/98). Since the KO call (105/98) was constructed with: − 1.0714 put (91.47) + call (105) by the previous equality, one gets:

$$\text{KIC } (105/98) = \text{call } (105) + 1.07 \times \text{put } (91.47) - \text{call } (105)$$
$$= 1.07 \text{ puts } (91.47)$$

Hence the replicating portfolio of the knock-in is the put (in some ratio) until the barrier is hit and then the call after the barrier is hit. The perfect replication would then entail executing the risk reversal at the barrier by swapping the put into a call. Table 19.3 plots the knock-in replication.

Case 2: Knock-In Call

The option constitutes a switch: At 98, when the passage from one to the other takes place, the risk reversal (in a ratio of 1 call to 1.0714 puts) is

Table 19.3   Knock-in Replication

				Replication (long 1.0714 puts above the barrier, long 1 call below the barrier)
		Ratio: 1.0714		
Asset Price	KI 105/98	Call 105	Put 91.47	
91	0.48	0.48	4.07	0.48
92	0.59	0.59	3.62	0.59
93	0.73	0.73	3.20	0.73
94	0.88	0.88	2.82	0.88
95	1.06	1.06	2.47	1.06
96	1.26	1.26	2.16	1.26
97	1.49	1.49	1.88	1.49
98	1.74	1.74	1.63	1.74
99	1.50	2.03	1.40	1.50
100	1.29	2.35	1.21	1.29
101	1.10	2.70	1.03	1.10
102	0.94	3.08	0.88	0.94
103	0.79	3.49	0.75	0.79
104	0.67	3.94	0.63	0.67
105	0.56	4.42	0.53	0.56
106	0.47	4.93	0.45	0.47
107	0.39	5.48	0.37	0.39
108	0.33	6.05	0.31	0.33
109	0.27	6.66	0.26	0.27
110	0.22	7.30	0.21	0.22

worth exactly 0. So the knock-in represents a switch from one to the other at that particular price.

Benefits of the Method.   Viewing the barrier as an embedded risk reversal presents three major results:

1. **Pricing the skew.** The slope of the skew should be kept in mind when analyzing the barrier. This is a methodology similar to the binary option analysis. Later in the chapter, a methodology will be derived to incorporate the skew and take into account its effect on structures.

2. **Pricing the volatility curve.** The term structure of volatility matters significantly, as will be seen later with the concept of stopping time. It is interesting, however, to see that the decomposition of the barrier leads to two options of a different duration on the volatility ladder. In the case of the knock-out call, the put leg of the risk reversal reacts to

Option Wizard: The Skew Revisited

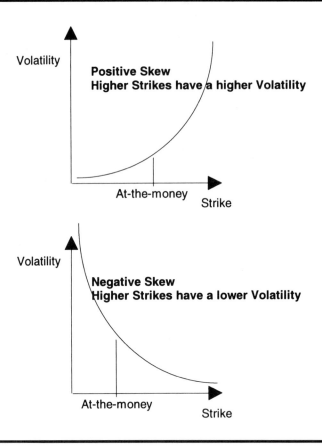

one period while the call leg reacts to another. In the case of knock-in options, the analysis is even more complex.

3. **Hedging.** A barrier option, like a risk reversal, is composed of two polar components. At any time, only one of them dominates when the market trades in its neighborhood. This holds for barriers (out of the money when they knock out or in), not so for reverse barriers where the large payoff is dominating. In the previous examples, the call comes alive and dominates in the rally and weakens in the sell-off with the put taking over. The option will therefore show a long gamma in a rally and a short gamma in a sell-off. Would a risk reversal hedge the structure? In most cases—but not all.

Pitfalls of the Method.   The method of hedging through the risk reversal is grounded on the following assumptions:

- Stable (preferably constant) skew.
- Flat and constant forward curve (no drift or premium/discount in the forward curve).

Making the skew unstable would cause a higher imprecision in the hedge. Initially, whether the operator entered the trade at a positive or negative skew, the position would be locally matched, owing to the incorporation of the skew price into it. Later on, the skew, being unstable, could shift and eventually reverse, causing the trade to become divorced from the skew slope. This is in addition to the possible ravages of time. This possible divorce occurs because the skew hedge may not adequately match the duration of the barrier. Even worse, there might not be a real duration susceptible of hedging the skew owing to the instability of the stopping time.

Making the interest rates or carry for the asset extremely positive or negative would invalidate the method as, by the rules expressed earlier in the chapter, the barrier option might no longer behave exactly like a risk reversal above the barrier. The next section provides a digression on the behavior of the gamma of a structure with a flat forward curve and that of a structure with an exaggerated interest rate differential.

Gammas of Structures Compared with That of the Risk Reversal.   Assuming a flat forward curve, the knock-out gamma would resemble the right half of a risk reversal (Figure 19.15).

The knock-in gamma would resemble the gamma of one call on one side of the hill (the right side) and that of the put on the left side of the hill (Figure 19.16). The risk reversal is shown in Figure 19.17.

Introducing an interest rate differential provides a more complicated situation, as depicted in Figure 19.18.

So what if a trader were to look at Mexico or an emerging market yielding 45% interest rate differential? Assume he examines a one-year option, knock-out call on the US dollar, put, on Mexico scaled at 100, with a knock-out price at 105 and a strike at 102. He can safely use a 50% volatility. This

---

Option Wizard: Where There Is Skew, There Is Skew Instability

Traders notice that the existence of a skew is accompanied by a noticeable shifting of the third moment (i.e., a strong fifth moment). Distributions with strongly positive or negative third moment will have strongly positive or negative fifth moment and a higher fourth moment.

That a market needs a skew in its option volatility surface is a consequence of asymmetry and a sign of structural instability.

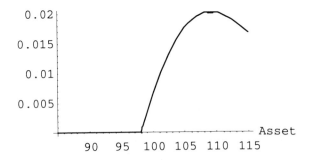

Figure 19.15 Knock-out gamma.

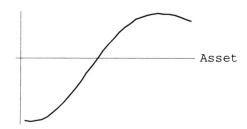

Figure 19.16 Knock-in gamma.

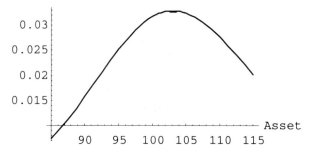

Figure 19.17 Risk reversal gamma.

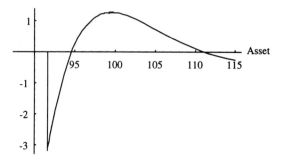

Figure 19.18 Knock-out gamma with a mild/positive drift.

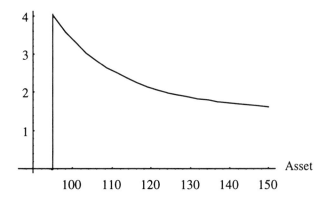

Figure 19.19   Deltas for a knock-out option on high yielding asset.

will help the reader understand why institutions chronically mismanage their emerging market positions.

Figures 19.19 and 19.20 show that, in these conditions, the barrier option behaves like a **full** risk reversal, not like a **half** risk reversal as depicted in Figure 19.15. In other words, its gamma **changes in sign** to the right of the barrier, quite a confusing matter.

To price that "Mexico effect" on any path-dependent option, it is necessary to use the Dupire-Derman-Kani techniques explained later in the book.

Barrier Decomposition under Skew Environments[2]

If in Case 1 (the knock-out call) the puts traded at a premium (i.e., the lower strikes traded at a premium to the higher strikes), the operator could afford to sell the barrier cheaper.

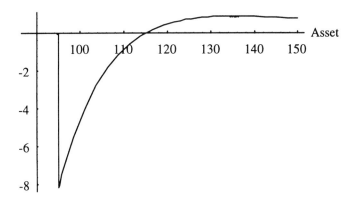

Figure 19.20   Gamma of a high yielding position.

Option Wizard: Long Skew/Short Skew (Last Comment on the Skew)

Long skew means having the vega (and/or gamma) increase in the rally and decrease in the sell-off.

Short skew means having the vega (or gamma) decrease in the rally and increase in the sell-off.

Long skew means benefiting from a positive third moment. Short skew means benefiting from a negative third moment.

> *Trading Rule:* Assuming a flat calendar, in a positive skew (higher strikes at a premium), the knock-out call option will be cheaper than in a flat world. The opposite applies to the negative skew. The opposite also applies to the put (assuming the put is a regular knock-out, not a reverse knock-out).

In general, if the trigger is higher than the strike, the knock-out option is short the skew, and vice versa.

The skew procedure will be analyzed in two steps. The first one is to ignore first exit time and simplify the world to look at the skew in a spatial dimension. After acquiring some familiarity with stopping time, it should be possible to examine the skew in two dimensions.

Thus this analysis (for pedagogical reasons) takes place in the flat calendar world, which means that options trade at the same volatility regardless of expiration.

The trader may attempt to quantify the skew for Case 1.

If the replicating portfolio is priced on the skew curve, the trader would have to find the portfolio that can be worth 0 at the trigger time. That portfolio includes selling a put further out of the money. Case 1 would not produce in a skew environment a call (K) − ratio $\times$ put$(K') = 0$. Say that the skew traded at a slope making the 91.47 trade at 1.7 volatility points over the 105 calls. The trader tries the replication of Case 1 (Table 19.4).

Obviously, it does not work. The risk reversal has a residual value of (0.45) at the barrier. So he needs to scale put/call symmetry to introduce some skew effect to it. He looks for the put that, combined with the call, satisfies the replicating portfolio value of 0 at the barrier.

The put is 89.92, which he found by iteration; he solved for the strike of the put that would be worth 1.74, the call value, when multiplied by the square root of 105/strike. He also found it to trade at 2 volatility points over the 105 call. The 89.92 put has a value of 1.62 at 98, which multiplied by $\sqrt{105/89.92}$ becomes 1.74, the exact value of the call.

Table 19.4   Case 1—Replication Attempt under Skew Environment

			Ratio:	1.0714
Asset Price	KO (priced at flat vols)	Call 15.7 vols	Put 2 vols higher than call	Risk Reversal (long 1 call short 1.0714 puts)
94	0.00	0.88	3.29	
95	0.00	1.06	2.94	
96	0.00	1.26	2.61	
97	0.00	1.49	2.31	
98	0.00	1.74	2.05	(0.45)
99	0.53	2.03	1.80	(0.10)
100	1.06	2.35	1.58	0.65
101	1.59	2.70	1.38	1.22
102	2.14	3.08	1.21	1.78
103	2.69	3.49	1.05	2.36
104	3.27	3.94	0.91	2.96
105	3.85	4.42	0.79	3.58
106	4.46	4.93	0.68	4.20
107	5.08	5.48	0.58	4.85
108	5.72	6.05	0.50	5.51
109	6.39	6.66	0.43	6.19
110	7.07	7.30	0.36	6.91

The hint: Because the trader sold a put that is further out-of-the-money, the entire structure would behave differently than before. The first lesson in skew trading is learning that options that trade at different volatilities exhibit unequal time decay. The trader solved for a replicating portfolio that has no residual value *today* upon reaching the trigger. Tomorrow, however, there will be a residual value at the trigger, given that the 89.92 put that he is short, will decay at a higher speed than the 105 call.

Result: The positive skew drops the value of the barrier.

Table 19.5 verifies that the replicating portfolio above the barrier would provide a residual value that would let a trader executing the trade against a barrier option priced at fat skew eke out a profit.

This confirms any skew trader's intuition: The put/call symmetry obtained on a skew would decay favorably. The last column shows the difference. The difference will peak but reach 0 if the market does not move, as all the options would then expire worthless.

The dependence of the skew premium on time to expiration shown in Figures 19.21 and 19.22 shows traders the need for a more complex pricing tool in the presence of a skew, any skew, in the market. Currently, there is no known closed formula for that purpose. It also illustrates the need to use a numerical method factoring the skew to price barrier options.

Table 19.5   Skew Risk Reversal through Time

	3 Months Later				Ratio:	1.0714	
Asset Price	KO	3-Month Change	Call	Put	Risk Reversal	3-Month Net Change	Net Replication P/L
	—		0.10	1.86			
92	—		0.14	1.53			
93	—		0.19	1.24			
94	—		0.27	1.00			
95	—		0.36	0.79			
96	—		0.47	0.62			
97	—		0.62	0.49			
98	—		0.80	0.38	0.40	0.40	0.40
99	0.38	(0.15)	1.01	0.29	0.70	0.20	0.35
100	0.77	(0.29)	1.26	0.22	1.03	0.02	0.30
101	1.17	(0.42)	1.55	0.16	1.38	(0.16)	0.26
102	1.60	(0.54)	1.89	0.12	1.76	(0.31)	0.22
103	2.06	(0.64)	2.27	0.09	2.18	(0.44)	0.19
104	2.54	(0.72)	2.71	0.06	2.64	(0.56)	0.17
105	3.06	(0.79)	3.19	0.05	3.13	(0.64)	0.15
106	3.62	(0.84)	3.71	0.03	3.68	(0.71)	0.13
107	4.22	(0.86)	4.28	0.02	4.26	(0.75)	0.11
108	4.85	(0.87)	4.90	0.02	4.88	(0.77)	0.10
109	5.53	(0.86)	5.56	0.01	5.55	(0.77)	0.09
110	6.24	(0.83)	6.26	—	6.26	(0.74)	0.08

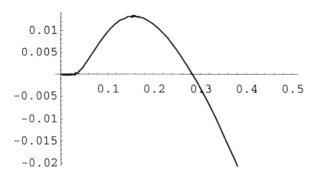

Figure 19.21   Skew premium and the time to expiration.

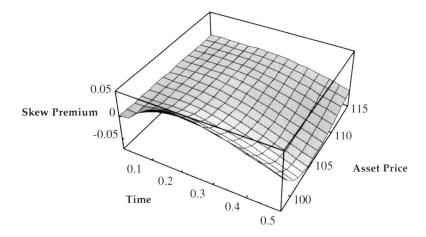

Figure 19.22   Skew premium in time and space.

The T decomposition formula is:

$$\begin{matrix} \text{Barrier option} \\ \text{(skew)} \end{matrix} = \begin{matrix} \text{Barrier option} \\ \text{(No skew)} \end{matrix}$$

$$+ \text{Expected value the residual}$$
$$\text{of the replicating portfolio/Conditional on hitting time}$$

The reflection principle and the Girsanov theorem will augment insight into this method.

The Reflection Principle

Another way of looking at the barrier symmetry is through the reflection principle (see Figure 19.23).[3] For a random walk, the paths from a point a to

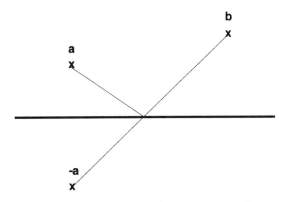

Figure 19.23   The reflection principle.

a point b that do not go through the origin (zero) are equal to the number of paths from −a to b.

This principle works on arithmetic paths only. To accommodate financial markets, it is necessary to trick it by using the logarithm of the prices.

This links back to the notion of option symmetry (see Figure 19.24). Using the regular example of a market trading at 100, with a 98 knock-out barrier, the number of paths from 100 to any point higher than it that does not touch the barrier of 98 is equal to the number of paths from $98^2/100$ to the same point. Option symmetry can define the distance in logarithmic terms to accommodate a geometric Brownian motion. So Log (100/98) = Log (98/96.04).

Example. Binomial Tree (Simplified):   From here we can proceed to an intuitive understanding of the skew with the barrier option. This example will also allow the reader to review binomial option pricing. Figure 19.25 shows the paths from 100 leading to in-the-money parts on the map (higher than 100). It is assumed that there are 20 trading days (one month) with movement of .99 per day, risk neutral, simply chosen for pedagogical reasons (ignore lognormality for such an interval and assume a "fudge," to have the up-probability initially equal to the down-probability[4]). Path 1 shows the number of paths from 100 leading to each terminal node (i.e., the vanilla option). Path 2 shows the number of paths from 96.04 to the same end nodes (i.e., the difference between the vanilla and the barrier).

For the vanilla, option pricing is commonly done by multiplying the intrinsic value on the end node by the *risk-neutral* probability of occurrence. The trader should be careful to consider such risk-neutrality as an arbitrage derivation (i.e., an option = expected cost of gamma P/L as explained in Module B). Here it is readily computed as the number of paths at the node divided by the total number of possible paths times the payoff.

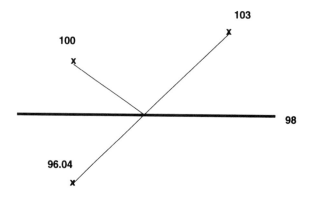

Figure 19.24   Extension to option symmetry.

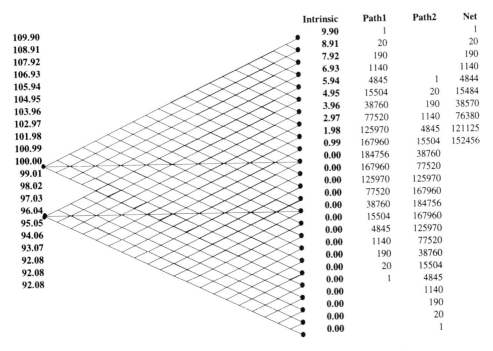

	Intrinsic	Path1	Path2	Net
109.90	9.90	1		1
108.91	8.91	20		20
107.92	7.92	190		190
106.93	6.93	1140		1140
105.94	5.94	4845	1	4844
104.95	4.95	15504	20	15484
103.96	3.96	38760	190	38570
102.97	2.97	77520	1140	76380
101.98	1.98	125970	4845	121125
100.99	0.99	167960	15504	152456
100.00	0.00	184756	38760	
99.01	0.00	167960	77520	
98.02	0.00	125970	125970	
97.03	0.00	77520	167960	
96.04	0.00	38760	184756	
95.05	0.00	15504	167960	
94.06	0.00	4845	125970	
93.07	0.00	1140	77520	
92.08	0.00	190	38760	
92.08	0.00	20	15504	
92.08	0.00	1	4845	
	0.00		1140	
	0.00		190	
	0.00		20	
	0.00		1	

Figure 19.25   Sample paths and the reflection principle.

$$\frac{\text{Expected value}}{\text{at the node}} = \frac{\text{Intrinsic at}}{\text{the node}} \times \frac{\text{Number of paths leading to the node}}{\text{Total number of possible paths}}$$

In Figure 19.25, the total number of paths is $2^{20} = 1{,}048{,}576$ paths. Expected payoff at any node is equal to intrinsic value times probability. Probability equals number of possible paths/total number of paths. So looking at the column Path 1, expected payoff at node $103.96 = 3.96 \times 38760/1048576 = .1463$.

The reader can also verify risk neutrality with no drift: Every possible outcome weighted by its probability adds up to 100. It is called the "conditional expectation of the future asset price at time t," *conditional* means that the expectation is based on information at the present.

The reader can also price the vanilla call struck at 100. It is equal to intrinsic times the probability of every level, as shown in Table 19.6.

The value of the vanilla option can be intuitively derived as the sum of the expected values at every node. The precision increases with the higher number of steps.

In Figure 19.25, Path 2 shows the number of paths that do not go through the barrier using the reflection principle. The value of the barrier option would therefore be the payoff (column labeled "Intrinsic") times the column net/total number of paths.

Table 19.6   Vanilla Valuation

Final Price	Intrinsic	Number of Paths	Probability (%)	Expected Value
109.90	9.90	1	0.00	0.00001
108.91	8.91	20	0.00	0.00017
107.92	7.92	190	0.02	0.00144
106.93	6.93	1,140	0.11	0.00753
105.94	5.94	4,845	0.46	0.02745
104.95	4.95	15,504	1.48	0.07319
103.96	3.96	38,760	3.70	0.14638
102.97	2.97	77,520	7.39	0.21957
101.97	1.98	125,970	12.01	0.23787
100.99	0.99	167,960	16.02	0.15858
100.00	—	184,756	17.62	—
	Total (all paths)	**1,048,576**		**0.872**

Repeating the exercise of Table 19.6, the trader derives the price of the same option but with a knock-out barrier at 98 (see Table 19.7).

This leads to the equality: In the absence of skew and drift, a regular knock-out option (that knocks out while out of the money), when the asset trades at S, with a strike K and barrier H is equal to the vanilla option of the same strike and maturity minus the same vanilla option priced with the spot at S' such that S' is the symmetrical reciprocal of S centered

Table 19.7   Knock-Out Valuation

Asset Price	Intrinsic	Path 1	Path 2 (Reflected Paths)	Net	Probability (%)	Expected Value
109.9	9.9	1		1	0.0000	0.000
108.91	8.91	20		20	0.0000	0.000
107.92	7.92	190		190	0.0002	0.001
106.93	6.93	1140		1140	0.0011	0.008
105.94	5.94	4845	1	4844	0.0046	0.027
104.95	4.95	15504	20	15484	0.0148	0.073
103.96	3.96	38760	190	38570	0.0368	0.146
102.97	2.97	77520	1140	76380	0.0728	0.216
101.98	1.98	125970	4845	121125	0.1155	0.229
100.99	0.99	167960	15504	152456	0.1454	0.144
100	0.00	184756	38760	145996	0.1392	—
	Total	1048576			Total	0.844

around H (S S' = H^2). The amounts need to be adjusted by their adequate ratio $\sqrt{(S/S')}$.

> *Example:*   A 3-month knock-out call strike 100, spot 100, barrier at 98 is equal to the price of the vanilla minus 100/98 times the same vanilla priced at 96.04.

This can lead to the notion of risk reversal. Applying put/call parity, as well as the change of numeraire method, a call with a strike price of 100, priced with a 96.04 spot will be equal in price to the 96.04 put priced with the spot at 100. This proves the skew rules shown earlier.

An **extension** of this notion is that, with a reverse knock-out option or a regular knock-out that presents a rebate, the rules are more complicated as one needs to add the payoff of the corresponding American binary.

Girsanov

It is easy to introduce the drift in the preceding framework to mix it with the reflection principle. This would be done in assuming different probabilities on exactly the same path structure, to compensate for the drift. The path remaining the same, the probabilities are shifted to alter the payoff without changing the paths.

Assume that over the same period, the spot needs to earn .99% per month. It means that we expect that the resulting price after one month would be 100.99.

The Girsanov theorem allows traders to change the probability of every outcome upward or downward to allow for the expected return of 100.99. In the example, the trader will have to shift the final probabilities. The module {pricing contingent claims} presents a more formal presentation of the method. Figure 19.26 shows the payoffs.

Repricing the option shows that the value of the package changed (Table 19.8).

Effect of Time on Knock-Out Options

With regular knock-outs, the effect of time is not truly perfidious, unlike reverse knock-outs where it can be harrying. Time makes the underlying option lose its value faster but at the same time increases discontinuity at the barrier, which mitigates the effect: What would be knocked out will have less and less value. Figure 19.27 shows this effect.

With knock-in options, however, the barrier has less effect in dominating the structure because there are no conflicting options in the structure. Figure 19.28 illustrates this effect.

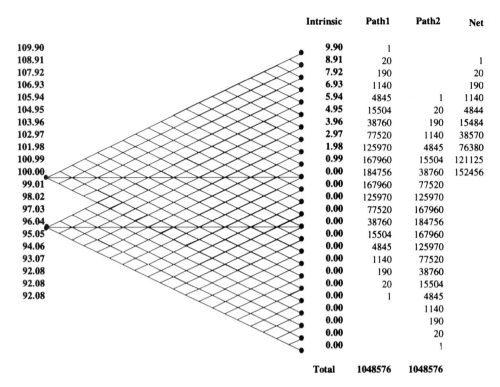

	Intrinsic	Path1	Path2	Net
109.90	9.90	1		
108.91	8.91	20		1
107.92	7.92	190		20
106.93	6.93	1140		190
105.94	5.94	4845	1	1140
104.95	4.95	15504	20	4844
103.96	3.96	38760	190	15484
102.97	2.97	77520	1140	38570
101.98	1.98	125970	4845	76380
100.99	0.99	167960	15504	121125
100.00	0.00	184756	38760	152456
99.01	0.00	167960	77520	
98.02	0.00	125970	125970	
97.03	0.00	77520	167960	
96.04	0.00	38760	184756	
95.05	0.00	15504	167960	
94.06	0.00	4845	125970	
93.07	0.00	1140	77520	
92.08	0.00	190	38760	
92.08	0.00	20	15504	
92.08	0.00	1	4845	
	0.00		1140	
	0.00		190	
	0.00		20	
	0.00		1	
Total		**1048576**	**1048576**	

Figure 19.26 The reflection principle with changes of probability measure.

First Exit Time and Its Risk-Neutral Expectation

■ The expected **first exit time (or stopping time)** is the time an asset price is expected to cross a given point in the market, conditional on an expiration date. Module G (Pricing Contingent Claims) provides the calculation for both the distribution of the first exit time and its expectation.

A barrier option unlike a European binary needs to be hedged using instruments that have a similar duration. This necessitates the knowledge at all times of the expected first exit time, which is in this case the time when the barrier is hit. The difference between the nominal expiration and the expected stopping time will correspond to the dominance of the barrier in the structure. When the barrier is weak (by exerting a small influence on the risks of the structure), the expected exit time is equal to the nominal duration. When the barrier is strong, it will be considerably shorter.

Table 19.8   Knock-Out Value after Change of Probabilities

Asset Price	Intrinsic	Path 1	Path 2	Net	Probability (%)	Expected Value
110.89	10.89	1		1	0.0000	0.000
109.9	9.90	20		20	0.0000	0.000
108.91	8.91	190		190	0.0002	0.002
107.92	7.92	1140		1140	0.0011	0.009
106.93	6.93	4845	1	4844	0.0046	0.032
105.94	5.94	15504	20	15484	0.0148	0.088
104.95	4.95	38760	190	38570	0.0368	0.182
103.96	3.96	77520	1140	76380	0.0728	0.288
102.97	2.97	125970	4845	121125	0.1155	0.343
101.98	1.98	167960	15504	152456	0.1454	0.288
100.99	0.99	184756	38760	145996	0.1392	0.138
100.00	0.00	1048576			Total	1.369

The expected first exit time can thus be represented as shown in Figure 19.29.

As volatility increases, the option shortens and the barrier starts dominating. When volatility is low, the underlying option dominates and the expected first exit time becomes the maturity of the vanilla.

Trading Rule: The certainty that first exit time is shorter than or equal to the nominal maturity makes any nonarbitrage static replication of a barrier with combination of vanillas imperfect.

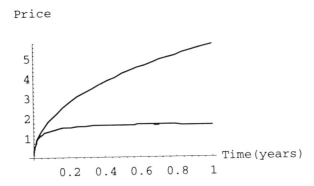

Figure 19.27   Knock-out option and a vanilla with time (100 calls, barrier 98).

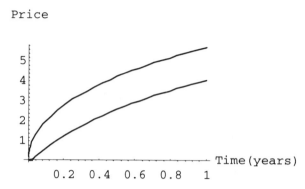

Figure 19.28 Knock-in option and a vanilla with time (100 calls, barrier 98).

Many simplistic methods of option hedging have been used, such as the static replication with a risk reversal presented earlier. Their not taking into account the fuzziness of the duration can be downright dangerous.

Many software vendors took the simplified homoskedastic (constant volatility) pricing tools available in the early academic literature and dumped them on the traders. Using only one volatility when there is a possibility of the barrier expiring earlier leads to overpricing when the volatility term structure is upward sloping and underpricing in a backwardized volatility curve.

Figure 19.29 Risk-neutral expected first exit time: 3-month, 100 call/knock-out 98, volatility 5, 15, and 20%.

The consequences of the risk management rule are:

- Any vega hedge against the barrier needs to take into account the first exit time for the matching of the barrier payoff.
- Hedging the forward exposure stemming from the barrier needs to be done carefully. First exit can move, and may lengthen or shorten. A lengthening of the expected first exit would necessitate a lengthening of the maturity of the hedge. This rebalancing can consume massive transaction costs. It is therefore recommended to hedge at a shorter maturity than the nominal one.
- First exit time depends on the volatility. Where there is a volatility curve in the market, positive and negative, the first exit time would lengthen or shorten.

Issues in Pricing Barrier Options

Since the first exit time is uncertain, it is necessary to know where it is located on the term structure for pricing purposes. Currently, most systems offered to traders present an erroneous system of pricing. There are two methods of fudging matters:

1. *The single volatility fudge.* It is less computer intensive but lacks accuracy. This author recommends using it only to patch up the flaws in the pricing formulas. It provides a half-answer.

2. *The pricing on a forward-forward curve* (the Dupire method). It is more computer intensive but is generally accurate in determining the real value and the appropriate hedges. Some people complain about the burdening implementation and convergence difficulties.

The Single Volatility Fudge

- *Step 1.* Determine the implied spot volatility curve in the market.

Month	1	2	3	4	5	6	7	8	9
Volatility	9.9	10.25	10.5	10.7	10.85	10.95	11.1	11.2	11.3

- *Step 2.* Find the expected stopping time. Notice that it is a distribution, not a fixed point in time. Assume the expected stopping time was derived to be close to 6 months. Therefore, interpolating on Figure 19.30, the volatility to use is 10.95, which should define that of the knock-out option.
- *Step 3.* Price the knock-out option using a synthetic risk reversal. The major option (the 105 call in the previous example) needs to be

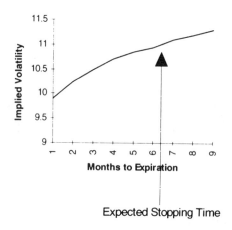

Figure 19.30 Stopping time: Volatility term structure.

priced as an option maturing with the nominal value. The second option needs to be priced using the parameters of first exit time. Thus a skew dimension would be added to the risk reversal.

- *Step 4.* Find the forward-forward between the stopping time and the end date. Using the formula of Chapter 9, the reader will obtain FFwd (6,9) = 12%. This number is useful in determining the value of the knock-in of the same nominal duration.

Finally, the fact that the stopping time is not fixed but has a distribution makes it necessary to specify the following rule.

Risk Management Rule: The hedges in forward assets that correspond to an option position need to be scattered to match the distribution of first exit time.

A More Accurate Method:
The Dupire-Derman-Kani Technique

In 1992, Dupire presented the seminal notion of a two-dimensional volatility process. Between one point and another in space (spot/strike) and time (to expiration) there is a volatility implied by both the skew and the forward-forward volatility in the market.[5] This was followed by breakthrough research by Dupire (1993) and Derman and Kani (1994). They arrived at a numerical technique that breaks up time into smaller sections between the nodes, thus constituting a calendar-based time-speed function (one can even call it diagonal). The method entails the use of some form of flexible nodes in the binomial (or multinomial) tree.

The method of pricing on the tree has serious implications for any path-dependent structure. Since a barrier depends not just on one single volatility but on that of every node, the pricing can more precisely establish the value of the barrier using a two-dimensional volatility surface. In effect, both the forward-forward problem and the estimation of the stopping time can thus be skirted.

Independently, in Berkeley, Marc Rubinstein discovered the notion of implied binomial tree and studied the lateral volatility between two asset prices derived from option prices. In other words, as Dupire and Derman and Kani explored the process between a point in space (asset price) and time (S, t) and $(S + \Delta S, t + \Delta t)$, Rubinstein was independently discovering the implied process betwen (S, t) and $(S + \Delta S, t)$.

A few issues, however, have marred the implementation of these techniques. The primary problem is that a high number of steps is needed to make the binomial tree (or trinomial) converge to a stable price. This could be time consuming and many efforts at finding numerical techniques to speed up the calculations and deliver feasible techniques of option pricing are under way.

To this date, no commercially available system implements such a method.

Additional Pricing Complexity: The Variance Ratios

Option traders hedge themselves at a given frequency, say an observable time interval. They concern themselves with the volatility at the time scale of their intervention. A trader who hedges himself every few minutes will not be concerned with tick volatility. A barrier option, however, responds to the infinitesimal volatility. The two can be markedly different as shown in Chapter 6.

Barrier options are priced on the assumption of the distribution of the minimum of the maximum of a Brownian motion that follows the same volatility as the Brownian motion itself. The most intuitive way to look at the barrier is to assume the risk-neutral (alas) discounted probabilistic pay-off of a vanilla option (i.e., $S - K$ for the call and $K - S$ for the put) *conditional* on the stopping time not being attained during that period. Putting that condition on the regular option represents the difference from a vanilla.

The condition of the stopping time, however, may react to the distribution of the minimum of maximum. The analysis of the Parkinson number (see Chapter 6) hinted that the distribution of the extremes on a particular day may be markedly different from what would be expected from a log-normal (or even normal as it does not matter much within one day) distribution.

> *Trading Rule:*   In a mean-reverting market, the barrier component of a barrier option is overpriced. In a trending market, it is underpriced.

The explanation for this effect is that the knock-out option is more likely to be knocked out when the market has a high level of intraday negative auto-correlation and options are priced on the close-to-close volatility. Remember that the structure is triggered off a price printing on the screen, not a terminal state for the asset.

Since this is not an econometrics course but general guidelines for option hedging, the trader must decide on whether the market follows one particular process or another, or whether one particular condition is more permanent than the other.

From this author's experience, every market, including markets involved in a trend (one-week sampled volatility is higher than daily samples) will exhibit mean reversion within a one-day framework. This is due to the execution slippage of the participants, to widening of the bid-offer spread in the event of higher volatility than normal, and several other factors.

Another way to examine it is to use the Parkinson number rule:

> *Trading Rule:*   If the close-to-close volatility is lower than the Parkinson number, the barrier component is underpriced by the regular method. Otherwise, it could be considered overpriced.

EXERCISE: ADDING THE PUTS

As an exercise, the reader could redo the previous examples by pricing a 98 put knocking out at 105 and the same one knocking in at 105. The author subscribes to the notion that a put is nothing but a synthetic call and prefers to spend appropriate time on the differences where they might arise.

Chapter **20**

Barrier Options (II)

The only thing I like about a knock-out option is that it knocks out.

N. Zeidan

This chapter focuses on reverse barrier options and double barrier options.[1]

REVERSE BARRIER OPTIONS

Reverse Knock-Out Options

■ A **reverse knock-out** is a barrier option that terminates in the money, therefore causing a large discrepancy between the values on each side of the barrier.

Reverse knock-outs are almost decomposable into regular knock-outs *plus* an American bet. However, one ends up with the opposite gap delta. Because a large number of horror stories attend their risk management, it will prove helpful to study reverse knock-outs separately.

A three-month call is generally worth 3.11% of face at 15.7% volatility. A reverse knock-out that terminates at 108 with no rebate will be worth .55% only. Strangely enough, the reverse knock-out call will sometimes present a negative delta (its price will decrease when the market rallies), which newcomers to the exotics club find difficult to conceive since ordinary options gain in value when their intrinsic value increases. In this case, however, the intrinsic value disappears at one point so the price decreases as the market rallies close to the barrier. The conflicting pull between the barrier and the regular underlying vanilla will show a serious conflict throughout the life of the instrument.

Reverse knockouts appear to be priced abnormally low, with their value generally moving inversely to time: they decay negatively. Such a feature makes them an attractive selling instrument to corporates. The same feature creates nightmares for option traders and sleepless night fraught with cold sweats, as will be shown later.

The best intuitive way to view reverse knock-out and knock-in options is to consider them American binary options with a high payout. Since the payoff is in the form of a deep-in-the-money option with a high intrinsic and little time value, they look very little like an option when close to the barrier and more like a bet.

Figures 20.1 and 20.2 show the unusual behavior of a reverse knock-out, terminating at 10, with 6 months on the clock. The reader will detect a mildly short gamma for the owner, as well as a short delta.

Figure 20.3 shows the nasty effect of time near the barrier, reminiscent of that of an American binary.

Figure 20.4 shows the effect of time on a reverse KO (100,105) and 20.5 shows the difference with an American binary: below 100 the trade is short gamma, therefore will *earn* time decay (even when there is no carry).

Case Study: The Knock-Out Box

The following real-life trade (only slightly modified) took place in the dollar against French Franc.

As the dollar dropped steadily against the European currencies during the 1990s, many French corporate treasuries found themselves under water on their speculative positions. It had been fashionable in Parisian circles to call the turn of the U.S. currency as travelers were invoking economic equilibrium theories and other notions that made the dollar look underpriced in their eyes. It was rare for this author to enter conversations with Parisians without hearing purchasing-parity comparisons such as the cost of a compact disk sold by Chinatown peddlers and the exact same item sold at

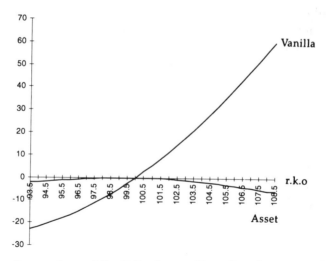

Figure 20.1   Comparison of the P/L of a vanilla call and a reverse knock-out.

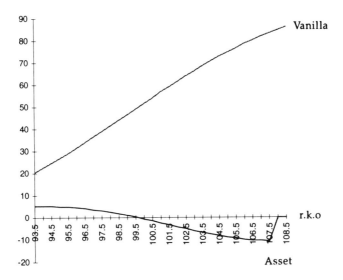

Figure 20.2 Comparison of the delta of a vanilla call and a reverse knock-out.

Roissy Airport. So macroeconomists-traders went long the dollar massively around 5.60 to the French franc, some 12% higher than the rest of the story. Many corporates without real marks-to-market rules found it easy to carry a position without the discipline of a stringent stop-loss. However, they needed at some point to swallow the bullet and show a loss.

As the franc was hovering around 5.00, some derivatives house presented them with the following gimmick: Here is a chance for you to be "hedged"

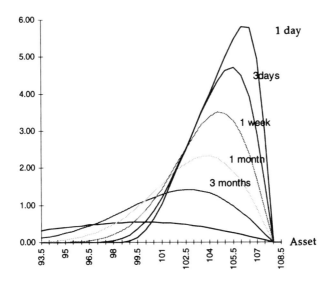

Figure 20.3 Effect of time on the price of a reverse knock-out.

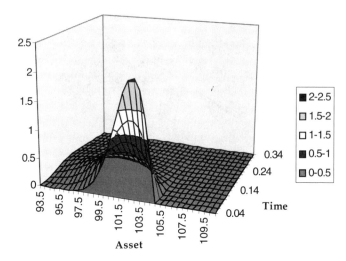

Figure 20.4 Reverse KO (100, 105) at different levels of volatility.

against your dollar exposure. So they sold them the quack medicine described below.

Customer is long dollars at 5.60 in the amount of $100 Mil. Therefore the losses are around $12 Mil since spot USD-FRF is at the round 5.00. The quack medicine would allow the customer to get it back.

Customer buys a 5.60 knock-out put on the dollar (call on the FF) for a relatively small price. It knocks out, however, at 4.85 (not very far from where spot is) and has an entire year to go. The cost of the trade is very small: around .8% of the face value of the position, which corresponds to $800,000 (including the bank's profit margin). At expiration, if the option has not been knocked out, the trader would make back his $12 Mil as

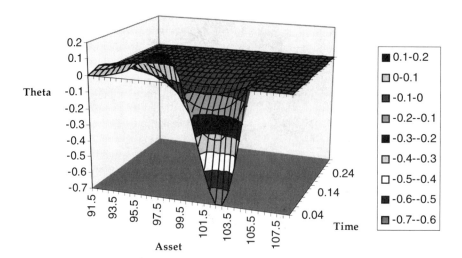

Figure 20.5 A theta that changes in sign.

Option Wizard: How Bad Salespeople Fool Their Customers

There is an old trick bad salespeople use to fool their customers into trades that generate profits for their employer and keep them in the game: taking advantage of their statistical misperception. It is easier to fool someone with a distributional confusion.

Covered Writes, for example, allowed brokers to kill the upside of their customers and generate steady flows of commissions. A customer is long the stock and sells calls against it. If the customer loses money on the calls, the broker could argue that the customer made money on the stock. Should the customer lose money on the stock, the broker would not fail to point out that the customer was spared further losses thanks to the income brought by the calls.

Until customers gained in sophistication, covered writes were the best game in town. As customers started understanding a little more statistics, the game moved to the fancier exotic options payoffs. The distributional confusion moved to the notion of path dependency.

The Wall Street firms that survive are those who cater to their clients' needs.

---

he would be able to go short the dollar back at 5.60 where the entire matter would be closed. The trader would be able to start a new life as a dollar bull again if he so wishes. Great trade. It sold very well, like a *Le Monde* issue on election day.

"Fair value" for the trade using a Black-Scholes-Merton type valuation (one constant volatility) shows the trade to be worth .63% at 11.5% volatility, 6% domestic U.S. rates, and 7% French rates.

The profile of the trade by itself is first examined. Figure 20.6 shows the value of a 5.60 put on the dollar (call on the FRF) KO at 4.85, with one year

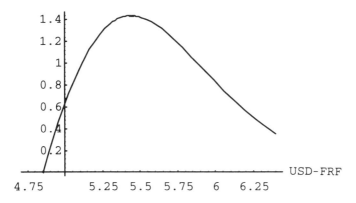

Figure 20.6   The salvation trade. Premium in mil dollars.

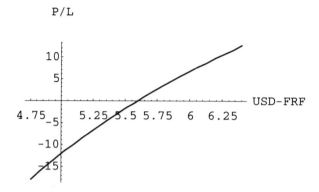

Figure 20.7   The position without the salvation trade.

to go and a volatility of 11.5%. The price is expressed in total dollar value of the premium for a $100 million dollar trade.

Figure 20.7 shows the initial position without the salvation trade while Figure 20.8 shows the position after. A drop in the bucket, one may say.

It is enlightening to compare it to the position with the Salvation Trade.

So today the trade does not do much for the hapless Frenchman. Tomorrow, however, there might be some hope. Look at the profile around expiration in Figure 20.8. A zone of break-even can be seen between 4.85 and 5.60 on the overall package (less the premium spent on the Salvation trade).

Trading Rule: Some institutions fool the gullible investors by taking advantage of their lack of knowledge of probability theory, and truncating the distribution of profits. The investors, particularly when under pressure, tend to believe in Santa Claus.

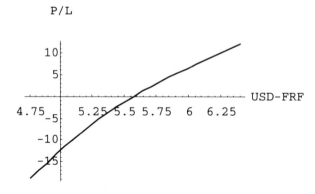

Figure 20.8   The position with the salvation trade.

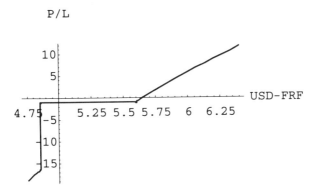

Figure 20.9   But there is some hope.

It does not improve the customer's condition to see the graph in Figure 20.9. But the broker now has a story to tell in cases of success and failure.

Further analysis of the trade shows that the reason such protection is cheap is precisely because its first exit time is very short. The trade is entirely dominated by the barrier, so the odds of the 5.60 put remaining an option are very low.

With time, the value of the option would increase, and, should (for some reason) the market become stationary, the structure would look like a real protection. Such an event has an infinitely small probability of surviving the next year. The salesperson would show the customer the pictures in Figures 20.9 and 20.10 but would fail to tell him that such a picture represents not the expiration P/L like a regular option but shows the P/L if USD-FRF *never* trades below than 4.850001. There is a massive difference between a path in dependent expiration P/L and a path-dependent one. Most customers have not been trained nor are they used to looking at such graphs properly.

Finally, the positive time decay from the trade, provided the USD-FRF remained totally frozen, shows in Figure 20.11.

Option Wizard: Fooled by the Expiration Profile

The expiration profile is a great way to delude a potential customer into entering a good trade (good for the seller). It has already been established that the statistical sense of people is rather weak, even in the examination of a regular risk profile.

When looking at a path-dependent profile "at expiration," the customer may not realize that he has mentally correct for the payoff probabilities. This is difficult when the report is made to look like a static payoff with a small mention at the bottom.

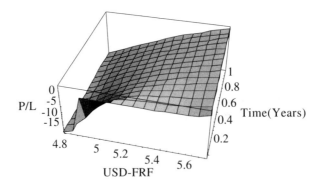

Figure 20.10 Profile until expiration.

Note: This example does not take into account that a trader who lost $12 million would incur interest charges on the losses. In fact, some trades escape such treatment but are penalized by their not getting any interest on their profits.

Some customers after a while could come back and tell their salesperson that perhaps the trade might not always work in all circumstances. They may be paying $800,000 (actually the bank might be charging them up to $1,000,000 for the trade under the illusion that every penny above Black-Scholes-Merton value is profits) just to buy a butterfly. So here is the answer.

Making the Trade Debit-Free. By entering the trade for no debit, or perhaps a small credit, the customer might complain very little in the event of being knocked-out of the trade. So the new idea is to perform, in addition to the "Great Salvation," a covered write.

The customer can thus, at no cost, keep performing the trade until the day, way down the road, when he would break even. A statistician can probably estimate that day to be a few hundred years away.

P/L (Spot USD-FRF 5.00)

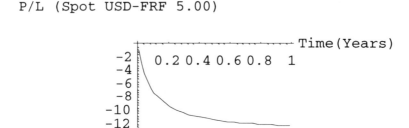

Figure 20.11 Static (no spot movement) view of the P/L.

To turn the trade into a debit trade, the dealer could make the gullible customer-underwater sell some 5.60 dollar calls for some premium. This is the late 1990s, however, and this kind of trade belongs to the preexotic structures of earlier days. Moreover, the customer could then decompose the trade by himself, trade it on his own and deprive them of the profits. Finally, then, should the customer sell a 5.60 call on the dollar, the structure could cause a problem in the event of the KO being terminated and the other leg staying naked to prevent the renewal of the structure.

What to do then? The package could include a call knock-out that would vanish also at 4.85. The no-debit rule can be achieved. In addition, the trader could even get some cushioning income from it. The terms would be as follows:

> Length: one year. Customer buys 5.60 put on dollar KO 4.85, sells 5.60 call on dollar KO 4.85 for no premium. Should, at the end of the 1.5 years, the dollar stay above 4.75, the customer would get back his $12 million losses.

However, should the structure be knocked out, which means that the dollar dropped below 4.85, the trader would have his global position lose even more money. That, the derivatives house would not mention.

What in effect the customer was led to do was truncating his distribution, cutting off any hope of making money back against the possibility of keep trying the trade forever, until he can spend one entire year without hitting a barrier.

Figure 20.12 shows the profile of the entire package at expiration. The principal difference between Figure 20.12 and Figure 20.9 is that, above the barrier of 485, Figure 20.12 shows perfect breakeven.

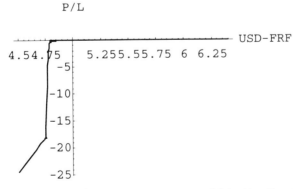

Figure 20.12   The customer truncated his distribution.

Hedging Reverse Knock-Outs: A Graphical Case Study

Reverse knock-outs are principally difficult to hedge. The following case study will examine the reverse knock-out from the vantage point of the trader and illustrate the possible hedges. The presentation will go through the Greeks and examine their relevance—or lack of it.

The trade will be examined from the standpoint of the seller of the option, and it will be hedged step by step.

The trader sells $100 million of one-year 5.60 dollar-put FRF call for $800,000, with a KO feature at 4.85, only 3% away from the market.

The Deltas.   The operator is short calls but an inexperienced trader might be surprised to see the deltas move from positive to negative. This occurs because close to the barrier the option structure weakens and is dominated by the bet. The trade becomes cheaper as the market approaches the barrier. Close to the other end, however, the trade becomes cheaper again as it resembles a long put in a rally. In between the two poles, the trade could be somewhat confusing.

The delta is expressed in percentage of face value (in dollars, not currencies). Figure 20.13 shows the changes in the delta of the structure. The reader can see the drop from the cliff at the barrier price of 4.75.

As time, however, moves closer, the deltas would give a little bit of heartbeat. Look at it with one day to go (Figure 20.14).

The delta one day from expiration reaches 2000 level, which, for, a $100 million position, will represent serious deltas. The face value of the position is actually larger for a dollar-based person since it corresponds to being short the equivalent of 100 million FRF at 5.6, 560 million FRF, which would be by the two-country paradox constant FRF but at 4.85 would turn

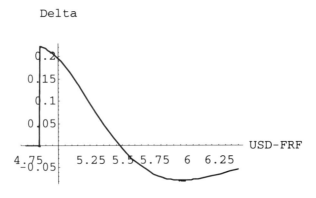

Figure 20.13   Delta one year to expiration.

Delta

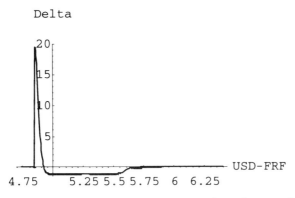

Figure 20.14   Deltas on expiration day (in number of times the position).

into $100 \times 5.60/4.85 = \$115.4$ million. So 2000 deltas would be 20 times $115.4 = \$231$ billion. The intrinsic value of the option would, by the same token, be worth \$15.5 million, quite an impressive time decay given that a year before, it is worth just between \$600,000 and \$800,000, the price at which the traders sold it.

Figure 20.15 shows the accelerated changes in the value of the option from the passage of time. In trading, acceleration means instability. Such instability increases at the barrier, provided the structure does not knock-out before the end of its life. So this scenario, while perhaps being the most beastly, is no doubt the least likely of all. There are very small chances for the market spending one year near a barrier without touching it.

The reader will find in Figure 20.16 two possible scenarios: The change in value at a USD-FRF rate of 4.76 (close to the barrier) and at 5.55 (away

{Option Value}

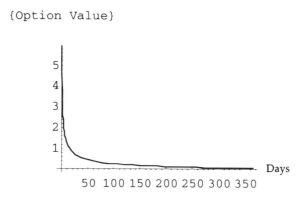

Figure 20.15   Changes in value with time at the trigger.

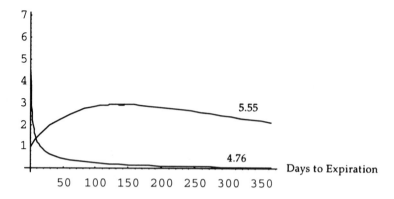

Figure 20.16   Value through its life at exchange rate 4.76 and exchange rate 5.55.

from the barrier). At 4.76 the trade undergoes a harrying negative time decay for the seller. At 5.55, however, the trade decays positively. The trader executes his delta. He sold the KO put and is therefore long dollars (short FRF). He sells dollars, buys FRF against the position in 19% of the dollar value (at 5.00 the dollar value is 100 × 5.60/5.00 = $112 mil so 19% is $21.2 mil).

Figures 20.17 through 20.23 will examine the various risks assuming dynamic hedging. Figures 20.17 through 20.20 will assume delta neutrality and the remaining figures will assume, in addition to delta neutrality, vega neutrality. Given the difference between the local behavior of the Greeks and their global behavior, the graphs will examine the sensitivity both using a microscope (for a local sensitivity assuming a small change in the parameters) and a telescope (assuming large changes).

Figure 20.17 shows the delta sensitivity through the microscope, in the neighborhood of a USD-FRF of 5.00. It looks like simple long gamma, with the "V" Shape of the P/L. Figure 20.18 shows the same sensitivity at a

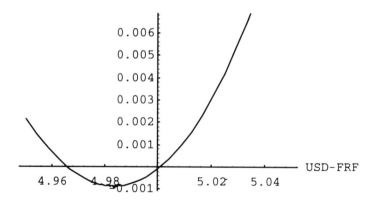

Figure 20.17   Hedged P/L in the microscope.

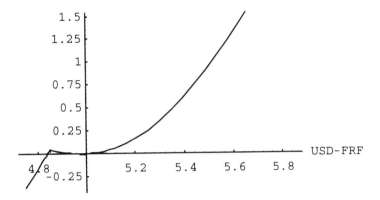

Figure 20.18   Hedged P/L in larger increments.

larger scale, with a jump at the barrier. Figure 20.18 shows the real need to liquidate the delta hedge at the barrier, one of the problems in managing a barrier option.

Gamma and Vega.   Figure 20.19 shows the disturbing gamma, as it is centered in the neighborhood of 5.30 USD-FRF. Figure 20.20 shows now that, 5 week from expiration, the gamma peaks at a level close to the barrier, and turns negative in the neighborhood of 5.35. The difference between Figure 20.19 and Figure 20.20 represents the reason traders are scared of reverse knock-out options, since they cannot be trusted to retain any characteristic for long.

Before looking at the necessary vega hedges, examine the stability of the measure. Figures 20.21 and 20.22 show the position at current spot. Figure 20.21 shows the volatility sensitivity of the position with 1 year left and Figure 20.22 shows the same sensitivity one month from expiration. It is

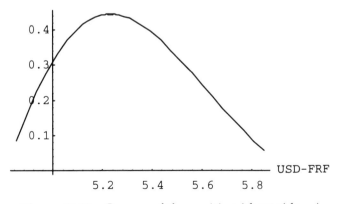

Figure 20.19   Gamma of the position (short side −).

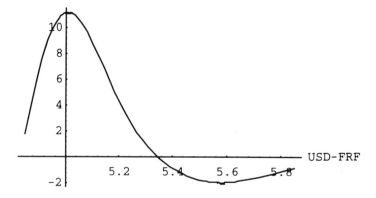

Figure 20.20 Gamma 5 weeks before expiration.

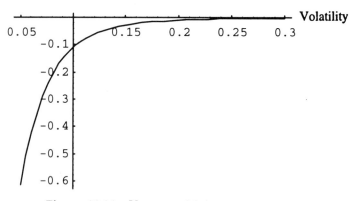

Figure 20.21 Vega sensitivity one year to go.

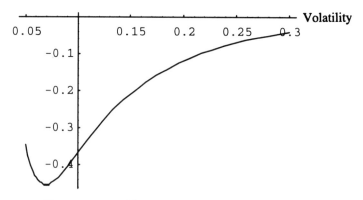

Figure 20.22 Vega sensitivity one month to go.

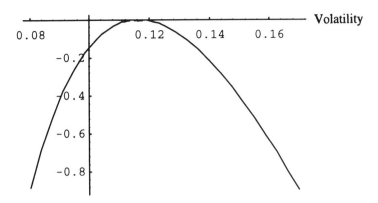

Figure 20.23 Vega neutral P/L.

noticeable that both the vegas and the vega convexity increase with time to expiration, in the neighborhood of the barrier.

It is worthy mentioning that the vega sign is negative: the owner is short vega. The trader who sold the option will have to sell vega to offset a long volatility position.

By looking at the gamma sheet for immediate moves, the trader would notice that the gamma peaks at around 5.30. So will the vega (for a single option gamma and vega peak at the same level). So the trader will sell an option that peaks around that level. The trader selects a 3-month option struck around USD-FRF of 5.30, which leaves him with a vega-neutral position. Figure 20.23, which is a graph of the vega combination, shows that vega neutrality will be very transitory for the next move.

It is never pleasant for traders to be in a situation where the vega of the position increases when volatility comes down and decreases in a rally. It means that vega neutrality will be a sure loser.

Figure 20.24 shows the vega of the structure unhedged across spot across volatility levels. Comparing Figure 20.24 to Figure 20.23 would certainly show it to be more favorable. Perhaps, after all, it would have been better to avoid selling the 3 month options as a hedge.

Finally, Figure 20.25 shows the hedged exposure across the exchange rate moves, to show that not just the volatility changes can bother the vega, but spot moves as well.

To conclude the case study, perhaps it would have been better to leave the trade without a vega hedge. As a trader the author prefers a dangerous trade left roughly *unhedged* than accurately *mishedged*.

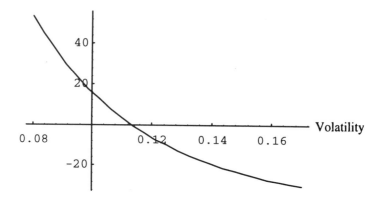

Figure 20.24 Vega of the structure.

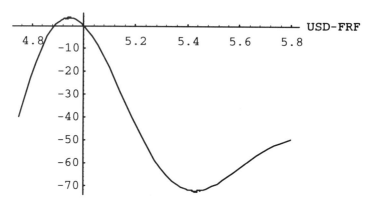

Figure 20.25 A dangerous vega hedge.

DOUBLE BARRIER OPTIONS

Double barrier options are structures that expire when either of the two barriers is touched by the market. In structures on a single asset (that is a one-dimensional option), there can only be two barriers, one higher than the market and another one lower. With multidimensional options, there could only be twice as many barriers as dimensions.

Figure 20.26 compares the value of a double barrier with that of a simple barrier. In both cases the option is a 1 year call struck at 100. The single barrier has an upper outstrike at 110 while the double barrier has an upper outstrike at 110 and a lower one at 90.

The following are basic rules about double barriers:

- Typically, the first exit time is so short that the underlying option's characteristics will be of little relevance. At best, the structure would

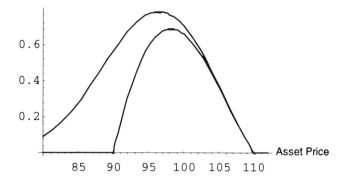

Figure 20.26   Value comparison between a reverse and a double barrier.

look like a reverse knockout. At the worst, it would seem to want to expire imminently.

- Consequently, the best way to study them is to examine American double bets.

Rebate

The rebate is a simple American binary option that pays a certain sum on the termination of the barrier. A knock-out option with a rebate is therefore a straight knock-out plus an American bet of the same strike.

Suppose that a reverse knock-out call of strike 100 and knock-out trigger 109 paid $9 on termination. The structure will simply be additive: one knock-out call 100 trigger 109 *plus* one $9 face value bet, which means that the bet pays $9 if the trigger 109 is reached at any point during its life.

Exercise: Adding the Knock-In

The reader should try, as an exercise, to repeat the study with knock-in options, using the methodology of the comparison between regular knock-out and regular knock-in options.

Alternative Barrier Options

These are also called outbarrier options. They belong to both the path-dependent and correlation families of exotic options.

A trader may have an option on one asset with a barrier, typically a knock-out, in another one.

Example: A SCUD, a second currency underlying, is an option on one asset in one currency with a barrier struck on the exchange rate.

Examples are a Deutsche mark cap with a dollar-mark barrier, or a Nikei Index put option with a knock-out on a lower dollar yen.

The SCUD assumes that the customer no longer needs the option protection when the price of the asset moves in such a way as to create a profit from the currency alone.

Say that a dollar-based fund is long Japanese stocks. A lower dollar, stronger yen would be sufficient to create a profit. He can simply purchase a protection against an adverse movement in the Japanese market that terminates if the currency appreciates. Should the option terminate, the investor can then unwind the entire package for a profit.

Another example is for a U.S.-based investor to borrow in short-term DM and roll over his borrowing periodically. He can buy a cap for his borrowing but with a knock-out should the DM depreciate. In the event of his being knocked out, he will be able to satisfy his short-term DM liability by buying back the currency for a profit.

The following are key trading issues:

- The correlation between assets makes the alternative barrier resemble a regular one. Independence makes the barrier become a bet on the other option.

- The structure will end up having two correlated deltas, one positive in the asset A and one, on the opposing side of the barrier, for the asset B in which the barrier is struck (see Chapter 22, "Multiasset Options").

The Exploding Option

An exploding option is one that presents a certain payout if and when a certain price is reached between the initiation and maturity. It is said then to "explode."

Assume that the underlying is trading at 100. A 102 call "exploding" at 107 pays 5 points when 107 is touched. It offers an alternative to a call spread or a put spread since the owner of the exploding option can thus take profits without having to incur transaction costs. The drawback of such an option is that should the owner change his mind about the position before expiration, the spread costs would be greater than those of a regular option.

An exploding option is equivalent to a reverse knock-out with a rebate equal to the exploding payoff at the time of the termination of the option.

Figures 20.27 and 20.28 show the difference between a regular call and an exploding option. The regular call is struck at 100 while the exploding option is struck at 100 and terminates at 105. Figure 20.27 considers a termination payoff of 2 while Figure 20.28 considers a payoff of 10.

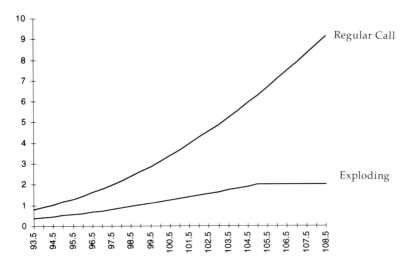

Figure 20.27   The 100 call that pays $2 on termination compared with the regular 100 call with 90 days until expiration.

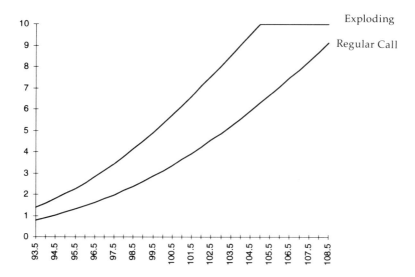

Figure 20.28   The 100 call that pays $10 on termination compared to the regular 100 call with 90 days until expiration.

Capped Index Option

A capped index option, called CAPs, is best described as a reverse knock-out that pays a rebate on termination equal to the difference between strike and outstrike. It is made to appear to be a call spread or put spread that offers a payout equal to the difference between the two strikes. One other intricacy is that unlike most knock-outs that are triggered if touched, this one needs the settlement price (in some cases) to be at or through the second strike.

CAPs are different from *exploding options* in that they are only terminated at the official closing price of the asset while the exploding option is commonly knocked out at any time. It is then said to explode. As explained in Chapter 18, the at-settlement options act like American binaries (i.e., monotonously long or short vega) except close to expiration day when they become European and can thus present mixed gamma features.

> *Example:* Figure 20.29 compares the P/L value of the CAPs 100-105 (i.e., a 100/105 capped call spread) with that of a regular call struck at 100 with the market at 100. The initial purchase price of the CAP is 2.72 compared with 3.11 for a regular call. Assume that volatility is 15.7% annualized.

CAPs are commonly difficult to trade compared with other structures because they only terminate if the underlying assets go through the settlement price, regardless of what can happen during the trading day. While this feature may appear of small consequence to the nonhedging user, it carries some significant risks or some significant opportunities to the hedger.

In a traditional barrier option, the trader knows exactly when to unwind his hedge. When a market maker is short the CAP and has a position in the underlying asset against it, he would work an order close to his CAP price. In an ordinary barrier, he would get out of his hedge at *close to* the

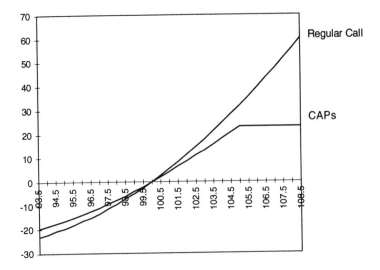

Figure 20.29 Comparison between a CAPs 100-105 and a 105 call 90 days to expiration.

Option Wizard: The Legality of the Triggering

Operators often disagree on what constitutes an incontrovertible termination of a barrier structure. If a trader owns a knock-out option that was terminated according to the counterparty, he would like to see clear signs that the market earnestly traded there without manipulation.

Manipulation is possible (some say likely) in illiquid over-the-counter markets. Listed exchanges do have a procedure in place for preventing two traders from consummating a trade at a fictitious price. A trade cannot be recorded at a price lower than existing bids or higher than existing offers. Such protection is not afforded by the over-the-counter traders who do not have a centralized place to exchange contracts.

The need for such protection caused banks and dealers to establish elaborate contracts specifying that the barrier-triggering conditions would be met only with a proof of the trade on more than an independent forum (i.e., more than one broker). Some firms are usually unhappy about such terms. They consider that a *market if touched* condition would be preferable, as in the heat of the battle, it would be impossible to predict whether the option was knocked out if the operator has to wait to gather information on the number of times it traded and where. The operator needs certainty. Knowing immediately whether he has been knocked out is of the utmost significance. Having to wait for the proof might be costly as the information lag causes slippage.

The best solution is to require the bank short the knock-out (or long the knock-in) to leave a stop-loss with a designated list of third parties (considered reputable from both sides). Thus the party long the barrier (i.e., having to place a *stop-loss* order against the market move as opposed to having a limit order) can satisfy the proof that the barrier was triggered with a simple confirmation slip.

---

knock-out price and close his risk. In this case, he does not know the exact price, which can, ironically give rise to some opportunity.

Take the example of the 100/105 CAPs structure. The trader is short $100 million and long $48 million of the underlying asset. At the 105 knock-out price, the market maker has his delta change from 48% to zero instantaneously. But should that happen during the day, the trader will not know whether to cover entirely by selling back the $48 million. He could sell a portion of it and wait to see whether the market goes higher, in which case he could sell the balance at a higher price if he gains confidence that the structure would be terminated. Should the market head lower through the barrier he could buy back the hedge for a profit, and hope for a repeat of the operation. So in this example, the trader has an invaluable option in his hand.

Option Wizard: Barriers and Price Manipulation

There are famous cases of traders defending their barriers, as with the well publicized case of the Venezuelan par bonds. One firm owning knock-in puts allegedly tried to buy massive amounts of the bond to satisfy the trigger conditions while the party short the puts left massive sell orders to prevent the price from going through the limit. A flash screen update caused one party to consider that the option was knocked in while the counterparty thought otherwise. The Securities and Exchange Commission (SEC) was alerted by the abnormal trading volume and its concentration among few players.

The lesson from such an event is that in an illiquid market the seller of the barrier option (i.e., the party benefiting from the hitting and therefore leaving a *stop* order) can easily manipulate markets with quantities small enough to make such manipulation worthwhile. The payoff at the barrier is large enough to make the risks of the attempt of triggering it very small in comparison. According to the contamination principle, this represents no less than a free option.

There are similar situations with cash-settled options where small buying a few minutes prior to expiration can lead to massive profits, without the penalty of the slippage in getting out of the trade.

Lesson: One should never get involved in a knock-out option in an illiquid market unless one gets proper compensation for the risk of liquidity holes.

The example shows that the *owner* of the structure would be at a disadvantage if he engaged in dynamic hedging.

READING A RISK MANAGEMENT REPORT

This section includes the following material:

- A report on the way Greeks are commonly disclosed to trading risk managers.
- Examples of the Greeks as treated (or mistreated) by a conventional risk management system.
- An example of the pin risks at the barrier.
- An opportunity through the gap report to examine the difference between *mined* and *clear* markets.

The discussion of the barrier option risk precedes the introduction of a standard risk management report (i.e., the kind used by banks' risk management departments in their daily monitoring of the risks). Because few institutions today have positions without barriers, the author believes in holistic risk management: Have all possible positions on one underlying cumulated in one report.

Risk managers get a hint of the risks of a particular position through common scenario analysis reports showing the sensitivity of the options to all manners of parameters. The principal such report is the spot sensitivity. It outlines the risks of P/L stemming from the changes in asset price.

Note that some firms generate "shadow" reports (i.e., showing shadow gamma, as defined in Chapter 8) while others, unfortunately, limit themselves to straight reports.

The risk reports of straight option positions are simple to look at as the risk manager does not need to make any assumption about the potential actions of traders. With barrier options, managers need to consider the risks of execution of hedges on hitting the strike.

Two reports are included in this section: One takes into account the liquidation of a barrier option position (Figure 20.30), and the other does not (Figure 20.31). The example will illustrate some of the concepts we covered and will show the variety of risks faced by risk managers in dealing with explosive products. For the sake of simplicity, the position only contains one delta-neutral position in a flat drift flat term structures of volatility environment.

It is assumed that the Syldavian currency trades at SYD 1.00 to the dollar (the report will show 100 as per reporting convention). The trader has only one position in his inventory: He is short 100 million dollar equivalent of the 3-month call on SYD put on the USD struck at 105.00 with a knock-out feature at 97.00. Typically, traders can carry positions with thousands of strikes, but there is no loss of generality from studying an exposure with a small number of positions.

The report provides the following information:

- *Variable: Spot.* The report changes the spot and does not allow for any change in other parameters. It is therefore a "straight gamma" sensitivity, incorporating no correlation structure between the spot levels and either the interest rates or volatility.

- *Pair.* The unit the trader is concerned with, assuming such position is entirely stand-alone.

- *P/L cur.* The currency in which the P/L is computed. It matters to have it in the numeraire currency and to have the delta expressed in countercurrency (as with the two-country paradox).

- *The dates.* The evolution of the P/L between the dates 8/13/96 and 8/13/96 (in this case the same day). The horizon date could have been longer.

Credit Bank of Syldavia - New York Branch

Report	6					Trader	M.
						Dept	332
Variable	SPOT	From	8/13/96	Incr (STD)	0.25	Portfolio	103B
Pair	SYD_USD	to	8/13/96	Min	94.5	Audited	ON
P&L cur	USD	Center	100.00	Max	105.5	Barrier	Analytic
Delta cur	SYD	Rounding	000			American	Cox-Ross
Vega cur	SYD	Barrier	OFF			Iterations	90 O/E
Gamma cur	SYD		10				

Spot	P&L	Delta	Gamma	Mvega	Theta	Rhod	Rhof
105.50	(5,301)	(20,660)	(4,400)	-1851	172	-1309	1392
105.25	(4,798)	(19,570)	(4,360)	-1833	170	-1276	1356
105.00	(4,332)	(18,490)	(4,320)	-1819	169	-1243	1319
104.75	(3,874)	(17,420)	(4,280)	-1803	167	-1209	1282
104.50	(3,452)	(16,340)	(4,320)	-1783	166	-1175	1245
104.25	(3,056)	(15,280)	(4,240)	-1761	163	-1141	1208
104	(2,688)	(14,230)	(4,200)	-1736	160	-1106	1170
103.75	(2,345)	(13,190)	(4,160)	-1709	158	-1072	1133
103.5	(2,028)	(12,160)	(4,120)	-1678	154	-1037	1095
103.25	(1,737)	(11,150)	(4,040)	-1645	151	-1002	1057
103.00	(1,470)	(10,160)	(3,960)	-1609	147	-967	1019
102.75	(1,228)	(9,190)	(3,880)	-1570	144	-932	981
102.50	(1,010)	(8,240)	(3,800)	-1529	140	-896	943
102.25	(816)	(7,320)	(3,680)	-1485	135	-860	905
102.00	(644)	(6,420)	(3,600)	-1389	131	-824	866
101.75	(494)	(5,550)	(3,480)	-1337	125	-788	828
101.5	(366)	(4,710)	(3,360)	-1283	121	-752	789
101.25	(259)	(3,900)	(3,240)	-1226	116	-715	750
101	(171)	(3,130)	(3,080)	-1167	110	-678	710
100.75	(102)	(2,380)	(3,000)	-1106	105	-640	671
100.50	(51)	(1,680)	(2,800)	-1043	99	-603	631
100.25	(17)	(1,020)	(2,640)	-977	93	-564	590
100.00	-	(390)	(2,520)	-910	87	-526	549
99.75	2	180	(2,280)	-841	80	-487	508
99.50	(8)	720	(2,160)	-770	74	-447	466
99.25	(33)	1,210	(1,960)	-697	67	-406	424
99.00	(69)	1,650	(1,760)	-624	61	-365	381
98.75	(115)	2,050	(1,600)	-548	54	-323	337
98.50	(171)	2,400	(1,400)	-472	47	-280	292
98.25	(235)	2,700	(1,200)	-395	40	-237	246
98	(306)	2,940	(960)	-317	33	-192	199
97.75	(382)	3,140	(800)	-238	25	-146	152
97.5	(462)	3,270	(520)	-159	17	-98	102
97.25	(545)	3,360	(360)	-79	9	-50	52
97.00	(630)	35,000	Error!!!	0	0	0	0
96.75	(1,505)	35,000	-	0	0	0	0
96.50	(2,379)	35,000	-	0	0	0	0
96.25	(3,254)	35,000	-	0	0	0	0
96.00	(4,129)	35,000	-	0	0	0	0
95.75	(5,004)	35,000	-	0	0	0	0
95.50	(5,879)	35,000	-	0	0	0	0
95.25	(6,754)	35,000	-	0	0	0	0
95.00	(7,629)	35,000	-	0	0	0	0
94.75	(8,504)	35,000	-	0	0	0	0
94.50	(9,379)	35,000	-	0	0	0	0

Figure 20.30 Report 1 with the barrier stop-loss off.

Credit Bank of Syldavia - New York Branch

Report	6					Trader	M.
						Dept	332
Variable	SPOT	From	8/13/96	Incr (STD)	0.25	Portfolio	103B
Pair	SYD_USD	to	8/13/96	Min	94.5	Audited	ON
P&L cur	USD	Center	100.00	Max	105.5	Barrier	Analytic
Delta cur	SYD	Rounding	000			American	Cox-Ross
Vega cur	SYD	Barrier	STOP ON			Iterations	90 O/E
Gamma cur	SYD						

Spot	P&L	Delta	Gamma	Mvega	Theta	Rhod	Rhof
105.50	(5,301)	(20,660)	(4,400)	-1851	172	-1309	1392
105.25	(4,798)	(19,570)	(4,360)	-1833	170	-1276	1356
105.00	(4,332)	(18,490)	(4,320)	-1819	169	-1243	1319
104.75	(3,874)	(17,420)	(4,280)	-1803	167	-1209	1282
104.50	(3,452)	(16,340)	(4,320)	-1783	166	-1175	1245
104.25	(3,056)	(15,280)	(4,240)	-1761	163	-1141	1208
104	(2,688)	(14,230)	(4,200)	-1736	160	-1106	1170
103.75	(2,345)	(13,190)	(4,160)	-1709	158	-1072	1133
103.5	(2,028)	(12,160)	(4,120)	-1678	154	-1037	1095
103.25	(1,737)	(11,150)	(4,040)	-1645	151	-1002	1057
103.00	(1,470)	(10,160)	(3,960)	-1609	147	-967	1019
102.75	(1,228)	(9,190)	(3,880)	-1570	144	-932	981
102.50	(1,010)	(8,240)	(3,800)	-1529	140	-896	943
102.25	(816)	(7,320)	(3,680)	-1485	135	-860	905
102.00	(644)	(6,420)	(3,600)	-1389	131	-824	866
101.75	(494)	(5,550)	(3,480)	-1337	125	-788	828
101.5	(366)	(4,710)	(3,360)	-1283	121	-752	789
101.25	(259)	(3,900)	(3,240)	-1226	116	-715	750
101	(171)	(3,130)	(3,080)	-1167	110	-678	710
100.75	(102)	(2,380)	(3,000)	-1106	105	-640	671
100.50	(51)	(1,680)	(2,800)	-1043	99	-603	631
100.25	(17)	(1,020)	(2,640)	-977	93	-564	590
100.00	-	(390)	(2,520)	-910	87	-526	549
99.75	2	180	(2,280)	-841	80	-487	508
99.50	(8)	720	(2,160)	-770	74	-447	466
99.25	(33)	1,210	(1,960)	-697	67	-406	424
99.00	(69)	1,650	(1,760)	-624	61	-365	381
98.75	(115)	2,050	(1,600)	-548	54	-323	337
98.50	(171)	2,400	(1,400)	-472	47	-280	292
98.25	(235)	2,700	(1,200)	-395	40	-237	246
98	(306)	2,940	(960)	-317	33	-192	199
97.75	(382)	3,140	(800)	-238	25	-146	152
97.5	(462)	3,270	(520)	-159	17	-98	102
97.25	(545)	3,360	(360)	-79	9	-50	52
97.00	(630)	0	Error!!!	0	0	0	0
96.75	(630)	0	0	0	0	0	0
96.50	(630)	0	0	0	0	0	0
96.25	(630)	0	0	0	0	0	0
96.00	(630)	0	0	0	0	0	0
95.75	(630)	0	0	0	0	0	0
95.50	(630)	0	0	0	0	0	0
95.25	(630)	0	0	0	0	0	0
95.00	(630)	0	0	0	0	0	0
94.75	(630)	0	0	0	0	0	0
94.50	(630)	0	0	0	0	0	0

Figure 20.31 Report 2 with the barrier stop-loss on.

- *Incr.* In standard deviations (self-explanatory). The report is for .25 standard deviations.

- *Rounding.* 000 means that amounts are in thousands.

- *Audited ON.* A flag that shows the risk management report was issued from a database audited by the controllers. It signifies that the report produced can be read but cannot be altered by the trader, on a read-only mode. The trader cannot (in theory) hide positions and take risks that do not show on the report.

- *Barrier: Analytic.* The pricing of the barrier options is performed on a simple model without any attempt at using more sophisticated tools. Analytic means that the system uses a closed-form solution.

- *American: Cox-Ross* (the Rubinstein in Cox-Ross-Rubinstein is undeservedly missing because of the narrowness of the field on the report). Indicates that a binomial model is implemented for American options. The field Iterations item shows 90 O/E, which means that the tree will have 90 iterations but will flip between odd and even as a precision optimizing trick.

- *Barrier: ON or OFF.* This is where the beef is: Some reports assume that the trader has a stop-loss to unwind the hedge at the barrier (in this case, 35 mil SYD at 97.00), and Report 2 with the flag ON makes such assumption. Typically, if the stop-loss is triggered, the trader has a documented proof that the market traded at such level as required by the contract and finished off the option. So it appears safe that, conditional upon a firm order in the market, the risk manager would be interested in seeing the rest of the position post-stop-loss.

Matters are not that easy, however: What if the barrier stop-loss was not executed at the desired price? There is the nefarious slippage, as defined in Chapter 4. Beyond that, there might be the more severe gap risk: the discontinuous moves as the market can snap through the barrier, thus causing liquidation at lower than 97.00. Every point lower would cost $3.5 million dollars in execution costs. This shows the need for another risk report, the **gap risk.** Traders assume that markets in foreign exchange trade on a 24-hour basis, but there is the risk of the discontinuity caused by the weekend. In addition, there are political announcements that can cause such gap risks: The news that the Syldavian king has some cardiovascular problems can hit the screens, thus causing a large and sudden *gapping* drop in the currency.

Many risk managers suggested to the author that the stop-loss be placed before the official knock-out trigger (slightly higher than a lower barrier and slightly lower than a higher barrier). This is a bad idea as it creates a negative gamma should the barrier not be reached (a phenomenon commonly called a "bounce" by traders trying to defend their barriers).

At another level, banks would be choked with risk and stopped from trading unless they eliminated the triggered barriers from the risk reports. Unlike the regular short option gamma, the barrier is a one-time hit, not a permanent danger. Assume that the trader sold the $3.5 million SYD on a stop-loss basis. The trade confirmation would be the proof that the barrier was knocked out. Should the market rally higher or continue dropping, the position would not exist at all.

The best solution for a risk manager is to have Report 2 with the barrier stop-loss ON (not Report 1 with the stop-loss OFF) as well as a gap report showing the potential execution risks.

This risk management issue illustrates why dynamic hedgers often go through the difficult task of trying to explain the P/L swings to their boss. The "I thought you were hedged" is an answer by managers unfamiliar with the product (or too burned out to try to learn about it) and the best remedy is the gap risk report.

Risk Management Rule: Traders and managers need to make a clear distinction on a report between the contractually path-dependent positions (i.e., barriers) and the securities that are path dependent owing to dynamic hedging (vanilla options).

A brief explanation of the report columns follows:

- P&L (column 2) shows the profits from the origin (*Center* on top shows 100). It assumes no shadow gamma, no changes in volatility. To compute the shadow gamma resulting P/L, one needs to make assumptions about the volatility behavior conditional on a move. Assume the trader thinks that at 102 the volatility would be (for the period concerned) one point higher, an extremely safe assumption. Being that he is short modified vega (the same as simple vega) in the amount of $139,000 per point the P/L at 102 would then be $-644,000 - 139,000 = -\$783,000$ at such spot level.

- Gamma in this report is conventional except that it blows up at the barrier where it becomes a Dirac. The report shows an error sign.

- The modified vega (expressed in 100 not 1,000 for reasons of convention) assumes curve shifts that are weighted in 3-month equivalent. Whatever amount is seen corresponds to the 3-month move with the previous month a function of it, according to some empirical observed weightings. It assumes the move to be one point in the 3-month, .5 in the 1-year, and so on. Because the model is using an analytical model in place of the Dupire-Derman-Kani, it is safe to assume that the modification will not be very precise for a barrier since the barrier reacts to the entire curve.

- Rhod shows the exposure to parallel shifts in the numeraire currency and Rhof shows the shifts in the countercurrency. Both are unweighted, an extremely bad idea. Rhod is higher than rhof because it includes the exposure to the carry of the premium.

Gaps and Gap Reports

■ The **gap report** shows and quantifies the possible execution risks of the gap delta (the deltas that need to be unloaded on a stop-loss on the termination of the structure). These are one-time slippage costs.

The second column of the gap report shown in Figure 20.32 shows the amount of deltas that need to be sold at 97.00. The system at the Credit Bank of Syldavia estimated the gap risk to be on weekdays $634,000 (Column 3), which corresponds to a gap of .20 (the risk of having the order filled on average at 96.80) and three times such amount when the market gaps over the weekend (Column 4).

The magnitude of the gap risk is a function of the number of options and will remain independent of the duration of the portfolio or stopping time. Moreover, the market has a tendency, after a period of high volatility, of cleaning up some range in the market of stop-losses. This often has some serious impact on volatility. It suggests the notion of mined markets.

■ A **mined market** is one that has many knock-outs and knock-in gap-delta orders placed in it and will therefore experience a high level of "whipping" and mean reverting volatility around these prices. A **cleared market** is one that has no such orders in it.

As the open interest in barrier options builds up, so will the gap orders by operators. Traders monitor the recent high and low (say for one month), and when such difference remains narrow for a few weeks, they can expect the

Credit Bank of Syldavia - New York Branch						
Report	7			Trader	M.	
Pair	SYD_USD			Dept		332
Delta cur	SYD	Date	8/13/96	Portfolio		103B
Amount	0			Audited		ON
Spot	Delta Gap	Week-day	Week-end			
	-					
97.00	31,700	634,000	2,536,000			

Figure 20.32   The gap report for the previous position.

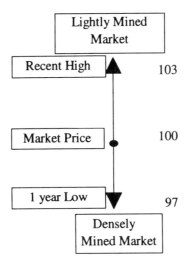

Figure 20.33   Mined markets.

buildup of gap delta orders below the low and above the high. As soon as the market enters a "mined" zone, a chain of liquidity holes is triggered. The market then clears out. This phenomenon is called the "driftwood effect" as all barrier option orders will be pushed out to the recent high and low range (see Figure 20.33).

Risk Management Rule: The expected slippage costs of gap deltas need to be increased when the risk manager has adequate information to conclude that their level is located in a densely mined market range.

Chapter *21*

Compound, Choosers, and Higher Order Options

Hiring an option trader with P/L volatility is the most common manifestation of a compound option.

Compound options are options that deliver another option. They are particularly present in the extendible option variety and other structures where the owner of the structure has, somewhere along the way, the possibility of extending his choice against the payment of a fee.

Compound options are extremely sensitive to higher derivatives with respect to spot, particularly the fourth moment of the distribution, which traders call volatility of volatility, in addition to the second moment with respect to volatility (somewhat related). They are commonly mispriced because of that effect. More than regular options, they depend on the thickness of the tails of the distribution. This makes a constant volatility type model, written in early days, dangerous to use. This chapter also gives warning of a more complex modeling technique that includes the volatility of volatility owing to the difficulties in both its estimation and its association with the underlying price behavior.

At the time of this writing, there is no known formula nor publicly available method to price compound options correctly (using stochastic volatility), other than a few numerical techniques this author dabbled with. So in this presentation, the author will use what poor formula is available and try to work around it by *estimating* the appropriate markup.

■ A **compound option,** or second-order option, is an option on a European option. It consists in the right to buy or sell a European option (called underlying option) of a given strike and maturity for a predetermined price.

A third-order option is an option on a compound option, and so forth. A compound option has one final strike price and one final expiration date (the equivalent to a vanilla). In addition, it will have intermediate strikes and intermediate dates. So a second-order option will be

$$\text{Second-order option } (\Phi_1 K_1, \, \Phi_{final} K_{final}, t_1, t_{final})$$

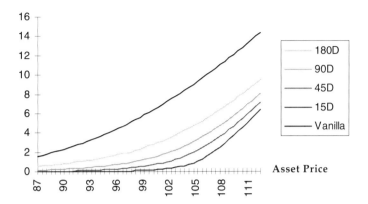

Figure 21.1 Compound option: OTM calls on 1-year call, 16% volatility.

with K_{final} and t_{final} the strike price and the time left to expiration of the vanilla. K_1 and t_1 will be the intermediate dates K_1 the strike price at which one has the right to buy or sell the option (K_{final} and t_{final}) at time t_1. Also, t_1 needs to be shorter than the final date. Note that every strike price will need the further specification of whether it is a put or a call (i.e., the right to buy or the right to sell), which is done through the indicator Φ.

A higher order option will have the following specifications:

nth order option ($\Phi_1 K_1, \ldots \Phi_n K_n, \Phi_{final} K_{final}, t_1, \ldots t_n, t_{final}$)

with $t_1 < t_2 < \ldots < t_n < t_{final}$

Example: Figure 21.1 shows the prices of a call on call struck for $1, at 16% volatility, assuming a flat forward curve.

Figure 21.2 displays an out-of-the-money put on a call. Figure 21.3 illustrates the straddle.

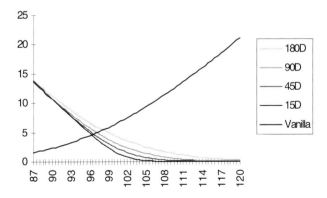

Figure 21.2 Compound option: Put on 1-year call.

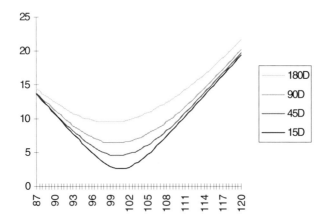

Figure 21.3 Straddle on 1-year call.

VEGA CONVEXITY: THE COSTS OF DYNAMIC HEDGING

Vega convexity can be best illustrated with the following case study (see Table 21.1). The underlying option has tenure of 2 years, struck at 100, with a flat forward, and 15% volatility. Assume for simplicity that the volatility curve is flat. As the price of the option is initially 8%, the trader buys a 16% out-of-the-money call on the call and hedges it vega neutral in the underlying security.

To simplify, assume that vega neutrality can be done without the adjustment factors. Adjustment factors, or weightings, add nothing to the example. Figure 21.4 shows the instability of vega neutrality. What a trader gets

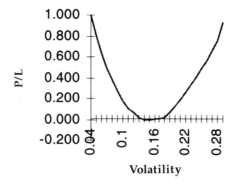

Figure 21.4 Long the higher moments: Compound versus vanilla long a 6M call on ATM 2-year call, 16% strike.

Table 21.1   Vega Effect

vol	Price	Vanilla P/L	Compound P/L	P/L
0.04				0.000
0.05	**0.000**	**2.062**	−1.065	0.997
0.06	**0.000**	**1.874**	−1.065	0.809
0.07	**0.015**	**1.687**	−1.050	0.637
0.08	**0.061**	**1.499**	−1.004	0.495
0.09	**0.129**	**1.312**	−0.936	0.376
0.1	**0.210**	**1.125**	−0.855	0.270
0.11	**0.305**	**0.937**	−0.760	0.177
0.12	**0.420**	**0.750**	−0.645	0.105
0.13	**0.564**	**0.562**	−0.501	0.061
0.14	**0.710**	**0.375**	−0.355	0.020
0.15	**0.878**	**0.187**	−0.187	0.000
0.16	**1.065**	**0.000**	0.000	0.000
0.17	**1.256**	**−0.187**	0.190	0.003
0.18	**1.449**	**−0.375**	0.384	0.009
0.19	**1.646**	**−0.562**	0.581	0.019
0.2	**1.878**	**−0.750**	0.813	0.063
0.21	**2.126**	**−0.937**	1.061	0.124
0.22	**2.378**	**−1.125**	1.313	0.188
0.23	**2.634**	**−1.312**	1.569	0.257
0.24	**2.893**	**−1.499**	1.828	0.329
0.25	**3.157**	**−1.687**	2.092	0.405
0.26	**3.424**	**−1.874**	2.359	0.485
0.27	**3.696**	**−2.062**	2.631	0.569
0.28	**3.971**	**−2.249**	2.906	0.657
0.29	**4.255**	**−2.437**	3.190	0.754
0.3	**4.611**	**−2.624**	3.546	0.922

when he goes vega neutral against a long compound option is a straddle on volatility.

USES OF COMPOUND OPTIONS: HEDGING BARRIER VEGA

Because barrier options present extreme vega concavity as a package, it seems sounder to execute the hedge of the vega with the use of a compound, should these be available at no higher cost in the market.

CHOOSER OPTIONS

■ **Chooser options** are options that could turn into either a put or a call at some predetermined time.

They have the following specifications:

Simple Chooser $(K, t_{intermediate}, t_{final})$

The more complex "Gutspin" Chooser $(K_2, K_1, t_{intermediate}, t_{final})$

with K the strike price, $t_{intermediate}$ the time until the owner of the structure would have to decide on whether he prefers to own the put or the call. The "gutspin" chooser allows for two strike prices, and the owner would certainly choose the one that is the furthest in the money.

A European chooser option that has the intermediate date equal to the end date would then be identical to a straddle. At the other extreme, a chooser that has very little time before the decision deadline would be priced at the highest of the put or the call.

Figure 21.5 shows a 2-month option (strike = 100, no drift) with a choosing period that floats between the immediate need for a decision and a time to decision equal to the end date. At one extreme, as the choosing period is equal to zero, the structure will be priced at the value of a 2-month call or put (they are equal in this case). At the other it will be valued at the price of the straddle.

Ironically, the chooser resembles a rainbow option because the trader has to pick one of two assets. It reaches its maximum (i.e., the straddle price) when the correlation between the two assets (the put and the call) is

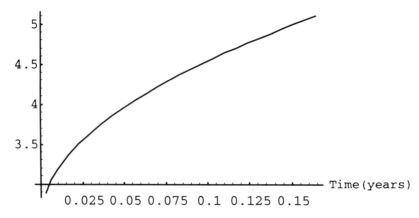

Figure 21.5   Chooser option price sensitivity to choosing period.

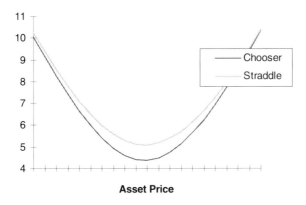

Asset Price

Figure 21.6 Comparison between a chooser and a straddle.

exactly equal to −1, which is the case close to expiration. The reader should go through the mental exercise of thinking that a put and a call are two negatively correlated assets.

Figure 21.6 provides a pictorial comparison between a chooser and a straddle.

There are few interesting things to say about the chooser except that it comes halfway between a vanilla and a straddle. Its sensitivity to volatility would be very linear when it is at the money and more convex than an out-of-the-money vanilla as it becomes deep in the money (a chooser has the characteristic or never being out of the money in the simple one-strike case).

Figure 21.7 shows the difference in vega convexity between an out-of-the-money vanilla and the deep-in-the money corresponding chooser. Spot trades at 100, with the chooser and the vanilla call) struck at 110. Volatility is the usual 15.7%. Both have 60 days to expiration, with the chooser 30 days to decision date.

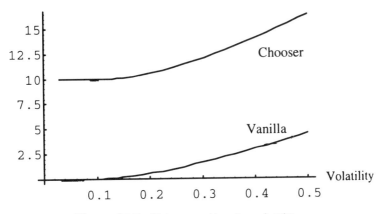

Figure 21.7 Price reaction to volatility.

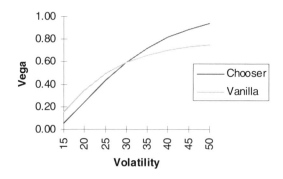

Figure 21.8   Vega changes with volatility: Convex vanilla versus chooser.

The vega representation shows the additional convexity of the chooser, though not as exaggerated as with the true compound (see Figure 21.8). The option has no vega below the 10% volatility: At low volatility, the in-the-money compound has decided that it was going to be a call and became insensitive to vega. At a higher volatility, the possibility of a switch from put to call becomes increasingly prominent.

A Few Applications of the Higher Order Options

- *Caption, Floortions.* They are options on caps and options on floors, themselves a SDF *(smallest decomposable fragment)* sum of options on independent forward Eurodeposit (or other form of interest rates) instruments called caplets and floorlets. Hence, captions and floortions are options on baskets (a basket of Euros) and compound options at the same time. The first characteristic allows traders to use covariance matrices in the analysis. The second necessitates a thorough analysis of the volatility of volatility.

- The compound element in captions and floortions is not remarkable, as the volatility of the basket will pull down that of the entire structure. The back contracts will not have the same sensitivity to volatility as the front ones. In addition, the first contract will not be very volatile.

- The multivariate element is not as dominating as with regular interest rate instruments. The correlation between the prices of caplets and floorlets presents more stable features than that of the underlying forward Eurodeposits.

Chapter **22**

Multiasset Options

The principal difference between a quant and a trader is that a quant favors a flawless model based on imperfect assumptions while the trader prefers an imperfect model based on flawless assumptions.

Multi-asset options range from the basket option to the rainbow. However, any structure in a pair not involving the home currency as a numeraire could be interpreted as a multiasset option. This chapter will cover the essential risk in most of the categories but will focus most on building the intuition of their risk management with a simplified dual-asset option structure.

Mathematicians have the habit of solving problems in the lower dimensions, then generalizing to $\mathbf{R}^n$. The reader should in the same fashion generalize structures from the lower into the higher dimensions. This is where the quantitative trading starts: While pure trader judgment and intuition can be relied on in the lower dimensions, a more mathematical framework and matrix analysis become essential in the higher dimensions.

Multiasset structures include:

- *Choice.* Options involving a choice between two or more instruments: best of, worst of, rainbow options, etc. A sample will be analyzed with the rainbow options.

- *Linear Combinations.* Options involving baskets, spreads. This chapter offers a brief examination of baskets. Unlike the product and others, a sum of two exponential Brownian motions is not an exponential Brownian. These instruments resemble Asian options in the sense that they will present some pricing complications in addition to some minor *skew* exposure when hedged with other instruments.

- *Product or Quotients.* Options involving a product between two or more instruments. They are easy to price, often more difficult to hedge. The chapter includes an analysis of a sample with the Mexican structured note.

A basic understanding of the risk management of multiasset options can be obtained with the rainbow option. There are indeed many possible structures but the same dynamic hedging method applies to all of them, which makes it unnecessary to fill up a phone book with combinations.

CHOICE BETWEEN ASSETS: RAINBOW OPTIONS

■ **Rainbow options** are options that include more than one strike price on more than one underlying asset.

They are usually specified as having one expiration date and a payoff that is equivalent to the largest in-the-money portion of any of the strike prices:

$$\text{Rainbow } (\Phi_1, K_1, \Phi_2, K_2, \ldots \Phi_n, K_n, t)$$

with Φ_i indicating whether it is a put or a call (it could be a call on asset 1 and a put on asset 2) and one time to expiration in the simple case (structurers could complicate life a little bit by including a multiple expiration date structure).

This simple example shows an option on "either or" two assets A and B, each currently trading at 100, with two strike prices of 100 for asset A and 100 for asset B. The reader will initially consider the sensitivity of the structure with 30 days to expiration then will extend the maturity to 6 months for a better analysis. Both assets trade at 15.7% volatility. Assume an initial 50% correlation between the two assets.

Note that one could rescale the assets to a different base than 100 provided that both the prices and the strikes are multiplied by the same amount.

The reader can intuitively see that the final payoff (Figure 22.1) covers more areas than either of the two options each taken separately but somewhat less than the sum of the two independent options (see Figures 22.2 and 22.3).

Using the contamination principle, it is possible to see that the price of the structure with time until expiration would look like an inflated balloon that would start sticking to the surface of Figure 22.1 as either volatilities or time until expiration decrease.

The structure is sensitive, in addition to the usual battery of Greeks, to correlation. As a matter of fact, it has a correlation vega, usually overlooked by researchers, as some tend to write off correlation as constant, owing to improper training in the physical sciences.

Figure 22.4 displays the sensitivity of the structure to correlation. As correlation is bounded between -1 and 1, the trader does not have to simulate very far for a two-asset option structure. For a higher dimension structure, the trader would need to perform the more difficult matrix analysis.

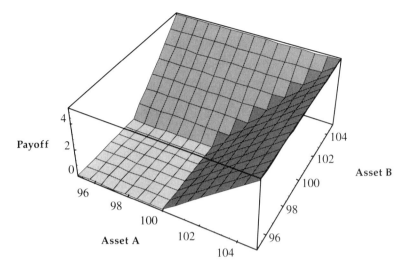

Figure 22.1   Dual strike expiration payoff.

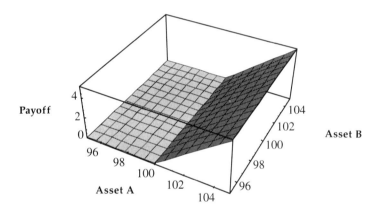

Figure 22.2   Single asset A expiration payoff.

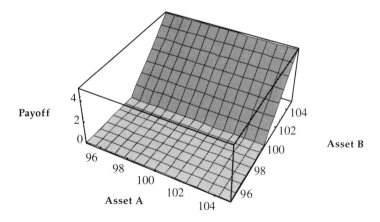

Figure 22.3   Single asset B expiration payoff.

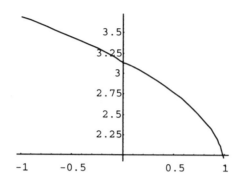

Figure 22.4 Sensitivity of the dual strike to correlation.

At a correlation of 1, the fact that the option has two assets becomes irrelevant. Because the two assets are valued at the same volatility, the option structure would trade at the price of either of the two. If there is (for some reason attributable to the cross-volatility between *A* and *B*) a difference between the volatilities of the assets, the structure would follow the highest of the two volatilities.

At a correlation of −1, the structure would trade at twice the value of a regular option because it is guaranteed to be in-the-money in one of the two assets. For every down-move in one asset, the operator is guaranteed an antithetic up-move in the other so one of the assets would be in the money.

Note. This example uses dual call options. A structure with a call on one asset and a put on the other (only one of which could be exercised at maturity) would have opposite results: negative correlation would depress the price.

■ A **correlation vega** for a dual asset structure corresponds to the change in price in the structure that results from a change in correlation.

For a multiasset option including more than two assets, there are many correlation vegas, one for every possible pair. So for a structure that has 4 assets:

$$\text{Vega} \begin{bmatrix} \rho_{12} & \rho_{13} & \rho_{14} \\ & \rho_{23} & \rho_{24} \\ & & \rho_{34} \end{bmatrix}$$

The diagonal is, of course, 0 since every asset has a 1 correlation with itself. Only half the matrix is shown because the correlations are mirror image with each other (correlation between asset 1 and asset 2 will be equal to that between asset 2 and asset 1).

There is a sensitivity to each one of these correlations.

This method could be pushed one step further and placed in the context of a covariance matrix (i.e., the risk of the overall portfolio). The author will call the covariance matrix for a portfolio, symbol Σ, the matrix showing the covariances between the assets. Traders usually learn to view the Σ as the equivalent of the volatility for an asset:

$$
\Sigma = \begin{bmatrix}
\sigma_{11} & \sigma_{12} & \sigma_{13} & \sigma_{14} \\
 & \sigma_{22} & \sigma_{23} & \sigma_{24} \\
 & & \sigma_{33} & \sigma_{34} \\
 & & & \sigma_{44}
\end{bmatrix}
$$

with σ_{ij} the covariance between asset i and that of asset j. σ_{ij} The total matrix needs to satisfy some restrictions,[1] and the correlations and volatilities need to conform to some boundary or the matrix would turn negative, the equivalent of a volatility being negative, something even experienced option traders have not yet encountered.

Correlated and Uncorrelated Greeks

The dual asset option presents more than one delta, and some assumptions need to be made by the hedger (Figure 22.5). A believer in the stability of correlations would necessarily trade the structure differently from a conspiracy theorist.

It is therefore necessary to build the *gradient*, also called total delta and correlated delta, composed of *partial deltas*.

$$
\nabla = \begin{bmatrix} \Delta_A \\ \Delta_B \end{bmatrix}
$$

Δ_A, called partial delta in A, represents the sensitivity of the structure to changes in the price of asset A assuming that asset B moves according to its correlation to A.

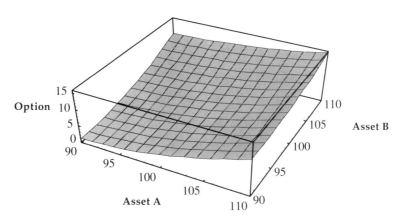

Figure 22.5 Time value of the dual strike.

Δ_B, called partial delta in B, represents the sensitivity of the structure to changes in the price of asset B assuming that asset A moves according to its correlation to B.

The gradient, ∇, also called the correlated delta, represents the sensitivity of the structure to the changes in the price of the assets A and B assuming that A would move according to its correlation to B and B according to its correlation to A.

Figure 22.6 shows two simulated runs for asset A. One varies A without a corresponding correlated move in asset B while the other takes B into account.

Asset A moving alone gives a different result than when the asset A move is accompanied by a correlated one with B.

The real risk then needs to be seen in two deltas, Δ_A and Δ_B as well as in the total deltas. It will be useful to compare the deltas of the total structure.

Table 22.1 shows the sensitivity of the option partial delta A to the asset A alone (asset B remains frozen).

To measure the total, or uncorrelated delta, requires more involved matrix analysis:

$$\text{Total delta: } \nabla^T \Sigma \nabla$$

which can be computed for our two-asset position as:

$$[\Delta_A \; \Delta_B] \begin{bmatrix} \sigma_A^2 & \sigma_{AB} \\ \sigma_{AB} & \sigma_B^2 \end{bmatrix} \begin{bmatrix} \Delta_A \\ \Delta_B \end{bmatrix}$$

This leads to the notion of partial gamma.

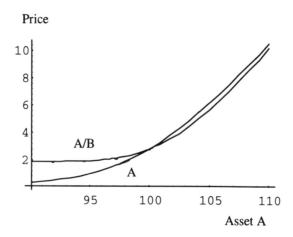

Figure 22.6   Correlated and uncorrelated moves.

Table 22.1 Partial Delta

Asset A	Δ_A
95	.18
96	.22
97	.27
98	.29
99	.31
100	.37
101	.42
102	.45
103	.46
104	.51
105	.57

As each structure has four possible deltas, it will also have the following gammas: Only the realistic correlated gammas will be examined:

$$\begin{bmatrix} \text{Gamma}AA & \text{Gamma}AB \\ \text{Gamma}BA & \text{Gamma}BB \end{bmatrix}$$

GammaAA = Changes in the Δ_A stemming from the changes in A
    (B moves according to its correlation)

GammaAB = Changes in the Δ_A stemming from the changes in B
    (A moves according to its correlation)

GammaBA = Changes in the Δ_B stemming from the changes in A
    (B moves according to its correlation). Both GammaAB and
    GammaBA yield the same result.

GammaBB = Changes in the Δ_B stemming from the changes in B
    (A moves according to its correlation)

Another option involving choice is the outperformance option.

■ An **outperformance option** (between two assets) is an option that entitles the owner to buy or sell one asset against the other at a predetermined rate. They are generally calls on the maximum, puts on a minimum.[2]

Outperformance options are a useful tool in the study of *numeraire* issues. An interesting way to view them is with index allocation. A fund manager who does not have a fixed allocation can assume that he has a theoretical delta that is similar to that of such option. He would then use the delta vectors and gamma matrices to continuously adjust his position.

An outperformance option can easily be seen as a spread option once it is specified:

$$Max(S1, S2) = [S1 + Max(0, S2 - S1)]$$

which means that an outperformance option is nothing but one asset plus a spread between two of the assets. As to spread options, it is better to view them from the vantage point of a basket by seeing that one of the assets has a negative weight.

Perhaps the mother of all outperformance options is the option on the bond future. It entitles the short future party to deliver the cheapest of the eligible bonds. As such it becomes an option on the minimum of several assets.

LINEAR COMBINATIONS

■ An option on a **linear combination** of assets has the following specifications:

$$\text{Option}\left(\sum_{i=1}^{n} w_i S_i\right)$$

The category contains basket options, spread options, and any combination one would dream of. In addition, Asian options can be included in it, as will be seen.

Example

- With $n = 2$ and $w_1 = w_2 = 1$. The option will be a call, put, or other (e.g., digital) on an underlying that is the sum of two assets.
- With $n = 2$ and $w_1 = 1$ $w_2 = -1$. The option will be a call, put, or other on an underlying that is the spread between two assets. Such option is generally called a Margrabe option.[3]
- With $n = 500$ and the w_i variable. The underlying basket would be a stock index, and so on.

Linear combinations between assets pose the problem of lognormality, which does not occur with other structures. To illustrate, assume that assets A and B are both lognormal:

$$A_t = A_0 \exp(-\tfrac{1}{2}\,\sigma_A^2\,\Delta t + \sigma_A\,\sqrt{\Delta t}\,Z_A)$$
$$B_t = B_0 \exp(-\tfrac{1}{2}\,\sigma_B^2\,\Delta t + \sigma_B\,\sqrt{\Delta t}\,Z_B)$$

with Δt the time until expiration of the structure, A_0 and B_0 the initial price of the assets, σ_A and σ_B the volatilities, Z_A and Z_B Wiener processes independent identically distributed with unit variance and 0 mean.

It is easy to see that the sum $W = A + B$ cannot be put in a geometric Brownian shape

$$W = A_0\exp(-\tfrac{1}{2}\,\sigma_A^2\,\Delta t + \sigma_A\,\sqrt{\Delta t}\,Z_A) + B_0\exp(-\tfrac{1}{2}\,\sigma_B^2\,\Delta t + \sigma_B\,\sqrt{\Delta t}\,Z_B)$$

nor would $W = A - B$ whereas setting $W = AB$, results in

$$W = A_0 B_0\exp(-\tfrac{1}{2}\,(\sigma_A^2 + \sigma_B^2)\,\Delta t + (\sigma_A Z_A + \sigma_B Z_B)\,\sqrt{\Delta t}),$$

or if setting $W = A/B$ gets

$$W = A_0/B_0\exp(-\tfrac{1}{2}\,(\sigma_A^2 - \sigma_B^2)\Delta t + (\sigma_A Z_A - \sigma_B Z_B)\,\sqrt{\Delta t}),$$

both of which are geometric Brownian.

Basket Options

Basket options are options on a weighted sum of two or more assets. They typically have a strike price on the net weighted sum. Basket options are omnipresent, since often many products are considered a basket of some subcomponent.

These options will not receive much attention here, as they can be simply analyzed as options on a product, the product being the underlying basket. Two hitches—lognormality and the correlation between the underlying assets—represent some singularities, however.

Lognormality

Problems in hedging basket options can be of some significance when dealing with markets that exhibit a strong skew.

Many operators price basket options as if the underlying basket were a commodity on its own following a stochastic process similar to that of other commodities, with its volatility derived from its own time series. This, however, conflicts with the fact that an average (or any linear combination) of assets with a lognormal distribution does not follow a lognormal distribution. So there is a conflict between saying that the SP100 components are lognormal and that the SP100 as a commodity is. In such cases, operators resort to assuming arbitrarily that the most traded of the basket or the components is going to be the lognormal product.

This problem arises in swaps and Eurodollar options. It is well known that a strip is a basket of Eurodollar contracts strung together and weighted by some discounting factor. An option on a strip is therefore a basket option. Which one needs to be lognormal?

A mitigating factor with stock indices and fixed income products is that when the correlation between the components is high the sum would come closer to a lognormally distributed asset.

The following example illustrates the problem.

Example: There are two uncorrelated assets A and B, with prices S_A and S_B, independently lognormally distributed with volatilities σ_A and σ_B.

The basket rule indicates that the volatility of the basket S containing both assets A and B would be the weighted square root of the volatilities minus correlation, in this case zero. Therefore

$$S\sigma = \sqrt{w_A^2 \sigma_A^2 S_A^2 + w_B^2 \sigma_B^2 S_B^2}$$

with w_A and w_B the weights imparted to each (a more general formula will be presented in the next section).

Figure 22.7 graphically displays why the process, the volatility of which is known, is not lognormal.

Assume no drift and equal weights of .5, S_A, and S_B both initially at 100 and 50% volatility. So the operator can expect the resulting sensitivity of a position that is long a combination of the options of the assets and short the basket (in ratio satisfying gamma neutrality): It looks like a risk reversal. Figure 22.7 shows such position at a high volatility. A more acute version of this problem will be discussed with Asian options.

Correlation Issues

The multiasset structure will be considered on n underlying securities. Ignoring the lognormality issue[4] the operator could consider the structure a pseudovanilla option and price it by assuming its volatility is that of the basket. To derive the correlation sensitivity, he would reprice the structure at different levels of correlation. This is best approximated by multiplying the vega by the effect of the correlation on the volatility.

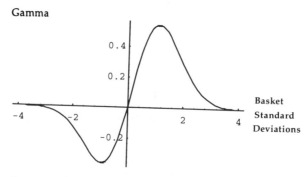

Figure 22.7 Gamma of a portfolio long asset options, short the basket options.

Option Wizard: A Pseudovanilla

A pseudovanilla option is an option used for risk management purposes to test some of the sensitivities of a more complex product.

The pseudovanilla for a basket is the option that trades at the net volatility of the basket. It could only be used to test some of the sensitivities.

A pseudovanilla for a barrier is, as seen earlier, a risk reversal, provided one only tested for the skew effect. It could also be (yes, indeed), a calendar spread, provided one tested only for the sensitivity to the term structure of volatility.

Before gauging the effect of an increase in any of the volatilities over the overall structure, the trader must get some formulas updated on a spreadsheet.

Assume that a basket S is a sum using the individual weights w_1 of assets X_i through X_n, that is:

$$S = w_1 X_1 + w_2 X_2 + \ldots w_n X_n$$

Using σ_S the volatility of the basket and σ_i that of asset i, $cov(i,j)$ the covariance between assets i and j, $\rho_{i,j}$ the correlation between assets i and asset j, the operator has

$$\sigma_S^2 = \frac{1}{S^2} \left(\sum_{i=1}^{n} w_i^2 \, var(X_i) X_i^2 + 2 \sum_{i<j}^{n} w_i \, w_j \, cov(X_i, X_j) \, X_i \, X_j \right)$$

which, since the correlation is the ratio of the covariances to the product of the individual variances, is equivalent to

$$\sigma_S = \frac{1}{S} \sqrt{ \sum_{i=1}^{n} w_i^2 \sigma_i^2 X_i^2 + 2 \sum_{i<j}^{n} w_i w_j \rho_{i,j} \sigma_i \sigma_j X_i X_j }$$

It follows that the *correlation vega* (as we can call it) of the structure is:

$$\frac{\delta \sigma_S}{\delta \rho_{i,j}} = \frac{w_i w_j \sigma_i \sigma_j X_i X_j}{S 2 \sigma_S}$$

Example (simplified): A 1-year option on the average of USD-DEM and USD-JPY, struck at 1.19 (for simplicity, divide yen by 100), which is at-the-money presently. USD-DEM trades at 1.42 and USD-JPY at 100. Rates are 5% for the USD, 5% for the DEM and 1% for the JPY. Note: To compute the forward of a basket, linear weightings of the forwards can be used. There are no complications (owing to the homogeneity of the function) as:

$$\text{Forward } (\Sigma w_i S_i, t) = \Sigma \, w_i \text{ Forward } (S_i, t).$$

Hence, the operator can ignore the forward (taking into account no shadow gamma) and simply use spot for the volatility computation.

The 6-month volatilities of USD-DEM and USD-JPY are 11.85% and 11% respectively. Assume that the weights are each .5. The correlation between the instruments is .60. Ignoring lognormality for now, the option on the basket can be priced as a vanilla with the volatility equal to:

$$(1.19 \; .5 + 1.42 \; .5)^{-1} (.5^2 \; .11^2 \; 1.19^2 + .5^2 \; .1185^2 \; 1.42^2 \\ + 2 \; .5 \; .5 \; .6 \; .11 \; .1185 \; 1.42 \; 1.19)^{\frac{1}{2}} = 10.28\%$$

Should the correlation go to .5, the volatility of the basket would decrease to 9.96%. Should correlation go to −1, the effect would be to compress the option price.

Table 22.2 shows the simplified example, with the arbitrage aberrations at the extremes of 0.9 and −0.9.

Table 22.2   Correlation Vega of a Basket Option

Correlation	Basket	Price	Correlation Vega
1.0	11.50%	4.58	
0.9	11.21	4.47	0.11
0.8	10.91	4.35	0.11
0.7	10.60	4.23	0.12
0.6	10.29	4.10	0.12
0.5	9.96	3.97	0.13
0.4	9.63	3.84	0.13
0.3	9.28	3.70	0.13
0.2	8.91	3.55	0.14
0.1	8.54	3.40	0.15
0.0	8.14	3.24	0.15
−0.1	7.72	3.08	0.16
−0.2	7.28	2.90	0.17
−0.3	6.82	2.71	0.18
−0.4	6.31	2.51	0.20
−0.5	5.77	2.30	0.21
−0.6	5.16	2.05	0.24
−0.7	4.48	1.78	0.27
−0.8	3.67	1.46	0.32
−0.9	2.62	1.04	0.41

> ***Risk Management Rule: The Correlation Trap.*** A basket option needs to trade below the level imparted by a correlation of 1 and above the level imparted by a correlation of −1 where either of the volatilities is independently (or partially independently) variable. This is a simple extension of the contamination principle. It results because a correlation becomes convex for the seller when it neighbors 1 and for the buyer when it neighbors −1.

Another related option is a quanto option. This is an option where the residual from the trade (i.e., the P/L) depends on a foreign rate that may be correlated with it. This represents a weak correlation effect to take into account.

Composite Underlying Securities

■ A **composite underlying security** is a security whose payoff is linked to a formula related to the price of two or more securities. Typically, operators bundle in such categories options on assets that are combined in such a way as to prevent uncorrelated delta neutrality.

Being tailor-made, these securities have no stable specifications. These securities can be ratios or weighted combinations (linear or nonlinear). Linear combinations have been addressed. The following case study examines an indexed note (a combination involving a quotient).

Defining the categories is a generally difficult task so each one of them must be tailor-priced, generally through numerical techniques. Complications can arise when a sum is involved: A ratio of two log-normal returns is lognormal, but not the sum, which brings the operator back to the basket problem.

Often correlations are involved in such instruments. Operators need to exercise great care, however, in finding the partial derivatives (partial delta, partial gamma, etc.), as the correlation measures will show serious instability.

Without probing into the firms' motivations when they issue such instruments, this author would warn potential customers not to look at path-dependent payoffs without a correcting lens as the final term sheets can be seriously misleading when conditional on some path, as seen with the French-Franc case study.

Quantitative Case Study: Indexed Notes

This case study affords the reader a study of a composite underlying security that can only be decomposed using a correlation analysis.

> *Mathematical Note:* This indexed note, in addition, illustrates a classical problem of instruments that are presented in incomplete markets and that need to be priced on a statistical (expected expiration value), non-arbitrage basis.
>
> In consequence, instantaneous volatility and correlation can no longer be used, but rather term (expiration) volatility and correlations. We also recommends the use of trader's sense in describing the discrete possible states as opposed to continuous-time finance.

Background

A friend of the author was told by some indexed notes salesperson that the following note "embedded a currency option" making it more valuable in the eyes of his firm. The friend, seasoned enough to discount salespeople's opinions, especially on such matters as option valuation asked the author to tie the note with the topics covered in the book. This examination will be limited to an intuitive approach; the attempt at pricing the note aims only at the general qualitative sensitivity rather than at establishing the elusive fair value.

Terms of the Note

Mexico issued on December 5, 1995, a USD-denominated note paying the following (using the notation of the term sheet):

Face Value (in USD) × Max (CETES option or LIBOR option) on November 27, 1996.

- With LIBOR option = $FV \times (1 + \text{USD LIBOR} \times \text{Actual days}/360)$ known on the issue date with certainty.
- LIBOR = 12 month USD LIBOR rate 2 days before the issue. Assume that the LIBOR option will be fixed at 1.056.

$$\text{CETES option} = FV\, \text{MXN}_A\, \text{MXN}_B / \text{USD}_R$$

- MXN_A = MXN-USD (i.e., number of pesos per 1 U.S. dollar) 2 days prior to the issuance of the note. Assume it to be fixed at 7.7.
- MXN_B = 1 + Max (CETES rate on expiration minus 2 days (annualized actual/360) − .06, 0). The CETES rate is the Mexican government note. The analysis ignores that the CETES rate will be

compounded from the issue date, which causes some differences, up to 30 basis points.

- USD_R = Peso rate MXN-USD on expiration minus 2 days.

The term sheet explains that the government of the United States of Mexico would be glad to accommodate the holder in local currency should it run out of dollars. This can be interpreted as meaning that the owner is not exempt from the well-known default, or convertibility risk: Governments have gotten into the bad habit of making the transfer of money illegal whenever they face a shortage of foreign reserves. The note may thus end up paying back in nonconvertible pesos forcing the holder to brush up his Spanish and elect some peaceful existence near a Mexican golf course.

Where Is the Underlying?

Using revised terminology, the note's value (in dollars) will be:

$$\exp(-rt)\,\text{Max}\,(7.7\,(1 + c_t) \times 1/\text{MXN-USD}, 1.056) - \{\text{Default risk}\}$$

or roughly,

$$\exp(-rt)\,\text{Max}\,(7.7\,(1 + c_t) \times 1/\text{MXN-USD} - 1.056, 0) + 1 - \{\text{Default risk}\}$$

since the 1 + LIBOR at inception will be equal to the financing rate $\exp(r)$; r is the continuously compounded rate used in these formulas; c is the CETES rate. Therefore it could be:

$$1 + \text{Call on } U \text{ with a strike price of } 0 - \{\text{Default risk}\}.$$

With

$$U = 7.7\,(1 + c_t) \times 1/\text{MXN-USD} - 1.056$$

Barring the default risk, this note seems to be a simple call on an underlying security that we first need to define. The security is principally composed of the product of the CETES and the currency (in American terms) or the division of the CETES and the currency (in peso terms). Is this product a currency? Not very likely, unless one of the terms (the CETES rate) remains frozen. Also the note would be a call on the CETES rate if the currency remained frozen. Somehow, the cases where one would move and the other remain frozen are limited to spreadsheet exercises. Assume that both CETES and the currency move in opposite directions when expressed in dollar terms (the rates go up when the peso weakens) and in the same direction when the operator looks at the currency in peso terms (the rates go up when the dollar rallies against the peso). So the underlying for the currency option will be conditionally linked to the currency or the CETES.

The potential buyer could therefore start correcting the salesperson. He should have said, "This note has an embedded option on an instrument that I cannot quite define but that is related somewhat to a currency."

Should such a product exist in the market, it would be easy for the holder of the note to go delta-neutral against it, and apply all the great rules of dynamic hedging. But the salesperson no doubt would show no intention to make such a market. It is therefore necessary to study the structure as a multiasset by design, as defined in Chapter 1. This is similar to a currency option on a bizarre pair that the owner needs to hedge by triangular decomposition only, therefore having to look at such matters as correlation.

As to the default risk, it could be best priced by considering it an American binary option on a percentage of the face value, itself correlated to the currency rate.

Triangular Decomposition

Omit the 1 from the formula for a while. Look at the payoff at expiration (Figure 22.8).

The figure shows that most of the payoff of the note corresponds to areas Northeast, which corresponds to a higher CETES and a stronger Mexican peso, something not very likely to occur in real life. It is unnecessary to price it to see that such an area is not very likely: Operators generally expect high-yielding currencies to raise their rate when they weaken and

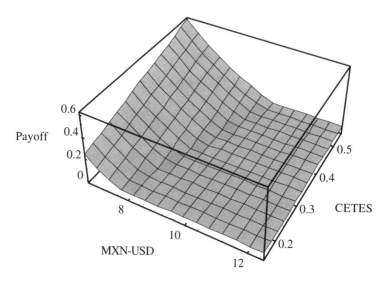

Figure 22.8 Expiration payoff.

lower it during the (rare) times of strength. The embedded currency option only comes into play in such areas.

Furthermore the expected return from the Mexican peso is far to the right of the inception rate, because the Mexican forward trades at a discount (the dollar at a premium).

Assuming 1-year forward rates = CETES (a simplification as the yield curve is being eliminated for pedagogical reasons)

Mu = interest rate differential. Assume it to be .225% (the difference between the United States and Mexican rate to use only the information available on the sheet).

Forward Mexico = Spot exp (−Mu t) the equivalent of 9.64 peso to the dollar. Additional pricing information will be relegated to the technical note.

- The first conclusion is that, as the salesperson initially said, such note has some form of "optionality" in it (in the absence of default risk) because it pays nothing in most parts of the map and *could* pay something somewhere. By the rule of stochastic dominance it needs to be worth some premium.
- The next step is to evaluate the optionality by computing the probability of ending up on each spot on the map. Intuitively, the operator has already established that the raised areas are quite unlikely.

Next, it is necessary to estimate the probability environment at some high correlation between the two elements MXN-USD and CETES. Figure 22.9 shows the probability of being on every spot of Figure 22.8 assuming a 75% correlation:

- *A warning.* One needs to be careful about correlation. This map is an expiration map and requires the use of longer term correlation. Using daily correlations will include some noise that will be of small significance with such an abnormal market as Mexico. Another way to look at it using the variance ratio method of analysis is that there may be a bias linked to the frequency of sampling: Shorter sampling periods would show a lower correlation measure. Finally, up-correlation is usually different from down-correlation, a point discussed in Chapter 15.
- *Another warning.* When deriving fair value for such a security, one needs to be careful about the horizon. Assuming that the operator is with either a mean-reverting process or any process with some heteroskedasticity, one needs to be warned against the risks

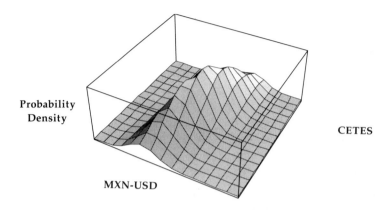

Probability
Density

CETES

MXN-USD

Figure 22.9   Probability map with a 75% correlation.

of assuming that $\sqrt{\Delta t}$, the square root of time notion works (i.e., the variance is linearly proportional to the time horizon). Therefore one cannot use the notion of daily measured volatility to price the final payoff. See the discussion in Chapter 6.

The reader can mentally combine the two maps to examine the conditional nature of the payoff. We do not need additional mathematics to see that the area Northeast of the mountain will show increased country default risk, a risk that is not rewarded for, as if it would force the owner of the note to retire in Mexico. There is indeed a tautological relationship between higher interest rates in a country, weaker currency, and increased default risk.

An examination of the sensitivities shows:

- The note *statically* gains in value if either the CETES or the currency gain in volatility. This can be visible on the map: the mountain in Figure 22.10 would become thicker and cover more payoff areas.

- The note *statically* gains in value if the correlation weakens between the two. It would also make the area of the mountain less diagonal (see Figure 22.11).

If Mexico was defined as a biased asset, as in Chapter 15, the operator would have expectations of a behavior that is conditional on market regimes: Mexico would have a higher volatility in some panic conditions that are linked to the position of the currency on some spots over the map. The definition of biased asset also stated that the down-correlation is higher than the up-correlation, a result of a negative-Poisson that affects both the rates and the currency pair.[5] If the two are governed by a diffusion plus a negative jump that affects both of them, it becomes conceivable that the

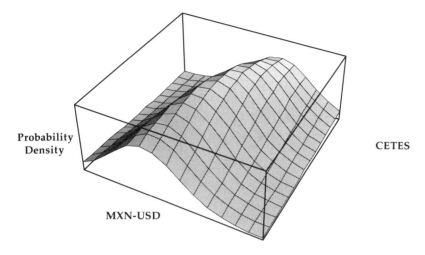

Figure 22.10 Higher CETES and currency volatilities.

currency and the rates exhibit some form of relative independence (diffusion, hence lower correlation) outside of periods of panic (jumps, hence high correlation).

The point to be stressed is that static examination of the Greek derivatives bears no true benefit. This analysis therefore will skip the sensitivity analysis.

The conclusion is that correlation-dependent products, particularly those in biased assets, are too difficult to listen to casual opinion.

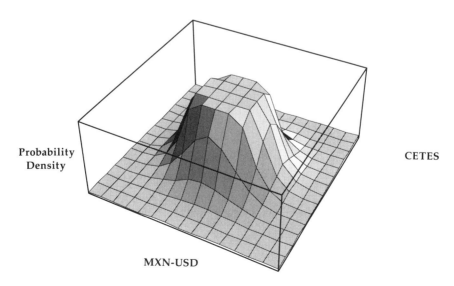

Figure 22.11 Lower correlation.

Pricing note (advanced topic):[6] USD-MXN is the Mexican rate expressed using the dollar as the numeraire.

$$\text{USD-MXN} = \text{USD-MXN}_0 \exp\{(\text{Mu} - .5\, \sigma_M^2)\, t + \sqrt{t} \times \sigma_M\}$$

with Mu = .225 the interest rate differential and $\text{USD-MXN}_0 = 1/7.7$. x is a random variable normally distributed with unit variance and 0 mean. σ_M is the volatility of the MXN-USD dollar pair (it is the same as that of the USD-MXN).

The operator needs to study the process for MXN-USD not USD-MXN as the numeraire is (so far) in USD. He has the expected rate period t

$$E_0(\text{rate period } t) = \int_{-\infty}^{\infty} \text{USD-MXN}_0 \exp\{(\text{Mu}_M - .5\, \sigma_M^2)\, t + \sqrt{t} \times \sigma_M\}\, \rho(x)\, dx$$
$$= \text{USD-MXN}_0 \exp(\text{Mu } t)$$

$\rho(x)$ is the centered normal density function. Remarkably if he chooses MXN-USD as numeraire, he would have as process:

$$\text{MXN-USD} = \text{MXN-USD}_0 \exp(-\text{Mu} - .5\, \sigma_M^2)\, t + \sqrt{t} \times \sigma_M$$

$$E_0(\text{rate period } t) = \int_{-\infty}^{\infty} \text{MXN-USD}_0 \exp\{(\text{Mu}_R - .5\, \sigma_M^2)\, t + \sqrt{t} \times \sigma_M\}\, \rho(x)\, dx$$
$$= \text{MXN-USD}_0 \exp\{(-\text{Mu} + \sigma_M^2)\, t\}$$

So the expectations for USD-MXN are 9.645, while those of the MXN-USD are at 35% volatility in the currency, at 10.90. This is another illustration of the two-country paradox.

As to the CETES rate, the trader uses:

$$c_t = c_0 \exp\{(d - .5\, \sigma_R^2)\, t + \sqrt{t}\, (\rho x + \sqrt{(1 - \rho^2)} y)\, \sigma_R\}$$

with d as the drift of the CETES rate and ρ its correlation with the currency.

The fair value of the note would therefore be:

$$\exp(-r\, t) \int_{-\infty}^{\infty} \int_{-\infty}^{\infty} (\text{Max}\, (7.7\, (1 + c_t) \times 1/\text{MXN-USD} - 1.056, 0) + 1)\, p(x)\, p(y)\, dx\, dy$$

which can be computed using standard pricing techniques.

Chapter 23

Minor Exotics: Lookback and Asian Options

A veteran trader-intellectual friend of the author, waxing philosophical after a few sips of a remarkable Bordeaux, pointed at the bottle and uttered: "A trader with a good mind, like good wine, improves with age. A bad trader rapidly turns into vinegar."

This chapter presents some options that, despite the plethora of research publications on their subject, do not represent any meaningful trading novelty on their own. They are called minor exotics as most of the information has been included in the previous chapters on exotics.

Lookback and Ladder Options

■ **Lookback options** are options that allow the owner to sell the high or buy the low over a set period.

As such, they are called "floating strike." There are other varieties of lookback options, such as the *fixed strike* where the owner of the structure owns an at-the-money option that will be exercised at the maximum over the period. Such varieties will not be examined here.

The major problem with lookback options is that they do not customarily trade, owing to their high price. They are indeed very costly: as a rule of thumb, approximately twice the premium of a conventional option.

> *Example:* The structure presented in Figure 23.1 allowed the owner to sell the high over the period. The high turned out to be 116.92. The owner became the happy owner of a put struck at 116.92.

There are many ways to view lookback options for risk management. Exotic option traders grounded in barrier options usually have no real difficulty understanding the skew exposures stemming from the product.

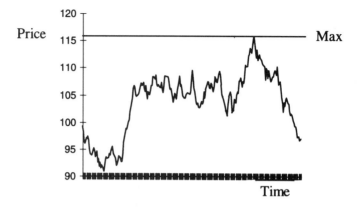

Figure 23.1   Maximum of a sample path.

The principal risk is the gamma. It becomes easy to see that the option has a gamma that is "one-sided," as it requires action on one side of the market and not the other. A lookback option that has reached a maximum, say 117 (as in Figure 23.1), and dropped below such maximum, would not really present any major gamma for the seller unless the market reaches a new high. This is called a one-sided gamma exposure. Such a situation is reminiscent of barrier options where the gamma changes in style beyond a barrier.

The Rollover Option

Lookback options can be viewed for risk management from two angles: the roll-over replication on one hand and the limit decomposition on the other. The original pricing by Goldman, Sosin, and Gatto[1] was inspired by the following replicating strategy.

Assume that the dealer sells a lookback call to the customer; that is, the right to buy the low over the next year. The dealer would initially buy a one-year at-the-money call. Should the market rally immediately, the trader would be relieved as the risk would no longer require dynamic hedging. The markets, however, have a bad tendency of swinging a little. To guarantee owning a call struck at the low, the dealer would have to roll his option position into a lower strike call every time the market dropped. Such a roll includes a cash expenditure. The additional cost could be easily calculated with the aid of a stochastic integral. The lookback option would then be the sum of the two components:

1. The original option.
2. The costs of the call spread "roll-down."

The stochastic integration (in present value) of the cost function corresponds to the markup over an at-the-money option. Such an option is known as a "strike bonus."

Using this framework to analyze lookbacks can provide the operator with the intuition of the real problem with their trading: the skew. A lookback call will be more valuable with a downside skew (when lower strikes are more expensive) because its maximum gamma will always be positioned at the lowest price the market reached over the lifetime of the option. Likewise, a lookback put in such a skew environment would be less valuable because its gamma would be located at upper levels. The reader should know by now that in down-skewed markets the upside is not where the gamma should be located.

Risk Management Rule: The lookback option has a third moment exposure that is not possible to hedge with vanilla options.

The reason for the rule is that the gamma of the lookback would always be maximum at the recorded extreme during its lifetime. A vanilla option that would initially match the gamma risk would rapidly move away from the money in a continuous sell-off while the lookback would retain its gamma.

One consolation, however, is that the lookback gamma remains one-sided. The operator would not be whipped both ways. Figure 23.2 shows the exact issue: The gamma of the option follows a bell-shaped curve around the strike while that of the lookback looks like a cliff with a flat top.

Before looking at the second method of pricing the lookback for hedging purposes, the reader should examine some form of combination involving them.

■ **Ladder options** are lookback options giving the owner the right to sell the high or buy the low at some set discrete increments. They are also called discrete lookbacks.

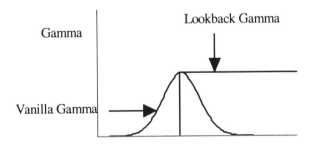

Figure 23.2 Lookback gamma.

Example: The same lookback as before allows the owner to sell the high but in $5 increments. It can sell 105, 110, 115, 120, and so forth. The high was 116.90 but the owner of the structure was able to sell at 115, which is not disastrous.

Figure 23.3 shows that the ladder resembles a lookback that is "rounded" in price. They will come cheaper because their payoff is capped at that of he lookback. In the previous example, the ladder paid off $1.90 less than the lookback.

Mathematicians know that applied problems can be approached from several different disciplines to yield identical results: The same applies to option valuation. The ladder option can be viewed as a lookback when the *strike bonus* part is only calculated off a set price increment. It can also be seen a strip of knock-in options.

Assume that the option gives the right to sell the asset at the best high rounded to the lowest 5 points, say 100, 105, 110, 115, and so on for the next year. Also assume an asset price of 100. Such option can be decomposed into the following, using the notation *KI(strike, trigger)*:

Long	1 *KI*(100,100) (that would be knocked in immediately)
Short	1 *KI*(100,105)
Long	1 *KI*(105,105)
Short	−1 *KI*(105,110)
Long	1 *KI*(110,110)
Short	1 *KI*(110,115)
Long	1 *KI*(115,115)
Short	1 *KI*(115,120)
Long	1 *KI*(120,120)

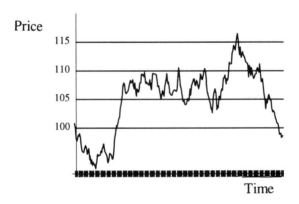

Figure 23.3   Ladder levels.

and so forth until the difference between the $KI(S,S)$ and the $KI(S,S + 5)$ vanishes to a small number.

Now the skew: The reader can calculate the skew for knock-in options using the method in Chapter 19, thus building a more accurate model for both ladders and the general lookback.

The lookback option can be viewed as a limiting case of such decomposition as the difference between strikes becomes very narrow. The general formula is:

$$\text{Laddermax} = \text{limit } \epsilon \rightarrow 0 \text{ Sum}(KIP(S_i,S_i) - KIP(S_i,S_i + \epsilon))$$
$$\text{from } i = 1 \text{ to infinity, with } \epsilon \text{ as increment.}$$

The ladder minimum is the same mirror constructed with knock-in calls. Skew-minded traders will not fail to improve on the formula by using a volatility function, that is related to the strike price of the barrier. Typically, this will raise the price of the lookback considerably.

Figure 23.4 shows how the price of a strip of knock-in options will converge away from that of a lookback as the trader increases the size of the difference between the legs of the knock-in. The graph depicts an at-the-money, one-year option with no drift and 10% volatility. At the extreme left, is the price of a lookback, close to twice the price of a vanilla. At the extreme right is the value of a vanilla.

In addition to the skew, the product shows the "driftwood" effect as traders tend to call it, which is the same chronic problem as that incurred with barrier options. This is the concentration of strikes right below the recent lows and above the recent highs. It results in considerable *bad gamma,* which is the gamma the operator will start incurring as the cost of covering it turns onerous.

Finally, it is worthy mentioning another application of the omnipresent Arcsine law of the random walk that was used for the distribution of the profits or loss of an individual trader in Chapter 3 (see Figure 23.5). The distribution of the *extrema* of any Brownian motion will be such that it will be maximal very early on or very late in the game.

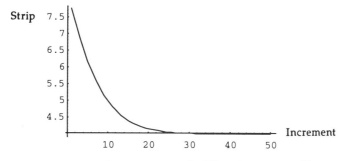

Figure 23.4 Convergence of a KI strip to a vanilla.

Frequency

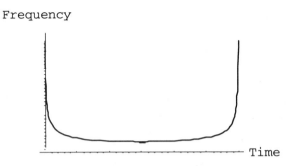

Figure 23.5 ArcSine law.

Why?

Starting in the middle of the period makes the concept easier to grasp. Assume that the option has six months to expiration and that the market just made new lows. The probability of the new low of being the low of the next six months is very weak as the market has a high probability of moving down further. It is as if the trader were standing with an entirely new lookback option in front of him.

Look at the beginning of the period: The possibility of the market having reached one of its extremes is very high as any trend will build up on the other side. If one throws dice and make three winnings, the cumulative P/L is three. The trend is such that the probability of the lows (here 0) being close to the origin is highest.

A Footnote on Basket Options: Asian Options

Asian options are commonly entrusted to junior traders owing to the regularity of their risks and the ease of their management.

■ **Asian options** refer to options on averages.[2] Their payoff depends on a weighted combination of events through a certain period.

Asian options include the *average floating strike* where, as with the lookback, the owner becomes entitled to a strike price through time, and the *fixed strike,* an option that has a known strike and that settles at the weighted average during a certain time window. There are several types of averages: Geometric and arithmetic are the most common. The usual Brownian motion is, this time discretized in equal intervals of one step for the sake of simplicity (and no drift):

$$S_t = S_{t-1} \exp(-\tfrac{1}{2} \sigma^2 t + \sigma \sqrt{t}\, z)$$

where σ is the volatility, t the time until expiration, and z a centered normal variate.

- Geometric average:

$$\left(\prod_{i=1}^{n} S_i^{w_i} \right)^{1/P}$$

with the w_i such that their product is equal to p. The author has never seen any trade but it is necessary to analyze it to view the difference between it and the arithmetic one, as the geometric average is more natural in the financial markets.

- Arithmetic average:

$$\frac{1}{n} \sum_{i=1}^{n} w_i S_i$$

with the w_i such that their sum equals n.

As with the exercise of Chapter 22, the following will help the reader understand some of their pricing difficulty.

Assume an average of four days. One would have the following process:

$$
\begin{aligned}
\text{Geometric average} &= (S_0\, S_0 \exp(-\tfrac{1}{2}\, 1/365\, \sigma^2 + \sigma\sqrt{(1/365)}\, z_1)\, S_0 \exp(-\tfrac{1}{2}\, 2/365\, \sigma^2 \\
&\quad + \sigma\sqrt{(1/365)}(z_1 + z_2))\, S_0 \exp(-\tfrac{1}{2}\, 3/365\, \sigma^2 \\
&\quad + \sigma\sqrt{(1/365)}(z_1 + z_2 + z_3))^{1/4} \\
&= S_0 \exp(-\tfrac{1}{2}\, 6/365\, \sigma^2 + \sigma\sqrt{(1/365)}(3\, z_1 + 2\, z_2 + z_3))^{1/4}
\end{aligned}
$$

The process takes an exponential shape and can easily yield some closed form results using simple Black-Scholes-Merton.

The arithmetic average, however, will be more illuminating. Look at the process for the same four days:

$$
\begin{aligned}
\text{Arithmetic average} &= \tfrac{1}{4}(S_0 + S_0 \exp(-\tfrac{1}{2}\, 1/365\, \sigma^2 + \sigma\sqrt{(1/365)}z_1) \\
&\quad + S_0 \exp(-\tfrac{1}{2}\, 2/365\, \sigma^2 + \sigma\sqrt{(1/365)}(z_1 + z_2)) \\
&\quad + S_0 \exp(-\tfrac{1}{2}\, 3/365\, \sigma^2 + \sigma\sqrt{(1/365)}(z_1 + z_2 + z_3)))
\end{aligned}
$$

exactly as if the user were looking at a linear combination of options on independent assets of the same volatility (it is known that $z_1, z_2, \ldots z_n$ are independent). There is little lognormality to it as the process cannot be summarized in the form $S_t = S_0 \exp(something)$. In other words, one cannot obtain dS/S a normally distributed variable.

This complication has caused some ink to flow. As a trader, the author was rapidly put to sleep by Asians. As an amateur probabilist, he discovered the process to be quizzical.[3]

The remaining of the chapter will focus on the few points that matter for hedging. The pricing methods currently in place attempt to fudge the process of the average $\Sigma w_i S_i$ by finding some form that can track the bias between the lognormal distribution and that of the averages.

The reader will be happy to learn that such bias is the skew. Most fudging methods attempt to replicate the distribution by detecting its moments and coming up with a lognormal distribution function that satisfies such moments. Still most traders are satisfied and resort to the more entertaining Monte Carlo engines as will be seen.

By comparing the distribution of the average to that of the underlying itself, it is possible to see that the ratio of the second moments of the distributions is close to $1/\sqrt{3}$. So the instantaneous local variance can be mitigated with a ratio hedge of equal amounts:

- The trader buys an Asian option and sells a corresponding vanilla in proper gamma neutral ratios of approximately 1.73 to 1. Figure 23.6 compares each position independently.
- Figure 23.7 shows the spread between them, as expected, short the skew.

A helpful way to understand the effect is through the notion of compounding. A sum of exponentials does not compound in the same way as an exponential of a sum. A sum of exponentials, say $\exp(n) + \exp(m)$, that are equal to another $\exp(a + b)$ will not track the growth when they are all multiplied by 2. The result is $\exp(2n) + \exp(2m)$ compared to

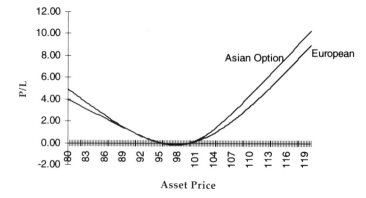

Figure 23.6 Asian and European option (locally delta-neutral gamma-neutral ratio).

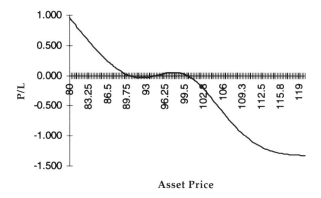

Figure 23.7 Hedging the Asian option with the European.

exp(2(*a* + *b*)). The reader can try it as an exercise to see one of the convex qualities of the exponential.

When pricing an Asian option, the reader is recommended to use forward volatility and interest rates (i.e., the entire curve) as every bucket matters. It is also recommended to use a Monte Carlo whenever volatility rises above 30%. In most other cases, a pricing model based on the usual approximations would do. More precision in the approximation is minuscule compared with the precision lost in the use of the homoskedastic model.

A few final points:

- *Bucketing.* Asian options require a schedule of bucket vegas and a distribution of forwards. Strangely, the middle point for forward hedges resembles visually that of the stopping time.
- *A Catch.* An arithmetic average is not invertible, by Jensen's inequality. An average on USD-DEM is not equal to 1/average on DEM-USD.

PART **IV**

MODULES

Brownian Motion on a Spreadsheet, a Tutorial

This module provides an introduction to the random walk.

■ A **random walk** for security prices means that a share of the price changes of the security over a given period of time is random. The share of the price change that is not expected to be random is called the drift.

Financial instruments, for reasons of efficiency, are assumed to follow a random process that we will let the reader create on a spreadsheet.

Brownian motion = Random walk + Drift

These exercises will focus on the random component. The drift will be covered in Module B.

THE CLASSICAL ONE-ASSET RANDOM WALK

Think of a drunk man on Madison Avenue. Dead drunk, he will have no memory as to where he was last. He can only move forward and will keep moving at the same pace. Each one of his steps will be exactly one forward + left or one forward + right, as shown in Figure A.1.

After 10 steps, the following combinations are possible: 10 forward + 10 left on one extreme and 10 forward + 10 right on the other extreme, with all the combinations in between.

Figure A.1 Random walk.

Securities markets are assumed to follow a similar walk, with one hitch: The size of the steps increases in function of the asset's price. Creating a random walk on an Excel™ spreadsheet will provide a good illustration of the concept:[1]

Open a new spreadsheet
Tools → Data analysis → Random number generation
Number of variables = 1
Number of random numbers = 248
Distribution = Normal
Mean = 0
Standard deviation = 1
Output range = B4
→ OK

Excel will generate 248 random numbers. The average will be close to 0. These numbers are then called normally distributed with a mean of 0 and a standard deviation of 1.

Put the number 100 in cell A3. This will be the initial asset price. Next, put the volatility of the asset (say .157) in cell A2. This means that the annual standard deviation is $\sqrt{248} = 15.7\%$ (a daily equivalent of 1% on a 248-day year). In cell A4, put the following formula:

$$A3 \times EXP(-.5 \,.\$A\$2^\wedge 2 \times (1/248) + \$A\$2 \times (1/15.\,7) \times B4)$$

and copy it down to A251. This would be the path of daily returns:

$$S_t = S_{t-1} \times Exp(-1/2\ \sigma^2 t + \sigma \times \sqrt{t} \times W_t)$$

Equating the cells to the preceding formula is accomplished as follows:

S_t = A4
S_{t-1} = A3
t = 1/248
$\sqrt{t}$ = SQRT (1/248) since every line is one day, so $\sqrt{t}$ = SQRT(1/15.7)

W_t is the random number with mean 0 and average positive 1 and negative -1.

Next select (A3:A251) and graph it. Figure A.2 will result.

Repeating the random number generation to get a fresh series of "white noise" numbers causes new paths to form on the screen.

Increasing the volatility magnifies the movement.

Brownian Motion

Figure A.2 Geometric Brownian motion.

SOME QUESTIONS

Question 1 (a question that is invariably asked): How does one go from the drunk man with equal size steps to the unequal steps W_t? (W_t can be any number between minus infinity and infinity, and take on a wide array of values like .56, 1.03.)

The answer lies at the core of probability laws and involves breaking up time in infinitely small fractions of $\frac{1}{10}$ of a second where such movement takes place in digital form $+1$ and -1.

The sum of the moves after 1 second (composed of 10 moves) will average 0 but will be spread between -10 and $+10$. Assuming the $+1$ and -1 came from a "fair" random number generator, the resulting histogram of the 1-second moves will present a clearly defined bell shape. The reader can try that in a spreadsheet by creating a tree, with up-branch $+1$ and down-branch -1. There will be 1024 combinations called sample paths leading to 11 possible outcomes. After 10 steps, the outcome can only be an even number of steps. The final proportions are shown in Table A.1 and plotted in Figure A.3.

This represents a heuristic derivation of the central limit theorem (in its simplest form: DeMoire-Laplace). The sum of a $+1$, -1 series of random steps approaches the bell-shaped distribution shown in Figure A.3 when one increases the number of observations. An apparent constraint is that the steps need to be the same size at all times. The law is simpler to understand in that context, except that it is perhaps the most misinterpreted law in the history of mathematics.

Question 2 Why is the standard deviation the square root of time?

In the preceding scenario, it was assumed that every step for the $+1$, -1 distribution is a unit of time. The standard deviation is the square

Table A.1 Number of Paths

Up	Down	Total Move	Number of Occurrences
10	0	10	1
9	1	8	10
8	2	6	45
7	3	4	120
6	4	2	210
5	5	0	252
4	6	−2	210
3	7	−4	120
2	8	−6	45
1	9	−8	10
0	10	−10	1
		Total	1024

root of the sum of the square of the moves. Here the moves all square up to $(-1)^2$ and $(1)^2$, which equals 1. In addition the mean $E(W) = 0$

$$\text{Hence } \sigma = \sqrt{\sum_{i=1}^{n} \frac{(W_i - \overline{W})^2}{n}}$$

$$= \sqrt{\sum_{i=1}^{n} \frac{W_i^2}{n}}$$

and since all the $W^2 = 1$, and t, the time equals n, $\sigma = \sqrt{t}$

Therefore the standard deviation of the binary $+1$, -1 is equal to the square root of the number of steps. It is apparent that the standard deviation in this exercise would equal to $\sqrt{10} = 3.16$. Roughly two-thirds of the paths lie between $+3.16$ and -3.16.

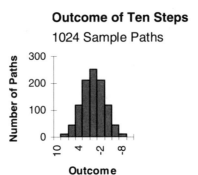

Outcome of Ten Steps

1024 Sample Paths

Figure A.3 (Almost) bell shaped.

Option Wizard: The Diffusion

The random walk on a spreadsheet illustrates a diffusion process.

The principal property of a diffusion is that, no matter how small time is sliced, the function remains jagged. It will always look geometrically like the following sample path:

The same sample path with more frequent observations would look like this:

Slicing time in even smaller increments would not make the picture any "rounder" in any of its segments. Although it is continuous, it is nowhere differentiable and does not become so any time. A fashionable term to describe such jaggedness is the "fractal" structure. Students taking college calculus learn, through Taylor methods, that any function in a very narrow segment could be expanded into a polynomial involving its derivatives.

$$f(x + \Delta x) = f(x) + f'(x)\, \Delta x + \tfrac{1}{2}\, f''(x)(\Delta x)^2 + \ldots + 1/n\, f^n(x)(\Delta x)^n$$

They also learn that, for a function S of time t, when the partitions become very small, $(\Delta S)^2 \to 0$ when $t \to 0$. One of the fundamental rules of stochastic calculus is that no matter how small time is sliced, ΔS^2 does not vanish owing to the random element in it. As a matter of fact $\Delta S^2 \to \sigma^2\, \Delta t$.

For an option trader, such intuition is important: If there is a possible smoothness on the curve of the underlying, then the manufacturing costs of the option through gamma rebalancing would be lowered provided the operator picked a frequency of hedges that matched such increment. Black-Scholes-Merton does not allow for such: Even if the trader rebalanced every billionth of the second, the cost of the option would not go down.

A Two-Asset Random Walk: An Introduction
to the Effects of Correlation

As the single-asset random walk has been used in connection with the drunk man, think of a drunk bird in space. Its location at any time will be determined by the elevation and position on the map (north-south and east-west). So the location of the bird requires three pieces of information. It is therefore considered in three dimensions.

The two-asset random walk can easily be simulated on the computer, and it does not require very complex matrix algebra. The hitch is that three parameters must be estimated: volatility of asset A, volatility of asset B, correlation between the assets.

Note. The reader can ignore matrix algebra for now and take the results for granted.

As in the example before, the reader can simulate the same Brownian motion.

The example can be done on a similar spreadsheet as before but with cells defined as names for ease of computation.

There are two assets A and B:

Go to Excel™

Open a new spreadsheet

Tools → Data analysis → Random number generation

Number of variables = 2

Number of random numbers = 252

Distribution = Normal

Mean = 0

Standard deviation = 1

Output range = B4

→ OK

As in the previous example, there are two series of independent random numbers. The first asset A will be independent. The second will need to be bridged to the first by the corresponding correlation:

Cell A1:Type Vol1   Cell B1 type 1 → Insert → Name → Define. Name Vol1

Cell A2: Type Vol2   Cell B2 type 1 → Insert → Name → Define. Name Vol2

Cell A3: Type Correl Cell B3 type 0 → Insert → Name → Define. Name Correl

Thus the cells are named. Vol1 is 100 times the daily volatility. Assume for the example that it was 1% and enter 1.

Next create the covariance matrix. It is necessary to create a 2 by 2 matrix with the following:

Cell C1: type Cov Matrix

Cell C2: type = Vol1^2

Cell D2: type = Correl × Vol1 × Vol2

Cell C3: type = Correl × Vol2 × Vol1

Cell D3: type = Vol2^2

Next, a special matrix called Cholesky is needed to decompose the previous matrix.[2] Familiarity with such decomposition is not essential (see Table A.2).

Cell E1: type Cholesky

Cell E2: type = SQRT(C2)

Cell E3: type = C3/E2   Cell F3: type = SQRT(D3 − E3^2)

Next, give names to the Cholesky matrix:

Name E2 a_11

Name E3 a_12

Name F3 a_22

Next, start looking at pairs of returns.

Then, to generate logarithmic returns for the securities that agree with the correlation matrix.

Cell C7: type RET A

Cell D7: type RET B

Cell C8: type A8 × a_11 copy down to cell C 261

Cell D8: type a_12 × A8 + a_22 × B8 copy down to cell D261

Table A.2   The Spreadsheet

Cells	A	B	C	D	E	F
1	Vol1	1	**Cov**	**Matrix**	Cholesky	
2	Vol2	1	1	0	1	
3	Correl	0	0	1	0	1

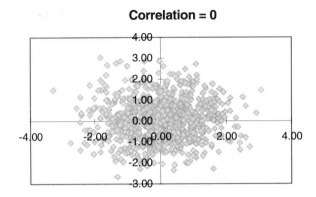

Figure A.4   Daily moves for a two-asset random walk.

Now there are streams of paired returns. Since a22 = 0, returns B are completely independent from returns A.

Figure A.4 shows a graph of the pairs: The returns are plotted for columns C8:C261 and D8:D261.

A circle is apparent with the density of the points very high in the center and diminishing away from it. Just as traders look at the market for a distribution of one asset as a bell-shaped curve, they need to look at that of a pair of assets in concentric circles. The transformation is shown in Figure A.5 and in Figure A.6.

Next, change the correlations and examine the resulting returns.

Figure A.7 shows that the curves compress toward the center forming one line as the correlation increases toward one. As the correlation tends toward negative one, again only one line is forming; the returns will be equal but with opposite signs.

Figure A.8 allows the reader to compare the example with correlations in the real world.

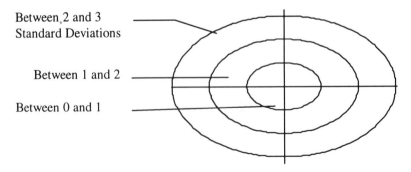

Figure A.5   Standard deviation of returns for two assets.

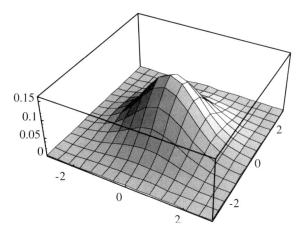

Figure A.6   In three dimensions.

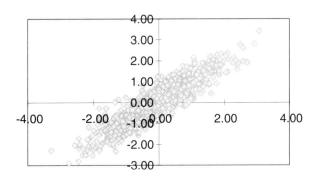

Figure A.7   Two-asset Brownian motion: 90% correlation.

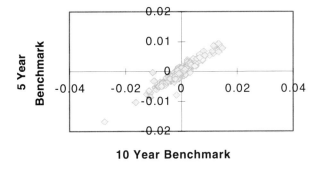

Figure A.8   A high correlation: The 5- and 10-year U.S. bonds; percentage change in bonds (prices: 3/94–5/95).

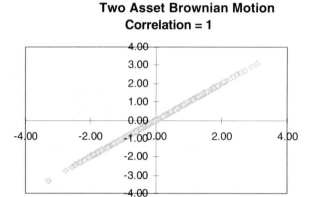

Figure A.9   Increasing the correlation.

Figure A.9 shows the results of a correlation of 1.

To add a third security, the process is the same. The relation of the third return to the first two will be similar to that of the second return to the first.

EXTENSION: A THREE-ASSET RANDOM WALK

As the returns of two assets can be represented, the end arrival of the combination of three uncorrelated assets can be viewed as a sphere (Figure A.10). A

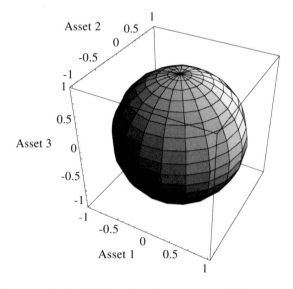

Figure A.10   One standard deviation for the returns of three uncorrelated assets.

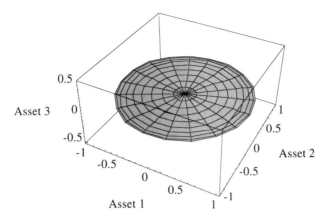

Figure A.11 One standard deviation for the returns of three assets, with one degenerate.

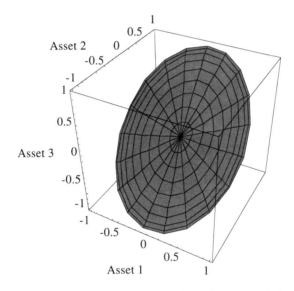

Figure A.12 One standard deviation when the other two of the three assets are 100% correlated.

small sphere for 1 standard deviation, a second one for 2, and so on, would replace the concentric circles.

When one of the assets has no volatility (and is said to be "degenerate") it reduces to a two-asset world (Figure A.11).

When two of the assets are perfectly correlated (100%), the result is a two-asset environment (Figure A.12).

When the three assets are perfectly correlated, the result is a line.

Module **B**

Risk Neutrality Explained

The risk-neutral argument of financial theory is explored in this module. It is essential for the understanding any arbitrage pricing of a contingent claim. The reader needs to get a notion of it to comprehend that all probabilities used in the text will be "tricked" into their risk-neutral equivalent.

STEP 1. PROBABILISTIC FAIRNESS, THE "FAIR DICE" AND THE SKEW

In this example, start by assuming an economy without rates.

The expected payoff of the security is each final price times its probability. In the example shown in Figure B.1, it will be $101.01 \times .499 + 98.99 \times .501 = 100$ minus the initial price, which sums up to 0. The security is therefore priced at a level where, based on information about possible events and their probability, it constitutes a fair game for a trader.

On a binomial tree, the following equality would occur.[1]

$$p = \text{probability of moving up}$$

$$q = (1 - p) = \text{probability of moving down}$$

$$S_u(t + 1) = e^u S(t) \text{ the up-price period } t + 1$$

$$S_d(t + 1) = e^d S(t) \text{ the down-price}$$

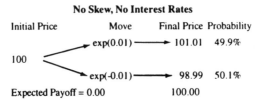

Figure B.1 No skew, no interest rates.

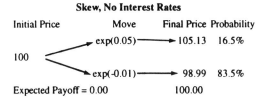

Figure B.2 Skew, no interest rates.

In the absence of all rates (to be introduced later), the user has:

$$S(t + 1) = p\, S_u + (1 - p)\, S_d = S(t)$$

hence

$$p\, e^u\, S(t) + (1 - p)\, e^v\, S(t) = S(t)$$

$$\text{so:}\ p\, e^u + (1 - p)\, e^v = 1$$

being satisfied at all times in the economy. This, in a nutshell, is called the probability fairness or "no free lunch."

It has been simplified to allow for discrete steps between prices in the market.

What if there was a skew? Assume that the market can move up by a u considerable larger than v. To make it probability neutral, the larger size of the up-steps needs to be compensated with a reduced probability of the event.

In Figure B.2, each outcome is multiplied by its probability: $105.13 \times .165 = 98.99 \times .835 = 100$.

STEP 2. ADDING THE REAL WORLD: THE RISK-NEUTRAL ARGUMENT

The Drift

Assume the asset that the operator is concerned with commanded a rate of return μ in the economy. It would then be necessary to assume that the expected return from holding the stock would be μ multiplied by the time horizon, $\mu\, \Delta t$, the "drift" return. What if the rate μ was different from the risk-free rate in the economy because it includes a premium for "something" that could be called risk?

The answer lies in the Black-Scholes-Merton breakthrough. There could not have been an option-pricing formula without the following argument: Arbitrage derivation of security prices means replication. Option replication eliminates the delta and the exposure to the asset change of direction (i.e., the return) and would let the operator only concern himself with the volatility of the asset not its required rate of return, nor the operator's risk preference. Black-Scholes-Merton constituted a self-financing (cash-flow neutral) delta-neutral portfolio that would attempt to replicate the option through continuous rebalancing (the buying and selling of the underlying asset against buying or selling a risk-free bond with the residual cash thus obtained). The value of the option would then correspond to the replication costs of the portfolio, themselves depending on the volatility of the asset and the risk-free rate in the economy. Module G includes a demonstration of the **Black-Scholes-Merton magic trick.**

This leads to the following result: For arbitrage trading and option valuation, the drift of the underlying non-interest-paying asset needs to be replaced by the risk-neutral rate in the economy.

On this tree, one needs to earn the "risk-free" rate of .11 for the period. There are many ways finance academia has adjusted for it. The first would be to increase the difference between up-steps and down-steps. The second, for reasons that will appear handy with the pricing of barrier options, consists in changing the probability of every move (while satisfying that the sum remains 100%). Figure B.3 shows the risky asset returns.

The operator tricks the distribution by fictitiously changing the probabilities to make believe (for derivative security valuation purposes only) that the expected payoff is that of a riskless asset. This is called a change of probability measure. Figure B.4 shows the result.

Say that r is the risk-free in the economy and that the asset concerned has an expected future payoff of μ.

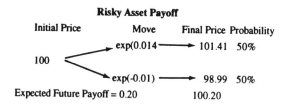

Figure B.3 Prechange of measure—risky asset payoff.

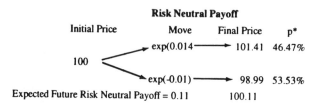

Figure B.4 Postchange of measure—risk-neutral payoff.

The operator defines the up-and-down prices:

$$S_u(t + \Delta t) = S(t)\, e^u$$
$$S_d(t + \Delta t) = S(t)\, e^d$$

with the following restriction:

$$p\, S_d(t + \Delta t) + (1 - p)\, S_u(t + \Delta t) = S(t)\, e^{u \Delta t}$$

So at the note $t + \Delta t$, the trader has

$$p\, e^u + (1 - p)\, e^d = e^\mu$$

He creates a new probability measure p^*, which should satisfy the fictitious replication values at the same period:

$$p^* e^u + (1 - p^*)\, e^d = e^r$$

Option Wizard: Why Traders Know the Risk-Neutral Argument

The risk-neutral argument is easier for traders to understand once they consider the simpler put-call parity rules. Assume that the asset is expected to grow at 23%. The asset, however, can be "rolled" (sold and bought back to avoid delivery) every day at 11% annualized, the differential between the financing and its carry, which makes its forward price one day hence lower by the annualized 11%. If the call traded at premium to the "roll" (hence the put at a discount to the "roll"), then the operator can sell the call, buy the put and own the asset that would cost him only 11% per day (annualized). Hence all puts and calls need to be priced at the "roll," the net of the risk-free rates.

Another way to view it is to see that the forward for an asset is risk neutral (cash and carry makes it trade at the risk-free rate minus its yield). Given that neutrality, the puts and calls need to synthetically replicate the forward owing to the equality for European options:

Call − Put = Forward

"Bullishness" would normally raise the value of the call. But arbitrage would also raise the value of the put, to satisfy the equality, which is a paradox: Bearishness would also raise the value of the put. Hence one's preferences should not affect the option's fair value.

This gives a hint of the technique of changing the probability measure to satisfy some purpose. This method, based on the Girsanov theorem[2], will present more applications in option pricing.

An option theory generalization is that the risk-neutral **drift** used for a pair is the difference between the two risk-neutral drifts. For a dividend-paying stock, it becomes the differential of carry (dividend minus the risk-free rate), for a bond it becomes the difference between its carry and the financing rate, and so forth.

Risk Management Rule: A dynamic hedger should use risk-neutral probabilities at all times.

Module **C**

Numeraire Relativity and the Two-Country Paradox

■ A base currency for an operator, also called a **numeraire,** is one in which his final P/L is expressed. A **countercurrency** is the one that corresponds to the number of units traded.

A numeraire could also be any possible unit. An operator can have his numeraire defined as a stock index or a bond fund, as many unwittingly do.

The numeraire problem[1] is well known to option traders with experience in the currencies. Unlike other contracts where the trading is exclusively done in units per dollar (or, if the contract is traded in France, in units per French franc), trading in currencies is done in pairs where the unit could be either of the two currencies. The relativity is of the utmost importance as the hedging amounts will depend on the base currency.

The notion is counterintuitive because in most people's minds a currency pair is invertible. A *JPY* against the USD is the inverse of the USD against the JPY. However, although the equality will apply to the price, it will not apply to the profits and losses since the P/L will be caused by currencies diverging and that such divergence will cause a change in the yardstick.

As will be seen a put on a currency is a call on the countercurrency. Likewise, a call on a SP500 can be viewed as a put on cash. The governing notion that a stock market can only go to zero as expressed in dollar terms can be stood on its head: Cash can go to infinite. For a SP500-based person, a call on the index (put on cash) can have a limited potential, while the put on the index (call on cash) can have an unlimited upside. This notion is largely ignored by fund managers, to the detriment of their hedging precision.

As is the convention, the currencies in this module are expressed in pairs, with the first currency the countercurrency and the second one the base currency.

The following symbols are used in the book (and the market):

USD is the U.S. dollar.

DEM is the German mark.

GBP is the British pound (the "G" stands for Great).

ITL is the Italian lira.

FRF is the French franc.

SP500 is the SP500 index.

USD-DEM will therefore be the DEM units expressed in marks per dollar (called the European convention). *DEM-USD* will be the dollars per mark (American convention). *GBP-USD* is the number of dollars one pound can buy. *GBP-DEM* is the number of German marks per pound sterling.

SP500 will be the SP500 expressed in USD (as implied). SP500-GBP is the GBP-denominated SP500. However a GBP-SP500 will be the units of pounds expressed in units of SP500.

Following is an example outlining the importance of the choice of numeraire.

> *Example:* Assume the operator is trading USD-DEM (as is the convention in the over-the-counter market, since worldwide USD-DEM is quoted in dollar, not currency, face value). He buys 10 million of US dollars at 1.40 DEM per USD. The market rallies to 1.50 and he sells $10 million. He will have the pleasant profits of DEM 1,000,000. For a dollar-based entity, these profits need to be hedged, whereas for a German company there is no risk since its profits were in its base currency.
>
> A counterexample: If the trader is dollar-based, he would trade instead 14 million DEM at the inverse rate (DEM-USD), 1/1.40 = .7142. Should the market drop to .6666, he would sell back 14 million DEM for a profit of $666,400.
>
> However, the contract is defined in USD-DEM, and the over-the-counter unit for the currency is in dollars. So mentally, the trader would go to the market and quote amounts that are constant foreign currency. In the preceding example, the trader would have had to trade $10 million and then exit by trading the dollar amount that represents a constant 14 million DEM, namely $9,333,333.

Risk Management Rule: A position in a numeraire is considered neutral. A residual long the numeraire will be positive P/L, a residual short the numeraire will be negative P/L. By residual is meant a position that arose from a trade.

Conversely, the hedger considers any position in a unit that is not a numeraire to be an "open" position, long or short.

A DEM balance for a German is considered square, while the U.S.-based person needs to have his residual balance in USD. A person from a country with hyperinflation might think of anything not denominated in hard assets as an open position.

EXTENSION: THE TWO-COUNTRY PARADOX

Two traders (one German and one American) were discussing dollar-mark (USD-DEM). The dollar was trading then at 1.42 and volatility was high. Interest rates were equal so the forward traded at "flat" with the cash, namely 1.42. Both had a view on the other's currency being weaker. Both were somehow right.

Consider the following (the reader should examine the description of the Brownian motion that asset prices are assumed to follow): Assume that assets follow the log normal distribution with expected volatility 20% per annum.

The risk neutrality forces the operator to have the expected price at any time in the future, given the spot, equal to the spot. This leads to:

Price period t = up-price period $(t + 1) \times$ probability of going up

$\qquad$ + down-price period $(t + 1) \times$ probability of going down.

Or:

$$S(t) = S_u (t + 1) p + S_d (t + 1) (1 - p)$$

with S_u the up-price, S_d the down-price, p the probability of going up, $1 - p$ that of going down since the sum of both should be equal to 1.

The operator has as the process followed by spot (as explained in Module G):

$$S_u (t + 1) = S(t) \exp(\sigma \sqrt{t})$$
$$S_d (t + 1) = S(t) \exp(-\sigma \sqrt{t})$$

which solves for p

$$p = (1 - d)/(u - d)$$

with

$$u = \exp (\sigma \sqrt{t}) \text{ and } d = \exp (-\sigma \sqrt{t})$$

So a tree can be built with two six-month nodes:

1. The asset price at the preceding node $\times$ Exp($+ .20 \times$ Sqrt(.5)) with a probability of 46.47%.
2. The asset price at the preceding node $\times$ Exp($- .20 \times$ Sqrt(.5)) with a probability of 53.52%.

Table C.1 Dollar Mark Expectations (for the German)

Volatility	20%			
	6 Months	1 Year	Probability	Expected Price
		1.8841	$p^2 = .2159$	.4068
	1.6375			
1.42		1.42	$2p(1-p) = 0.4975$	.7064
	1.2327			
		1.0707	$(1-p)^2 = 0.2865$	.3066
		Expected		
		USD-DEM		1.42

The expected final asset price is computed by the final outcome times its probability. Table C.1 shows the German's position.

So far so good: The German expects his currency, in the absence of drift and interest rate differential, to remain the same at the end of one year. To see at every node what he expects the inverse of dollar-mark to do, one would take the same table and replace dollar-mark by 1/dollar-mark (see Table C.2). The first cell will be $1/1.42 = .7042$.

So the German expects his currency to remain the same in dollar-mark terms, but to appreciate considerably in mark-dollar terms. This paradox is rather unsettling in a global economy.

Table C.3 shows the marks per dollar point of view. Table C.4 shows the reverse at every node.

The American, too believes that his currency would increase against the other's.

Chapters 7 and 17 present an extension of the paradox: A call on dollar-mark will therefore not have the same delta as a put on mark-dollar. An intuitive way to see it is by considering a move up in dollar-mark to the infinite. For a dollar-based investor, the move in the currencies is down to zero, therefore limited.

Table C.2 Mark-Dollar Expectations for the German

Move	20%			
	6 Months	1 Year	Probability	
		$1/1.8841 = .5307$	$p^2 = .2159$	.1146
	$1/1.6375 = .6135$			
$1/1.42 = 0.7042$		$1/1.42 = 0.7042$	$2p(1-p) = 0.4975$	.3503
	$1/1.2327 = .8112$			
		$1/1.0707 = .9344$	$(1-p)^2 = 0.2865$	.2677
		Expected		
		DEM-USD		.7327
		Equivalent		
		USD-DEM		1.3648

Table C.3   Marks per Dollar Expectations (for the American)

Volatility	20% 6 Months	1 Year	Probability	Expected Price
		.9344	$p^2 = .2159$	.2018
	.8115			
.7042		.7042	$2p(1-p) = 0.4975$	.35
	.6113			
		.5307	$(1-p)^2 = 0.2865$	.1520
		Expected DEM-USD		.7042

■ **Numeraire flipping** consists of switching the unit in which the numeraire is expressed from base currency to counterasset *t*.

A call on *S*, with strike *K*, with risk-neutral rate rd and counterasset rate *d* can be priced as a put on $1/S$ with strike $1/K$, risk-neutral rate *d*, and counterasset rate rd.

Traders need to be warned that numeraire flipping obtains exactly the same price equivalent (except for Asian and digital options), but the delta will be different.[2]

Conclusion

Any risk manager/trader should be aware of the real, true numeraire before proceeding to analyze and measure risks. This issue crops up at either a higher volatility or in situations where many pairs are traded against each other without any dominant home currency.

The next section is intended for the mathematical stickler.

Table C.4   Mark-Dollar Expectations for the German

Move	20% 6 Months	1 Year	Probability	
		1.07	$p^2 = .2159$	.23
	1.2328			
1/.7042 = 1.42		1.42	$2p(1-p) = 0.4975$	.7065
	1.6358			
		1.8843	$(1-p)^2 = 0.2865$	.5399
		Expected USD-DEM		1.4775
		Equivalent DEM-USD		.6768

Mathematical Note[3]

The preceding situation is a direct extension of Jensen's inequality: A convex[4] function of an expectation will be lower than the expectation of the function.

If Φ is convex

$$\Phi(E[x]) \leq E[\Phi(x)]$$

applying for the reciprocal of the defined as (asset1–asset2) = 1/(asset2–asset1) then

$$1/E(x) \leq E(1/x)$$

A more complete method is to use Ito's lemma and examine the effect of the change of variable. This would allow the operator to take the drift into account and get an exact figure. It can be done by creating a 1/x function of the underlying security and deriving its expectation.

Starting with a Brownian motion:

$$\frac{dS}{S} = \mu dt + \sigma dZ$$

with S the security, σ the volatility, and Z a Wiener process.

Set $U(S) = 1/S$ the inverse of the rate (countercurrency) and using Ito's lemma:

$$dU = \frac{\partial U}{\partial t} dt + \frac{\partial U}{\partial S} dS + \frac{\partial^2 U}{\partial S^2} (dS)^2$$

we have

$$\frac{\partial U}{\partial t} dt = 0$$

$$\frac{\partial U}{\partial S} dS = -\frac{1}{S^2} dS = \frac{-1}{S} (\mu dt + \sigma dZ)$$

$$\frac{\partial^2 U}{\partial S^2} (dS)^2 = \frac{1}{S} (\mu dt + \sigma dZ)^2$$

using the Ito multiplication table:

$$dt^2 = 0$$

$$dt\, dZ = 0$$

$$dZ^2 = dt$$

which obtains

$$\frac{dU}{U} = (\sigma^2 - \mu)dt - \sigma dZ$$

while dS/S has expectation $\mu\, dt$, dU/U has expectation $(\sigma^2 - \mu)\, dt$.

Conclusion

Every operator will be subjected to a special risk-neutral stochastic process as a function of his numeraire.[5]

Correlation Triangles: A Graphical Case Study

This section is necessary preparation for the analysis of multiasset options.[1] The analysis is limited to implied volatility and correlations stemming from European options.

Assets can be represented for delivery in a given maturity (the assets themselves, not the quoted pairs), as points in a Euclidean space. The "distance" between the points will correspond to the implied volatility between them. This method can facilitate the understanding of the relationships between volatilities and the effect the correlation has on all the possible pairs.

The definition of an asset for that purpose is a unit that needs to be paired with some other unit for it to become tradable. So corn could be an asset, gold another asset, the U.S. dollar a third one. One could easily see a contract defined as an option for corn against gold, a vanilla product for individuals whose home currency is corn or gold.

It is always easier to analyze currencies in that light because currencies lend themselves very well to changes in numeraire. A currency trader can easily see a dollar-yen option on the same footing as a yen-Mongolian Tugrit. A currency, by definition, is a numeraire, but so could any other unit, including baseball tickets, for those who are too centered on the matter and see everything else translated into baseball ticket equivalence.

- The implied volatility of a pair (for a given maturity) is measured with the distance between the points represented by their coordinates in a Euclidean space.

- In a two-dimensional universe, the formula of the distance between two assets with coordinates (x_1, x_2) and (y_1, y_2) is

$$d(x,y) = \sqrt{(x_1 - y_1)^2 + (x_2 - y_2)^2}$$

It is easy for the mathematical stickler to see that the volatility function thus defined satisfies the conditions for a metric, or distance function. Hence, $v(x,y)$ will represent the volatility of the tradable pair x-y, or x in terms of units of y:

1. $v(x,y)$ is strictly positive if x is different from y. In addition, $v(x,x) = 0$: The volatility of the asset expressed in terms of itself as a numeraire is nil. It suffices to see that the volatility of cash in terms of cash is 0.

2. $v(x,y) = v(y,x)$. The volatility of y in terms of x as a numeraire is equal to the volatility of y in terms of x as a numeraire.

3. $v(x,y)$ is at all times lower or equal to $v(x,z) + v(z,y)$.

In a n dimensional space, the formula of the distance between two assets with coordinates $x = (x_1, x_2, \ldots, x_n)$ and $x = (y_1, y_2, \ldots, y_n)$ is

$$v(x,y) = \sqrt{\sum_{i=1}^{n} (x_i - y_i)^2} \tag{1}$$

Start by assuming that one-month DEM volatility is a point in a Euclidean space (the one-month space) with coordinates {7,12.12}. Also pick USD to be (0,0). It is always recommended, for the sake of simplicity, to use the point (0,0) for the numeraire, the commodity in which the P/L is computed.

To conform to market standards, the notation $v(x,y)$ will be used to write $v(x\_y)$, which should read "volatility of the pair x_y". $v(\text{USD-DEM})$, the metric between point {0,0} and the point {7,12.12} shown in Figure D.1 will be $\sqrt{7^2 + 12.12^2} = 14$, which puts the USD-DEM volatility at 14% (example is rescaled by 100 for simplicity). By the same token, the $v(\text{DEM-USD})$, the DEM-USD volatility is seen at 14% as well.

Next, add the JPY. Assume that USD-JPY is trading at 12% volatility so USD-JPY is a vector of length 12. But there are many possibilities to put it on the chart as the coordinates could represent an entire circle of radius 12 around the (0,0) point (Figure D.2).

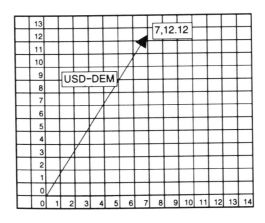

Figure D.1   A two-currency world.

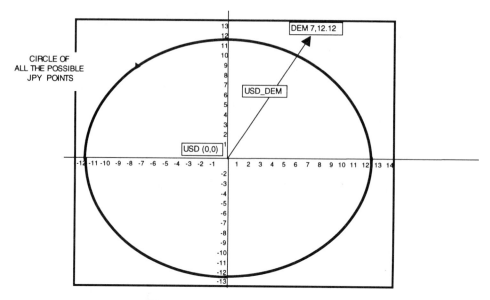

Figure D.2 Possible JPY points.

The coordinates are arbitrarily set to be (x_1, x_2), a point that would be on the circle. There are infinite possibilities as the $\sqrt{x_1^2 + x_2^2} = 12$ gives rise to many combinations. Pick $x_1 = 11$, so x_2 would be $\sqrt{12^2 - 11^2}$, and the point for JPY would, as a result, be (11,4.79).

Now there are three points in space: USD = (0,0), DEM = (7,12.12), JPY = (11,4.79). These three points should be capable of providing additional information. According to formula (1), v(DEM-JPY) will be sqrt{$(7 - 11)^2 + (12.12 - 4.79)^2$} = 8.35.

Note that the same triangle equality shown in Figure D.3 would have been satisfied with the yen on the other side (i.e., with the coordinates {−1.35,11.92}).

Before proceeding to the what-if analysis, examine the correlation. It is well known that the correlation between the volatility segments will be the cosine of the angle cornering them.

Let the point $n = (n_1, n_2, \ldots n_n)$ be defined as a *numeraire*:

$$\cos(b) = (x - n) \cdot (y - n) / \, v(x,n) \, v(y,n),$$

b being the angle between the segments with the dot product, the "inner product," $(x - n) \cdot (y - n) = \Sigma(x_i - n_i)(y_i - n_i)$ and it is already known that the metric $v(x,n) = \sqrt{\Sigma(x_i - n_i)^2}$.

It could be made easier by assuming that X and Y have $(x_1, x_2), (y_1, y_2)$ for coordinates.

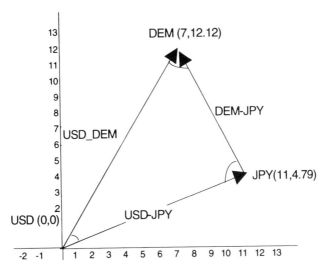

Figure D.3 Adding the yen.

CORRELATION TRIANGLE RULE

$$\cos(b) = \text{correlation}(x\text{-}n, y\text{-}n) = ((x_1 - n_1)(y_1 - n_1)$$

$$+ (x_2 - n_2)(y_2 - n_2))/\sqrt{[(x_1 - n_1)^2 + (x_2 - n_2)^2]}\sqrt{[(y_1 - n_1)^2 + (y_2 - n_2)^2]}$$

It is easy to see that correlation $(x\text{-}n, y\text{-}n)$ = correlation $(n\text{-}x, n\text{-}y)$; in other words, the correlation between the asset x measured against the numeraire n and the asset y measured against the numeraire n is equal to the correlation between the asset n measured against the numeraire x and the asset n measured against the numeraire y.

It is now possible to return to the example and calculate the correlations imparted by the three-currency world. Compute the correlation between USD-DEM segment and the USD-JPY:

$$\text{Corr(DEM-USD,JPY-USD)} = (7 - 0)(11 - 0)$$
$$+ (12.12 - 0)(4.79 - 0)/\sqrt{(49 + 146.89)}\sqrt{(121 + 22.94)} = .8035$$

Corr(DEM-JPY/USD-DEM) = .52

Corr(DEM-JPY/USD-DEM) = .09

For correlation to remain constant, the volatilities of the sides should increase by the same percentage amount (Figure D.4). This would cause the

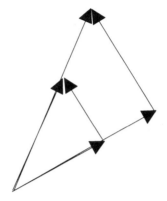

Figure D.4 Correlation unchanged.

third volatility to increase as well. It is somewhat hard to imagine that DEM-JPY now increases in volatility because both components gained in volatility against the dollar. This author spent some precious time trying to convince fellow colleagues who were reluctant to accept the notion.

Furthermore, when the third leg rotates (as in Figure D.5), the volatilities remain constant and correlation shifts.

To add a currency to this world would necessitate increasing the dimensions by 1. Including the GBP requires adding one dimension to all the others. Using an $\{x,y,z\}$ coordinate system, the result (displayed in Figure D.6) is

$$USD(numeraire) = \{0,0,0\}$$

$$DEM = \{7,12.12,0\}$$

$$JPY = \{11,4.79,0\}$$

$$GBP = \{0,9.57,2.91\}$$

Figure D.5 Volatility unchanged, correlation decreases.

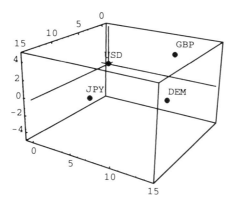

Figure D.6   A four-currency world.

What if a user added the SP500? He would now have five units, four dimensions for a possible representation. However, he could eliminate one unit every time for representation purposes.

The trader represents the subuniverse USD,SP,DEM,JPY (without the GBP). He removes the third line accordingly for the representation, representing (n1,n2,n4) to accommodate the fact that even traders can only view the world in three dimensions.

$$USD = \{0,0,0\}$$

$$DEM = \{7,12.12,0\}$$

$$JPY = \{11,4.79,0\}$$

$$SP = \{0,0,10\}$$

The pair SP500-USD satisfies no correlation with any other segment. The reader could, as an exercise, verify that. The implication is apparent, as corr(2 segments) = 0 infers the cos(angle) = 0, which results in a right angle between SP-USD and JPY-USD, as well as with SP-USD and DEM-USD, as shown in Figure D.7.

Result: The world of volatilities can be represented as a universe of points.

Absence of volatility/correlation arbitrage requires that all the volatilities in the market (and the correlations stemming from it) satisfy the same metric between points. Any shift of a point to the left, right, up, or down should then result in arbitrage.

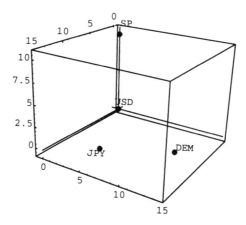

Figure D.7   Three currencies and the SP500.

CALCULATING AN IMPLIED CORRELATION CURVE

Having the different sides makes it possible to build a correlation curve, which is the correlation implied by the rules of the triangle (Table D.1).

Table D.1   Derived Implied Correlations*

	DM	FF	DM/FF	CORR
1m	13.40	10.30	4.80	0.95
2m	13.40	10.40	5.00	0.94
3m	13.35	10.45	5.35	0.93
4m	13.35	10.45	5.50	0.92
5m	13.30	10.40	5.60	0.92
6m	13.25	10.45	5.70	0.91
7m	13.15	10.35	5.70	0.91
8m	13.15	10.35	5.70	0.91
9m	13.15	10.45	5.70	0.91
10m	13.10	10.40	5.70	0.91
11m	13.10	10.40	5.70	0.91
12m	13.10	10.50	5.70	0.91

* *Source:* Tradition Financial Services, October 30, 1995, closing prices.

The Value-at-Risk

Abyssus abyssum invocat (The abyss calls for the abyss).[1]
Latin Proverb

Below is a presentation of a risk management method that, like portfolio insurance, can only work if a small number of people are using it. It is a paradox, discussed in Taleb (1997), that states that it can only work (and succeed) if it is unsuccessful.

- **Value-at-risk**[2] is a method of estimating the maximum loss for a portfolio at a confidence level assuming a knowledge of the process governing its components.

The VAR can present some useful short-term hedging tools for traders, as we examined with the discussion on stacking in Chapter 12. However, it led to seriously disputed applications by risk management firms that led (perhaps innocently) their customers to believe they possessed tools to summarize the overall market risks for a position, a unit, a department, or an entire firm, in one simplified numerical exposure, without standard error.

As the concept is evolving in its applications, the presentation here will be limited to a rapid intuitive exposition.

Value-at-risk[3] is growing in use among the banks and corporations both for adequate risk allocation and appropriate quantification of the risk-adjusted returns on capital. The idea of disclosing the overall exposure as *one simple quantity* appeals to most corporate board members and regulators, many of whom are uninitiated into the nuances and complexities of financial market risks. They can easily be impressed by the "scientific" tools used.

The condensation of complex factors naturally does not just affect the accuracy of the measure. Critics of VAR (including the author) argue that simplification could result in such distortions as to nullify the value of the measurement. Furthermore, it can lead to *charlatanism:* Lulling an innocent investor or business manager into a false sense of security could be a serious breach of faith. Operators are dealing with unstable parameters, unlike those of the physical sciences, and risk measurement should not just be understood to be a vague and imprecise estimate. This approach can easily lead to distortions. The most nefarious effect of the VAR is that it has allowed people who have never had any exposure to market risks to express their opinion on the matter.

In brief, it cannot be used to say, "Within 99.7% (or within 90% or something of the sort), you are not expected to lose in the next month more than 1 million dollars." The innocent treasurer or company official would believe himself to be listening to a scientific statistic similar to statistics on airplane crashes. It could, however, be used to say: "You are expected to lose no more than 100,000 dollars within the next two hours with a 66% accuracy, provided you do not try to liquidate your position and the other similar firms do not have the same portfolio."

SIMPLIFIED EXAMPLES

In these examples, the VAR corresponds to the risk for 1 standard deviation (66% of the time), not 3 standard deviations as expressed in the common literature.

Assume for this series of examples that the universe offered to a trading desk is composed of the following four items:

USD-DEM: USD against the German mark currency pair as quoted in the interbank market.

USD-JPY: USD against the Japanese yen currency pair as quoted in the interbank market.

Treasury Bond futures: As traded on the Chicago Board of Trade (the example translates units into face value exposure).

SP500 Index futures: As quoted on the Chicago Mercantile Exchange.

The example uses data as of May 23, 1995.
Annualized nine-month historical volatilities (percentage) are as follows:

USD-DEM   12.1
USD-JPY   12.3
Bonds   8.5
SP500   9.33

Volatility is defined as the standard deviation of the log of the returns (unweighted).

Table E.1 Correlation Matrices (9 Month)

	USD-DEM	USD-JPY	Bonds	SP500
USD-DEM	1.00	0.74	0.30	0.23
USD-JPY	0.74	1.00	0.26	0.30
Bonds	0.30	0.26	1.00	0.45
SP500	0.23	0.30	0.45	1.00

Example 1. No Diversification

The trader has a $20 million face value limit and decides to invest in going long one of the four instruments, but does not know which one. Table E.2 shows the net exposure that would correspond to each undiversified position. The net exposure is defined arbitrarily for one daily standard deviation of the moves in the market, which should (in theory, unless the distribution changes) represent 67% of all events. It should also resemble the average daily swing in the portfolio. Should the trader decide to include wider events, like 3 standard deviations, he could multiply the exposure by 3: It would then show the total maximum possible loss with a 99.7% confidence. However, the management of that trader has heard of fat tails and prefers to see 1 standard deviation as a benchmark for a comparative purpose.

Example 2. A Cross-Position

The trader might desire to get involved in cross-positions. Would he benefit from a positive correlation?

It is apparent here that the VAR stemming from a cross-currency position as shown in Table E.3, owing to the higher correlation of changes between dollar/mark and dollar/yen would correspond to 71% of the risk of a dollar/mark position.

Obviously, the diversification works. Since he has not fully drawn on his gross limit, he can add to the position and utilize the balance of $10 million in a diversified manner (Table E.4).

The overall position is thus reduced from the undiversified Example 1: The capital at risk for 1 standard deviation corresponds to at least half the risks of any of the initial four positions.

Table E.2   The Risk of Each Position

	Position (in $ mil)	Net Exp
USD-DEM	20	$153,700
USD-JPY	20	$156,240
Bonds	20*	$107,971
SP500	20†	$118,514

*20 million exposure in Treasury bonds corresponds to 182 contracts, computed by dividing 20,000,000 by the face value of every contract ($100,000) times 110 the price.
†20 million exposure in the SP500 futures corresponds to 77 contracts, which is computed by dividing 20,000,000 by 523 (the contract price) times 500 (the contract is defined as paying 500 time the index).

Table E.3   VAR for a Cross-Currency Position

	Position (in $ mil)	Net Exp
USD-DEM	5	$38,425
USD-JPY	−5	$39,060
Bonds	0	—
SP500	0	—
VAR		**$27,944**

Example 3. Two Possible Trades

USD-DEM and USD-FRF are two highly correlated currencies. The trader can position himself in one, in the other, or in the cross.

Correlation Matrix:

	USD-DEM	USD-FRF
USD-DEM	1	0.97
USD-FRF	0.97	1

Volatilities:

	vol
USD-DEM	12.1
USD-FRF	11

The Cross-Position Risk:

	Position (in $ mil)	Net Exp
USD-DEM	−80	$614,798
USD-FRF	80	$558,908
VAR		$154,080

The risk of a cross-position corresponds to 25% of the risks of each. The VAR of the equivalent position could have been computed through the

Table E.4   Full Use of the Capital ($20 million)

	Position (in $ mil)	Net Exp
USD-DEM	5	$38,425
USD-JPY	−5	$39,060
Bonds	5	$26,993
SP500	5	$29,628
VAR		**$54,868**

volatility of the resulting DEM-FRF currency pair: 3.03%. The alternative risk profile is as follows:

	Vol	Position (in $ mil equivalent)	Net Exp
DEM-FRF	3.03	−80	$154,080
VAR			$154,080

Problem 1. Assumed Homoskedasticity of Markets.   (This argument is developed in Chapter 15.) The models being used rely heavily on the "normality" of the markets (i.e., price changes follow a bell-shaped curve, a fact that is extremely rare). "Fat tails" and "high peaks" are familiar to any option trader with a thorough understanding of the weakness of the models.

While the normality assumption could be acceptable for some applications, such as the pricing of at-the-money options, such approximation of the distribution could be considered inappropriate for the measurement of "worst-case" risks. Risks are located in the tails, which is where the distribution is the least known.

Assuming that the volatility of markets is not constant, the rule of the $\sigma \sqrt{t}$ no longer holds. Result: In a heteroskedastic market, the variance is not a multiple of the time horizon. One-week (5-day) dollar volatility is not 2.23 times that of one day.

In addition, correlations not being constant (as dicussed in Chapter 6), the "joint tails" of several assets are fuzzier to model.

Risk Management Rule: The VAR provides an admirable short-term hedging tool but is by no means a risk management device.

Problem 2. Liquidity Risks.   (This argument is developed in Chapter 4.) The VAR method makes no allowance for the fact that liquidity could represent the largest risks in some markets. In some less mature instruments, liquidity costs become indistinguishable from market risk. The selling of a large block of securities, particularly in the event of a forced liquidation, can lead to total market collapse.

Those not interested in the liquidation value of their portfolio need not be concerned about its market price risk.

Problem 3. Behavior of Parameters at Times of Stress.   The essence of the VAR concept is correlation and diversification. The widespread use of these techniques leads to the simultaneous breakdown of both at times of excessive stress in the markets. Typically, low correlation between assets tends to rise in consequence to stressful events, therefore reducing the diversification effect. A severe example of that is provided by the "bond market crash" of 1994 as all the bond markets sank together. Similarly, the high correlation drops abruptly, sometimes even turning negative, in the face of such events: The cross-maturity hedges cease to work. The yield curves shift, often causing nonpredicted deformations, at times of high volatility.

There is a significant conflict between a multiasset risk model and the stress-testing approach. One relies on known relationships while the second has grounding in a statistics-free world. Relying exclusively on the first would mislead grossly at times of uncertainty. Relying exclusively on the second would prevent firms from trading.

Problem 4. Dangers of Generalized Use.   Assume that everyone used the value at risk and that the market moved abruptly. The fact that such a system became a benchmark would cause a snowball effect.

The chain would be as follows: In a schematic world of a small number of homogeneous leveraged players, everyone would end up with close to the same portfolio constitution and weights owing to the diversification scheme (the optimal portfolio) {A,B,C} with weights w_A, w_B, w_C, in such a way that they reduced their risks to fit the optimal allocation. They would all invest more lulled with the knowledge of being comfortably diversified as they were properly taught by the risk management consultant.

Assume that A went down in price causing the total portfolios to drop in value. Assume that the volatility of A increased. To maintain a constant VAR, the weights would need to be adjusted down, so the operator would have to sell some stocks of B and C. The quantities, though small, would be large enough to push prices lower and make operators race each other to the state of near-bankruptcy. The factor would cause the correlation between the components to rise, weakening the diversification effect in an unexpected way. The same effect would take place if one of the weights is negative and the operators are "hedging." An interesting parameter in hedges is that they only work when they are not identified as hedges by the multitude. If most other similar institutions needed to act in a similar manner in similar circumstances, there would be a dynamical system traders would need to account for.[4]

> *Risk Management Rule:*   The market will follow the path that will thwart the higher number of possible hedgers.

Problem 5. Computational Problems.   Severe computational issues are associated with the VAR. Large firms do not cumulate all their position in one place from where they could be retrieved easily and in a timely way. Missing one simple position could cause sufficient distortions to invalidate the measurements. The way the VAR is computed makes it necessary to merge all the individual positions together, not add up the VAR of different departments and branches.

Again, the value at risk of a sum is not the sum of the VARs. Despite the sophistication of operators, most active firms experience data-gathering lags. The complexity of their operations led them to account for units by using a pyramid of net numbers. The VAR project would necessitate the handling of every single position in every single branch, not easy for institutions with a large network.

Another problem arises when the instruments become too numerous, creating a large matrix. Estimating the covariances will create some rounding and estimation errors, and when such errors cumulate, they will prevent the matrices from being positive definite. This makes large matrices impracticable.[5]

Problem 6. What Is Volatility? So far, volatility has been discussed as if it were some observed physical phenomenon. Because it is unstable, traders need to consider modeling and all the resulting problems. Which volatility? Implied or historical? Over which horizon? and so on.

Problem 7. Do Not Even Dream of Applying It to Derivatives. The subject matter of this book stresses the difficult interplay of parameters traders must face in evaluating the risks of an option position, owing to its multidimensional nonlinearity. The notion of higher moments also underscores that there is no way of tracking the risks of complex portfolios with one simplified Greek.

Conclusions. Many efforts are under way to correct the inherent defects of the system. Most promising results, typically in the shape of nonparametric methods for stress testing, are presently outside the public domain.

Formulas. The problem is being approached from the angle of the correlation matrix instead of the simpler covariance because of conventions in the software market.

E is the Net exposure = Position (Face value) $\times$ 1 Daily stdev. (computed by computing the annualized standard deviation used in option pricing by the square root of 252). **M** is an m by m correlation Matrix. **VAR** is the value at risk, amount risked for n standard deviations.

$$\text{VAR} = n \text{ SQRT}(\mathbf{E}^{\mathrm{T}} \mathbf{M} \mathbf{E})$$

Example: Say that in a world of four instruments an operator had the following vector:

Volatilities:

$$V = \begin{bmatrix} \sigma_1 \\ \sigma_2 \\ \sigma_3 \\ \sigma_4 \end{bmatrix}$$

Position:

$$P = \begin{bmatrix} P_1 \\ P_2 \\ P_3 \\ P_4 \end{bmatrix}$$

The trader gets the net exposure **E** (expected risks per standard deviation):

$$E = \frac{1}{\sqrt{252}} \begin{bmatrix} P_1\sigma_1 \\ P_2\sigma_2 \\ P_3\sigma_3 \\ P_4\sigma_4 \end{bmatrix}$$

Then he pulls the correlation matrix:

$$M = \begin{bmatrix} 1 & \rho_{12} & \rho_{13} & \rho_{14} \\ & 1 & \rho_{23} & \rho_{24} \\ & & 1 & \rho_{34} \\ & & & 1 \end{bmatrix}$$

The lower triangle is the mirror of the upper one since $\rho_{12} = \rho_{21}$.

Finally the value at risk is computed by multiplying the transpose of **E** (1,4) by **M** (4,4) and multiplying the resulting (1,4) matrix by **E** (4,1) to get one number. The square root of the number will be the **VAR**.

Probabilistic Rankings in Arbitrage

RANKING OF SECURITIES

The value of a security can be established by ranking. If security A is worth more than security B and less than security C, a book runner can thus get some orientation on how to price it. This is particularly easy when the prices are readily available for the comparative "straddling" securities and when the comparative securities are close in price to each other.

This instrument pricing and hedging method is based on the rule of stochastic dominance.[1] When an instrument or combination of instruments is at least as valuable as another set, the author will use the sign $\geq$ to express the inequality. Instrument $A \geq B$ means that A in all possible events (under all parameter changes) is deemed to be at least equal to instrument B, or that under no event will B be worth more than A. Such rules can be used to price options given the availability of other prices in the market. They certainly can be extended to portfolio management.

European Option Rules

The following notation will be used: $C(S, t)$ is a European call expiring period t with a strike price S. $P(S, t)$ is a European put. A $C(S, t, H_L)$ is a call with a barrier below the market (down and out) at a price H_L and a $C(S, t, H_H)$ is a call with a barrier higher than market (up and out) at price H_H, also called a reverse knock-out. A call (S, t, H_L, H_H) is a double barrier:

$$C(S, t) \geq C(S + \alpha, t)$$

A 101 call will be worth more than a 102 call of the same expiration under all circumstances. This rule is obvious:

$$P(S + \alpha, t) \geq P(S, t)$$

A 101 put will be worth more than a 100 put under all circumstances.
The butterfly rules:

$$C(S - \alpha, t) + C(S + \alpha, t) \geq 2\,C(S, t)$$

Two 101 calls are worth less than one 100 call and one 102 call together. It means that the 100/101/102 butterfly should be worth at least 0. The reason is that it will have a value of 0 everywhere except in the "eye"; at the center, it may have a value of 1.

By put/call parity:

$$P(S - \alpha, t) + P(S + \alpha, t) \geq 2\,P(S, t)$$

Two puts at 101 should be worth more than one 100 put and one 102 put together.

These rules may seem simplistic but veteran option traders on the exchanges who pride themselves on trading without "sheets" have been able to operate by these butterfly rules alone. They can price the entire spectrum using a small number of options.

By extension:

$$P(S, t) + C(S, t) \geq P(S - \alpha, t) + C(S + \alpha, t)$$

a straddle is necessarily more valuable than a strangle.

Calendar Rules

With τ strickly positive,

$$P(S, t + \tau) + C(S, t + \tau) \geq P(S, t) + C(S, t)$$

(In present value: It is more appropriate to deduct financing.)

This means that a longer straddle should be worth more than a shorter one, after taking financing into account. The rule always holds for "serial" options, options on only 1 future (like a 1-month 2-month option on a 3-month future). It does not unconditionally apply to options where the underlying security S is not "fixed," and such weakness gets exacerbated with nonfungible assets (i.e., live cattle. Exceptions can occur when a security cannot be swapped into a longer maturity).

Barrier and Digital Rules

An American digital is worth more than a European one. An American digital of the "if touched" variety where the bet is satisfied if some event takes place at all times during the life of the instrument is worth more than a bet that an event would take place at expiration only.

Example: A note that pays off one dollar if the security goes above 103 at any point in the next year is worth more than a note that pays off one dollar if the security is above 103 on expiration day:

$$C(S, t) \geq C(S, t, H_H) \text{ and } \geq C(S, t, H_L)$$

An option with no barrier is always worth more than an option cum barrier, since there are possibilities of losing the option before expiration:

$$C(S, t, H_H) \geq C(S, t, H_H + \alpha)$$
$$C(S, t, H_L) \geq C(S, t, H_H - \alpha)$$

Any option cum barrier is more valuable than the same option with a barrier closer to the money:

$$C(S, t, H_H) \geq C(S, t, H_L, H_H)$$
$$C(S, t, H_L) \geq C(S, t, H_L, H_H)$$

Any single barrier option is more valuable than a double barrier if they share a common trigger H.

Correlation Rules

These boundary rules apply for at-the-money options. They work for at-the-money (forward) straddle prices or implied volatility of options.

The possible currencies are Currency A (used for numeraire), Currency B, and Currency C. The notation $v(A\text{-}B)$ is used to designate the volatility for the pair A against B.

Triangle Inequality

$$v(A\text{-}B) + v(B\text{-}C) \geq v(A\text{-}C)$$

Correlation and Volatility.   Using $\rho(A\text{-}B, A\text{-}C)$, the correlation of the pair $A\text{-}B$ and the pair $B\text{-}C$:

$$v(B\text{-}C)^2 = v(A\text{-}B)^2 + v(A\text{-}C)^2 - 2\,\rho(A\text{-}B, A\text{-}C)\,v(A\text{-}B)\,v(A\text{-}C)$$

Example:

$$v(\text{USD-DEM}) + v(\text{DEM-FRF}) \geq v(\text{USD-FRF})$$

(This rule seems to be often violated.)

$$v(\text{USD-FRF}) + v(\text{DEM-FRF}) \geq v(\text{USD-DEM})$$

It implies that given three security pairs, implied volatility between them cannot be such that one of the implied correlations exceeds 1 in absolute value.

Furthermore, by the rule of contamination, no combination between options should allow for a combination yielding a correlation higher than 1 in absolute value.

Warning. This does not represent full arbitrage (i.e., a locked-in profit or loss) since the P/L of combinations with the numeraire can be predicted with certainty, whereas the "cross" (in this case, DEM-FRF for a dollar-based person) can yield a P/L that depends on the performance of the components with respect to the base currency.

A **generalization** based on the preceding is that an implied covariance matrix (implied from at-the-money option prices) needs to be positive definite (its eigenvalues need to be positive definite). It is an extension of the boundary rules for a three-currency world. Otherwise an operator would be able to arbitrage it by getting some combination of options for free (or for a credit).

$$v(\text{USD-DEM}) = \sigma_1$$

$$v(\text{USD-FRF}) = \sigma_2$$

$$\text{"Cross" vol (DEM-FRF)} = \text{Volatility of FRF-DEM} = \sigma_c$$

Thus the following covariance matrix results:

$$\Sigma = \begin{bmatrix} \sigma_1^2 & \sigma_{12} \\ \sigma_{21} & \sigma_2^2 \end{bmatrix} \text{ with } \sigma_{12} = \sigma_{21} = \sigma_1^2 + \sigma_2^2 - \sigma_c^2$$

σ_{12} and σ_{21} being the covariance between USD-DEM and USD-FRF.

It is easy to check whether the matrix is "clean," or arbitrage-free. As volatility cannot possibly be negative, Σ needs to be positive definite, which requires the eigenvalues to be positive. In this example, the aberrations for a 2 by 2 matrix can be visible to the naked eye while those of a 20 by 20 matrix would require computer crunching.

In the next example, there are restrictions on one of the elements the matrix (considering it to be symmetric with covariance 1, 2 = covariance 2, 1). Assume that vol USD-DEM is 14% and DEM-FRF (the cross) is 4%. Then the restriction is on USD-FRF to be between 10% and 18%. Outside that band, arbitrages are possible. Below 10%, an operator could buy the USD-FRF and DEM-FRF volatilities and sell the USD-DEM. He would be completely bounded as this operation is equivalent to being "short" correlation at 1. Any drop in correlation at any time between the two currencies would benefit the trader.

Likewise, "buying" correlation at -1 could be perfected by buying USD-DEM at 14%, buying DEM-FRF at 4%, and selling USD-FRF at 18%. Any rise in the correlation above -1 would result in profits.

A more involved matrix can be created by adding a security to the matrix. It becomes much more difficult to see with a naked eye the implications of an arbitrage-free situation:

$$\Sigma = \begin{bmatrix} \sigma_1^2 & \sigma_{12} & \sigma_{13} \\ \sigma_{21} & \sigma_2^2 & \sigma_{23} \\ \sigma_{31} & \sigma_{32} & \sigma_3^2 \end{bmatrix}$$

Take the asset 1 = USD-DEM, asset 2 = USD-FRF, asset 3 = USD-CHF, assets 12 and 21 = DEM-FRF, assets 13 and 31 = DEM-CHF, and the illiquid assets 23 and 32 FRF-CHF. With vol USD-DEM at 15%, USD-FRF at 12%, USD-CHF at 18% and crosses USD-FRF at 4%, CHF-FRF at 6% and DEM-CHF 5%, one of the eigenvalues flags a negative number that causes the computer to beep. The matrix above is faulty. The arbitrage can be constructed through a combination of options.

Remember that enough currencies are there to allow for some arbitrage, or at least to construct a trade with a high expected return.

Warning. The rule of the positive eigenvalues does not hold for a comparison between implied volatilities of options that are not at-the-money forward.

CORRELATION CONVEXITY RULES

The next few rules emanate from the contamination principle.

One can easily see from the previous examples that a structure that is set up short a "high" correlation (close to 1), that is, that should benefit from correlation dropping, or long a low correlation (close to -1), is stronger than a structure that is set up in a correlation that is closer to 0, everything else being equal. Say that a trader in a three-asset world pays 11% for USD-FRF and 4% for DEM-FRF and sells USD-DEM at 14%. He really disbursed the equivalent of one volatility, or sold correlation at 97%. It is an application of the following formula:

$$\sigma_{cross} = \sqrt{\sigma_1^2 + \sigma_2^2 - 2\rho\sigma_1\sigma_2}$$

from which is derived a correlation ρ of .97.

In the real world, correlations are unstable. Therefore, a trade that has a better chance of benefiting from changes in correlation than losing from it is of higher grade than a trade that presents the opposite characteristic.

GENERAL CONVEXITY RULES

> *Risk Management Rule:*   A security that is convex with respect to a nonconstant parameter should, everything else being equal, be worth more than a security that is not as convex with respect to the same parameter.

In a flat-yield-curve environment and assuming the back-month maturities have the same volatility, it is preferable to own the bond with the highest convexity.

A **corollary** is that a portfolio of options that presents a symmetric convexity in its vega is worth more than a similar portfolio that presents none.

> *Example:*   Two portfolios are long vega in the amount of $100,000 per volatility point (from 16% down to 15%). Portfolio A's vega increases as volatility rallies and decreases in a sell-off, while portfolio B's vega decreases in the rally and increases in a sell-off. On that account alone, the options that constitute portfolio A are more valuable than those that constitute portfolio B.
>
> It is preferable to be square vega and own the second derivative of vega than have a position (through binary options hedged with vanilla) that loses money when vega moves. These instruments are therefore deemed "inferior."

> *Risk Management Rule:*   A portfolio of options that presents symmetric convexity in its vega with respect to underlying A is worth more than a similar portfolio of options of the same symmetric convexity with respect to underlying B if underlying B is less heteroskedastic than underlying A.
>
> A portfolio of options long vega through shorting a barrier option is less valuable than a portfolio of options that is long vega through out-of-the-money options.

Figure F.1 shows the difference between convex and concave vega.

Concave Vega

Convex Vega

Figure F.1   Convex and concave vega.

Option Pricing

Ito's Lemma Explained

Ito's lemma is an important tool in option pricing. Without spending an excessive amount of time on theory, this module will provide a heuristic definition, couching as much of it as possible in terms practitioners can understand.

The gist of Ito's method is that a function of a random walk (not smooth) is smooth and differentiable. The module of the Brownian motion on a spreadsheet (Module A) goes into the details of the lack of smoothness.

The random walk has already been intuitively defined:

$$\Delta W = W(t + \Delta t) - W(t) = \mu(W, t)\Delta t + \sigma(W, t)\Delta Z \tag{1}$$

with $\Delta Z = \sqrt{\Delta t}\, U(0, 1)$, $U(0, 1)$ an i.i.d. process following a normal distribution[1] with mean 0 and unit variance. The shortcuts σ and μ for $\sigma(W, t)$ and $\mu(W, t)$ will be used.

Equation (1) means that the change in W, over time Δt, is composed of a drift and of a stochastic element the magnitude of which is determined by the variance.

It is established that no matter how small one defines the increments Δt, the function will not be smooth anywhere. It will remain jagged and nowhere differentiable. This is analogous to a coastline that no one can accurately measure because of its infinite jaggedness.

Select time in tranches so small that any smaller increment would be 0. Anything that is multiplied by time would vanish.

It is possible to check that:

$E(\Delta W) = \mu\Delta t$ since $E(\Delta Z) = 0$

$V(\Delta W) = E\{\Delta W\} - E(\Delta W)^2\}^2 = E\{0 + \sigma^2\Delta t\ U^2\}$

so

$$V(\Delta W) = \sigma^2\Delta t$$

this leads to the following Ito multiplication table:

	dt	*dW*
dt	0	0
dW	0	$\sigma^2 dt$

From here, (1) can be written as what is known as an Ito process:

$$dW = \mu(W, t)dt + \sigma(W, t)dZ \tag{2}$$

at the limit. This differential form should be always seen as a shorthand for a stochastic integral, not a true partial differential equation.

Let $F(W, t)$ be a security that is function of both W and time. Expanding, leads to:

$$dF = \frac{\partial F}{\partial t} dt + \frac{\partial F}{\partial W} dW + \frac{1}{2} \frac{\partial^2 F}{2\partial W^2} (dW)^2 + \frac{1}{2} \frac{\partial^2 F}{\partial t^2}(dt)^2$$

$$+ \frac{\partial^2 F}{\partial W \, \partial t}(dW \, dt) \tag{3}$$

since:

1. Unlike ordinary calculus, the stochastic expansion does not stop at dW since dW^2 does not vanish, like the coastline that remains jagged at all scales and

2. Anything multiplied by dt vanishes,

so (3) becomes

$$dF = \frac{\partial F}{\partial t} dt + \frac{\partial F}{\partial W} dW + \frac{1}{2} \frac{\partial^2 F}{\partial W^2} (dW)^2 \tag{4}$$

expanding dW and $(dW)^2$ results in

$$dF = \left[\frac{\partial F}{\partial t} + \mu(W, t)\frac{\partial F}{\partial W} + \frac{1}{2} \frac{\partial^2 F}{\partial W^2} \sigma^2(W, t)\right] dt + \frac{\partial F}{\partial W}\sigma(W, t)dW \tag{5}$$

It is easy to see how this can lead to the Black-Scholes equation. As a first step, consider that dS/S is an Ito process:

$$\frac{dS}{S} = \mu dt + \sigma dZ \tag{6}$$

Examine the process of the log dS with the aid of the Ito transform:

$$d \, \text{Log} S = \frac{dS}{S} + \frac{(dS)^2}{2S^2} \text{ and since } \left(\frac{dS}{S}\right)^2 = (\mu dt + \sigma dZ)^2 = \sigma^2(dZ)^2 = \sigma^2 dt$$

$$d \, \text{Log} S = \left(\mu - \frac{\sigma^2}{2}\right) dt + \sigma dW$$

S_{t0} a period shorter than period t (usually t_0 is the present).

$$\text{Log}S_t - \text{Log}S_{t0} = \int_{t0}^{t} \left(\mu - \frac{\sigma^2}{2} \right) dr + \sigma \int_{0}^{t} dW_r$$

$$= \left(\mu - \frac{\sigma^2}{2} \right)(t - t_0) + \sigma(W_t - W_{t0})$$

This leads to:

$$S_t = S_{t_0} e^{(\mu - \sigma^2/2)(t - t_0) + \sigma\sqrt{(t - t_0)}u} \tag{7}$$

Equation (7) is used with most of the option pricing tools in this book. In addition, (7) satisfies

$$E_0(S_t) = S_{t_0} e^{(\mu - \sigma^2/2)(t - t_0)} \int_{-\infty}^{\infty} e^{\sigma\sqrt{(t - t_0)}u} n(u)du \tag{8}$$

$$= S_{t_0} e^{(\mu - \sigma^2/2)(t - t_0)} e^{\sigma^2/2(t - t_0)}$$

since the right integral in (8) is the moment-generating function M of the Gaussian distribution

$$\int_{-\infty}^{\infty} e^{\sigma\sqrt{(t - t_0)}u} n(u)du = M_{\sigma\sqrt{(t - t_0)}}(u) = e^{\sigma^2(t - t_0)}$$

hence

$$E_0(S_t) = S_{t_0} e^{\mu(t - t_0)} \tag{9}$$

With the results, operators can proceed to price options, in several ways.

- By using the Black-Scholes (1973) argument of delta neutrality leading us to ignore the utility curve of operators and possible risk premiums establishing that $\mu = r$. The argument will be displayed further down.

- A more modern method consists in using the Harrison and Kreps (1979) and Harrison and Pliska (1981) generalization that allows the extension of the previous argument to any type of contingent claims, under some conditions of **market completeness** (as far as all of the instrument affecting the derivative are concerned) that can easily be summarized as: *allowing full replication through dynamic (hence static) hedging*.

- Other methods, such as Feynman-Kac, which are being used in modern finance to integrate Ito's lemma and derive an underlying process under risk-neutralized paths.

The Feynman-Kac solution of a large class of stochastic differential equations as the probabilistic expectation of a function (under some regularity conditions on the drift and the variance, see Dana and Jeanblanc-Piqué, 1994 for a clear review) allows operators to use **probabilistic methods,** rather than the more burdening (and less intuitive) partial differential equations, in order to tackle option pricing. More simply, one can price a path independent option (and a large class of soft path dependent options such as barriers) as the expectation of the terminal payoff **assuming that the asset price follows a risk neutral diffusion.** The solution is then said that

$$\exp\left(-r\left(t-t_0\right)\right) E^Q \{f(S)\}$$

for a path independent option, and

$$\exp\left(-r\left(t-t_0\right)\right) E^Q \{f(S)/t < \tau\}$$

for a soft path dependent one (like a barrier), with Q the risk neutral probability measure, $f(S)$ the final payoff function, t the time to expiration and τ the stopping time (when hitting the barrier). It facilitates Monte Carlo methods (of averaging the payoffs in a series of random paths). It presents the special advantage of allowing the use of numerical integration, a method which this author finds extremely flexible to program (owing to the widely available subroutines). Numerical integration can be lengthier in computer time but saves in considerable programming labor and presents a smaller error rate.

The operator can go about his business, provided he can ascertain that $E_0\left(S(t)\right)$ is risk neutral.

Ito's Lemma for Two Assets

It is easy to generalize Ito's lemma to multiple assets (Table G.1)

The example can be speeded up by showing the results of a function of two Ito processes and time:

$$dF = \frac{\partial F}{\partial t}\, dt + \frac{\partial F}{\partial W_1}\, dW_1 + \frac{\partial F}{\partial W_2}\, dW_2 + \frac{\partial^2 F}{\partial W_1 \partial W_2}\, dW_1 dW_2$$

with σ_1 and σ_2 the volatility of each asset W_1 and W_2 and ρ the correlation between their moves.

Table G.1   Two-Asset Ito Multiplication Table

	dt	dW_1	dW_2
dt	0	0	0
dW_1	0	$\sigma_1^2\, dt$	$\rho\,\sigma_1\sigma_2 dt$
dW_2	0	$\rho\,\sigma_1\sigma_2 dt$	$\sigma_2^2 dt$

BLACK-SCHOLES EQUATION

The Risk-Neutral Argument

First it is necessary to get the drift out of the equation. Say that the operator sold a European call C on a dividend paying asset S and bought a bond B with the proceeds.[2] The bond pays r, the underlying asset is r, the asset is expected to return μ rate of return. The call is defined as the Max(S-K, 0) and expires at period t.

Say that the operator would remain delta neutral at all times. So he would have on his balance sheet the following portfolio P composed of:

$$P = -C + \partial C/\partial S\; S + B = 0$$

hence

$$B = C - \partial C/\partial S\; S$$

and would have B equal of the difference between the cash raised from the call and the dollars invested in the stock S. The portfolio earns interest at the risk-free rate and earns dividends on the stock held. Setting $\Delta P = 0$ for the portfolio to be cash-flow insensitive, gives:

$$-\Delta C + \partial C/\partial S \times \Delta S + \Delta B = 0$$

so, for infinitesimally small increments and using Ito's expansion:

$$-\partial C/\partial t\; dt - \partial C/\partial S\; dS - \tfrac{1}{2}\; \partial^2 C/\partial S^2 dS^2 + \partial C/\partial S \times dS + dB = 0$$

with

$dS = S\,(\mu\, dt + \sigma\, dW)$

$dS^2 = S^2\,(\mu\, dt + \sigma dZ)^2 = S^2\sigma^2 dt$ from the Ito multiplication tables

$dB = rB$, the interest earned on the bond portfolio (or paid, if negative)

$dB = (r\,C - \partial C/\partial S\; S\, r - \partial C/\partial S\; S\, d)\, dt = r\,C\, dt - \partial C/\partial S\; S\,(r - d)\, dt$

Thus:

$$-\partial C/\partial t\; dt - \tfrac{1}{2}\partial^2 C/\partial S^2\; S^2\sigma^2 dt + r\,C\, dt - \partial C/\partial S\; S\,(r - d)\, dt = 0$$

hence:

$$\partial C/\partial t + \tfrac{1}{2}\partial^2 C/\partial S^2\; S^2\sigma^2 - r\,C + \partial C/\partial S\; S\,(r - d) = 0 \qquad (10)$$

One can see dS coming out of the equation, along with μ. The only rates left are the risk-free and the payout rate.

From here on, m will be called the risk-neutral drift, equivalent to $r - d$. The operator can proceed and price the differential equation (10) under boundary conditions. Or he could integrate the diffusion to yield the same results as before in (7) but with $(r - d)$ in place of μ:

$$C = \exp\left(-r(t - t_0)\right) \int_{-\infty}^{\infty} \max\left(S_{t_0} \exp(r - d) - \frac{\sigma^2}{2}(t - t_0)\right.$$
$$\left. + \sigma\sqrt{(t - t_0)}\, x - K_0\right) n(x)d(x)$$

x being a centered Gaussian random variable. The solution for the integral from here is tedious but only requires slight manipulations. Users end up with the value of the call, using $t_0 = 0$ to simplify as:

$$C = \exp(-dt)\, S_0 N(d1) - \exp(-rt)\, K\, N(d2)$$

with:

$$d1 = [\log(S_0/K) + (r - d)t]/[\sigma\sqrt{t}] + \sigma\sqrt{t}/2$$
$$d2 = [\log(S_0/K) + (r - d)t]/[\sigma\sqrt{t}] - \sigma\sqrt{t}/2$$

A numeraire change will easily give the put value. The put/call parity rules can also be used to derive it as a mirror image to the call.

Following are the formulas and techniques used in the book. Most of the thrust was on numerical methods as the author—thanks to a Pentium chip received as a birthday gift—did not need to find closed form solutions to many of the exotic options and the stochastic volatility model.

Most of the numerical methods implemented were part of a Mathematica™ Nintegrate command that is based on the Konrod quadrature method. One integrates between −5 and 5 in lieu of positive or negative infinity as the error beyond becomes very small. These methods are outperforming in cases where early exercise is excluded and mix rather well with options priced partially analytically. Being still a trader, the author did not have to subscribe to academic elegance and drew on the comfort of computer power.

STOCHASTIC VOLATILITY MODEL

It is assumed that both the security and the volatility follow a Brownian motion. This is to illustrate the effect of heteroskedasticity on option prices. The process is being used for simple purpose: to gauge the value of the portfolio at expiration assuming the operator hedged both the delta and the gamma of the options. It is inspired by stochastic volatility models, such as

Hull and White[3] (1987), that did attempt to replicate the volatility in a risk-neutral way (through the buying and selling of options), akin to the Black-Scholes method for the asset itself. This formula assumes that there exists a risk-neutral replication, which allows for Feynman-Kac final payoff pricing. As the model below assumes independence between asset return and volatility, a numerical "fudge" is provided that considers that the quadratic norm of the volatility process

$$\sigma_t = \sqrt{\frac{1}{t - t_0} \int_{t0}^{t} \sigma_s^2 ds}$$

could be numerically computed as one single evolution between t_0 and t.

$$S_t = S_0 \exp (r - d)(t - t_0) - \frac{1}{2} \int_{t0}^{t} \sigma_s^2 ds + \sqrt{\frac{1}{t - t_0} \int_{t0}^{t} \sigma_s^2 ds} \sqrt{(t - t_0)z}$$

$$\sqrt{\frac{1}{t - t_0} \int_{t0}^{t} \sigma_s^2 ds} = \sigma_0 \exp \left(-\frac{1}{2} V^2 (t - t_0) + V \sqrt{t - t_0} z' \right)$$

r is the risk-free rate, d the counterrate (foreign rate for a currency, dividend rate for a stock, etc.), S_t the asset price at time t, $\sigma(t)$ the volatility of the asset at time t; V is the standard deviation of volatility; z and z' are Wiener processes each independent and normally distributed with 0 mean and unit variance.

For simplification, assume that $t_0 = 0$. The no-free lunch rules must be satisfied:

$$E_0(S_t) = \int_{-\infty}^{\infty} \int_{-\infty}^{\infty} S_t n(z) n(z') dz dz' = S_0 e^{(r - d)t}$$

$$E_0(\sigma_t) = \int_{-\infty}^{\infty} \sigma_t n(z') dz' = \sigma_0$$

$n(z)$ is the normal density function of z with mean 0 and variance 1.

Another simplification is to make the expectation uniform with time, in order not to include a term structure of volatility. This allows the use of a model for the values from period t only.

The price of the European option follows:

option(S_t, K, σ, r, d, vvol)

$$= \exp (- rt) \int_{-\infty}^{\infty} \int_{-\infty}^{\infty} \text{Max}(\Phi S_t - \Phi K, 0) n(z) n(z') dz dz'$$

With $\Phi = 1$ when the option is a call and $\Phi = -1$ when the option is a put. The double integral could be simplified by integrating a Black-Scholes-Merton call over different σ_t.

As usual, numerical integration methods are used, using the Mathematica™ that this author received for the holidays. The table of the results was presented in Chapter 15.

MULTIASSET OPTIONS

Take two assets A and B. The risk neutral process will be:

$$S_A(t) = S_{A0} \exp((r - d_A - \frac{1}{2}\sigma_A(t)^2)(t - t_0) + \sigma_a \sqrt{t - t_0}z)$$

$$S_B(t) = S_{B0} \exp((r - d_B - \frac{1}{2}\sigma_B(t)^2(t - t_0) + \sigma_B \sqrt{t - t_0}(\rho z + \sqrt{1 - \rho^2}z')))$$

r is the risk-free rate; d_A the counterrate for asset A (foreign rate for a currency, dividend rate for a stock, etc.); $S_A(t)$ and $S_B(t)$ the asset prices A and B respectively at time t; σ_A and σ_B the volatilities of assets A and B respectively; z and z Wiener processes each independent and normally distributed with 0 mean and unit variance; ρ the instantaneous correlation between A and B.

With the following model, traders can price several varieties of multiasset options using expectation of final payoff thanks to Feynman-Kac.

To add a third asset C, the same process would take place, but with C depending on a Wiener process.

$$S_c(t) = S_{c0} \exp ((r - d_c - \frac{1}{2}\sigma_c(t)^2)(t - t_0) + \sigma_c \sqrt{t - t_0} LZ)$$

where L is the (3,1) vector that is the 3rd row of C, the (3,3) lower triangular Cholesky decomposition such that $C\ C^T$ becomes the correlation matrix of the returns of the 3 securities and Z is the vector composed of z, z' and the additional z''' for asset C.

Rainbow Options

They are options on two assets with one strike price:

option$(S_{A0}(t), S_{B0}(t), K_A, K_B, \sigma_A, \sigma_B, r, d_A, d_B)$

$$= \exp(- rt) \int_{-\infty}^{\infty}\int_{-\infty}^{\infty} Max(\Phi_A S_A(t) - \Phi_A K_A, \Phi_B S_B(t) - \Phi_B K_{AB}, 0)n(z)n(z')dzdz'$$

With $\Phi_A = 1$ when the option is a call and $\Phi_A = -1$ when the option is a put, $n(z)$ the normal density function with mean 0 and variance 1. We assume for simplification in the rest of the module that $t_0 = 0$.

Outperformance Options

$$\text{option}(S_{A0}(t), S_{B0}(t), \sigma_A, \sigma_B, r, d_A, d_B)$$

$$= \exp(-rt) \int_{-\infty}^{\infty} \int_{-\infty}^{\infty} Max(S_A(t) - S_B(t), S_B(t) - S_A(t)) n(z) n(z') dz dz'$$

Spread Options

$$\text{option}(S_{A0}(t), S_{B0}(t), K, \sigma_A, \sigma_B, r, d_A, d_B)$$

$$= \exp(-rt) \int_{-\infty}^{\infty} \int_{-\infty}^{\infty} Max((\Phi S_A(t) - \Phi S_B(t)) - \Phi K, 0) n(z) n(z') dz dz'$$

with K the strike price of the spread defined as $S_A - S_B$ and $\Phi = 1$ when the option is a call on the spread and $\Phi = -1$ when the option is a put on the spread.

COMPOUND AND CHOOSER ORDER OPTIONS

Unlike before, the formulas introduce a term structure of volatility, interest, and carry rates. The same univariate process is used as before, with:

K_2 the strike price of the "mother" options.
Φ_2 equals 1 if the mother is a put, -1 if it is a call.
t_2 is the time to expiration of the mother option.
K_1 is the strike price of the "daughter" options.
Φ_1 equals 1 if the daughter is a put, -1 if it is a call.
t_1 is the time to expiration of the daughter option.

In addition to the conventional models, the following will be included:

σ_1 and σ_2, r_1 and r_2, d_1 and d_2, respectively the spot volatility and interest rates until the expiration of the daughter and the forward (or forward-forward) between the expiration of the daughter and that of the mother.

These rates are not the spot rates in the market but need to be derived using forward-forward break-even formulas, such as the forward volatility described in Chapter 9.

Compound Options

The compound option will be priced as:

$$\text{Compound}(S_0, \Phi_1 K_1, \sigma_1, r_1, d_1, \Phi_2 K_2, \sigma_2, r_2, d_2)$$

$$= \int_{-\infty}^{\infty} \text{Max}(\Phi_1 BS(S_2, \Phi_2 K_2, \sigma_2, r_2, d_2) - \Phi_1 K_1, 0) n(z) dz$$

with BS a Black-Scholes-Merton vanilla and

$$S_2 = S_0 \exp(r_1 - d_1 - \frac{1}{2}\sigma^2 + \sigma_1 \sqrt{t_1} z)$$

Chooser Options

Integrate the Max(Put, Call), using BSP as the Black-Scholes-Merton valued put and BSC the call keeping the same notations as well as the same notion of forward-forward interest rates and volatilities between the exercise date of the mother and that of the daughter:

$$\text{Chooser}(S_0, K, \sigma_1, r_1, d_1, \sigma_2, r_2, d_2)$$

$$= \int_{-\infty}^{\infty} \text{Max}(BSC(S_2, K, \sigma_2, r_2, d_2), BSP(S_2, K, \sigma_2, r_2, d_2)) n(z) dz$$

with

$$S_2 = S_0 \exp(r_1 - d_1 - \frac{1}{2}\sigma^2 + \sigma_1 \sqrt{t_1} z)$$

BARRIER OPTIONS

There are two ways to price barrier options. The first, most intuitive, way, is to approach it through stopping time and say that the option is the Feynman-Kac expectation under risk neutral probability Q, times the risk neutral probability of the option not being knocked-out before expiration (which is equivalent to the probability of stopping time being longer than expiration). The second, more convenient, is to use the reflection principle as described in Chapter 19, which allows for simple results with single barriers.

It is worthy to note that the study of the joint distribution of the triplet (upper range, lower range, Brownian motion) was investigated early on in probability theory. Its premonition was attributed to a later (and no less precursor) Bachelier by Geman and Yor (1996). More recent results for option pricing were obtained by Kunitomo and Ikeda (1992).

Thanks to the reflection principle and the Girsanov theorem, one can use closed form solutions for barriers. There are two classes of pricing formulas for barriers:

1. Closed form Black-Scholes-Merton based formulas, unfortunately weak because they assume constant volatility and constant interest rates between time 0 and expiration, a method that misprices options when there is either a sloping implied volatility or interest rate curve.

2. Numerical methods, none of which is presently in the public domain. They range from heavy-duty Monte Carlo simulators to trees with accurate local volatility between the nodes.

The Reflection Principle

As described in Chapter 19, the reflection principle allows users to determine the number of conditional Brownian paths between two points. It will be used here to compute the risk-neutral probability density of the paths that reach a given destination *without going through* the barrier. They will be the complement (i.e., the sum equals 100%) of:

- The number of paths that reach a destination going through the barrier (the difference between knock-in and knock-out).

- The number of paths that do not reach the final destination.

Let W_t be defined as a standard Brownian motion (0 drift) and l a given limit underneath it. The reflection principle (see Karatzas and Shreve, 1991; Grimmet and Stirzaker, 1992; Lamberton and Lapeyre, 1991) allows the following transformation:

$$W\hat{}_t = W_t \text{ if the barrier is not touched,}$$

and

$$W\hat{}_t = 2l - W_t \text{ if the barrier is touched.}$$

Hence, options can be priced using the difference between the two processes as described in Chapter 19. However, a hitch would appear if there is a drift, which forces us to use the Girsanov theorem.

Girsanov's Theorem

What Girsanov's theorem allows users is to create a new fictitious probability density to replace the previous one, the new density being the risk-neutral one.[4] Most presentations of Girsanov present arduous features whereas, explained to traders, it appears rather simpler to digest once stripped of measure theory. A stripped-down version of the theorem is presented here as it becomes a lot less complicated in situations where the drift is constant.

The principal result is that it eliminates the drift and, instead, integrates it within the probability distribution by shifting the expectation accordingly.

Define W_t as a standard Brownian motion with (0 drift and unit variance) under a probability measure P.

Girsanov's theorem establishes that the process defined by

$$W'_t = \lambda t + W_t$$

a standard Brownian motion under probability measure Q_t with Radon-Nikodym derivative:

$$dQ_t/dP = \exp{(\tfrac{1}{2}\lambda^2 t - \lambda W'_t)}$$

A function V of the payoff of a Brownian motion (i.e., a derivative security) will be priced so its expectation under probability measure Q is the expectation under probability measure P times the derivative of the two measures:

$$E^Q(V) = E^P(dQ_t/dP\ V)$$

so

$$E^Q(V) = E^P(\exp{(\tfrac{1}{2}\lambda^2 t - \lambda W'_t)}\ V)$$

With these elements, the reader can build the pricing intuition for barrier options.

Pricing Barriers

The results below are inspired by Douady (1996).

The trader begins with the call up-and-out and builds the intuition of the pricing:

- Call up-and-out CUO = Under probability measure P (risk-neutral), the discounted, by $\exp(-rt)$, expectation of the Max $(S - K, 0)$ as before with the Black-Scholes-Merton formula, but *conditional* on the barrier H_L not being touched.

Therefore, the trader should start with $S_0 < H$; otherwise the option would be terminated from the beginning. Hence, using Girsanov, the process $W'_t = 1/\sigma \log(S_t/S_0)$ is a Brownian motion without drift under the probability:

$$Q_t = \exp\left(\frac{1}{2}\lambda^2 t - \lambda W'_t\right) P$$

with $\lambda = (r - d)/\sigma - \sigma/2$

Hence,

- CUO = Under probability measure Q, $\exp(- rt)$ times the expectation of the $\exp(- \frac{1}{2}\lambda^2 t - \lambda/\sigma\log(S_t/S_0))$ times (Max $(S - K, 0)$, *conditional* on the barrier H not being touched.
- Using the reflection principle, the density of the process (under Q) of S_t is, conditional on the barrier H_H not being touched, equal to that of the process of H^2/S_t.

This allows jumping to:

- CUO = Expected (discounted) price of distribution of the $S_t > K$ minus the expected price of the paths that touch the barrier H:

$$CUO = \exp(- rt)\,(P1 - P2),$$

with

$$P1 = \int_k^h \exp(-\frac{1}{2}\,\lambda^2 t + \lambda\sqrt{t}\,z)\,(S_0\,\exp(\sigma\,\sqrt{t}z - K)\,n(z)dz$$

$$P2 = \int_k^h \exp(-\frac{1}{2}\lambda^2 t + \lambda\sqrt{t}\,z)\,(S_0\,\exp(\sigma\,\sqrt{t}z - K)\,n(2h - z)dz$$

with

$$h = \left(1/\left(\sigma\sqrt{t}\right)\right)\log\,(H/S_0)$$

$$k = \left(1/\left(\sigma\sqrt{t}\right)\right)\log\,(K/S_0)$$

Setting

$$\lambda' = \lambda + \sigma = (r - d)/\sigma + \sigma/2$$
$$\alpha = (H/S_0)^{2\lambda/\sigma}$$
$$\alpha' = (H/S_0)^{2\lambda'/\sigma}$$
$$d_1 = \lambda'\sqrt{t} - k$$
$$d_2 = \lambda\sqrt{t} - k$$
$$d_3 = \lambda'\sqrt{t} - h$$
$$d_4 = \lambda\sqrt{t} - h$$
$$d_5 = -\lambda\sqrt{t} - h$$
$$d_6 = -\lambda'\sqrt{t} - h$$
$$d_7 = -\lambda\sqrt{t} - 2h + k$$
$$d_8 = -\lambda'\sqrt{t} - 2h + k$$

$$\text{and } N(d_1) = \textit{cumulative normal distribution of } d_1$$

$$\int_K^h \exp\left(-\frac{1}{2}\lambda^2 t + \lambda\sqrt{t}\,z\right) n(z)\, dz = N(-d_4) - N(-d_2) = N(d_2) - N(d_4)$$

$$\int_K^h \exp\left(-\frac{1}{2}\lambda^2 t + \lambda'\sqrt{t}z\right) n(z)\, dz = \exp\{(r-d)t\}(N(d_1) - N(d_3))$$

$$\int_K^h \exp\left(-\frac{1}{2}\lambda^2 t + \lambda\sqrt{t}z\right) n(2h - z)\, dz = \alpha(N(d_5) - N(d_7))$$

$$\int_K^h \exp\left(-\frac{1}{2}\lambda^2 t + \lambda'\sqrt{t}z\right) n(2h - z)\, dz = \alpha'\exp((2-d)t)(N(d_6) - N(d_8))$$

This leads to the following formulas.

Calls Up-and-Out.

$$\begin{aligned}
\text{CUO} = {}& \exp\{(-d)t\}S_0\{N(d_1) - N(d_3) - \alpha'(N(d_6) \\
& - N(d_8))\} - K\exp(-rt)\{N(d_2) - N(d_4) \\
& - \alpha(N(d_5) - N(d_7))\}
\end{aligned}$$

Using the technique, we can extend to all other options.

Calls Up-and-In.   Calls up-and-in are synthetically vanilla calls minus calls up-and-out. Hence:

$$\begin{aligned}
\text{CUI} = {}& \exp\{(-d)t\}\, S_0\, \{N(d_3) + \alpha'(N(d_6) - N(d_8))\} \\
& - K\exp(-rt)\{N(d_4) + \alpha(N(d_5) - N(d_7))\}
\end{aligned}$$

Puts Down-and-Out.   Puts down-and-out are priced like the call up-and-out but by an exact change of numeraire, which reverses the sign of the integral. Hence:

$$\begin{aligned}
\text{PDO} = {}& K\exp(-r\,t)\{N(d_4) - N(d_2) - \alpha(N(d_7) - N(d_5))\} \\
& - \exp(-d\,t)\,S_0\{N(d_3) - N(d_1) - \alpha'(N(d_8) - N(d_6))\}
\end{aligned}$$

Puts Down-and-In.

$$\begin{aligned}
\text{PDI} = {}& K\exp(-r\,t)\{1 - N(d_4) + \alpha(N(d_7) - N(d_5))\} \\
& - \exp(-d)t\,S_0\{1 - N(d_3) - \alpha'(N(d_8) - N(d_6))\}
\end{aligned}$$

Calls Down-and-Out.   Calls down-and-out will be priced in two different ways: When they are out-of-the-money (i.e., the strike K is higher than H) or when they knock-out with intrinsic.

Case 1: $K \geq H$

$$\text{CDO}_{K \geq H} = \exp\{(-d)t\}S_0\{N(d_1) - \alpha'(1 - N(d_8))\}$$
$$- K\exp(-rt)\{N(d_2) - \alpha(1 - N(d_7))\}$$

Case 2: $K \leq H$

$$\text{CDO}_{K \leq H} = \exp\{(-d)t\}\ S_0\ \{N(d_3) - \alpha'(1 - N(d_6))\}$$
$$- K\exp(-rt)\{N(d_4) - \alpha(1 - N(d_5))\}$$

Calls Down-and-In.   The same is true with calls down-and-in:

Case 1: $K \geq H$

$$\text{CDI}_{K \geq H} = \exp\{(-d)t\}\ S_0\ \alpha'(1 - N(d_8))$$
$$- K\exp(-rt)\ \alpha(1 - N(d_7))$$

Case 2: $K \leq H$

$$\text{CDI}_{K \leq H} = \exp\{(-d)t\}S_0\{N(d_1) - N(d_3) + \alpha'(1 - N(d_6))\}$$
$$- K\exp(-rt)\{N(d_2) - N(d_4) + \alpha(1 - N(d_5))\}$$

Puts Up-and-Out.

Case 1: $K \geq H$

$$\text{PUO}_{K \geq H} = K\exp(-rt)\{1 - N(d_2) - \alpha(N(d_7) - N(d_5))\}$$
$$- \exp(-d)t\ S_0\{1 - N(d_1) - \alpha'(N(d_8))\}$$

Case 2: $K \leq H$

$$\text{PUO}_{K \leq H} = K\exp(-rt)\{1 - N(d_4) - \alpha\ N(d_5)\}$$
$$- \exp(-d)t\ S_0\{1 - N(d_3) - \alpha'N(d_6)\}$$

Puts Up-and-In.   It is a natural option algebra equivalent to the vanilla *minus* the PUO. We know that if $S_0 > H$ it will be considered knocked-in and would be valued at exactly the same equivalent price as the vanilla option. Otherwise it will be:

Case 1: $K \geq H$

$$\text{PUI}_{K \geq H} = K \exp(-r\,t)\{N(d_4) - N(d_2) + \alpha N(d_5))\}$$
$$- \exp(-dt)S_0\{N(d_3) - N(d_1) + a'N(d_6)\}$$

Case 2: $K \leq H$

$$\text{PUI}_{K \leq H} = K\{\exp(-r\,t)\alpha N(d_5)\} - \exp(-dt)S_0\{1 - N(d_3) - \alpha'N(d_6)\}$$

Rebates and American Barrier Options. The SDF of a barrier *cum* rebate is a barrier without rebate (priced with the formulas above) *plus* an American binary option.

Calls Double Knock-Out. Geman and Yor (1996) offer a new methodology based on excursions theory to provide the Laplace transform of double barrier options, which can be inverted using the Geman-Eydeland technique. Below is the earlier Kunitomo-Ikeda model. Use a high barrier H_H and a low barrier H_L.
Set:

$$h_H = 1/\sigma\sqrt{t} \log (H_H/S_0)$$
$$h_L = 1/\sigma\sqrt{t} \log (H_L/S_0)$$
$$\delta = h_H - h_L$$

Case 1: $H_L < K < H_H$

$$\text{CDB}_{HL < K < HH} = \exp(-dt)S_0 \sum_{n=-\infty}^{\infty} I_n(\lambda'\sqrt{t}) - J_n(\lambda'\sqrt{t})$$
$$- \exp(-rt)\,K \sum_{n=-\infty}^{\infty} I_n(\lambda\sqrt{t}) - J_n(\lambda\sqrt{t})$$

with

$$I_n(x) = \exp(-2nx\delta)\,(N(h_h + 2n\delta - x) - N(k + 2n\delta - x))$$
$$J_n(x) = \exp\{2x(n\delta + h_h)\}\,(N(2h_h - k + 2n\delta + x) - N(h_H + 2n\delta - x))$$

Note that the summation converges rapidly and $-\infty$ can be replaced by -12, $+\infty$ by $+12$.

Case 2: $K \leq H_L$

$$\text{CDB}_{K \leq H_L} = \exp(-dt)S_0 \sum_{n=-\infty}^{\infty} I_n(\lambda' \sqrt{t}) - J_n(\lambda' \sqrt{t})$$
$$- \exp(-rt) K \sum_{n=-\infty}^{\infty} I_n(\lambda\sqrt{t}) - J_n(\lambda\sqrt{t})$$

(same as before) with

$$I_n(x) = \exp(-2nx\delta)\,(N(h_H + 2n\delta - x) - N(h_H + (2n-1)\delta - x))$$
$$J_n(x) = \exp\{2x(n\delta + h_H)\,(N(h_H + (2n+1)\delta + x) - N(h_H + 2n\delta + x))$$

Puts Double Knock-Out.

Case 1: $H_L < K < H_H$

$$\text{PDB}_{H_L < K < H_H} = \exp(-rt) K \sum_{n=-\infty}^{\infty} I_n(\lambda\sqrt{t}) - J_n(\lambda\sqrt{t})$$
$$- \exp(-dt)S_0 \sum_{n=-\infty}^{\infty} I_n(\lambda' \sqrt{t}) - J_n(\lambda' \sqrt{t})$$

with

$$I_n(x) = \exp(-2nx\delta)\,(N(k + 2n\delta - x) - N(h_h + (2n-1)\delta - x))$$
$$J_n(x) = \exp\{2x(n\delta + h_h)\,(N(h_h + (2n+1)\delta + x) - N(2h_H - k + 2n\delta + x))$$

Case 2: $H_H \leq K$

$$\text{PDB}_{H_H \leq K} = \exp(-rt) K \sum_{n=-\infty}^{\infty} I_n(\lambda\sqrt{t}) - J_n(\lambda\sqrt{t})$$
$$- \exp(-dt)S_0 \sum_{n=-\infty}^{\infty} I_n(\lambda' \sqrt{t}) - J_n(\lambda' \sqrt{t})$$

(same as before) with

$$I_n(x) = \exp(-2nx\delta)\,(N(h_H + 2n\delta - x) - N(h_H + (2n-1)\delta - x))$$
$$J_n(x) = \exp\{2x(n\delta + h_H)\,(N(h_H + (2n+1)\,\delta + x) - N(h_H + 2n\delta + x))$$

Pricing Double Binary Options. In this book, the author tricked the preceding formulas for double barriers by pricing for situations where the option is deep in the money (the payoff becomes equal to intrinsic at trigger time). Deep calls were selected with strike close to 0.

Stopping Time and Its Expectation. The author avoided introducing stopping time in the analysis of barrier options in order to build on the intuitive approach of the reflection principle. Most papers introduce it in the derivation of the pricing of any barrier. The following formula is the calculation for the stopping time and its expectation.

Take as before $\lambda = (r - d)/\sigma - \sigma/2$ and the barrier $h = 1/\sigma \log H/S_0$, with H the barrier. The density of the unconditional stopping time is given with no drift:

$$P_H(t) = \left(h/\sqrt{2\pi t^3}\right)\exp(-h^2/2t)$$

and, adding the drift:

$$P_H(t) = \left(h/\sqrt{2\pi t^3}\right)\exp(\lambda h - \lambda^2 t/2 - h^2/2t)$$

As to the expectation of the exit time, that is the distribution of the minimum of τ the exit time and the time to expiration T:

$$E(\tau^T_H) = h/\lambda + (T - h/\lambda)\, N(h/\sqrt{T} - \lambda\sqrt{T})$$
$$- \exp(2\lambda h)(T + h/\lambda)\, N(-h/\sqrt{T} - \lambda\sqrt{T})$$

With a double barrier, the following can be computed.

$$h = 1/\sigma \log H/S_0$$

$$l = 1/\sigma \log L/S_0$$

The following formula provides the density of stopping line (starting inside the range).

$$P_{HL}(\tau) = \frac{\pi}{(h - l)^2}\exp\left(-\frac{\lambda^2}{2}t\right)\sum_{n=1}^{\infty}(-1)^{n-1}n\exp\left(-\frac{n^2\pi^2 t}{2(h - l)^2}\right)$$
$$\left(\exp(\lambda l)\sin n\pi\, \frac{h}{h - l} - \exp(\lambda h)\sin n\pi \frac{l}{h - l}\right)$$

As to its expectation, the user can break it up

$$E(\min\tau^T_{HL}) = E(\tau_{HL}) - D_T$$

where

$$E(\tau_{HL}) = ((h - l)(\exp(\lambda h)\sinh \lambda h - \exp(\lambda l)\sinh \lambda l)\cosh \lambda(h - l)$$
$$- (h\exp(\lambda l)\cosh \lambda h - l\exp(\lambda h)\cosh \lambda l)\sinh \lambda\,(h - l))/\lambda\sinh^2 \lambda(h - l)$$

$$D_T = \frac{\pi}{(h-l)^2} \sum_{n=1}^{\infty} (-1)^{n-1} \, n \, \frac{\exp(-u_n T)}{u_n^2} \, (\exp(\lambda l) \sin \frac{n\pi h}{h-l}$$

$$- \exp(\lambda h) \sin \frac{n\pi l}{h-l})$$

and

$$u_n = \frac{n^2 \pi^2}{2(h-l)^2} + \lambda^2$$

NUMERICAL STOCHASTIC INTEGRATION: A SAMPLE

A Mathematica™ Program

This program illustrates a general option pricing method that will gain in currency as the computer chip war rages on. The author used such integration techniques to find the numerical expectation of a stochastic integral.

```
(*Homoskedastic compound options*)
(*Nassim Taleb*)
gauss[x_]: = Exp[−x^2/2]/(Sqrt[2*Pi]);
Gauss[x_]: = (1 + Erf[x/Sqrt[2]])/2;
St[S_,x_,t1_,sig_]: = S Exp [sig Sqrt[t1] x]
(*computing Black-Scholes with no drift*)
d1[S_,k_,sig_,t1_]: = (Log[S/k] + sig^2(t1)/2)/(sig*Sqrt[t1]);
d2(S_,k_,sig_,t1_]: = (Log[S/k] − sig^2(t1)/2)/(sig*Sqrt[t1]);
call[S_,k_,sig_,t1_]: = S*Gauss[d1[S,k,sig,t1]] − k*Gauss[d2[S,k,sig,t1]]
put[S_,k_,sig_,t1_]: = call[S,k,sig,t1] − (S − k)
(*compound option*)
callcallpayoff[S_,k_,kopt_,sig_,x_,t1_,tint_]: = Max[call[S Exp[sig
Sqrt[tint] x],k,sig,(t1 − tint)] − kopt,0]
callcall[S_,k_,kopt_,sig_,t1_,tint_]: = NIntegrate[ callcallpayoff[S,k,kopt,
sig,x,t1,tint] gauss[x], {x, −4,4}]
(*for precision-minded people increase the integration band to −6 to 6*)
(*adding the drift is straight forward*)
```

Notes

PREFACE

1. This represents about 60 transactions per business day and the examination of about two batches of reports per day (with an average of about 17 different reports representing the different markets in which I ran option books). The total corresponds to 95,000 trades in the currency options, 30,000 in equity indices, 30,000 in Eurodeposits (Eurodollars, PIBOR, Euroyen, Euromarks), 1,000 in commodities (live cattle, oil, . . .), and the rest in swaptions and long bond options. I traded only 2 options on mortgages. (I opened and closed the trade disgustingly on the same day).

2. Throughout this book, see Bibliography for full reference citations: See Soros (1987), Derman (1996).

3. Black-Scholes (1973); Merton (1973).

4. There are very few books written by practitioners. One notable entry-level text used by traders is Natenberg (1995). The reader would find the prerequisites to understand option trading from the standpoint of the "producer" (as opposed to the consumer or the amateur theorist).

5. This rescaling is compatible with the analytical option pricing formulas, (see Merton, 1973, for the theorems):

    Black-Scholes-Merton value $V(\lambda S, \lambda K, \sigma, r, d) = \lambda V(S, K, \sigma, r, d)$

    (Black-Scholes-Merton is homogeneous degree one in the underlying asset price and the strike price.)

    It is also homogeneous degree one in S, K, H_H, H_L, (H_H is the high barrier, H_L is a low barrier):

    $$V(\lambda S, \lambda K, \lambda H_H, \lambda H_L, \sigma, r, d) = \lambda V(S, K, H_H, H_L, \sigma, r, d)$$

INTRODUCTION

1. Leland (1985) provides a clear review of the literature on the issue of discrete time dynamic hedging. He shows that the replicating portfolio value, composed of long the asset and short the option will not be 0 at all times once we start hedging infrequently. The reader will see in the Module F that the Black-Scholes price is derived from a strategy that would make the P/L stay at 0 the entire time. In reality it is not possible to buy and sell continuously. So in place of the continuous dt we opt for Δt, the time lapse between hedging revisions. The P/L will be, however, 0 in expectation. The variance of the package, he verified, decreased by $\sqrt{2}$ when Δt was cut by half. Similar results can be obtained using the functional central limit theorems by showing that as the sample paths is divided in infinitely small fragments the variance of the P/L would (uniformly, no less) converge to 0.

    One alarming fact for modern financial theory is that the package has a variance. It looks just like any other risky security. In other words: option replication has risks, which requires compensation.

Chapter 1 Introduction to the Instruments

1. Trading them, however, can be done in such a way as to cause dependence on the correlation between parts and make them akin to multiasset options.

2. The bond future includes a hidden option (the right to choose).

3. Dixit and Pyndick (1994) study the application of option theory to corporate financial management.

4. Most traders think in terms of the forward while the quants think in terms of the cash since the Black-Scholes (1973) formula views an option price as a function of the cash price of the asset. Merton's (1973) approach is more compatible with traders' methods. This distortion can lead to mishedging in cases of currency bands.

5. American options complicate the solution of the Black-Scholes-Merton partial differential equation under, among other boundary conditions, the early exercise rules of $Q(t)$, an optimal exercise path where the derivative security is equal to $\phi(S - K)$. Such time-dependent boundary condition is causing much ink to flow. Worse, there might be two boundaries as will be shown.

6. More complex analysis would use stochastic interest rates and take into account the possibility of changes in the structure of the interest rate differential. On that, see Amin and Jarrow (1991) for a treatment of currency option pricing with stochastic interest rates.

7. There is, ironically, a flood of academic papers attempting to value American options precisely while parameters affecting their value are imprecise.

8. A simple application of Ito's lemma gives these results.

9. By convention, any rate r in this book will be the continuously compounded zero coupon rate.

10. While Eurodollars are quoted in $100 - \text{yield}$ for all purpose of analysis (like the computation of volatility and correlations), we use the derived yield as the variable.

Chapter 2 The Generalized Option

1. In Durett (1991).

2. J. Piper, O'Connel, and Piper seminar, Chicago, December 4, 1995. It is remarkable that some veteran equity traders fear the "bad distribution" to the point of refusing to touch a put. Such phobias are part of the traders survival toolkit.

3. More advanced analysis would show that it harbors a measure of shadow gamma and shadow delta, characteristics that will be discussed later in this book.

Chapter 3 Market Making and Market Using

1. This case is easily replicated in the real world where the trader buys a one-year at-the-money European binary option for $2.5 mil paying either zero or $5 mil at expiration if the SP500 closes at or above 668.00.

2. See Grossman and Miller (1988).

3. See Ho and Stroll (1980); Silber (1984); Garman (1976) and O'Hara (1995) for a review.

4. See D. Guillaume et al. (1995), Roll (1984).

5. Sampling of six currency market makers by the author, June 1995.
6. See Feller I (1968).
7. A clear way to view it is to compare the P/L of a trader to a Brownian motion with a drift. The real "skills" of the trader would correspond to the drift.

    Let P be the profits of the trader, with $P_0 = 0$, Z a Wiener process and σ the volatility of the trader's P/L:

    $$dP = \mu\, dt + \sigma dZ$$

    an arithmetic Brownian motion (the P can be allowed to be negative). The reader should view the μ as the "edge"; if he believes he has a 51% against 49% edge on the market during a given period of time, the drift is 2% of the net amounts involved. The σ is simply the volatility of the market in which the trader has the drift. It becomes clear that the volatility of the trader will dominate the drift in most cases. Counterintuitively, the σ will typically drown the μ.
8. Private conversation with the author, New York, April 1996.
9. See Dubins and Savage (1965). Also see Billingsley (1986).
10. A submartingale (the expected wealth next period is higher than that of the present).
11. A supermartingale (the expected wealth next period is lower than that of the present).
12. See Feller I (1968).
13. In one of the essays in Taleb (1997), I show that traders subjected to a stop loss present a high-right moment, a skewness with a small sample property that weakens the power of the Sharpe ratio.

CHAPTER 4   LIQUIDITY AND LIQUIDITY HOLES

1. There is an abundant market microstructure literature. The goal in this chapter is to portray liquidity from a practitioner's vantage point.
2. See the excellent and comprehensive review in Brock and de Lima (1995).
3. See Brock, Hsieh, and LeBaron (1991).
4. A Markov process is formally defined as: $P(X_n = s/X_0 = x_0, X_1 = x_1, \ldots, X_{n-1} = x_{n-1})$ $= P(X_n = s/X_{n-1} = x_{n-1})$ for all $n \geq 1$. It means that the conditional probability of the next price X_n depends only on the price preceding it, not the sequence of prices that led there.
5. At the time of this writing, it is five minutes of suspension if the open is within 500 points from the previous close, then half an hour if it is within 2000 points, then until the end of the session if the market hits the 3000 points third limit.
6. See Leland (1992).
7. Grossman (1988) distinguishes between strategies and securities and shows how an Arrow-Debreu state of nature cannot be replicated dynamically. Because of the way trades convey information, a real option will therefore present a different payoff than a program traded replication.
8. Implicit bid-offer spread is the true bid offer spread, and is wider than the visible, or explicit, bid-offer spread. It corresponds to the adjustment of the prices upward or downward in response to a large order.

CHAPTER 5   ARBITRAGE AND THE ARBITRAGEURS

1. These are applied definitions of arbitrage largely stripped of the dimension in micro-economics and financial theory. The text will introduce the notion of self-financing strategies in connection with option values.

2. Oxford English Dictionary (1971).

3. If there is a multivariate Ito process then the link is stochastic (see Module G) in terms of Z_1 through Z_n. If both securities share the same random component, then the link is deterministic.

4. It is uncertain whether one can use risk neutral probabilities when pricing the value of a passive arbitrage.

CHAPTER 6   VOLATILITY AND CORRELATION

1. The simplification is pedagogical but valid at the limit of very small increments. The process for asset prices $dS/S = \mu\, dt + \sigma\, dz$ with boundary $S(t_0) = S_0$ has for solution $\log\,(S_t/S_0) = (\mu - \tfrac{1}{2}\sigma^2)(t - t_0) + \sigma\,\sqrt{t - t_0}Z$, hence $S_t = S_0\,\exp\,((\mu - \tfrac{1}{2}\sigma^2)(t - t_0) + \sigma\,\sqrt{t - t_0}Z))$ with S the asset price, σ the volatility, t time, and Z a random variable normally distributed with unit variance and zero mean.

2. Some assets, according to Raphael Douady, can exhibit overgeometric behavior, with their volatility increasing in higher levels and decreasing at lower ones.

3. See Cox and Rubinstein (1985).

4. Some traders use μ, the risk-neutral drift in a commodity, as a mean, in accordance with the Black-Scholes-Merton prescription.

5. See Hamilton (1994) for a presentation of state-space models.

6. See Parkinson (1980); see Atilgan (1996). Notice that Cox and Rubinstein (1985) calculates the estimation of volatility based on the average S_H/S_L, which biases the estimator downward by a factor of 91%.

7. Option traders call gamma trading the subsequent delta adjustments emanating from a long or short gamma position.

8. See Taleb (1996b).

9. Lo and McKinley (1988).

10. There are many potent methods, such as the Brock-Dechert-Scheinckman BDS test of nonlinearity. The variance ratio is satisfactory enough for traders and risk managers to gain a knowledge of the structure of the volatility. See Brock, Hsieh, and LeBaron (1991) for a complete analysis of nonlinear dependence (including a presentation of the correlation integral).

11. See Kritzman (1994).

12. One should note that the variance ratio is another way to look at autocorrelation. It corresponds to the summation of the autocovariance function over the corresponding lags. For a good intuition, see Harvey (1993) and the excellent book by Bloomfield (1976).

CHAPTER 7   ADAPTING BLACK-SCHOLES-MERTON: THE DELTA

1. See Black (1988).

2. If pair (N, A) has a constant volatility (N is a numeraire) and pair (N, B) has a constant volatility, and pair (B, A) has a constant volatility, then the correlation between (N, A)

and (N, B) will be constant. When cross options trade heteroskedasticity means unstable correlations.

3. This is attributable to the issue of *discrete-time convergence*. Options, therefore, converge in value to Black-Scholes-Merton but not in the higher derivatives.

4. This is another facet of the *discrete-time convergence* problem. A binomial leads to a continuous time valuation of the option. But the delta and higher Greeks will not converge. This issue is easier to see with a portfolio of options.

5. Cash equivalent position = $\frac{\partial C}{\partial U} \Delta U + \frac{1}{2} \left(\frac{\partial^2 C}{\partial U^2} \right) \Delta U^2 + \frac{1}{6} \left(\frac{\partial^3 C}{\partial U^3} \right) \Delta U^3$ etc.

The Taylor expansion thus can be pushed to include, in addition to the delta, the gamma—the DgammaDspot (i.e., the stability of the gamma) in the measurement. But for a portfolio with many options, the expansion needs to cover higher and higher order derivatives to track the risks. It becomes intuitive that the VAR does not apply to a book. We will see in Chapter 11 why, since a book is not "compact" and since higher orders or ΔU do not vanish, we need more powerful ways to look at the risks.

CHAPTER 8   GAMMA AND SHADOW GAMMA

1. I owe the coining of the term "shadow gamma" to one of my former coworkers, Lenny Dundennen.

2. Sig(x) is the change in volatility resulting from the changes in asset price between x_0 and x.

3. Shadow gamma should not be confused with stochastic volatility techniques. Implied volatility here is defined to be a direct, deterministic function of the move as *predicted* by the trader and added to Black-Scholes-Merton. Traders can thus assert that volatility would be higher by 100 basis points should the market drop by 1% and establish a map of volatility changes. Another way to view the difference is that shadow gamma is concerned with implied volatility (as measured by Black-Scholes-Merton), whereas stochastic volatility is concerned with a pricing model that tracks more accurately the distribution of the actual volatility. The latter assumes that volatility is randomly distributed around some mean, similar to the underlying itself, often correlated with the asset price.

4. Organization for Economic Cooperation and Development.

5. European Rate Mechanism.

CHAPTER 9   VEGA AND THE VOLATILITY SURFACE

1. It is assumed that one Brownian motion affects the volatility for one maturity and that the rest of them follow in some known proportion.

2. Taleb (1996a).

3. The author's strong reservations about the value-at-risk system do not apply to the volatility curve for the following reasons: (1) This method is an aid in short-term hedging not worst-case scenario analysis. In the "tail" events, volatility buckets matter less than the gamma exposure getting there. In addition, the cross-vega generally vanishes in the tails; (2) this could be considered a *second-degree* value-at-risk method since the principal instrument is the expectation of the second moment.

4. This corresponds to the floor traders' designation of calendar spreads as "horizontal" and strike spreads as "vertical," with the mixture called "diagonal."

5. The local volatility is the volatility between two points with coordinates (S, t) and $(S + \Delta S, t + \Delta t)$. A local volatility between (S, t) and $(S, t + \Delta t)$ is called a forward volatility, as discussed earlier.

6. Dupire's (1996) volatility spot forward is expressed as $\sqrt{(2\partial F/\partial t)/(\partial^2 F/\partial K^2)}$ with K the strike price, F the derivative security value, and t time to expiration. The second derivative of the option price with respect to the strike presents what Breeden and Litzenberger (1978) deemed to be the *local* risk-neutral density of the underlying asset.

7. Some operators build the volatility surface as a function of the delta of the option instead of the spot/strike. We avoided the pitfall of having to determine the delta as it is well known that the delta is a function of volatility.

8. The following polynomial function was estimated:

$$x:\text{ time (days)},\; y = ln(fwd/K)$$

$$\text{Volatility} = 11.9257 + 0.110067\,\text{Sqrt}[x] + 5.77624\,y + 350.516\,y - /\,\text{Sqrt}[x]$$

$$+ 153.843\,y^2 - 1088.23\,y^3 - 1805.65\,y^4 + 21942.8\,y^5$$

CHAPTER 10   THETA AND MINOR GREEKS

1. For the pair numeraire-asset.

2. It is always preferable to derive the numerical, not the analytical, exposure for the rho. The analytical exposure would sum up the microscopic derivatives of every option multiplied by the size. The numerical method reprices the portfolio and can thus deal with changing derivatives.

3. This section can be skipped at first reading.

4. It can be computed using the classical Black-Scholes-Merton differential equation (eliminating the drift):

$$\frac{\partial V}{\partial t} = -\frac{1}{2}\sigma^2 S^2 \frac{\partial^2 V}{\partial S^2}$$

5. To bridge the alpha with fair value, the trader can consider that the expected theta given a volatility would be negative where one "pays up" for the alpha. Expected theta for a Black-Scholes-Merton hedger is the net of time decay after hedging in a market of a given volatility. Using θ as time decay, Γ the gamma, α as the alpha, σ as implied volatility, and σ' as actual over the period, we get the expected theta:

$$E(\theta) = \alpha(\sigma)\,\Gamma(\sigma) - \alpha(\sigma')\Gamma(\sigma')$$

We see that expected time decay is positive if $\sigma' > \sigma$ and negative if $\sigma' < \sigma$.

6. This section was added because it came to the author's attention that traders tend to use these measurements, not because of their risk management value.

7. *Mathematical Note.* The percentage difference is inaccurate for large moves because of the asymmetry in lognormal markets. It is more mathematically correct to use Log (spot/barrier). The difference becomes larger when the barrier is away from the money.

8. Gamma is a special case of convexity (i.e., convexity with respect to the asset price). However, its precision required presentation in a separate section.

9. Using the best fit method given the limited number of points, the author found:

$$\text{Factor} = 1.30825 - .03789\,x + .0007419\,x^2, \text{ with } x \text{ the maturity (in years)}.$$

10. The mathematical way to price such a convexity is through Ito's change of variable as described in Module G. There is an Ito term in the payoff of the Eurodollar. The Eurodollar futures could be interpreted as a function of a random variable with a payoff equal to $dr \times \exp\{r(t - to)\}$ with the random variable r following a Brownian motion.

CHAPTER 11   THE GREEKS AND THEIR BEHAVIOR

1. This topic is necessary for the study of exotic option structures.

CHAPTER 12   FUNGIBILITY, CONVERGENCE, AND STACKING

1. Again, this topic is presented from a practitioner's perspective, not from a theoretical viewpoint.
2. The ensuing academic dispute provides a rather interesting, if not entertaining exchange for traders. On that, see Culp and Miller (1994), Canter and Edward (1995).

CHAPTER 13   SOME WRINKLES OF OPTION MARKETS

1. A quarterly option on a future is one whose expiration corresponds to that of a future. Otherwise, the option is called a serial option on futures.
2. There is another type of barrier—the absorbing state—from which one cannot exit. A trader who has a bad run knows he has hit the absorbing state when clearing firm representatives show up in the middle of the pit to take away his trading privileges (sometimes they require the help of security guards to draw the hapless trader out of the pit).
3. *Mathematical Note.* If we bound a random walk to $W_t < W_{max}$. It becomes clear that as W_t becomes close to W_{max}, volatility needs to drop for the market to remain in a "fair" game. Another solution is for the market to have excessive skew.
4. Flood and Garber (1992) demonstrate how stabilizing exchange rates lead to an increased interest rates volatility.
5. Confirmed by two major brokerage firms, Tradition Financial Services and BCMG, about their volume in New York, Singapore, London, and Tokyo.

CHAPTER 15   BEWARE THE DISTRIBUTION

1. Heteroskedasticity for a normal distribution leads to a fourth moment higher than 3 times the square of the second moment.
2. See Hull and White (1987). To make the volatility process risk-neutral, we can safely assume the existence of a volatility future contract.
3. I studied in Taleb (1997) the dynamics of a generalized switching regime process.
   Let $X_t = \text{Log}(P_t/P_{t-\Delta t})$, the natural *log-returns* between time $t - \Delta_t$ and time t of an observed variable P_t.

Let $X_{At} \sim N(m_1, \sigma_1^2)$, in other words the associated price P_{At} follows a geometric Brownian motion with mean $m1$ and variance σ_1^2, since $dP_A/P_A = m_1 \, dt + \sigma_1 \, dW$, W a unit variance-zero mean Wiener process.

and $X_{Bt} \sim N(m_2, \sigma_2{}^2)$

The random variable X_t is then said to follow a *Brownian mixture* of X_A and X_B if:

• $X_t = X_{At}$ with probability p
• $X_t = X_{Bt}$ with probability $(1 - p)$

This note simplifies the Markov chain by assuming that p (and $1 - p$) are the ergodic probabilities (i.e., the long term average spent in any of the two states).

The moment generating function defined as $\Phi_x(s) = \int_\Omega e^{-sx} \, p(x) \, dx$ becomes the mixture of the m. g. f. of X_A and X_B. $\Phi_x(s) = p \, \Phi_{XA}(s) + (1 - p) \, \Phi_{XB}(s)$. See Feller (1971) for the theorem.

Since X_A and X_B are both normally distributed:

$$\Phi_{XA}(s) = \exp(m_1 s + \tfrac{1}{2} \sigma_1^2 s^2)$$

and

$$\Phi_{XB}(s) = \exp(m_2 s + \tfrac{1}{2} \sigma_2^2 s^2)$$

then

Denoting $\Phi'^{\,n}$ the nth derivative of Φ, and μ_n the nth moment we obtain the following:

• $\mu_1 = \Phi'^{\,1}_x(0) = m_1 p + m_2(1 - p) \, \sigma_2$
• $\mu_2 = \Phi'^{\,2}_x(0) = p \, \sigma_1^2 + (1 - p) \, \sigma_2^2 + p \, m_1^2 + (1 - p) \, m_2^2$
• $\mu_4 = \Phi'^{\,4}_x(0) = 3p\sigma_1^4 + 3(1 - p)\sigma_2^4 + p \, m_1^4 + (1 - p)m_2^4 + 6 \, p \, m_1^2\sigma_1^2 + 6 \, m_2^2(1 - p)\sigma_2^2$

From which we see the "fatness of the tails". When $\sigma_1 \neq \sigma_2$ and $p\epsilon(0,1)$, $\mu_4/\mu_2^2 > 3$.

4. The constant elasticity of variance linking asset prices to their volatility seems to explain some of this behavior. However, the analysis is static. It is concerned with absolute levels, not changes in levels. See Cox (1975); Beckers (1980); or MacBeth and Merville (1980).

CHAPTER 16   OPTION TRADING CONCEPTS

1. See Derman (1995).

2. The matching cannot be perfect. It is necessary, therefore, to establish a cost function (typically the quadratic norm of the difference) and minimize it. In addition, some weights can be introduced to reflect the importance of the parameter risk.

3. To use market maker jargon, "below sheets." "Sheets" are spreadsheets with theoretical value that market makers carry on the exchanges. Below sheets means below theoretical value (assuming no shift in parameters).

4. This is analogous in probability theory to the Brownian bridge where possible paths are examined conditional on a final arrival point.

5. Assume, for simplicity, that the forward trades at flat with the spot and that the owner of an option incurs negligible carrying costs.

CHAPTER 17   BINARY OPTIONS: EUROPEAN STYLE

1. This resembles the Breeder-Litzenberger (1978) argument, where the infinitely narrow butterfly (the call spread being purchased against another one being sold)

is $C(k + h) - C(k) - (-C(k - h) + C(k)) = C(k + h) + C(k - h) - 2C(k)$. At the limit, the entity becomes the second derivative of the option price with respect to the strike.

2. The bet is the derivative with respect to the strike. Since

$$dC = \frac{\partial C}{\partial K} \, dK + \frac{\partial C}{\partial \sigma(K)} \, d\sigma(K) = \frac{\partial C}{\partial K} \, dK + \frac{\partial C}{\partial \sigma(K)} \, \frac{\partial \sigma(K)}{\partial K} \, dK$$

CHAPTER 18   BINARY OPTIONS: AMERICAN STYLE

1. Howard Savery's rule of thumb is that the American digital will be roughly twice the European. The reason is that in at the money American will be worth $1 (it terminates) while an European is worth $.50. This relationship will "contaminate" to lower prices.

CHAPTER 19   BARRIER OPTIONS (I)

1. The reader should be acquainted with liquidity holes (Chapter 4) before proceeding.
2. Advanced Topic. (It is recommended that the reader practice the skew decomposition method of the binary option prior to further reading of this section.)
3. See Grimmet and Stirzaker (1992); Karatzas and Shreve (1991).
4. The stickler can use an up node of exp $\{(a - \frac{1}{2}\sigma)t\}$ and a down node of exp $\{(- at)\}$ satisfying both risk neutrality and lognormality. Again there is no point complicating such exercise with true lognormal moves. Alan Brace told the author: "communication is more important than accuracy."
5. See Dupire (1992, 1993, 1994, 1996), Rubinstein (1994), and Derman and Kani (1994).

CHAPTER 20   BARRIER OPTIONS (II)

1. A thorough understanding of American binary options is necessary before proceeding.

CHAPTER 22   MULTIASSET OPTIONS

1. The matrix needs to be symmetric and positive definite.
2. Lee Stulz (1982).
3. See Margrabe (1978).
4. *Mathematical Note.* Since the exercise aims at finding sensitivity, not prices, it is possible to set aside the lognormality issue. The correlation vega does not vary markedly after an adjustment in the stochastic process. Only the odd moments (the ones linked to the skew) will be truly affected.
5. See Taleb (1997).
6. The devaluation risk is excluded in pricing; therefore the operator would focus on the option without the component.

CHAPTER 23   MINOR EXOTICS: LOOKBACK AND ASIAN OPTIONS

1. See Goldman, Sosin, and Gatto (1979).
2. Given the fluidity of market designations, the term *Asian* may bear some other meaning in some circles.
3. For an interesting approach to the problem, see Geman and Yor (1993) where the average of a geometric Brownian is decomposed in a series of subordinated Bessel processes.

MODULE A   BROWNIAN MOTION ON A SPREADSHEET, A TUTORIAL

1. This applies to any other spreadsheet program, provided the cells are respected.
2. Module D provides an explanation for the restrictions on the matrix, the equivalent of volatility having to be positive.

MODULE B   RISK NEUTRALITY EXPLAINED

1. See Cox, Ross, and Rubinstein (1979).
2. See Harrison and Kreps (1979), Harrison and Pliska (1981).

MODULE C   NUMERAIRE RELATIVITY AND THE TWO-COUNTRY PARADOX

1. See Geman, El Karoui, and Rochet (1995).
2. Such a method allows the pricing of puts as calls with the numeraire flipped.
3. This section can be omitted without any loss of the substance of the paradox.
4. For a definition of a convex function, see Chapter 1.
5. Changes of numeraire are used with term structure models as "glue" where every maturity uses the preceding forward as a base for the stochastic process.

MODULE D   CORRELATION TRIANGLES: A GRAPHICAL CASE STUDY

1. See Geman and Souveton (1996); Margrabe (1993).

MODULE E   THE VALUE-AT-RISK

1. A trader translation: "when it goes it keeps going."
2. See Markowitz (1959) for the breakthrough in minimum variance portfolio selection and the birth of modern portfolio theory. See Ingersoll (1986), Huang and

Litzenberger (1988), or the more accessible Elton and Gruber (1995) for a description of the notion of mean variance.

3. Similar to the VAR is an excellent technique called "generalized pairs trading," a short term trading method where, conditional upon the return vector $R_t = \{r_1, r_2, \ldots, r_n\}$ at time t of securities a vector $X_t = \{X_1, X_2, \ldots, X_n\}$ of security prices where a multivariate diffusion is assumed, one can find a linear combination $\alpha = \{\alpha_1, \alpha_2, \ldots, \alpha_n\}$ maximizing the conditional probability of making a profit on a portfolio $\alpha^T (X_t - X_{t+\Delta t})$ where α^T is the transpose α, if the market diffused properly between $(t - \Delta t)$ and $(t + \Delta t)$. In other words, the trader can thus detect which securities at times t behaved as an outlier with respect to the covariance matrix between securities as know at period $t - \Delta t$ and take action, hoping that this would correct by next period $t + \Delta t$. If two assets assumed to behave alike (that is highly correlated) parted way, there might be a trade (assuming no new information) with the certainty of a profit potential higher than 97%. The trader can buy one and sell the other if he attributes the statistical divergence to some liquidity factor. Unlike the VAR, such technique, handled by the professional, is impervious to a large amount of tail events as it forecasts the "body" of the distribution, not the rare occurrences.

4. This rule was inspired by a conversation with Raphael Douady.

5. There will be a combination of assets with *negative* volatility.

Module F   Probabilistic Rankings in Arbitrage

1. See Rothchild and Stiglitz (1970) for the presentation of the difference between the "risks" of two instruments.

Module G   Option Pricing

1. More formally, W is a Wiener process. Uncertainty about the process is represented by a filtered probability space "quadruple," $\{\Omega, P, F, F_t\}$ where Ω is the probability space, P the objective probability measure, F a σ-algebra (or, in this instance, a Borel tribe, which consists in a collection of all subsets of Ω which includes the empty set, all countable unions and all complements of subsets in Ω), F_t the *filtration,* the set of information about the process known at time t (which includes information known at all previous times), such that $F_t \subset F_s$ whenever $t \leq s$.

   See Billingsley (1985) for a pedagogical presentation of measure theory, Dothan (1989) and the excellent and comprehensive Duffie (1996) for applications to finance. The reader will see a clear presentation of stochastic integration in Oksendal (1995).

2. See Black and Scholes (1973); Merton (1973).

3. For further discussion of stochastic volatility techniques, see Scott (1987) and Bates (1993).

4. The results here are inspired by Douady (1996).

Bibliography

Essential Books for Traders

Cox, J., & Rubinstein, M.[1] (1985). *Option Markets*, Englewood Cliffs, NJ: Prentice Hall.

> The best book ever written on options; after more than a decade the book has not a speck of dust. It is written with rare intuitive depth of market sense. Imperative reading for anyone who enters a trading room.

Natenberg, S. (1995). *Option Volatility and Pricing Strategies* (2nd ed.), Chicago: Probus.

> Unencumbered with theory, it portrays option trading from the vantage point of a down-to-earth floor trader. It provides an essential introductory text for book runners and risk managers.

Baird, A. (1994). *Option Market Making*, New York: Wiley.

> More advanced than Natenberg, a compact reading for a market maker. The reader will find in it some introductory preparation for the concepts of risk management of an inventory.

Hull, J. (1993). *Option Futures and Other Derivative Securities* (2nd ed.), Englewood Cliffs, NJ: Prentice Hall.

> Clear, pedagogical, and up to date.

Recommended Books

Abramowitz, M., & Stegun, N. C. (1970). *Handbook of Mathematical Functions*, New York: Dover.

Bachelier, L. (1990). *Theorie de la speculation*, Annales de l'Ecole Normale Superieure, Paris: Gauthier-Villars.

Beck, P., & Sydsaeter, K. (1991). *Economist's Mathematical Manual* (2nd ed.), Heidelberg, Germany: Springer Verlag.

Billingsley, P. (1986). *Probability and Measure*, New York: Wiley.

Bloomfield, P. (1976). *Fourier Analysis of Time Series: An Introduction*, New York: Wiley.

Brock, W., Hsieh, D., & LeBaron, B. (1991). *Nonlinear Dynamics, Chaos and Instability*, Boston: MIT Press.

Burghardt, G., Belton, T., Lane, M., Luce, G., & McVey, R. (1991). *Eurodollar Futures and Options*, Chicago: Probus.

Dana, R. A., & Jeanblanc-Piqué, M. (1994). *Marchés financiers en temps continu*, Paris: Economica.

DeRosa, D. (1992). *Options on Foreign Exchange*, Chicago: Probus.

DeRosa, D. (1996). *Managing Foreign Exchange Risk* (2nd ed.), Homewood, IL: Irwin.

Dixit, A., & Pyndick, R. (1994). *Investment Under Uncertainty*, Princeton, NJ: Princeton University Press.

Dothan, M. (1990). *Prices in Financial Markets*, New York: Oxford University Press.

---

[1] The author owes his trading education to a smuggled copy of the manuscript for this book.

Dubins, L., & Savage, L. (1965). *How to Gamble If You Must,* New York: McGraw-Hill.

Duffie, D. (1988). *Security Markets Stochastic Models,* New York: Academic Press.

Duffie, D. (1996). *Dynamic Asset Pricing Theory,* Princeton, NJ: Princeton University Press.

Durett, R. (1991). *Probability: Theories and Examples,* Pacific Grove, CA: Wadsworth and Brooks/Coles.

Elton, E., & Gruber, M. (1995). *Modern Portfolio Theory and Investment Analysis* (5th ed.), New York: Wiley.

Enders, W. (1995). *Applied Econometric Time Series,* New York: Wiley.

Feller, W. (1968). *An Introduction to Probability Theory and Its Application* (Vol. I; 3rd ed.), New York: Wiley.

Feller, W. (1971). *An Introduction to Probability Theory and Its Application* (Vol. II; 2nd ed.), New York: Wiley.

Gastineau, G. L. (1992). *Dictionary of Financial Risk Management,* Chicago: Probus.

Grabbe, J. O. (1996). *International Financial Markets* (3rd ed.), Englewood Cliffs, NJ: Prentice Hall.

Grimmett, G. R., & Stirzaker, D. R. (1992). *Probability and Random Processes* (2nd ed.), Oxford: Oxford University Press.

Hamilton, J. D. (1994). *Times Series Analysis,* Princeton, NJ: Princeton University Press.

Harvey, A. C. (1993). *Time Series Models* (2nd ed.), London: Harvester Wheatsheaf.

Huang, C. F., & Litzenberger, R. (1988). *Foundations for Financial Economics,* Englewood Cliffs, NJ: Prentice Hall.

Ingersoll, J. (1986). *The Theory of Financial Decision Making,* Savage, MD: Rovoman & Littlefield.

Jarrow, R. (1995). *Modelling Fixed Income Securities and Interest Rate Options,* New York: McGraw-Hill.

Jarrow, R., & Rudd, A. (1983). *Option Pricing,* Homewood, IL: Irwin.

Karatzas, I., & Shreve, S. (1991). *Brownian Motion and Stochastic Calculus* (2nd ed.), New York: Springer Verlag.

Kennedy, P. (1992). *A Guide to Econometrics* (3rd ed.), Cambridge, MA: MIT Press.

Lamberton, D., & Lapeyre, B. (1991). *Introduction au calcul stochastique applique a la finance,* Paris: Ellipses.

Levy, P. (1948). *Processus stochastiques et mouvement brownien,* Paris: Gauthier-Villars.

Markowitz, H. (1959). *Portfolio Selection: Efficient Diversification of Investments,* New York: Wiley.

Merton, R. C. (1990). *Continuous-Time Finance,* Cambridge, MA: Blackwell.

Nelken, I. (Ed.). (1995). *The Handbook of Exotic Options,* Homewood, IL: Irwin.

Oksendal, B. (1995). *Stochastic Differential Equations* (4th ed.), Berlin: Springer.

Oxford English Dictionary. (1971). Oxford: Oxford University Press.

Pesaran, N. H., & Potter, S. M. (Eds.). (1993). *Nonlinear Dynamics, Chaos, and Econometrics,* London: Wiley.

Ray, C. (1993). *The Bond Market, Trading and Risk Management,* Homewood, IL: Irwin.

Russell, B. (1945). *History of Western Philosophy,* New York: Simon & Schuster.

Schwager, J. D. (1992). *The New Market Wizards, Conversations with America's Top Traders,* New York: Harper Business.

Shiller, R. J. (1989). *Market Volatility,* Cambridge, MA: MIT Press.

Shimko, D. (1992). *Continuous Time Finance: A Primer,* Miami, FL: Kolb Publishing.

Soros, G. (1994). *The Alchemy of Finance* (2nd ed.), New York: Wiley.

Stigum, M. (1990). *The Money Market* (3rd ed.), Homewood, IL: Irwin.

Taylor, H. M., & Karlin, S. (1981). *A Second Course in Stochastic Processes*, New York: Academic Press.

Taylor, H. M., & Karlin, S. (1994). *An Introduction to Stochastic Modeling*, New York: Academic Press.

Varian, H. (1993). *Economic and Financial Modeling with Mathematica*, Santa Clara, CA: Telos.

Wilmott, P., Dewynne, J., & Howison, S. (1993). *Option Pricing, Mathematical Models and Computation*, Oxford: Oxford Financial Press.

Wolfram, S. (1991). *Mathematica, a System for Doing Mathematics by Computer* (2nd ed.), Reading, MA: Addison-Wesley.

Recommended Articles

Amin, K., & Jarrow, R. (1991). "Pricing Foreign Currency Options under Stochastic Interest Rates," *Journal of International Money and Finance, 10*, 310–329.

Atilgan, T. (1996). *A General Review of Volatility Estimation Techniques*, unpublished manuscript.

Avellaneda, M., Levy, A., & Paras, A. (1995). "Pricing and Hedging Derivative Securities in Markets with Uncertain Volatilities," *Applied Mathematical Finance, 2*, 73–88.

Avellaneda, M., & Paras, A. (1994). "Dynamic Hedging Portfolios for Derivative Securities in the Presence of Large Transaction Costs," *Applied Mathematical Finance, 1*, 165–193.

Bailey, W. (1987, December). "An Empirical Investigation of the Market for Comex Gold Futures Options," *Journal of Finance, 42*(5), 1187–1194.

Bailie, R. T., & Bollerslev, T. (1989). "The Message in Daily Exchange Rates: A Conditional Variance Tale," *Journal of Finance, 44*(1), 167–182.

Bates, D. S. (1993). *Jumps and Stochastic Volatility: Exchange Rate Processes Implicit in PHLX Deutschemark Options*, National Bureau of Economic Research, Working Paper No. 4596.

Bauman, W. S., & Miller, R. (1994). "Can Managed Portfolio Performance be Predicted?" *Journal of Portfolio Management, 20*(4), 31–40.

Beckers, S., (1980). "The Constant Elasticity of Variance Model and Its Implications for Option Pricing," *Journal of Finance, 35*(3), 661–673.

Black, F. (1975). "Fact and Fantasy in the Use of Options," *Financial Analysts Journal, 31*(4), 36–41, 61–72.

Black, F. (1976). "Pricing of Commodity Contracts," *Journal of Financial Economics, 3.*

Black, F. (1988, August). "The Holes in Black-Scholes," in New Frontiers in Options, *RISK.*

Black, F., & Scholes, M. (1973). "The Pricing of Options and Corporate Liabilities," *Journal of Political Economy, 81*, 637–654.

Bollerslev, T. (1986). "Generalized Autoregressive Conditional Heteroskedasticity," *Journal of Econometrics, 31*, 307–327.

Bollerslev, T. (1987, August). "A Conditional Heteroskedastic Times Series Model for Speculative Prices and Rates of Return," *Review of Econometric Studies.*

Bowie, J., & Carr, P. (1994, August). "Static Simplicity," *RISK.*

Boyle, P. P. (1977). "Options: A Monte Carlo Approach," *Journal of Financial Economics, 4*(3), 323–338.

Boyle, P. P. (1989, March). "The Quality Option and Timing Option in Futures Contracts," *Journal of Finance, 44*(1), 101–114.

Boyle, P. P., Evnine, J., & Gibbs, S. (1989). "Multivariate Contingent Claims," *Review of Financial Studies, 2*(2), 241–250.

Breeden, D., & Litzenberger, R. (1978). "Prices of State-Contingent Claims Implicit in Option Prices, *Journal of Business, 51*, 621–651.

Brennan, M. J., & Schwartz, E. S. (1978, September). "Finite Difference Methods and Jump Processes Arising in the Pricing of Contingent Claims: A Synthesis," *Journal of Financial and Quantitative Analysis.*

Brock, W., & de Lima, P. J. F. (1995). *Nonlinear Time Series, Complexity Theory, and Finance,* Working Paper.

Carr, P. (1988, December). "The Valuation of Sequential Exchange Opportunities," *Journal of Finance.*

Carr, P. (1994). "European Put Call Symmetry," Cornell University, Working Paper.

Carr, P. (1995). *Static Hedging of Path Dependent Options,* Working Paper.

Carr, P., (1995). *Two Extensions to Barrier Option Valuation,* Working Paper.

Cox, J. (1975). *Constant Elasticity of Variance Diffusions,* Working Paper, Stanford University.

Cox, J. C., Ingersoll, J., & Ross, S. (1985a). "An Intertemporal General Equilibrium Model of Asset Prices," *Econometrica, 53*, 363–384.

Cox, J. C., Ingersoll, J., & Ross, S. (1985b). "A Theory of the Term Structure of Interest Rates," *Econometrica, 53*, 385–407.

Cox, J. C., & Ross, S. (1976). "The Valuation of Options for Alternative Stochastic Processes," *Journal of Financial Economics, 3.*

Cox, J. C., Ross, S. A., & Rubinstein, M. (1979). "Option Pricing: A Simplified Approach," *Journal of Financial Economics, 7.*

Culp, C. L., & Miller, M. H. (1994). "Hedging a Flow of Commodity Deliveries with Futures: Lessons from Metallgessenshaft, *Derivatives Quarterly, 1.*

Dacorogna, M. M., Muller, U., Embrechts, P., & Samorodnitsky, G. (1995). *Moment Conditions for HARCH(k) Models,* Working Paper, Olsen & Associates, Zurich, Switzerland.

Derman, E., Ergener, D., & Kani, I. (1995, Summer). "Static Option Replication," *Journal of Derivatives.*

Derman, E., & Kani, I. (1994, February). "Riding on a Smile," *RISK,* 32–39.

Derman, E. (1996). "Valuing Models and Modelling Value," *Journal of Portfolio Management, 22*(3), 106–114.

Douady, R. (1995). *Mouvement browniens cylindriques et optimisation de Heath-Jarrow-Morton,* Paris: Ecole Normale Superieure Working Paper.

Douady, R. (1995). *Options à limites,* Working Paper.

Douady, R. (1996). *De la distribution du temps de sortie et de son esperance,* Working Paper.

Dubourg, N., & Douady, R. (1995). "Energy Optimization and Optimal Hedging under Proportional Transaction Costs," *Societe Generale,* Paris.

Dupire, B. (1992). "Arbitrage Pricing with Stochastic Volatility," in *Proceedings of the A.F.F.I. Conference of June 1992.*

Dupire, B. (1993, September). "Model Art," *RISK.*

Dupire, B. (1994, January). "Pricing with a Smile," *RISK, 7*, 18–20.

Dupire, B., (1996). *A Unified Theory of Volatility,* Working Paper, Paribas Capital Markets.

Edwards, F., & Canter, M. (1995). "The Collapse of Metalgessellschaft: Unhedgeable Risks, Poor Hedging Strategy, or Just Bad Luck?" *Journal of Futures Markets, 15*(3), 211–264.

El Karoui, N., & Geman, H. (1994). "A Probabilistic Approach to the Valuation of General Floating Rate Notes with an Application to Interest Rate Swaps," *Advances in Options and Futures Research.*

Engle, R. (1982). "Autoregressive Conditional Heteroskedasticity with Estimates of the Variance of UK Inflation," *Econometrica, 50.*

Engle, R., & Rosenberg, J. (1995, Summer). "Garch Gamma," *Journal of Derivatives.*

Flood, R. P., & Garber, P. M. (1992). "The Linkage between Speculative Attack and Target Zone Models of Exchange Rates: Some Extended Results," in P. Krugman & M. Miller (Eds.), *Exchange Rate Targets and Currency Bands,* Cambridge, England: Cambridge University Press.

Fung, W., & Hsieh, D. (1996). *Global Yield Curve Event Risk,* Working Paper, Fuqua School of Business, Duke University.

Garman, M. (1976). "Market Microstructure," *Journal of Finance, 3,* 257–275.

Garman, M. (1989). "Immunizing Foreign Exchange Contracts against Swap Rate and Volatility Risks," *Journal of International Financial Management and Accounting, 1.*

Garman, M. (1992, December). "Spread the Load," *RISK.*

Garman, M., & Klass, M. J. (1980). "On Estimation of Security Price Volatilities from Historical Data," *Journal of Business, 53*(1), 67–78.

Garman, M., & Kohlhagen, S. W. (1983). "Foreign Currency Option Values," *Journal of International Money and Finance, 2*(3), 231–237.

Geman, H., El Karoui, N., & Rochet, J. C. (1995). "Changes of Numeraire, Changes of Probability Measure, and Option Pricing," *Journal of Applied Probability, 32,* 443–458.

Geman, H., & Souveton, R. (1996). "No Arbitrage between Economies and Correlation Risk Management," forthcoming in *Computational Economics.*

Geman, H., & Yor, M. (1993). "Bessel Processes, Asian Options, and Perpetuities," *Mathematical Finance, 3*(4), 349–375.

Geman, H., & Yor, M. (1996). "Pricing and Hedging Double Barrier Options: A Probabilistic Approach," forthcoming, *Mathematical Finance.*

Geske, R. (1979). "The Valuation of Compound Options," *Journal of Financial Economics, 7*(1), 63–82.

Geske, R., & Johnson, H. E. (1984, December). "The American Put Option Valued Analytically," *Journal of Finance, 39*(5), 1511–1524.

Geske, R., & Roll, R. (1984). "On Valuing American Call Options with the Black-Scholes European Formula," *Journal of Finance, 39*(2), 443–455.

Geske, R., & Shastri, K. (1985). "Valuation by Approximation: A Comparison of Alternative Option Valuation Techniques," *Journal of Financial and Quantitative Analysis, 20*(1), 45–72.

Goldman, B. M., Sosin, H. B., & Gatto, M. A. (1979). "Path Dependent Options: 'Buy at the Low, Sell at the High,'" *Journal of Finance, 34*(5), 1111–1127.

Grossman, S. (1987). "Insurance Seen and Unseen: The Impact on Markets," *Journal of Portfolio Management, 14*(4), 5–6.

Grossman, S. (1988). "An Analysis of the Implication for Stock and Future Price Volatility of Program Trading and Dynamic Hedging Strategies," *Journal of Business, 61*(3).

Grossman, S. J., & Miller, M. H. (1988). "Liquidity and Market Structure," *Journal of Finance, 43,* 617–633.

Guillaume, D., Dacorogna, M., Dave, R., Muller, U., Olsen, R., & Pictet, O. (1995, March). *From the Bird's Eye to the Microscope,* Working Paper, Olsen & Associates, Zurich, Switzerland.

Hamilton, J. (1993). "Autoregressive Conditional Heteroskedasticity and Changes in Regime," U. C. San Diego, Working Paper.

Hamilton, J. (1994). "Rational Expectations and the Economic Consequence of Changes in Regime," U. C. San Diego, Working Paper.

Hamilton, J., & Susmel, R. (1995). "Specification Testing in Markov Switching Time Series Models," U. C. San Diego, Working Paper.

Harrison, M., & Kreps, D. (1979). "Martingales and Arbitrage in Multiperiod Securities Markets," *Journal of Economic Theory, 20,* 381–408.

Harrison, M., & Pliska, S. (1981). "Martingales and Stochastic Integrals in the Theory of Continuous Trading," *Stochastic Processes and Their Applications.*

Heath, D., Jarrow, R., & Morton, A. (1987). *Bond Pricing and the Term Structure of Interest Rates,* Working Paper, Cornell University.

Heath, D., Jarrow, R., & Morton, A. (1990). "Bond Option Pricing and the Term Structure of Interest Rates: A Discrete Time Approximation," *Journal of Financial and Quantitative Analysis, 25,* 419–440.

Heath, D., Jarrow, R., & Morton, A. (1992). "Bond Pricing and the Term Structure of Interest Rates: A New Methodology for Contingent Claims Valuation," *Econometrica, 60,* 77–106.

Heynen, R., & Kat, H. (1994, June). "Crossing Barriers," *RISK,* 46–51.

Ho, T., & Stoll, H. (1980). "On Dealer Markets under Competition," *Journal of Finance, 35,* 259–267.

Ho, T., & Stoll, H. (1983). "The Dynamics of Dealer Market under Competition," *Journal of Finance, 38,* 1053–1074.

Hull, J., & White, A. (1987). "The Pricing of Options on Assets with Stochastic Volatilities," *Journal of Finance, 42*(2), 281–300.

Hutchinson, J., Lo, A. W., & Poggio, T. (1994, July). "A Non-Parametric Approach to Pricing and Hedging Derivative Securities via Learning Networks," *Journal of Finance, 49*(1), 27–36.

Irvin, S. H., Zulauf, C., & Ward, B. (1994, Winter). "The predictability of Managed Futures Returns," *Journal of Derivatives.*

Jackwerth, J. C., & Rubinstein, M. (1995). "Implied Probability Distributions: Empirical Analysis," Working Paper, U. C. Berkeley.

Jamshidian, F. (1989, March). "An Exact Bond Option Formula," *Journal of Finance, 44*(11), 205–210.

Johnson, H. (1987). "Options on the Maximum or the Minimum of Several Assets," *Journal of Financial and Quantitative Analysis, 22*(3), 277–284.

Johnson, H., Shanno, D. (1987, June). "Option Pricing When the Variance Is Changing," *Journal of Financial and Quantitative Analysis.*

Johnson, H., & Stulz, R. (1987). "The Pricing of Options with Default Risk," *Journal of Finance, 42*(2), 267–280.

Kemna, A. G. Z., & Vorst, A. C. F. (1990). "A Pricing Method for Options Based on Average Values," *Journal of Banking and Finance, 14,* 113–130.

Kim, D., & Kon, S. (1994). "Alternative Models for the Conditional Heteroskedasticity of Stock Returns," *Journal of Business, 67*(4), 563–598.

Kritzman, M. (1994). "About Serial Dependence," *Financial Analysts Journal, 50*(2), 19–22.

Kunitomo, N., & Ikeda, M. (1992). "Pricing Options with Curved Boundaries," *Mathematical Finance, 2*, 275–282.

Kuserk, G., & Locke, P. (1993). "Scalper Behavior in an Auction Market: An Analysis of Scalpers in Futures Markets," *Journal of Futures Markets, 13*, 409–431.

Kuserk, G., & Locke, P. (1994, Summer). "Market Maker Competition on Futures Exchanges," *Journal of Derivatives*, 56–66.

Leland, H. (1985). "Option Pricing and Replication with Transactions Costs," *Journal of Finance, 40* (5), 1285–1301.

Leland, H. (1992, December). "The Lessons of History," *RISK*.

Levy, E. (1992). "Pricing European Average Rate Currency Options," *Journal of International Money and Finance, 11*(4), 474–491.

Lo, A., & MacKinley, A. C. (1988). "Stock Market Prices Do Not Follow Random Walks: Evidence from a Simple Specification Test," *Review of Financial Studies, 1*, 41–66.

MacBeth, J., & Merville, L. (1980, May). "Tests of the Black-Scholes and Cox Call Option Valuation Models," *Journal of Finance, 35*(2), 285–303.

Margrabe, W. (1978). "The Value of an Option to Exchange One Asset for Another," *Journal of Finance, 33*(1), 177–186.

Margrabe, W. (1993, Fall). "Triangular Equilibrium and Arbitrage in the Market for Options to Exchange Two Assets," *The Journal of Derivatives, 1*.

Merton, R. (1973, Spring). "Theory of Rational Option Pricing," *Bell Journal of Economics*.

Merton, R. (1976). "Option Pricing When Underlying Stock Returns Are Discontinuous," *Journal of Financial Economics, 3*(1/2), 125–144.

Merton, R. (1982). "On the Mathematics and Economic Assumptions of Continuous-Time Models," in W. F. Sharpe & C. M. Cootner (Eds.), *Financial Economics: Essays in Honor of Paul Cootner*, Englewood Cliffs, NJ: Prentice Hall.

Nelson, D. B. (1990). "ARCH Models as Diffusion Approximations," *Journal of Econometrics, 45*, 7–38.

Parkinson, M. (1980). "The Extreme Value Method for Estimating the Variance of the Rate of Return," *Journal of Business, 1*.

Pechtl, A. (1995, June). "Classified Information," *RISK*.

Peterson, D. R., & Tucker, A. L. (1988). "Implied Spot Rates as Predictors of Currency Returns: A Note," *Journal of Finance, 43*(1), 247–258.

Rabinovitch, R. (1989). "Pricing Stock and Bond Options When the Default-Free Rate Is Stochastic," *Journal of Financial and Quantitative Analysis, 24*(4), 447–458.

Rendleman, R. J., Jr., & Bartter, B. J. (1979, December). "Two-State Option Pricing," *Journal of Finance*.

Roll, R. (1984). "A Simple Implicit Measure of the Effective Bid-Ask Spread in An Efficient Market," *Journal of Finance, 39*(4), 1127–1139.

Ross, S. A. (1989). "Information and Volatility: The No-Arbitrage Martingale Approach to Timing and Resolution Irrelevancy," *Journal of Finance, 44*(1), 1–18.

Rothchild, M., & Stiglitz, J. (1970). "Increasing Risk I: A Definition," *Journal of Economic Theory, 2*, 225–243.

Rubinstein, M. (1983, March). "Displaced Diffusion Option Pricing," *Journal of Finance*.

Rubinstein, M. (1984). "A Simple Formula for the Expected Rate of Return of an Option over a Finite Holding Period," *Journal of Finance, 39*(5), 1503–1509.

Rubinstein, M. (1985). "Nonparametric Tests of Alternative Option Pricing Models Using CBOE Reported Trades," *Journal of Finance, 40*(2), 455–480.

Rubinstein, M. (1991). *Exotic Options,* Finance Working Paper No. 220, U. C. Berkeley.

Rubinstein, M. (1994, June). "Implied Binomial Trees," *Journal of Finance, 49*(3), 771–818.

Scott, L. O. (1987, December). "Option Pricing When the Variance Changes Randomly: Theory, Estimation and Application," *Journal of Financial and Quantitative Analysis.*

Shimko, D. (1993, April). "Bounds of Probability," *RISK.*

Silber, W. (1984). "Marketmaking Behavior in an Auction Market: An Analysis of Scalpers in a Futures Market," *Journal of Finance, 39,* 937–953.

Stroll, H. R. (1989). "Inferring the Components of the Bid-Ask Spread: Theory and Empirical Tests," *Journal of Finance, 44,* 115–134.

Stulz, R. M. (1982). "Options on the Minimum or Maximum of Two Risky Assets: Analysis and Applications," *Journal of Financial Economics, 10,* 161–185.

Taleb, N. (1996). "Dynamic Hedging in Heteroskedastic Environments," presented at the Institute for Advanced Studies, Princeton, NJ.

Taleb, N. (1996). "Parkinson Statistic, Mean Reversion and Numerical Pricing of Barrier Options Using a Brownian Bridge," Working Paper.

Taleb, N. (1997). "Essays in Applied Option Theory," Working Paper.

Turnbull, S. M., & Wakeman, L. M. (1991, September). "A Quick Algorithm for Pricing European Average Options," *Journal of Financial and Quantitative Analysis.*

Vasicek, O. (1977). "An Equilibrium Theory of the Term Structure," *Journal of Financial Economics, 5,* 177–188.

Whaley, R. E. (1986). "Valuation of American Futures Options: Theory and Empirical Tests," *Journal of Finance, 41*(1), 127–150.

Whalley, A. E., & Wilmott, P. (1993). "Counting the Costs," *RISK, 6,* 10.

Index